PRINCIPLES

PRINCIPLES

RAY DALIO

SIMON & SCHUSTER

NEW YORK   LONDON   TORONTO   SYDNEY   NEW DELHI

Simon & Schuster
1230 Avenue of the Americas
New York, NY 10020

First Simon & Schuster hardcover edition September 2017

SIMON & SCHUSTER and colophon are registered trademarks of Simon & Schuster, Inc.

For information about special discounts for bulk purchases, please contact Simon & Schuster Special Sales at 1-866-506-1949 or business@simonandschuster.com.

The Simon & Schuster Speakers Bureau can bring authors to your live event. For more information or to book an event, contact the Simon & Schuster Speakers Bureau at 1-866-248-3049 or visit our website at www.simonspeakers.com.

Interior design by Rodrigo Corral Art & Design

Manufactured in the United States of America

20 19 18 17 16 15 14

Library of Congress Cataloging-in-Publication Data has been applied for.

ISBN 978-1-5011-2402-0
ISBN 978-1-5011-2405-1 (ebook)

To Barbara,
the half of me who has made me
whole for more than forty years.

PART I
WHERE I'M COMING FROM

1

1 My Call to Adventure: 1949–1967   5

2 Crossing the Threshold: 1967–1979   11

3 My Abyss: 1979–1982   27

4 My Road of Trials: 1983–1994   39

5 The Ultimate Boon: 1995–2010   67

6 Returning the Boon: 2011–2015   91

7 My Last Year and My Greatest Challenge: 2016–2017   117

8 Looking Back from a Higher Level   121

PART II
LIFE PRINCIPLES

131

1 Embrace Reality and Deal with It   132

2 Use the 5-Step Process to Get What You Want Out of Life   168

3 Be Radically Open-Minded   182

4 Understand That People Are Wired Very Differently   204

5 Learn How to Make Decisions Effectively   234

Life Principles: Putting It All Together   267

Summary and Table of Life Principles   272

PART III
WORK PRINCIPLES
279

Summary and Table of Work Principles   280

TO GET THE CULTURE RIGHT . . .   318

1   Trust in Radical Truth and Radical Transparency   322

2   Cultivate Meaningful Work and Meaningful Relationships   338

3   Create a Culture in Which It Is Okay to Make Mistakes and Unacceptable Not to Learn from Them   348

4   Get and Stay in Sync   356

5   Believability Weight Your Decision Making   370

6   Recognize How to Get Beyond Disagreements   384

TO GET THE PEOPLE RIGHT . . .   394

7   Remember That the WHO Is More Important than the WHAT   398

8   Hire Right, Because the Penalties for Hiring Wrong Are Huge   404

9   Constantly Train, Test, Evaluate, and Sort People   420

TO BUILD AND EVOLVE YOUR MACHINE . . .   444

10   Manage as Someone Operating a Machine to Achieve a Goal   448

11   Perceive and Don't Tolerate Problems   472

12   Diagnose Problems to Get at Their Root Causes   482

13   Design Improvements to Your Machine to Get Around Your Problems   496

14   Do What You Set Out to Do   518

15   Use Tools and Protocols to Shape How Work Is Done   524

16   And for Heaven's Sake, Don't Overlook Governance!   530

Work Principles: Putting It All Together   539

CONCLUSION   543

APPENDIX: TOOLS AND PROTOCOLS FOR BRIDGEWATER'S IDEA MERITOCRACY   545

BIBLIOGRAPHY   553

INDEX   555

ACKNOWLEDGMENTS   565

ABOUT THE AUTHOR   569

INTRODUCTION

Before I begin telling you what I think, I want to establish that I'm a "dumb shit" who doesn't know much relative to what I need to know. Whatever success I've had in life has had more to do with my knowing how to deal with my *not* knowing than anything I know. The most important thing I learned is an approach to life based on principles that helps me find out what's true and what to do about it.

I'm passing along these principles because I am now at the stage in my life in which I want to help others be successful rather than to be more successful myself. Because these principles have helped me and others so much, I want to share them with you. It's up to you to decide how valuable they really are and what, if anything, you want to do with them.

Principles are fundamental truths that serve as the foundations for behavior that gets you what you want out of life. They can be applied again and again in similar situations to help you achieve your goals.

Every day, each of us is faced with a blizzard of situations we must respond to. Without principles we would be forced to react to all the things life throws at us individually, as if we were experiencing each of them for the first time. If instead we classify these situations into types and have good principles for dealing with them, we will make better decisions more quickly and have better lives as a result. Having a good set of principles is like having a good collection of recipes for success. All successful people operate by principles that help them be successful, though what they choose to be successful at varies enormously, so their principles vary.

To be principled means to consistently operate with principles that can be clearly explained. Unfortunately, most people can't do that. And it's very rare for people to write their principles down and share them. That is a shame. I would love to know what principles guided Albert Einstein, Steve Jobs, Winston Churchill, Leonardo da Vinci, and others so I could clearly understand what they were going after and how they achieved it and could compare their different approaches. I'd like to know which principles are most important to the politicians who want me to vote for them and to all the other people whose decisions affect me. Do we have common principles that bind us together—as a family, as a community, as a nation, as friends across nations? Or do we have opposing principles that divide us? What are they? Let's be specific. This is a time when it is especially important for us to be clear about our principles.

My hope is that reading this book will prompt you and others to discover your own principles from wherever you think is best and ideally write them down. Doing that will allow you and others to be clear about what your principles are and understand each other better. It will allow you to refine them as you encounter more experiences and to reflect on them, which will help you make better decisions and be better understood.

HAVING YOUR OWN PRINCIPLES

We come by our principles in different ways. Sometimes we gain them through our own experiences and reflections. Sometimes we accept them from others, like our parents, or we adopt holistic packages of principles, such as those of religions and legal frameworks.

Because we each have our own goals and our own natures, each of us must choose our own principles to match them. While it isn't necessarily a bad thing to use others' principles, adopting principles without giving them much thought can expose you to the risk of acting in ways inconsistent with your goals and your nature. At the same time, you, like me, probably don't know everything you need to know and would be wise to embrace that fact. If you can think for yourself while being open-minded in a clearheaded way to find out what is best for you to do, and if you can summon up the courage to do it, you will make the most of your life. If you can't do that, you should reflect on why that is, because that's most likely your greatest impediment to getting more of what you want out of life.

That brings me to my first principle:

● Think for yourself to decide 1) what you want, 2) what is true, and 3) what you should do to achieve #1 in light of #2 . . .

. . . and do that with humility and open-mindedness so that you consider the best thinking available to you. Being clear on your principles is important because they will affect all aspects of your life, many times a day. For example, when you enter into relationships with others, your principles and their principles will determine how you interact. People who have shared values and principles get along. People who don't will suffer through constant misunderstandings and conflicts. Think about the people you are closest to: Are their values aligned with yours? Do you even know what their values or principles are? Too often in relationships, people's principles aren't clear. This is especially problematic in organizations where people need to have shared principles to be successful. Being crystal clear about my principles is why I labored so much over every sentence in this book.

The principles you choose can be anything you want them to be as long as they are authentic—i.e., as long as they reflect your true character and values. You will be faced with millions of choices in life, and the way you make them will reflect the principles you have—so it won't be long before the people around you will be able to tell the principles you are really operating by. The worst thing you can be is a phony, because if you're a phony you will lose people's trust and your own self-respect. So you must be clear about your principles and then you must "walk the talk." If inconsistencies seem to exist, you should explain them. It's best to do that in writing because by doing so, you will refine your written principles.

While I will be sharing my own principles, I want to make clear to you that I don't expect you to follow them blindly. On the contrary, I want you to question every word and pick and choose among these principles so you come away with a mix that suits you.

MY PRINCIPLES AND HOW I LEARNED THEM

I learned my principles over a lifetime of making a lot of mistakes and spending a lot of time reflecting on them. Since I was a kid, I've been a curious, independent thinker who ran after audacious goals. I got excited about visualizing things to go after, had some painful failures going after them, learned principles that would prevent me from making the same sort of mistakes again, and changed and improved, which allowed me to imagine and go after even more audacious goals and do that rapidly and repeatedly for a long time. So to me life looks like the sequence you see on the opposite page.

I believe that the key to success lies in knowing how to both strive for a lot and fail well. By failing well, I mean being able to experience painful failures that provide big learnings without failing badly enough to get knocked out of the game.

This way of learning and improving has been best for me because of what I'm like and because of what I do. I've always had a bad rote memory and didn't like following other people's instructions, but I loved figuring out how things work for myself. I hated school because of my bad memory but when I was twelve I fell in love with trading the markets. To make money in the markets, one needs to be

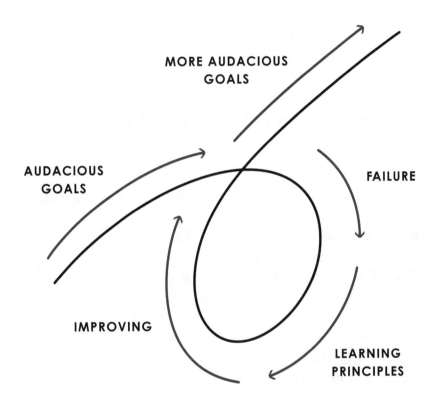

MORE AUDACIOUS
GOALS

AUDACIOUS
GOALS

FAILURE

IMPROVING

LEARNING
PRINCIPLES

an independent thinker who bets against the consensus and is right. That's because the consensus view is baked into the price. One is inevitably going to be painfully wrong a lot, so knowing how to do that well is critical to one's success. To be a successful entrepreneur, the same is true: One also has to be an independent thinker who correctly bets against the consensus, which means being painfully wrong a fair amount. Since I was both an investor and an entrepreneur, I developed a healthy fear of being wrong and figured out an approach to decision making that would maximize my odds of being right.

● Make believability-weighted decisions.

My painful mistakes shifted me from having a perspective of "I know I'm right" to having one of "How do I know I'm right?" They gave me the humility I needed to balance my audacity. Knowing that I could be painfully wrong and curiosity about why other smart people saw things differently prompted me to look at things through the eyes of others as well as my own. That allowed me to see many more dimensions than if I saw things just through my own eyes. Learning how to weigh people's inputs so that I chose the best ones—in other words, so that I believability weighted my decision making—increased my chances of being right and was thrilling. At the same time, I learned to:

● Operate by principles . . .

. . . that are so clearly laid out that their logic can easily be assessed and you and others can see if you walk the talk. Experience taught me how invaluable it is to reflect on and write down my decision-making criteria whenever I made a decision, so I got in the habit of doing that. With time, my collection of principles became like a collection of recipes for decision making. By sharing them with the people at my company, Bridgewater Associates, and inviting them to help me test my principles in action, I continually refined and evolved them. In fact, I was able to refine them to the point that I could see how important it is to:

● Systemize your decision making.

I discovered I could do that by expressing my decision-making criteria in the form of algorithms that I could embed into our computers. By running both decision-making systems—i.e., mine in my head and mine in the computer—next to each other, I learned the computer could make better decisions than me because it could process vastly more information than I could, and it could do it faster and unemotionally. Doing that allowed me and the people I worked with to compound our understanding over time and improve the quality of our collective decision making. I discovered that such decision-making systems—especially when believability weighted—are incredibly powerful and will soon profoundly change how people around the world make all kinds of decisions. Our principle-driven approach to decision making has not only improved our economic, investment, and management decisions, it has helped us make better decisions in every aspect of our lives.

Whether or not your own principles are systemized/computerized is of secondary importance. The most important thing is that you develop your own principles and ideally write them down, especially if you are working with others.

It was that approach and the principles it yielded, and not me, that took me from being an ordinary middle-class kid from Long Island to being successful by a number of conventional measures—like starting a company out of my two-bedroom apartment and building it into the fifth most important private company in the U.S. (according to *Fortune*), becoming one of the one hundred richest people in the world (according to *Forbes*), and being considered one of the one hundred most influential (according to *Time*). They led me to a perch from which I got to see success and life very differently than I had imagined, and they gave me the meaningful work and meaningful relationships I value even more than my conventional successes. They gave me and Bridgewater far more than I ever dreamed of.

Until recently, I didn't want to share these principles outside of Bridgewater because I don't like public attention and because I thought it would be presumptuous to tell others what principles to have. But after Bridgewater successfully anticipated the financial crisis of 2008–09, I got a lot of media attention and so did my principles and Bridgewater's unique way of operating. Most of those stories were distorted and sensationalistic, so in 2010, I posted our principles on our website so people could judge them for themselves. To my surprise, they were downloaded over three million times and I was flooded with thank-you letters from all over the world.

I will give them to you in two books—Life and Work Principles in one book, and Economic and Investment Principles in the other.

HOW THESE BOOKS ARE ORGANIZED

Since I have spent most of my adult life thinking about economies and investing, I considered writing Economic and Investment Principles first. But I decided to begin with my Life and Work Principles because they're more overarching and I've seen how well they work for people, independent of their careers. Since they go so well together, they are combined here in one book prefaced by a short autobiography, Where I'm Coming From.

Part I: Where I'm Coming From
In this part, I share some of the experiences—most importantly, my mistakes—that led me to discover the principles that guide my decision making. To tell you the truth, I still have mixed feelings about telling my personal story, because I worry that it might distract you from the principles themselves and from the timeless and uni-

versal cause-effect relationships that inform them. For that reason, I wouldn't mind if you decided to skip this part of the book. If you do read it, try to look past me and my particular story to the logic and merit of the principles I describe. Think about them, weigh them, and decide how much, if at all, they apply to you and your own life circumstances—and specifically, whether they can help you achieve your goals, whatever they may be.

Part II: Life Principles

The overarching principles that drive my approach to everything are laid out in Life Principles. In this section, I explain my principles in greater depth and show how they apply in the natural world, in our private lives and relationships, in business and policymaking, and of course at Bridgewater. I'll share the 5-Step Process I've developed for achieving one's goals and making effective choices; I'll also share some of the insights I've gained into psychology and neuroscience and explain how I've applied them in my private life and in my business. This is the real heart of the book because it shows how these principles can be applied to most anything by most anyone.

Part III: Work Principles

In Work Principles, you'll get a close-up view of the unusual way we operate at Bridgewater. I will explain how we've coalesced our principles into an idea meritocracy that strives to deliver meaningful work and meaningful relationships through *radical truth* and *radical transparency*. I'll show you how this works at a granular level and how it can be applied to nearly any organization to make it more effective. As you will see, we are simply a group of people who are striving to be excellent at what we do and who recognize that we don't know much relative to what we need to know. We believe that thoughtful, unemotional disagreement by independent thinkers can be converted into believability-weighted decision making that is smarter and more effective than the sum of its parts. Because the power of a group is so much greater than the power of an individual, I believe these work principles are even more important than the life principles on which they're based.

What Will Follow This Book

This print book will be followed by an interactive book in the form of an app that will take you into videos and immersive experiences so that your learning is more experiential. The app will also get to know you through your interactions with it in order to provide you with more personalized advice.

This book and the app will be followed by another volume containing two other parts, Economic and Investment Principles, in which I will pass along the principles that have worked for me and that I believe might help you in these areas.

After that, there will be no advice I can give that will not be available in these two books, and I will be done with this phase of my life.

Think for yourself!

1) What do you want?

2) What is true?

3) What are you going to do about it?

PART I

WHERE I'M COMING FROM

Time is like a river that carries us forward into encounters with reality that require us to make decisions. We can't stop our movement down this river and we can't avoid those encounters. We can only approach them in the best possible way.

When we are children, other people, typically our parents, guide us through our encounters with reality. As we get older, we begin to make our own choices. We choose what we are going after (our goals), and that influences our paths. If you want to be a doctor, you go to medical school; if you want to have a family, you find a mate; and so on. As we move toward these goals, we encounter problems, make mistakes, and run up against our own personal weaknesses. We learn about ourselves and about reality and make new decisions. Over the course of our lives, we make millions and millions of decisions that are essentially bets, some large and some small. It pays to think about how we make them because they are what ultimately determine the quality of our lives.

We are all born with different thinking abilities but we aren't born with decision-making skills. We learn them from our encounters with reality. While the path I went down is unique—being born to particular parents, pursuing a particular career, having particular colleagues—I believe that the principles I learned along the way will work equally well for most people on most paths. As you read my story, try to look through it and me to the underlying cause-and-effect relationships—at the choices I made and their consequences, what I learned from them, and how I changed the ways I make decisions as a result. Ask yourself what you want, seek out examples of other people who got what they wanted, and try to discern the cause-and-effect patterns behind their achievements so you can apply them to help you achieve your own goals.

To help you understand where I'm coming from, I am giving you an unvarnished account of my life and career, placing special emphasis on my mistakes and weaknesses and the principles I learned from them.

CHAPTER 1

MY CALL TO ADVENTURE:

1949–1967

I was born in 1949 and grew up in a middle-class Long Island neighborhood, the only son of a professional jazz musician and a stay-at-home mom. I was an ordinary kid in an ordinary house and a worse-than-ordinary student. I loved playing around with my pals—touch football in the streets and baseball in a neighbor's backyard when I was young, and chasing girls when I got older.

Our DNA gives us our innate strengths and weaknesses. My most obvious weakness was my bad rote memory. I couldn't, and still can't, remember facts that don't have reasons for being what they are (like phone numbers), and I don't like following instructions. At the same time, I was very curious and loved to figure things out for myself, though that was less obvious at the time.

I didn't like school, not just because it required a lot of memorization, but because I wasn't interested in most of the things my teachers thought were important. I never understood what doing well in school would get me other than my mother's approval.

My mother adored me and worried about my poor grades. Up until middle school, she would make me go to my room and study for a couple of hours before going out to play, but I couldn't bring myself to do it. She was always there for me. She folded and rubber-banded the newspapers I delivered and baked cookies for the two of us to eat while we watched horror movies together on Saturday nights. She died when I was nineteen. At the time, I couldn't imagine ever laughing again. Now when I think of her I smile.

My dad worked very late hours as a musician—until about three in the morning—so he slept late on weekends. As a result, we didn't have much of a relationship when I was young other than him constantly nagging me to take care of chores like mowing the lawn and cutting the hedges, which I hated. He was a responsible man dealing with an irresponsible kid. Memories of how we interacted seem funny to me today. For example, one time he told me to cut the grass and I decided to do just the front yard and postpone doing the back, but then it rained for a couple of days and the backyard grass became so high I had to cut it with a sickle. That took so long that by the time I was finished, the front yard was too high to mow, and so on.

After my mother died, my dad and I became very close, especially when I started my own family. I both liked and loved him. He had a casual, fun way about him the way musicians tend to, and I admired his strong character, which I assume came from living through the Great Depression and fighting in both World War II and the Korean War. I have memories of him from when he was in his seventies, not hesitating to drive through big snowstorms, shoveling himself out whenever he got stuck like it was no big deal. After playing in clubs and cutting records for most of his life, he began a second career in his midsixties, teaching music in high school and at a local community college, which he continued until he had a heart attack at eighty-one. He lived another decade after that, as sharp as ever mentally.

When I didn't want to do something, I would fight it, but when I was excited about something, nothing could hold me back. For example, while I resisted doing chores at home, I eagerly did them outside the house to earn money. Starting at age eight, I had a newspaper route, shoveled snow off people's driveways, caddied, bussed tables and washed dishes at a local restaurant, and stocked shelves at a nearby department store. I don't remember my parents encouraging me to do these jobs so I can't say how I came by them. But I do know that having those jobs and having some money to handle independently in those early years taught me many valuable lessons I wouldn't have learned in school or at play.

In my early years the psychology of the 1960s U.S. was aspirational and inspirational—to achieve great and noble goals. It was like nothing I have seen since. One of my earliest memories was of John F. Kennedy, an intelligent, charismatic man who painted vivid pictures of changing the world for the better—exploring outer space, achieving equal rights, and eliminating poverty. He and his ideas had a major effect on my thinking.

The United States was then at its peak relative to the rest of the world, accounting for 40 percent of its economy compared to about 20 percent today; the dollar was the world's currency; and the U.S. was the dominant military power. Being "liberal" meant being committed to moving forward in a fast and fair way, while being "conservative" meant being stuck in old and unfair ways—at least that's how it seemed to me and to most of the people around me. As we saw it, the U.S. was rich, progressive, well managed, and on a mission to improve quickly at everything. I might have been naive but I wasn't alone.

In those years, everyone was talking about the stock market, because it was doing great and people were making money. This included the people playing at a local golf course called Links where I started caddying when I was twelve. So I took my caddying money and started playing the stock market. My first investment was in Northeast Airlines. I bought it because it was the only company I'd heard of that was selling for less than $5 a share. I figured the more shares I bought, the more money I would make. That was a dumb strategy, but I tripled my money. Northeast Airlines was actually about to go broke and another company acquired it. I got lucky, but I didn't know it at the time. I just thought making money in the markets was easy, so I was hooked.

In those days, *Fortune* magazine had a little tear-out coupon you could mail in to get free annual reports from Fortune 500 companies. I ordered them all. I can still remember watching the mailman unhappily lugging all those reports to our door, and I dug into every

NORTHEAST AIRLINES EQUITY PRICE

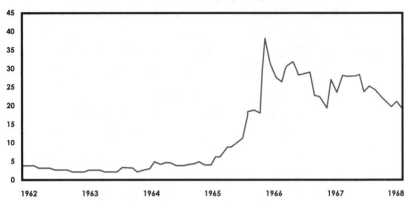

one of them. That was how I began building an investment library. As the stock market continued to climb, World War II and the Depression seemed like distant memories and investing seemed like simply a matter of buying anything and watching it go up. It would certainly go up, the common knowledge held, because managing the economy had developed into a science. After all, stocks had nearly quadrupled over the previous ten years, and some had done much better than that.

As a result, "dollar-cost averaging"—investing essentially the same dollar amount in the market every month, no matter how few or many shares it could buy—was the strategy most people followed. Of course, picking the best stocks was even better, so that's what I and everyone else tried to do. There were thousands to choose from, all neatly listed on the last few pages of the newspaper.

While I liked playing the markets, I also loved playing around with my friends, whether in the neighborhood when I was a kid, using fake IDs to get into bars when we were teens, or, nowadays, going to music festivals and on scuba-diving trips together. I've always been an independent thinker inclined to take risks in search of rewards—not just in the markets, but in most everything. I also feared boredom and mediocrity much more than I feared failure. For me, great is better than terrible, and terrible is better than mediocre, because terrible at least gives life flavor. The high school yearbook quote my friends chose for me was from Thoreau: "If a man does not keep pace with his companions, perhaps it is because he hears a different drummer. Let him step to the music which he hears, however measured or far away."

In 1966, my senior year of high school, the stock market was still booming and I was making money and having a blast, cutting school with my best friend Phil to go surfing, and doing what fun-loving high school boys usually do. Of course I didn't know it then, but that year was to be the stock market's top. After that, almost everything I thought I knew about the markets was proven wrong.

CHAPTER 2

CROSSING THE THRESHOLD:

1967–1979

I came into this period with the biases I had picked up from my experiences and the people around me. In 1966, asset prices reflected investors' optimism about the future. But between 1967 and 1979, bad economic surprises led to big and unexpected price declines. Not just the economy and the markets but social sentiment deteriorated as well. Living through that taught me that while almost everyone expects the future to be a slightly modified version of the present, it is usually very different. But I didn't know that in 1967. Certain that stocks would eventually rebound, I kept buying them, even as the market fell and I lost money until I figured out what was going wrong and how to deal with it. I gradually learned that prices reflect people's expectations, so they go up when actual results are better than expected and they go down when they are worse than expected. And most people tend to be biased by their recent experiences.

That fall, I started at a local college, C. W. Post. I got in on probation because of my C average in high school. But unlike high school, I loved college because I could learn about things that interested me, not because I had to, so I got great grades. I also loved living away from home and having independence.

Learning to meditate helped too. When the Beatles visited India in

1968 to study Transcendental Meditation at the ashram of Maharishi Mahesh Yogi, I was curious to learn it, so I did. I loved it. Meditation has benefited me hugely throughout my life because it produces a calm open-mindedness that allows me to think more clearly and creatively.

I majored in finance in college because of my love for the markets and because that major had no foreign language requirement—so it allowed me to learn what I was interested in, both inside and outside class. I learned a lot about commodity futures from a very interesting classmate, a Vietnam veteran quite a bit older than me. Commodities were attractive because they could be traded with very low margin requirements, meaning I could leverage the limited amount of money I had to invest. If I could make winning decisions, which I planned to do, I could borrow more to make more. Stock, bond, and currency futures didn't exist back then. Commodity futures were strictly real commodities like corn, soybeans, cattle, and hogs. So those were the markets I started to trade and learn about.

My college years coincided with the era of free love, mind-expanding drug experimentation, and rejection of traditional authority. Living through it had a lasting effect on me and many other members of my generation. For example, it deeply impacted Steve Jobs, whom I came to empathize with and admire. Like me, he took up meditation and wasn't interested in being taught as much as he loved visualizing and building out amazing new things. The times we lived in taught us both to question established ways of doing things—an attitude he demonstrated superbly in Apple's iconic "1984" and "Here's to the Crazy Ones," which were ad campaigns that spoke to me.

For the country as a whole, those were difficult years. As the draft expanded and the numbers of young men coming home in body bags soared, the Vietnam War split the country. There was a lottery based on birthdates to determine the order of those who would be drafted. I remember listening to the lottery on the radio while playing pool with my friends. It was estimated that the first 160 or so birthdays called would be drafted, though they read off all 366 dates. My birthday was forty-eighth.

I wasn't smart enough to be afraid of going to war because I naively thought nothing bad could happen to me, but I didn't want to go because I was charging forward with my life and to put it on hold for two years seemed like an eternity. My dad, though, was adamantly against the war and hell-bent against me going, even though he had believed in and fought in the prior two wars. He had me examined by a doctor who discovered I had hypoglycemia, which gave me an exemption. When I look back on that, I see that I got out of serving on a technicality—that my dad was essentially helping me dodge the draft—which now gives me mixed feelings. I feel guilty I didn't do my part, relieved I didn't experience the harmful consequences so many others suffered from the war, and appreciative of my dad for the love behind his effort to protect me. I have no idea what I'd do if I were faced with the same situation today.

As America's politics and economy deteriorated, the country's mood became depressed. The Tet Offensive in January 1968[1] seemed to convey the U.S. was losing the war; that same year Lyndon Johnson decided not to run for a second term and Richard Nixon was elected, beginning an even more difficult era. At the same time, France's president Charles de Gaulle was turning in his country's dollars for gold because he was concerned the U.S. was printing money to finance its spending. Watching the news and the market move together, I began to see the whole picture and understand the cause-effect relationship between the two.

Around 1970 or 1971, I noticed gold was starting to tick up in world markets. Until then, like most people, I hadn't paid much attention to currency rates because the currency system had been stable throughout my lifetime. But as currency events increasingly appeared in the news, they caught my attention. I learned that other currencies were fixed against the dollar, that the dollar was fixed against gold, that Americans weren't allowed to own gold (though I wasn't sure why), and that other central banks could convert their paper dollars into gold, which was how they were assured that they wouldn't be hurt if the U.S. printed too many dollars. I heard our government

---

[1] A surprise simultaneous attack by the North Vietnamese on more than one hundred cities and towns in South Vietnam.

officials pooh-pooh the worries about the dollar and the excitement about gold, assuring us that the dollar was sound and that gold was just an archaic metal. Speculators were behind the rising gold prices, they said, and they would get burned once things settled down. Back then, I still assumed that government officials were honest.

In the spring of 1971, I graduated college with a nearly perfect grade point average, which got me into Harvard Business School. The summer before I started at HBS, I got a job as a clerk on the floor of the New York Stock Exchange. By midsummer, the dollar problem began to reach a breaking point. There were reports that Europeans wouldn't accept dollars from American tourists. The global monetary system was in the process of breaking down, but that wasn't clear to me quite yet.

Then, on Sunday, August 15, 1971, President Nixon went on television to announce that the U.S. would renege on its promise to allow dollars to be turned in for gold, which led the dollar to plummet. Since government officials had promised not to devalue the dollar, I listened with amazement as he spoke. Instead of addressing the fundamental problems behind the pressure on the dollar, he continued to blame speculators, crafting his words to make it sound like he was moving to support the dollar while his actions were doing just the opposite. "Floating it," as Nixon was doing, and then letting it sink like a stone, looked a lot like a lie to me. Over the decades since, I've repeatedly seen policymakers deliver such assurances immediately before currency devaluations, so I learned not to believe government policymakers when they assure you that they won't let a currency devaluation happen. The more strongly they make those assurances, the more desperate the situation probably is, so the more likely it is that a devaluation will take place.

As I listened to Nixon speak, I wondered what those developments meant. Money as we'd known it—a claim check to get gold—no longer existed. That couldn't be good. It seemed clear to me that the era of promise that Kennedy had personified was unraveling.

Monday morning I walked onto the floor of the exchange expecting pandemonium. There was pandemonium all right, but not the sort

I expected: Instead of falling, the stock market jumped about 4 percent, a significant daily gain.

To try to understand what was happening, I spent the rest of that summer studying past currency devaluations. I learned that everything that was going on—the currency breaking its link to gold and devaluing, the stock market soaring in response—had happened before, and that logical cause-effect relationships made those developments inevitable. My failure to anticipate this, I realized, was due to my being surprised by something that hadn't happened in my lifetime, though it had happened many times before. The message that reality was conveying to me was "You better make sense of what happened to other people in other times and other places because if you don't you won't know if these things can happen to you and, if they do, you won't know how to deal with them."

Enrolling at Harvard Business School that fall, I was excited about meeting the extraordinarily intelligent people from all over the planet who would be my classmates. And high as my expectations were, the experience was even better. I lived with people from all over the world and we partied together in an exciting, eclectic environment. There was no teacher in front of a blackboard telling us what to remember and no tests to see whether we remembered it. Instead we were given actual case studies to read and analyze. Then we gathered in groups to thrash out what we would do if we were in the shoes of the people in those situations. This was my kind of school!

Meanwhile, thanks to the wave of money printing that had followed the demise of the gold standard, the economy and the stock market were soaring. Stocks were in again in 1972, and the fashion at the time was the Nifty 50. This group of fifty stocks had fast and steady earnings growth and were widely believed to be a sure thing.

As hot as the stock market was, I was more interested in trading commodities, so that spring I begged the director of commodities at Merrill Lynch to give me a summer job. He was surprised because people from places like Harvard Business School weren't typically interested in commodities, which were considered an obscure stepchild of the Wall Street brokerage industry. Up until then, as far as I know, no Harvard Business School student had ever worked in commodity futures anywhere. Most Wall Street firms didn't even have commodity futures divisions, and Merrill Lynch's was small, tucked away on a side street, and furnished with basic metal desks.

A few months later, when I was back for my second year at HBS, the first oil shock began, with prices quadrupling in a matter of months. The U.S. economy slowed, commodity prices soared, and in 1973 the stock market took a dive. Once again, I was blindsided—but in retrospect I could see that the dominoes had fallen in a logical sequence.

In this case, the debt-financed overspending of the 1960s had continued into the early 1970s. The Fed had funded this spending with easy-credit policies, but by paying back its debts with depreciated paper money instead of gold-backed dollars, the U.S. effectively defaulted. Naturally, with all this money printing the dollar plunged in value. That allowed for more easy credit, which led to even more spending. The inflationary surge that followed the breakdown of the currency system sent commodity prices even higher. In response, in 1973, the Fed tightened monetary policy, which is what central banks do when inflation and growth are too strong. This in turn caused the worst decline in stocks and the worst weakening of the economy since the Great Depression. The Nifty 50 were particularly affected, plunging severely.

The lesson? When everybody thinks the same thing—such as what a sure bet the Nifty 50 is—it is almost certainly reflected in the price, and betting on it is probably going to be a mistake. I also learned that for every action (such as easy money and credit) there is a consequence (in this case, higher inflation) roughly proportionate to that action, which causes an approximately equal and opposite reaction (tightening of money and credit) and market reversals.

I was beginning to see things happening over and over again, which led me to see that most everything is "another one of those": Most everything has happened repeatedly before for logical cause-effect reasons. Of course, being able to both properly identify which ones of those are happening and to understand the cause-effect relationships behind them remained difficult. Though most everything seemed inevitable and logical in retrospect, nothing was nearly as clear in real time.

Because people chase what's hot and avoid what's not, stock investing fell out of favor after 1973 and commodity trading became the thing to do. With my background in commodities and my Harvard MBA, I became a sought-after property. Dominick & Dominick, a middle-sized, hundred-year-old brokerage firm, hired me as director of commodities for $25,000 a year, which was near the top of what HBS graduate starting salaries were that year. My new boss paired me with an older, experienced guy who had lots of commodities brokerage experience, and we were assigned the task of setting up a commodities division. I was in way over my head, though I was too arrogant to realize it at the time. I probably would have learned a lot of painful lessons had the job continued, but the bad stock market took Dominick & Dominick under before we'd made much progress.

As the economy unraveled, the Watergate scandal dominated the headlines and I saw again how politics and economics intertwine, usually with economics leading. This downward spiral led people to become pessimistic, so they sold their stocks and the market continued to fall. Things couldn't have gotten much worse but everyone was afraid they would. It was the mirror image of what I'd witnessed in 1966 when the market hit its top, and just as it was then, the consensus was wrong. When people are very pessimistic, they sell out, prices typically get very cheap, and action to improve conditions has to be taken. Sure enough, the Fed eased its monetary policy and stocks hit bottom in December 1974.

At the time, I was single and living in New York; I was having a great time partying with friends from HBS and dating a lot. My roommate was dating a Cuban woman and he set me up on a blind date with one of her friends, an exotic woman from Spain named Barbara who could barely speak English. This wasn't a problem, because we communicated in different ways. She thrilled me for nearly two years before we moved in together, got married, had four sons, and shared an amazing life together. She still thrills me but is too private a person for me to say more about her.

While I worked in the brokerage business, I also traded my own account. Though I had many more winning positions than losing ones, I can only recall the losing ones now. I remember one big one when I owned pork bellies. For several days the market for them was limit down—meaning that the price had fallen so low that trading had to be stopped. I later described the impact of this experience to Jack Schwager, the author of *Hedge Fund Market Wizards*:

In those days, we had the big commodity boards, which clicked whenever prices changed. So each morning, on the opening, I would see and hear the market click down 200 points, the daily limit, stay unchanged at that price, and know that I had lost that much more, with the amount of potential additional losses still undefined. It was a very tactile experience . . . [and] it taught me the importance of risk controls, because I never wanted to experience that pain again. It enhanced my fear of being wrong and taught me to make sure that no single bet, or even multiple bets, could cause me to lose more than an acceptable amount. In trading you have to be defensive and aggressive at the same time. If you are not aggressive, you are not going to make money, and if you are not defensive, you are not going to keep money. I believe that anyone who has made money in trading has had to experience horrendous pain at some point. Trading is like working with electricity; you can get an electric shock. With that pork belly trade and other trades, I felt the electric shock and the fear that comes with it.

After Dominick & Dominick closed its retail business, I moved on to a bigger, more successful brokerage firm. During my short stay there, it took over numerous other firms and changed its name several times, eventually becoming Shearson, though Sandy Weill stayed in charge through it all.

Shearson put me in charge of its futures hedging business, which included both commodity futures and financial futures. I was the person helping clients who had price risks in their businesses manage them by using futures. I developed quite an expertise in the grain and livestock markets, which often led me down to West Texas and the agricultural areas of California. The Shearson brokers, cattle producers, and grain dealers I dealt with were great folks who brought me into their worlds, taking me to honky-tonks, dove hunts, and barbecues. We worked and had a blast together, and I built a second life with them that lasted several years—though my job at Shearson lasted only a bit more than a year.

Much as I loved the job and the people I worked with, I didn't fit into the Shearson organization. I was too wild. For example, as a joke that now seems pretty stupid, I hired a stripper to drop her cloak while I was lecturing at a whiteboard at the California Grain & Feed Association's annual convention. I also punched my boss in the face. Not surprisingly, I was fired.

But the brokers, their clients, and even the ones who fired me liked me and wanted to keep getting my advice. Even better, they were willing to pay me for it, so in 1975 I started Bridgewater Associates.

STARTING BRIDGEWATER

Actually, I *re*started it. Just after I graduated from HBS and went to work in commodities at Dominick & Dominick, I'd set up a little business with Bob Scott, a friend from HBS. Along with a few pals in other countries, we made halfhearted attempts to sell commodities from the U.S. to other countries. We called it Bridgewater because we were "bridging the waters" and it had a good ring to it. By 1975 there wasn't much left of this commodities company, but as it did already exist on paper, I used it.

I worked out of my two-bedroom apartment. When a pal from HBS who I shared the apartment with moved out, I made his bedroom an office. I worked with another friend I played rugby with, and we hired a great young woman who worked as our assistant. That was Bridgewater.

I spent most of my time following the markets and putting myself in the shoes of my corporate clients to show them how I would handle market risks if I were them. And of course I continued to trade my own account. Pursuing a mission with friends to help clients beat the markets was much more fun than having a real job. As long as my basic living expenses were covered, I knew I'd be happy.

In 1977, Barbara and I decided to have a child, so we got married. We moved into a rented brownstone in Manhattan and I moved the company there too. The Russians were buying lots of grain at the time and wanted my advice, so I took Barbara on a combined honeymoon–business trip to the USSR. We arrived in Moscow on New Year's Eve and rode by bus from the drab airport through a dusting of snow, past St. Basil's Cathedral to a big party with a lot of incredibly friendly, fun-loving Russians.

My business has always been a way to get me into exotic places and allow me to meet interesting people. If I make any money from those trips, that's just icing on the cake.

MODELING MARKETS AS MACHINES

I was really getting my head into the livestock, meat, grain, and oilseed markets. I loved them because they were concrete and less subject than stocks to distorted perceptions of value. While stocks could stay too high or too low because "greater fools" kept buying or selling them, livestock ended up on the meat counter where it would be priced based on what consumers were willing to pay. I could visualize the processes that led to those sales and see the relationships underlying them. Since livestock eat grain (mostly corn) and soymeal, and since corn and soybeans compete for acreage, those markets are closely related. I learned just about everything imaginable about them—what the planted acreage and typical yields were in each of the major growing areas; how to convert rainfall levels in different weeks of the growing season into yield estimates; how to project harvest sizes, carrying costs, and livestock inventories by weight group, location, and rates of weight gain; and how to project dressing yields, retailer margins, consumer preferences by cut of meat, and the amounts to be slaughtered in each season.

This wasn't academic learning: People with practice in the business showed me how the agricultural processes worked, and I organized what they told me into models I used to map the interactions of those parts through time.

For example, by knowing how many cattle, chickens, and hogs were being fed, how much grain they ate, and how fast they gained weight, I could project both when and how much meat would come to market and when and how much corn and soymeal would be consumed. Likewise, by seeing how much acreage was planted with corn and soybeans in all the growing areas, doing regressions that showed how rainfall affected the yields in each of these areas, and applying weather forecasts and rainfall data, I could project the timing and quantity of corn and soybean production. To me it all looked like a beautiful machine with logical cause-effect relationships. By understanding these relationships, I could come up with decision rules (or principles) I could model.

These early models were a far cry from the ones we use now; they were back-of-the-envelope sketches, analyzed and converted into computer programs with the technology I could afford at the time. At the very beginning, I did regressions on my handheld Hewlett-Packard HP-67 calculator, plotted charts by hand with colored pencils, and recorded every trade in composition notebooks. When the personal computer came along, I could input the numbers and watch them be converted into pictures of what would happen on spreadsheets. Knowing how cattle, hogs, and chickens progressed through their stages of production, how they competed for meat-eater dollars, what meat-eaters would spend and why, and how the profit margins of meatpackers and retailers would influence their behaviors (for example, which cuts of meat they would push in advertisements), I could see how the machine produced cattle, hog, and chicken prices that I could bet on.

As basic as those early models were, I loved building and refining them—and they were good enough to make me money. The approach to price determination I was using was different from the one I had learned in my economics classes where supply and demand were both measured in terms of quantities sold. I found it much more practical to measure demand as the amount spent (instead of as the quantity bought) and to look at who the buyers and sellers were and why they bought and sold. I will explain this approach in Economic and Investment Principles.

This different approach was one of the key reasons I caught economic and market moves others missed. From that point on, whenever I looked at any market—commodities, stocks, bonds, currencies, whatever—I could see and understand imbalances that others who defined supply and demand in the traditional way (as units that equaled each other) missed.

Visualizing complex systems as machines, figuring out the cause-effect relationships within them, writing down the principles for dealing with them, and feeding them into a computer so the computer could "make decisions" for me all became standard practices.

Don't get me wrong. My approach was far from perfect. I vividly remember one "can't lose" bet that personally cost me about $100,000. That was most of my net worth at the time. More painful still, it hurt my clients too. The most painful lesson that was repeatedly hammered home is that you can never be sure of anything: There are always risks out there that can hurt you badly, even in the seemingly safest bets, so it's always best to assume you're missing something. This lesson changed my approach to decision making in ways that will reverberate throughout this book—and to which I attribute much of my success. But I would make many other mistakes before I fully changed my behavior.

BUILDING THE BUSINESS

While making money was good, having meaningful work and meaningful relationships was far better. To me, meaningful work is being on a mission I become engrossed in, and meaningful relationships are those I have with people I care deeply about and who care deeply about me.

Think about it: It's senseless to have making money as your goal as money has no intrinsic value—its value comes from what it can buy, and it can't buy everything. It's smarter to start with what you really want, which are your real goals, and then work back to what you need to attain them. Money will be one of the things you need, but it's not the only one and certainly not the most important one once you get past having the amount you need to get what you really want.

When thinking about the things you really want, it pays to think of their relative values so you weigh them properly. In my case, I wanted meaningful work and meaningful relationships equally, and I valued money less—as long as I had enough to take care of my basic needs. In thinking about the relative importance of great relationships and money, it was clear that relationships were more important because there is no amount of money I would take in exchange for a meaningful relationship, because there is nothing I could buy with that money that would be more valuable. So, for me, meaningful work and meaningful relationships were and still are my primary goals and everything I did was for them. Making money was an incidental consequence of that.

In the late 1970s, I began sending my observations about the markets to clients via telex. The genesis of these *Daily Observations* ("Grains and Oilseeds," "Livestock and Meats," "Economy and Financial Markets") was pretty simple: While our primary business was in managing risk exposures, our clients also called to pick my brain about the markets. Taking those calls became time-consuming, so I decided it would be more efficient to write down my thoughts every day so others could understand my logic and help improve it. It was a good discipline since it forced me to research and reflect every day. It also became a key channel of communication for our business. Today, almost forty years and ten thousand publications later, our *Daily Observations* are read, reflected on, and argued about by clients and policymakers around the world. I'm still writing them, along with others at Bridgewater, and expect to continue to write them until people don't care to read them or I die.

In addition to providing clients with these observations and advice, I began to manage their exposures by buying and selling on their behalf. Sometimes I was paid a fixed fee each month and sometimes I received a percentage of the profits. Among my consulting clients during this period was McDonald's, which was a huge beef buyer, and Lane Processing, then the largest chicken producer in the country. I made them both a lot of money—especially Lane Processing, which did even better from its speculations in the grain and soy markets than it did from raising and selling chickens.

Around this time, McDonald's had conceived of a new product, the Chicken McNugget, but they were reluctant to bring it to market because of their concern that chicken prices might rise and squeeze their profit margins. Chicken producers like Lane wouldn't agree to sell to them at a fixed price because they were worried that their costs would go up and *they* would be squeezed.

As I thought about the problem, it occurred to me that in economic terms a chicken can be seen as a simple machine consisting of a chick plus its feed. The most volatile cost that the chicken producer needed to worry about was feed prices. I showed Lane how to use a mix of corn and soymeal futures to lock in costs so they could quote a fixed price to McDonald's. Having greatly reduced its price risk, McDonald's introduced the McNugget in 1983. I felt great about helping make that happen.

I identified similar types of price relationships in the cattle and meat markets. For example, I showed cattle feeders how they could lock in strong profit margins by hedging good price relationships between their cost items (feeder cattle, corn, and soymeal) and what they were going to sell (fed cattle) six months later. I developed a way of selling different cuts of fresh meat for future delivery at fixed prices far below frozen meat prices but that still produced big profit margins. Combining my clients' deep understanding of the way the "machines" of their own businesses operated with my knowledge of the way markets functioned worked to our mutual advantage, while making the markets more efficient overall. My ability to visualize these complex machines gave us a competitive edge against those who were shooting from the hip, and eventually changed the way these industries operated. And, as always, it was a kick to be working with people I liked.

On March 26, 1978, my wife gave birth to our first son, Devon. To have a child was the most difficult decision I ever made, because

I couldn't know what the experience would be like and it would be irrevocable. It turned out to be my best decision. While I won't delve too much into my family life in this book, I pursued it with the same sort of intensity with which I pursued my career, and I linked them. To give you an idea about how interwoven they were in my mind, Devon was named after one of the oldest breeds of cattle known to man, among the first breeds imported into the U.S. and renowned for its high fertility.

CHAPTER 3

MY ABYSS:

1979–1982

F rom 1950 until 1980, debt, inflation, and growth moved up and down together in steadily larger waves, with each bigger than the one before, especially after the dollar's link to gold was broken in 1971. In the 1970s, there were three such waves. The first came in 1971, as a result of the dollar's devaluation. The second, which came between 1974 and 1975, took inflation to its highest level since World War II. The Fed tightened the money supply, driving interest rates to record highs, which caused the worst stock market and economic downturn since the 1930s. The third and largest wave came in 1979–82 and was one of the greatest economic/market crescendos and reversals since 1929–32. Interest rates and inflation soared and crashed; stocks, bonds, commodities, and currencies went through one of their most volatile periods ever; and unemployment hit its highest level since the Great Depression. It was a time of extreme turbulence for the global economy, for the markets, and for me personally.

In 1978–80 (as in 1970–71 and in 1974–75) different markets began to move in unison because they were more influenced by swings in money and credit growth than by changes in their individual supply-demand balances. These big moves were exacerbated by the oil shock that followed the fall of the Shah of Iran. That oil market volatility led to the creation of the first oil futures contract, which gave me trading opportunities (by then, there were futures markets in interest rates and currencies as well, and I was making bets in all of them).

Because all markets were being driven by these factors, I immersed myself in macroeconomics and historical data (especially interest rates and currency data) to improve my understanding of the machine at play. As inflation began to rise in 1978, I realized the Fed would likely act to tighten the monetary supply. By July 1979, inflation was clearly out of control, and President Jimmy Carter appointed Paul Volcker chairman of the Federal Reserve. A few months later, Volcker announced that the Fed would limit the growth of the money supply to 5.5 percent. According to my calculations at the time, 5.5 percent money growth would break the inflation spiral—but it would also strangle the economy and markets and likely cause a catastrophic debt crisis.

A SILVER ROLLER COASTER

Just before Thanksgiving, I met with Bunker Hunt, then the richest man in the world, at the Petroleum Club in Dallas. Bud Dillard, a Texan friend and client of mine who was big in the oil and cattle businesses, had introduced us a couple of years before, and we regularly talked about the economy and markets, especially inflation. Just a few weeks before our meeting, Iranian militants had stormed the U.S. embassy in Tehran, taking fifty-two Americans hostage. There were long lines to buy gas and extreme market volatility. There was clearly a sense of crisis: The nation was confused, frustrated, and angry.

Bunker saw the debt crisis and inflation risks pretty much as I saw them. He'd been wanting to get his wealth out of paper money for the past few years, so he'd been buying commodities, especially silver, which he had started purchasing for about $1.29 per ounce, as a hedge against inflation. He kept buying and buying as inflation and the price of silver went up, until he had essentially cornered the silver market. At that point, silver was trading at around $10. I told him I thought it might be a good time to get out because the Fed was becoming tight enough to raise short-term interest rates above long-term rates (which was called "inverting the yield curve"). Every time that happened, inflation-hedged assets and the economy went down. But Bunker was in the oil business, and the Middle East oil producers he talked to were still worried about the depreciation of the dollar. They had told him they were also going to buy silver as a hedge against inflation so he held on to it in the expectation that its price would continue to rise. I got out.

On December 8, 1979, Barbara and I had our second son, Paul. Everything was changing very fast, but I loved the intensity of it all.

By early 1980, silver had gone to nearly $50, and as rich as he was, Bunker became a lot richer. While I had made a lot of money on silver's rise to $10, I was kicking myself for missing the ride to $50. But at least, by being out, I didn't lose money. There are anxious times in every investor's career when your expectations of what should be happening aren't aligned with what is happening and you don't know if you're looking at great opportunities or catastrophic mistakes. Because I had a strong tendency to be right but early, I was inclined to think that was the case. It was, but to have missed the $40 move up was inexcusable to me.

When the plunge finally did happen, in March 1980, silver crashed back down below $11. It ruined Hunt, and he nearly brought down the whole U.S. economy as he fell.[2] The Fed had to intervene to control the ripple effects. All of this pounded an indelible lesson into my head: Timing is everything. I was relieved that I was out of that market, but watching the richest man in the world—who was also someone I empathized with—go broke was jarring. Yet it was nothing compared to what was to come.

EXPANDING THE TEAM

Later that same year, a great guy named Paul Colman joined Bridgewater. We had become good friends from our dealings in the cattle and beef industry, and I respected his intellect and values, so I convinced him we should conquer that world together. He brought his wonderful

---

[2] His inability to meet his obligations, especially his margin calls at brokerage houses, could have led to cascading defaults.

wife and kids up from Guymon, Oklahoma, and our families became inseparable. We ran the business in a scrappy, seat-of-the-pants way. Because the office part of the brownstone where I lived and worked was generally such a mess—with chicken bones or other scraps from working through the previous night's dinner littering my desk—we held all our client meetings at the Harvard Club. Paul would hide a clean blue oxford shirt and tie amid the mess so I'd have something to wear. In 1981, we decided we wanted to raise our families in more of a country setting, so we all moved up to Wilton, Connecticut, to run Bridgewater from there.

Colman and I worked by challenging each other's ideas and trying to find the best answers; it was a constant back-and-forth, which we both enjoyed, especially at a time when there was so much to figure out. We would debate about the markets and the forces behind them late into the night, plug data into the computer before we went to bed, and see what it spit out in the morning.

MY BIG DEPRESSION CALL

The economy was in even worse shape in 1979–81 than it was during the financial crisis of 2007–08 and the markets were more volatile. In fact, some would say this was the most volatile period ever. The charts opposite going back to 1940 show the volatility of interest rates and gold.

As you can see, there had been nothing like it prior to 1979–82. It was one of the most pivotal times in the last hundred years. The political pendulum throughout the world swung to the right, bringing Margaret Thatcher, Ronald Reagan, and Helmut Kohl to power. "Liberal" had ceased to mean being in favor of progress and had come to mean "paying people not to work."

As I saw it, the Fed was stuck between a rock and a hard place. They either had to a) print money to relieve debt problems and keep the economy going (which had already pushed inflation to 10 percent in 1981 and was causing people to dump bonds and buy inflation-hedged assets), or b) break the back of inflation by becoming bone-crushingly tight (which would break the back of debtors because debt was at the

T-BILL RATE

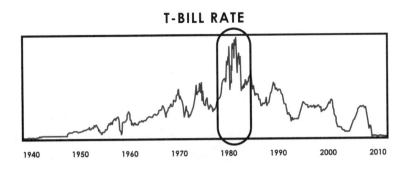

10 YR BOND YIELD

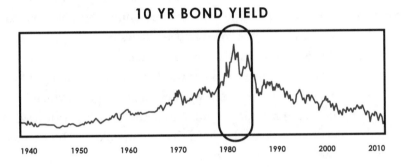

GOLD PRICE

highest levels since the Great Depression). The worsening problem showed up in both progressively higher levels of inflation and progressively worse levels of economic activity. Both appeared to be coming to a head. Debts continued to rise much faster than the incomes borrowers needed to repay them, and American banks were lending huge amounts—much more than they had in capital—to emerging countries. In March 1981, I wrote a *Daily Observation* entitled "The Next

Depression in Perspective" and concluded it by saying, "The enormity of our debt implies that the depression will be as bad or worse than that witnessed in the thirties."

This view was extremely controversial. To most people, "depression" was a scary word used by kooky and sensationalist people, not something thoughtful people took seriously. But I had studied debt and depressions back to 1800, done my calculations, and was confident that the debt crisis led by emerging countries was coming. I had to share my thinking with my clients. Because my views were so controversial I asked others to track my reasoning and point out to me where it was bad. No one could find any flaws in my logic, though they were all reluctant to endorse my conclusion.

Because I believed that the choice was between accelerating inflation and deflationary depression, I was holding both gold (which performs well in accelerating inflation) and bonds (which perform well in deflationary depressions). Up until that point, gold and bonds had moved in opposite directions, depending on whether inflation expectations rose or fell. Holding those positions seemed much safer than holding alternatives like cash, which would lose value in an inflation environment, or stocks, which would crash in a depression.

At first, the markets went against me. But my experience with silver and other trades had taught me that I had a chronic problem with timing, so I believed I was just early and what I was expecting would happen soon. That didn't take long to happen. By the fall of 1981, the tight Fed policies were having a devastating effect, my bond bets were beginning to pay off, and my kooky views were starting to look right on. In February 1982, the Fed temporarily added liquidity to avoid a cash crunch. In June, as the scramble for liquidity intensified, the Fed responded by printing money, increasing liquidity to its highest level since Paul Volcker's appointment. But it still wasn't enough.

THE GREATEST WHIPSAW EVER

In August 1982, Mexico defaulted on its debt. By then, it was clear to most everyone that a number of other countries were about to follow.

This was a huge deal, because U.S. banks had lent about 250 percent of their capital to other countries just as at risk as Mexico. Business loan activity in the U.S. ground to a halt.

Because I was one of the few people who had seen these things coming, I started to get a lot of attention. Congress was holding hearings on the crisis and invited me to testify; in November I was the featured guest on *Wall $treet Week with Louis Rukeyser*, the must-watch show for anyone in the markets. In both appearances, I confidently declared that we were headed for depression and explained why.

After Mexico's default, the Fed responded to the economic collapse and debt defaults by making money more readily available. This caused the stock market to jump by a record amount. While that surprised me, I interpreted it as a knee-jerk reaction to the Fed's move. After all, in 1929 a 15 percent rally was followed by the greatest crash of all time. In October, I laid out my prognosis in a memo. As I saw it, there was a 75 percent chance the Fed's efforts would fall short and the economy would move into failure; a 20 percent chance it would initially succeed at stimulating the economy but still ultimately fail; and a 5 percent chance it would provide enough stimulus to save the economy but trigger hyperinflation. To hedge against the worst possibilities, I bought gold and T-bill futures as a spread against eurodollars, which was a limited-risk way of betting on credit problems increasing.

I was dead wrong. After a delay, the economy responded to the Fed's efforts, rebounding in a noninflationary way. In other words, inflation fell while growth accelerated. The stock market began a big bull run, and over the next eighteen years the U.S. economy enjoyed the greatest noninflationary growth period in its history.

How was that possible? Eventually, I figured it out. As money poured out of these borrower countries and into the U.S., it changed everything. It drove the dollar up, which produced deflationary pressures in the U.S., which allowed the Fed to ease interest rates without raising inflation. This fueled a boom. The banks were protected both because the Federal Reserve loaned them cash and the creditors' committees and international financial restructuring organizations such as the International Monetary Fund (IMF) and the Bank for International Settlements arranged things so that the debtor nations could pay their debt service from new loans. That way everyone could pretend everything was fine and write down those loans over many years.

My experience over this period was like a series of blows to the head with a baseball bat. Being so wrong—and especially so publicly wrong—was incredibly humbling and cost me just about everything I had built at Bridgewater. I saw that I had been an arrogant jerk who was totally confident in a totally incorrect view.

So there I was after eight years in business, with nothing to show for it. Though I'd been right much more than I'd been wrong, I was all the way back to square one.

At one point, I'd lost so much money I couldn't afford to pay the people who worked with me. One by one, I had to let them go. We went down to two employees—Colman and me. Then Colman had to go. With tears from all, his family packed up and returned to Oklahoma. Bridgewater was now down to just one employee: me.

Losing people I cared so much about and very nearly losing my dream of working for myself was devastating. To make ends meet, I even had to borrow $4,000 from my dad until we could sell our second car. I had come to a fork in the road: Should I put on a tie and take a job on Wall Street? That was not the life I wanted. On the other hand, I had a wife and two young children to support. I realized I was facing one of life's big turning points and my choices would have big implications for me and for my family's future.

FINDING A WAY PAST MY INTRACTABLE INVESTMENT PROBLEM

Making money in the markets is tough. The brilliant trader and investor Bernard Baruch put it well when he said, "If you are ready to give up everything else and study the whole history and background of the market and all principal companies whose stocks are on the board as carefully as a medical student studies anatomy—if you can do all that and in addition you have the cool nerves of a gambler, the sixth sense of a clairvoyant and the courage of a lion, you have a ghost of a chance."

In retrospect, the mistakes that led to my crash seemed embarrassingly obvious. First, I had been wildly overconfident and had let my emotions get the better of me. I learned (again) that no matter how much I knew and how hard I worked, I could never be certain enough to proclaim things like what I'd said on *Wall $treet Week*: "There'll be no soft landing. I can say that with absolute certainty, because I know how markets work." I am still shocked and embarrassed by how arrogant I was.

Second, I again saw the value of studying history. What had happened, after all, was "another one of those." I should have realized that debts denominated in one's own currency can be successfully restructured with the government's help, and that when central banks simultaneously provide stimulus (as they did in March 1932, at the low point of the Great Depression, and as they did again in 1982), inflation and deflation can be balanced against each other. As in 1971, I had failed to recognize the lessons of history. Realizing that led me to try to make sense of all movements in all major economies and markets going back a hundred years and to come up with carefully tested decision-making principles that are timeless and universal.

Third, I was reminded of how difficult it is to time markets. My long-term estimates of equilibrium levels were not reliable enough to bet on; too many things could happen between the time I placed my bets and the time (if ever) that my estimates were reached.

Staring at these failings, I realized that if I was going to move forward without a high likelihood of getting whacked again, I would have to look at myself objectively and change—starting by learning a better way of handling the natural aggressiveness I've always shown in going after what I wanted.

Imagine that in order to have a great life you have to cross a dangerous jungle. You can stay safe where you are and have an ordinary life, or you can risk crossing the jungle to have a terrific life. How would you approach that choice? Take a moment to think about it because it is the sort of choice that, in one form or another, we all have to make.

Even after my crash, I knew I had to go after the terrific life with all its risks, so the question was how to "cross the dangerous jungle" without getting killed. In retrospect, my crash was one of the best things that ever happened to me because it gave me the humility I needed to balance my aggressiveness. I learned a great fear of being wrong that shifted my mind-set from thinking "I'm right" to asking myself "How do I know I'm right?" And I saw clearly that the best way to answer this question is by finding other independent thinkers who are on the same mission as me and who see things differently from me. By engaging them in thoughtful disagreement, I'd be able to understand their reasoning and have them stress-test mine. That way, we can all raise our probability of being right.

In other words, I just want to be right—I don't care if the right answer comes from me. So I learned to be radically open-minded to allow others to point out what I might be missing. I saw that the only way I could succeed would be to:

1. Seek out the smartest people who disagreed with me so I could try to understand their reasoning.
2. Know when not to have an opinion.
3. Develop, test, and systemize timeless and universal principles.
4. Balance risks in ways that keep the big upside while reducing the downside.

Doing these things significantly improved my returns relative to my risks, and the same principles apply in other aspects of life. Most importantly, this experience led me to build Bridgewater as an idea meritocracy—not an autocracy in which I lead and others follow, and not a democracy in which everyone's vote is equal—but a meritocracy that encourages thoughtful disagreements and explores and weighs people's opinions in proportion to their merits.

Bringing these opposing opinions into the open and exploring them taught me a lot about how people think. I came to see that people's greatest weaknesses are the flip sides of their greatest strengths. For example, some people are prone to take on too much risk while others are too risk averse; some are too focused on the details while others are too big-picture. Most are too much one way and not enough another. Typically, by doing what comes naturally to us, we fail to account for our weaknesses, which leads us to crash. What happens after we crash is most important. Successful people change in ways that allow them to continue to take advantage of their strengths while compensating for their weaknesses and unsuccessful people don't. Later in the book I will describe specific strategies for change, but the important thing to note here is that beneficial change begins when you can acknowledge and even embrace your weaknesses.

Over the years that followed, I found that most of the extraordinarily successful people I've met had similar big painful failures that taught them the lessons that ultimately helped them succeed. Looking back on getting fired from Apple in 1985, Steve Jobs said, "It was awful-tasting medicine, but I guess the patient needed it. Sometimes life hits you in the head with a brick. Don't lose faith. I'm convinced that the only thing that kept me going was that I loved what I did."

I saw that to do exceptionally well you have to push your limits and that, if you push your limits, you will crash and it will hurt a lot. You will think you have failed—but that won't be true unless you give up. Believe it or not, your pain will fade and you will have many other opportunities ahead of you, though you might not see them at the time. The most important thing you can do is to gather the lessons these failures provide and gain humility and radical open-mindedness in order to increase your chances of success. Then you press on.

My final lesson was perhaps the most important one, because it has applied again and again throughout my life. At first, it seemed to me that I faced an all-or-nothing choice: I could either take on a lot of risk in pursuit of high returns (and occasionally find myself ruined) or I could lower my risk and settle for lower returns. But I needed to have both low risk and high returns, and by setting out on a mission to discover how I could, I learned to go slowly when faced with the choice between two things that you need that are seemingly at odds. That way you can figure out how to have as much of both as possible. There is almost always a good path that you just haven't discovered yet, so look for it until you find it rather than settle for the choice that is then apparent to you.

As difficult as this was, I eventually found a way to have my cake and eat it too. I call it the "Holy Grail of Investing," and it's the secret behind Bridgewater's success.

CHAPTER 4

MY ROAD OF TRIALS:

1983–1994

C oming out of my crash, I was so broke I couldn't muster enough money to pay for an airplane ticket to Texas to visit a prospective client, even though the fees I'd earn were many times the cost of the fare—so I didn't make that trip. Still, I gradually added clients, revenue, and a new team. With time, my upswings increased in magnitude and my downswings were both tolerable and educational. I never thought of what I was doing as building (or rebuilding) a company; I was just getting the things I needed to play my game.

Computers were among the most valuable things I acquired, because of how they helped me think. Without them, Bridgewater would not have been nearly as successful as it turned out to be.

The first microcomputers (what would later be known as personal computers) had come on the market during the late 1970s, and I had been using them as econometricians did, applying statistics and computing power to economic data to analyze the workings of the economic machine. As I wrote in a December 1981 article, I believed (and still believe) that "theoretically . . . if there was a computer that could hold all of the world's facts and if it was perfectly programmed to mathematically express all of the relationships between all of the world's parts, the future could be perfectly foretold."

But I was a long way from doing that. Though my early systems provided valuable insights into where prices would eventually reach equilibrium, they hadn't helped me develop robust trading strategies; they just showed me that a particular bet would eventually pay off. For example, I'd run through my analysis and end up with a view that the price of some commodity should be, say, 75 cents or so. If it was currently 60 cents, I'd know I wanted to buy it, but I wouldn't be able to predict that the price would drop to 50 cents before climbing back to 75, and I wouldn't know when to buy and sell. Rarely, but still too often, the system would be dead wrong and I would lose a lot.

"He who lives by the crystal ball is destined to eat ground glass" is a saying I quoted a lot in those days. Between 1979 and 1982, I had eaten enough glass to realize that what was most important wasn't knowing the future—it was knowing how to react appropriately to the information available at each point in time. In order to do that, I would have to have a vast store of economic and market data to draw on—and as it happened, I did.

From very early on, whenever I took a position in the markets, I wrote down the criteria I used to make my decision. Then, when I closed out a trade, I could reflect on how well these criteria had worked. It occurred to me that if I wrote those criteria into formulas (now more fashionably called algorithms) and then ran historical data through them, I could test how well my rules would have worked in the past. Here's how it worked in practice: I would start out with my intuitions as I always did, but I would express them logically, as decision-making criteria, and capture them in a systematic way, creating a mental map of what I would do in each particular situation. Then I would run historical data through the systems to see how my decision would have performed in the past and, depending upon the results, modify the decision rules appropriately.

We tested the systems going as far back as we could, typically more than a century, in every country for which we had data, which gave me great perspective on how the economic/market machine worked through time and how to bet on it. Doing this helped educate me and led me to refine my criteria so they were timeless and universal. Once I vetted those relationships, I could run data through the systems as it flowed at us in real time and the computer could work just as my brain worked in processing it and making decisions.

The result was Bridgewater's original interest rate, stock, currencies, and precious metals systems, which we then combined into one system for managing our portfolio of bets. Our system was like an EKG on the economy's vital signs; as they changed, we changed our positions. However, rather than blindly following the computer's recommendations, I would have the computer work in parallel with my own analysis and then compare the two. When the computer's decision was different from mine, I would examine why. Most of the time, it was because I had overlooked something. In those cases, the computer taught me. But sometimes I would think about some new criteria my system would've missed, so I would then teach the computer. We helped each other. It didn't take long before the computer, with its tremendous processing power, was much more effective than me. This was great, because it was like having a chess grandmaster helping me plot my moves, except this player operated according to a set of criteria that I understood and believed were logical, so there was no reason for us to ever fundamentally disagree.

The computer was much better than my brain in "thinking" about many things at once, and it could do it more precisely, more rapidly, and less emotionally. And, because it had such a great memory, it could do a better job of compounding my knowledge and the knowledge of the people I worked with as Bridgewater grew. Rather than argue about our conclusions, my partners and I would argue about our different decision-making criteria. Then we resolved our disagreements by testing the criteria objectively. The rapidly expanding power of computers during that era was like a constant stream of gifts from the gods to us. I remember when RadioShack came out with an inexpensive handheld chess computer; we sent one to each of our clients with the message, "A Systemized Approach from Bridgewater." That little computer chess game could kick my ass on level two out of its nine levels. It was fun to put it up against each of my clients so they could see how hard it was to beat computerized decision making.

Of course, we always had the freedom to override the system, which we did less than 2 percent of the time—mostly to take money off the table during extraordinary events that weren't programmed, like the World Trade Center going down on 9/11. While the computer was much better than our brains in many ways, it didn't have the imagination, understanding, and logic that we did. That's why our brains working with the computer made such a great partnership.

These decision-making systems were much better than the forecasting systems I'd been using before, mostly because they incorporated our ongoing reactions to developments, allowing us to deal with a wider range of possibilities. They could also include timing rules. In a January 1987 piece called "Making Money vs. Making Forecasts," I explained that:

> *Truth be known, forecasts aren't worth very much, and most people who make them don't make money in the markets. . . . This is because nothing is certain and when one overlays the probabilities of all of the various things that affect the future in order to make a forecast, one gets a wide array of possibilities with varying probabilities, not one highly probable outcome. . . . We believe that market movements reflect economic movements. Economic movements are reflected in economic statistics. By studying the relationships between economic statistics and market movements, we've developed precise rules for identifying important shifts in the economic/market environment and in turn our positions. In other words, rather than forecasting changes in the economic environment and shifting positions in anticipation of them, we pick up these changes as they're occurring and move our money around to keep in those markets which perform best in that environment.*

Over the last three decades of building these systems we have incorporated many more types of rules that direct every aspect of our trading. Now, as real-time data is released, our computers parse information from over 100 million datasets and give detailed instructions to other computers in ways that make logical sense to me. If I didn't have these systems, I'd probably be broke or dead from the stress of trying so hard. We certainly wouldn't have done as well in the markets as we have. As you will see later, I am now developing similar systems to help us make management decisions. I believe one of the most valuable things you can do to improve your decision making is to think through your principles for making decisions, write them out in both words and computer algorithms, back-test them if possible, and use them on a real-time basis to run in parallel with your brain's decision making.

But I'm getting ahead of myself. Let's go back to 1983.

RESURRECTING BRIDGEWATER

By late 1983, Bridgewater had six employees. Up until then, I hadn't done any marketing; the business we got came from word of mouth and from people reading my daily telexes and seeing my public appearances. But clearly there was a growing demand for our research, and I realized we could sell it to supplement our consulting and trading income. So I hired a seventh employee, a former door-to-door Bible salesman named Rob Fried, and we hit the road, lugging around a projector and a huge stack of slides, hawking a $3,000-per-month research package with my daily telexes, weekly conference calls, biweekly and quarterly research reports, and quarterly meetings. Over the next year, Rob brought in a number of institutions and institutional investment managers, including General Electric, Keystone Custodian Funds, the World Bank, Brandywine, Loomis Sayles, Provident Capital Management, the Singer Company, Loews Corporation, GTE Corporation, and Wellington Management.

At that point, our business consisted of three main areas: consulting for fees, managing companies' risks for incentive fees, and selling the research packages. We worked with all sorts of corporate, financial, and government institutions that had market exposures—banks, diversified international businesses, commodities producers, food producers, public utilities, and more. For example, we would build a plan to help a multinational company deal with the currency exposure it faced from operating in different countries.

My approach was to immerse myself in a business until I got to a point where I felt that the strategies I was handing off were the ones I would use were I running the company myself. I would break each company down into distinct logical components and then come up with a plan for managing each part, using a variety of financial tools, especially derivative instruments. The most important components to separate were the profits coming from the core business and those that were speculative profits and losses coming from price changes. We would do this to show them what a "risk-neutral" position would look like, which is to say, the properly hedged position one would take if one didn't have a view of the markets. I would advise them to deviate from this position only when they wanted to speculate, which they should only do in measured ways and with full knowledge of the effects it could have on their core business. This approach was eye-opening for most of the firms we worked with. It gave them clarity and control, and yielded them better results. Sometimes they wanted us to speculate for them, which we would do for a share of the profits.

This approach to establishing a "risk-neutral" benchmark position and deviating from it with measured bets was the genesis of the style of investment management we would later call "alpha overlay," in which passive ("beta") and active ("alpha") exposures are separated. The return of a market (such as the stock market) itself is called its beta. Alpha is the return that comes from betting against others. For example, some people outperform the stock market and others underperform it; they are said to have positive or negative alpha. With alpha overlay, we were offering a way of making bets independent of underlying market performance. Approaching the market in this way taught me that one of the keys to being a successful investor is to only take bets you are highly confident in and to diversify them well.

One of our clients in the mid-1980s was Alan Bond, an audacious entrepreneur who was one of the richest people in Australia. A self-made man, he was famous for being the first non-American to win the

America's Cup yacht race in its then 132-year history. Like Bunker Hunt, he eventually bet badly and was forced to declare bankruptcy. I advised him and his team on their way up and stayed on through his downfall, so I watched the tragedy unfold from up close. His was a classic case of confusing business with speculation and only hedging when it was too late.

Bond borrowed U.S. dollars to buy assets like breweries in Australia. He did that because U.S. interest rates were lower than they were in Australia. Though he didn't realize it, he was speculating that the U.S. dollar, in which he would have to pay back his loans, would not rise. When the U.S. dollar did rise against the Australian dollar in the mid-1980s and his Australian-dollar beer-sales earnings weren't enough to pay his debts, his team called me for advice. I calculated what Bond Corp's position would be if they hedged on currencies and saw that doing so would lock in losses that would ruin them, so I advised them to wait. When the Australian dollar rallied, I advised them to put the hedges in place, but they didn't because they believed the currency problem had gone away. Before long, the Australian dollar plunged to new lows and they called me in for an emergency meeting. There wasn't much they could do without locking in ruinous losses, so they again did nothing, and this time the Australian dollar didn't rally. Seeing one of the richest and most accomplished men on the planet lose everything made a huge impression on me.

We also did one-off consulting projects related to the markets. In 1985, I worked with Paul Tudor Jones, a good friend and a great trader, to design a U.S. dollar futures contract (a tradable index tracking the price of the U.S. dollar against a basket of foreign currencies) that traded (and still trades) on the New York Cotton Exchange. I also worked with the New York Futures Exchange to help design and market their CRB futures contract (a tradable index that tracks the price of a basket of commodities).

Unlike most people who work in the markets, I never had any desire to build investment products, especially conventional ones, just because they would sell well. All I wanted was to trade the markets and build relationships, doing for our clients exactly what I would do if I were in their shoes. But I also loved building brand-new things, especially if they were great and revolutionary. By the mid-1980s, a couple of things were clear to me: First, we were making good calls in the interest-rate and currency markets, and the institutional investment managers who were buying our research were using it to make money. Second, we were successfully managing companies' interest-rate and currency exposures. With those two things going as well as they were, I figured we could become successful institutional investment managers ourselves. So I made the pitch to the people who ran the World Bank's pension fund, most importantly Hilda Ochoa, who was its chief investment officer at the time. Despite the fact that we had no assets under management and no track record, she gave us a $5 million U.S. bond account to manage.

That was a huge turning point for us, as it was the start of Bridgewater as we know it today. The strategy we used for the World Bank shifted between holding cash and holding twenty-year U.S. Treasury bonds, because these positions would give us leveraged bets on the direction of interest rates. When our systems indicated that the pressures on interest rates would cause them to fall, we would hold twenty-year Treasury bonds, and when the system pointed to rates rising, we would stay in cash. We did very well, and before long other large institutional investors gave us money to manage as well. Mobil Oil and Singer were our next two accounts and others followed in rapid succession. We went on to become the top-performing U.S. bond manager in the world.

VENTURING BEHIND THE "CLOSED DOOR" OF CHINA

Part of what was great about consulting was that it gave me opportunities to travel. The more unusual a place, the more interesting I found it. This curiosity drew me to Beijing in 1984. The only images I'd seen of China when I was growing up were of masses of people waving Mao's Little Red Book, so having an opportunity to go behind what was still a mostly "closed door" was alluring. I got the invitation because I had a small office in Hong Kong whose director was an advisor to CITIC, the "window company" that was the only business in China allowed to deal with the outside world. Beijing was filled with wonderful and incredibly hospitable people who introduced us to the tradition of drinking shots of Moutai while shouting *Ganbei!* (Bottoms up!) and generally showed us a great time. This first trip, which I made with my wife and a few other people, began an incredibly rewarding thirty-plus-year journey that has had a profound impact on my family and me.

There were no financial markets in China at the time; eventually a small group put together by nine Chinese companies (including CITIC) known as the Stock Exchange Executive Council began to develop them. They started in 1989, just before the Tiananmen Square incident, which set them back because such market developments were still seen as too capitalist. They operated out of a small hotel room and hardly had any financing. I can still picture the big garbage bin under the metal stairway going up to their office. I really respected the risks these young people were taking by doing this at such an unsettled time, so I made a small donation to give them a hand and was excited to share my knowledge with them. From nothing, these people built China's markets and the government's securities regulatory arm.

In 1994, I set up a company called Bridgewater China Partners. By then, I was convinced that China was poised to become the greatest economy in the world in the twenty-first century, but hardly anyone was investing in China yet; good deals could still be struck. I could bring money to the table by introducing my institutional investment clients to opportunities, and I could provide know-how by introducing Chinese companies to American ones. In exchange, we would get a stake in these companies. Essentially, I was setting up the first U.S.-based private equity firm in China.

I launched the company by bringing a small group of institutional investor clients, who together managed $70 billion in assets, to China for a visit. When we got back, we agreed to move forward by setting up a jointly owned merchant bank in Beijing. While I knew that entering a territory where few had been before would require a lot of experimentation and learning, I soon realized I had sorely underestimated the complexity of the task we had set for ourselves and the amount of time it would take. I found myself constantly on the phone at three in the morning, trying to make sense of the shaky accounting and questionable controls at the companies we were interested in—with all my Bridgewater responsibilities awaiting me when the sun came up.

After about a year of this, I could see that running both Bridgewater and Bridgewater China Partners wasn't going to be possible, so I closed its doors. Nobody made or lost any money, because I hadn't been comfortable enough with what I was seeing to make any investments. I'm sure that if I had devoted all my time to it, we would have had great success, but then Bridgewater would not be what it is today. Despite passing up this great opportunity, I don't regret my choice. I learned that if you work hard and creatively, you can have just about anything you want, but not everything you want. Maturity is the ability to reject good alternatives in order to pursue even better ones.

While I stepped away from that opportunity, China remained an important part of my own and my family's lives. We loved it, especially the people. In 1995, my wife, Barbara, our eleven-year-old son, Matt, and I decided together that Matt would spend a year in Beijing, attending an all-Chinese school and living with our friend Madame Gu, who had stayed with us in America during the Tiananmen Square days and whom Matt had visited in China with us when he was three. Standards of living in China were very different from what Matt was accustomed to in Connecticut. For example, the apartment Madame Gu and her husband lived in had hot water for showers only twice a week, and the school Matt attended didn't have heat until well into the winter, so the students wore their coats in the classrooms. Matt didn't speak Chinese and none of his classmates spoke English.

All of this was not just a huge adventure for Matt; it was completely unprecedented and required special permission from the Chinese government. I was excited for Matt because I knew he would see a different world and broaden his mind. Barbara needed a little convincing and a couple of visits to a child psychologist for reassurance, but she had lived all around the world herself and knew how it had benefited her, so she was ultimately receptive to the idea, even if she was less excited about being separated from her son. Matt's difficult but life-changing journey profoundly affected his values and goals. Because he fell in love with China (he says that he became part Chinese that year) and because he learned the value of empathy relative to the value of material wealth, he started a charity called China Care to help Chinese special-needs orphans when he was just sixteen. He ran it for twelve years (and, to a much lesser degree, still does), while shifting his efforts to reconceive what computing can be in the emerging world, which he is executing through his company Endless. I in turn learned a lot from Matt, especially about the joys of philanthropy, and we both learned the deep pleasures of great personal relationships. Over the years, I (and in turn Bridgewater) have also built meaningful relationships with many wonderful people in China, and we have helped its financial institutions grow from fledgling organizations to sophisticated giants.

China wasn't the only country whose people and governments Bridgewater would become involved with. Through their representatives, Singapore's, Abu Dhabi's, and Australia's government investment funds, and Russian and European policymakers, came knocking on our door. The experiences I have had, the perspectives I gained, and the help I was able to provide all added up to a package of rewards as large as any of the others that I got out of my career.

My contact with Singapore's people and institutions also thrilled me. There was and still is no leader I admire more than Lee Kuan Yew, who transformed Singapore from a mosquito-infested backwater to a model economy. That says a lot, as I have gotten to know and admire several world leaders. One of my most thrilling moments was a dinner I had with him at my house in New York, shortly before his death in 2015. Lee requested the dinner to discuss the state of the world economy. I invited former Fed chairman Paul Volcker (another hero of mine), former Treasury secretary Bob Rubin (whose breadth of experiences gave great perspective), and Charlie Rose (one of the most curious and insightful people I know). Besides answering his questions, we probed Lee on world affairs and world leaders. Since he had personally known virtually all of the world's leaders over the last fifty years, we asked Lee about the qualities that distinguished the great ones from the bad ones and what he thought of those who were leading at the time. He rated Angela Merkel as the best leader in the West and considered Vladimir Putin one of the best leaders worldwide. He explained that leaders must be judged within the context of the circumstances they encounter and then went on to share his view of how difficult it is to lead Russia and why he thought Putin was doing it well. He also reflected on his unique relationship with Deng Xiaoping, whom he regarded as the best leader of all.

I love getting to know interesting people from interesting places and seeing the world through their eyes. This is true whether they are rich or poor. Seeing life through the eyes of the indigenous people I got to know in Papua New Guinea was as illuminating for me as gaining the perspectives of the political and economic leaders, world-changing entrepreneurs, and cutting-edge scientists I've spent time with. I'll never forget the blind holy man I met in a mosque in Syria, who explained the Quran and his connection to God to me. Encounters like these have taught me that human greatness and terribleness are not correlated with wealth or other conventional measures of success. I've also learned that judging people before really seeing things through their eyes stands in the way of understanding their circumstances—and that isn't smart. I urge you to be curious enough to want to understand how the people who see things differently from you came to see them that way. You will find that interesting and invaluable, and the richer perspective you gain will help you decide what you should do.

MY FAMILY AND MY EXTENDED FAMILY

My family, my extended family of co-workers, and my work have all been extremely important to me. Juggling work and family has been as much a challenge to me as to anyone else, especially since I wanted both to be great, so I combined them whenever I could. For example, I took my kids on business trips. When at first I brought my son Devon and later Matt to my Chinese business meetings, our hosts were always very kind—they would give them cookies and milk. One great memory from Abu Dhabi was when my clients/friends took my son Paul and me to the desert to eat a freshly killed and roasted goat with our bare hands. I asked Paul, who was dressed in the traditional gown they'd given him, how he liked it and he said, "What could be better than to sit on the floor, dressed in pajamas, eating with my hands, with nice people?" We all laughed. I remember another time when my eldest son, Devon, then about 10 years old, brought back silk scarves from China he'd bought for $1 and sold for $20 in a shopping mall just before Christmas—which was just the first sign of his business savvy.

By the mid-1980s, Bridgewater had grown to about ten people, so I rented a big old farmhouse. Bridgewater occupied part of it and my family occupied the rest. It was extremely informal and family-like: Everyone parked in the driveway, we met around the kitchen table, and my kids would leave the door open while they sat on the toilet. The people I worked with would wave as they walked by.

Eventually, the farm was put up for sale so I bought a barn on the property and renovated it. My wife, our kids (eventually there were four), and I lived in a small apartment inside the barn, and I made the unfinished hayloft usable as an office by putting in electric baseboard heat, which I chose because it was cheapest to install. It was a great space for parties and there was enough land for us to play soccer and volleyball and have outdoor barbecues. For our company Christmas party, we'd have a big potluck dinner with my family. After a few drinks, Santa would show up and we'd all sit on his lap for a photo and find out who had been naughty or nice. The night always ended with a lot of dancing. We also had an annual "Sleaze Day" when everybody would dress up sleazy. You get the idea: Bridgewater was a small community of friends who worked hard and partied hard.

Bob Prince joined Bridgewater in 1986 when he was still in his twenties, and more than thirty years later we are still close partners as co-chief investment officers. From the very start, Bob and I "played great jazz together" whenever we'd go back and forth on ideas. We still love doing that and will until one of us dies. He is also a great teacher, both to clients and co-workers. Over time, he became like my brother as well as one of the most critical builders and pillars of Bridgewater.

Soon, Bridgewater began to look like a real company. We outgrew the barn and moved into a small office in a strip mall; there were twenty of us by the end of the 1980s. But even as we grew, I never thought of anybody I worked with as an employee. I had always wanted to have—and to be around people who also wanted to have—a life full of meaningful work and meaningful relationships, and to me a meaningful relationship is one that's open and honest in a way that lets people be straight with each other. I never valued more traditional, antiseptic relationships where people put on a façade of politeness and don't say what they really think.

I believe that all organizations basically have two types of people: those who work to be part of a mission, and those who work for a paycheck. I wanted to surround myself with people who needed what I needed, which was to make sense of things for myself. I spoke frankly, and I expected those around me to speak frankly. I fought for what I thought was best, and I wanted them to do so as well. When I thought someone did something stupid, I said so and I expected them to tell me when I did something stupid. Each of us would be better for it. To me, that was what strong and productive relationships looked like. Operating any other way would be unproductive and unethical.

MORE BIG TWISTS AND TURNS IN THE ECONOMY AND MARKETS

1987 and 1988 were filled with more of those big twists and turns that helped shape me and my approach to life and investing. We were one of the few investment managers who were short stocks ahead of "Black Monday," October 19, 1987, then the largest single-day percentage decline in the history of the stock market. We got a lot of attention because we were up 22 percent when most others were down a lot. The media dubbed us as among the "Heroes of October."

Naturally, I was feeling pretty good going into 1988. I had grown up in an era of high volatility and had learned that the best way to play it was to get a hold of a big move and ride it. We used our indicators to catch shifting fundamentals and our technical trend-following filters to confirm that price movements were consistent with what the indicators were suggesting. When they both pointed in the same direction, we had a strong signal; when they were at odds, we had little or no signal. But as it turned out there was hardly any volatility in 1988, and so our technical filters whipsawed us and we ended up giving back a bit more than half our 1987 gains. That stung, but it also taught us some important lessons and prompted Bob and me to replace our technical trend-following filter with better value measures and risk controls.

Until then our systems had been completely discrete—we would flip from a fully long position to a fully short one when we crossed a predetermined threshold (much as we switched from bonds to cash for the World Bank). But we weren't always equally confident in our views, and we'd also get killed paying transaction costs when we crossed back and forth. That drove Bob crazy. I can remember him running laps around the office building to calm himself down. So at the end of the year, we moved to a more variable system that allowed us to size our bets in relation to how confident we were. These and other improvements Bob made to our systems have paid off many times since.

Not everyone at Bridgewater saw things as Bob and I did. Some in the company doubted that systemization could work, especially when the systems didn't do well, which, like normal decision making, happened every now and then. It took a lot of reasoning to persuade some of the people I worked with to press on. But even if I couldn't convince them, they couldn't change my mind, because they couldn't show me why our approach of clearly specifying, testing, and systemizing our logic wasn't preferable to making decisions less systematically.

All great investors and investment approaches have bad patches; losing faith in them at such times is as common a mistake as getting too enamored of them when they do well. Because most people are more emotional than logical, they tend to overreact to short-term results; they give up and sell low when times are bad and buy too high when times are good. I find this is just as true for relationships as it is for investments—wise people stick with sound fundamentals through the ups and downs, while flighty people react emotionally to how things feel, jumping into things when they're hot and abandoning them when they're not.

Despite our relatively poor investment performance, 1988 was a great year for Bridgewater, because by reflecting on and learning from our poor performance, we made systematic improvements. I have come to realize that bad times coupled with good reflections provide some of the best lessons, and not just about business but also about relationships. One has many more supposed friends when one is up than when one is down, because most people like to be with winners and shun losers. True friends are the opposite.

I got a lot out of my bad times, not just because they gave me mistakes to learn from but also because they helped me find out who my real friends were—the friends who would be with me through thick and thin.

THE NEXT FOOTHOLD FOR BRIDGEWATER

As the 1980s came to an end, we were still a very small company, with just two dozen employees. Bob introduced me to Giselle Wagner in 1988. She would be my partner in running the noninvestment side of the business for twenty years. Dan Bernstein and Ross Waller joined in 1988 and 1989, respectively, both fresh out of Dartmouth College. At that time, and for quite a while longer, I tended to hire people just out of school who didn't have much experience but were smart, determined, and committed to the mission of making the company great.

I didn't value experience as much as character, creativity, and common sense, which I suppose was related to my having started Bridgewater two years out of school myself, and my belief that having an ability to figure things out is more important than having specific knowledge of how to do something. It seemed to me, young people were creating sensible innovation that was exciting. Older folks who did things in the old ways held no appeal. I should add, though, that putting responsibility in the hands of inexperienced people doesn't always work out so well. Some painful lessons that you'll read about later taught me that it can be a mistake to undervalue experience.

By now, the initial $5 million from the World Bank had grown to $180 million in investments that we were managing for a variety of clients, but we were still trying to grab a larger foothold in the institutional investment business. When Rusty Olson, CIO of Kodak's pension fund, approached us to solve an investment problem, we jumped at the chance. Rusty was a remarkable innovator and a man of great character who'd started at Kodak in 1954 and took over its pension fund in 1972; he was widely respected as a leader in the pension fund world. We'd been sending him our research for a while, and in 1990 he wrote us looking for our opinion on a big concern of his. The Kodak portfolio was heavily invested in equities and Rusty was worried about what would happen in an environment in which the value of his assets fell badly. He had been trying to come up with a way to hedge himself against this risk without reducing his expected return.

Rusty's fax arrived on a Friday afternoon and we leaped into action. Getting a client this prestigious and innovative would make a big difference to us. We knew we could do a uniquely great job for Kodak, because we knew a lot about bonds and financial engineering, and we had a historical perspective unmatched in the industry. Bob Prince, Dan Bernstein, and I worked nonstop through the weekend, analyzing the Kodak portfolio and the strategy Rusty was considering. Then we wrote him a long memo laying out our thoughts.

Just as I had deconstructed the business of a chicken producer in the 1970s and many other companies since, we broke down Kodak's pension fund into its constituent parts to better understand the "machine." Our proposed solutions drew on the portfolio-engineering ideas that would later become core to Bridgewater's unique way of managing money. Rusty invited Bob and me to Rochester, and we came home with the $100 million account. That was a game changer. Not only did it bring us a lot of credibility, it provided us with a reliable source of revenue at a time when we needed it.

DISCOVERING THE "HOLY GRAIL OF INVESTING"

From my earlier failures, I knew that no matter how confident I was in making any one bet I could still be wrong—and that proper diversification was the key to reducing risks without reducing returns. If I could build a portfolio filled with high-quality return streams[3] that were properly diversified (they zigged and zagged in ways that balanced each other out), I could offer clients an overall portfolio return much more consistent and reliable than what they could get elsewhere.

Decades earlier, the Nobel Prize–winning economist Harry Markowitz had invented a widely used model that allowed you to input a set of assets along with their expected returns, risks, and correlations (showing how similarly those assets have performed in the past) and determine an "optimal mix" of those assets in a portfolio. But his model didn't tell you anything about the incremental effects of changing any one of those variables, or how to handle being uncertain about those assumptions. By then I was terribly fearful about what would happen if my assumptions were wrong, so I wanted to understand diversification in a very simple way. I asked Brian Gold, a recently graduated math major from Dartmouth who'd joined Bridgewater in 1990, to do a chart showing how the volatility of a portfolio would decline and its quality (measured by the amount of return relative to risk) would improve if I incrementally added investments with different correlations. I'll explain it in more detail in my Economic and Investment Principles.

That simple chart struck me with the same force I imagine Einstein must have felt when he discovered $E=mc^2$: I saw that with fifteen to twenty good, uncorrelated return streams, I could dramatically reduce my risks without reducing my expected returns. It was so simple but it would be such a breakthrough if the theory worked as well in practice as it did on paper. I called it the "Holy Grail of Investing" because it

---

[3] By "return streams," I mean the returns that come from executing a particular decision rule—think of them as lines on a chart that track the value of an investment through time, and the decision to either let it continue to grow in value or sell.

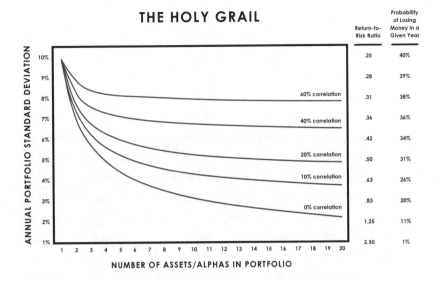

THE HOLY GRAIL

showed the path to making a fortune. This was another key moment in our education.

The principle we'd discovered applies equally well to all ways of trying to make money. Whether you own a hotel, run a technology company, or do anything else, your business produces a return stream. Having a few good uncorrelated return streams is better than having just one, and knowing how to combine return streams is even more effective than being able to choose good ones (though of course you have to do both). At the time (and still today), most investment managers did not take advantage of this. They managed investments in a single asset class: equity managers managed equities, bond managers managed bonds, and so on. Their clients gave them money with the expectation that they would receive the overall return of the asset class (e.g., the S&P 500 stock market index) plus some added returns from the bets managers took by over- and under-weighting particular assets (e.g., buying more Microsoft stock than was in the index). But individual assets within an asset class are generally about 60 percent correlated with each other, which means they go up or down together more than half the time. As the Holy Grail chart showed, an equity manager could put a thousand 60 percent-correlated stocks into their portfolios and it wouldn't provide much more diversification than if they'd picked only five. It would be easy to beat those guys by balancing our bets in the way the chart indicated.

Thanks to my process of systematically recording my investment principles and the results they could be expected to produce, I had a large collection of uncorrelated return streams. In fact, I had something like a thousand of them. Because we traded a number of different asset classes, and within each one we had programmed and tested lots of fundamental trading rules, we had many more high-quality ones to choose from than a typical manager who was tracking a smaller number of assets and was probably not trading systematically.

I worked with Bob and Dan to pull our best decision rules from the pile. Once we had them, we back-tested them over long time frames, using the systems to simulate how the decision rules would have worked together in the past.

We were startled by the results. On paper, this new approach improved our returns by a factor of three to five times per unit of risk, and we could calibrate the amount of return we wanted based on the amount of risk we could tolerate. In other words, we could make a ton more money than the other guys, with a lower risk of being knocked out of the game—as I'd nearly been before. I called it the "killer system" because it would either produce killer results for us and our clients or it would kill us because we were missing something important.

The success of this approach taught me a principle that I apply to all parts of my life: Making a handful of good uncorrelated bets that are balanced and leveraged well is the surest way of having a lot of upside without being exposed to unacceptable downside.

As excited as we were about this new approach, we proceeded cautiously. We gave the system a 10 percent weight initially and it made money in nineteen of the twenty months in our test period. As we got more confident, I decided to reach out to a select group of investors I knew well about investing in the strategy with $1 million trial accounts. I knew that asking these institutional investors to invest such relatively modest amounts would make it hard for them to turn us down. I called the new product "Top 5%" at first, because it comprised the best 5 percent of our decision rules; later I changed the name to Pure Alpha to convey that it consisted purely of alphas. Because Pure Alpha didn't have any betas, it didn't have any bias to go up or down along with any market. Its returns depended only on how good we were in outperforming others.

Our totally new "alpha overlay" approach allowed investors to receive the return of their chosen asset class (the S&P 500 stock market, a bond index, commodities—whatever) plus the return from the portfolio of bets that we were making across all asset classes. As unprecedented as our approach was, we explained our logic carefully, showing why it was actually much less risky than traditional approaches. We also showed them how we expected the cumulative performance to unfold and what the expected range of performance around that would be. For our clients, it was a bit like being presented with the design of a plane that had never flown before but looked radically better than any other plane on paper. Would anyone be courageous enough to get on board?

GROSS CUMULATIVE ALPHA VS. EXPECTATIONS (IN)

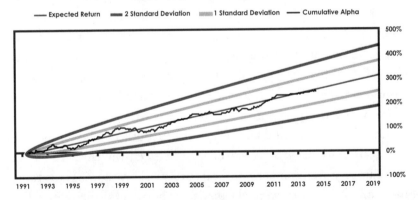

Some clients got the concepts and were excited to change the rules; others either didn't understand or worked for organizations that refused to try cutting-edge things. Frankly, we were thrilled that any of them were willing to try. For over twenty-six years now, that new type of plane has flown exactly as we anticipated, making money in twenty-three of these years (having only modest losses in the other three) and making more money in total for our clients than any other hedge fund ever. While the investment management concepts that underlie Pure Alpha eventually changed our industry, the journey from conception to general acceptance took many years of learning and grinding work by a group of dedicated partners.

GETTING OUR KILLER SYSTEM OUT INTO THE WORLD

Pure Alpha represented the best way we knew to actively manage money, but we also knew that if we wanted to manage a meaningful amount of institutional money, we had to accept the reality that only a limited number of innovative clients would try the approach. So while we tried to convince clients to adopt our way, by the end of the 1990s and into the early 2000s, Pure Alpha made up only around 10 percent of our total assets under management.

Even though we couldn't trade stocks and commodities in our pure bond accounts, we applied the portfolio structuring principles we'd discovered and used with Pure Alpha to give our bond clients higher returns at lower levels of risk. This included trading foreign government bonds, emerging market debt, inflation-linked bonds, corporate bonds, and the currency exposures that came with the foreign investments. In our most unconstrained bond portfolios, we would make about fifty different types of bets, way more than traditional bond managers traded. Doing so gave us a big edge and landed us at the top of many investment performance tables year after year.

Our Pure Alpha product was just the first of a number of innovative designs we brought to our clients. In 1991, we had become the first currency overlay managers for institutional investors. At the time, institutional investors were placing larger portions of their portfolios into global equity and bond markets. While investing internationally added valuable diversity, it also added unmanaged currency exposure. This was a big problem because the currency exposures added risk without adding any expected return. We had traded currencies for years and had developed expertise in portfolio engineering, so we were in a prime position to solve this problem. Eventually we became the largest active currency manager in the world.

We also produced several other new and effective ways of managing money that flew exactly as they were designed. With each one, we gave clients clearly stated performance expectations expressed in a chart that showed an accumulated profit line and the expected variations around that line. We could do this because the systemization of our decision-making process allowed us to stress-test the performance of our decision making under a wide variety of conditions.

SYSTEMIZING OUR LEARNING FROM MISTAKES

Of course we continued to make mistakes, though they were all within our range of expectations. What was great is that we made the most of our mistakes because we got in the habit of viewing them as opportunities to learn and improve. One of our most memorable mistakes happened in the early 1990s, when Ross, who was in charge of trading at the time, forgot to put in a trade for a client and the money just sat there in cash. By the time the mistake was discovered, the damage was several hundred thousand dollars.

It was a terrible and costly error, and I could've done something dramatic like fire Ross to set a tone that mistakes would not be tolerated. But since mistakes happen all the time, that would have only encouraged other people to hide theirs, which would have led to even bigger and more costly errors. I believed strongly that we should bring problems and disagreements to the surface to learn what should be done to make things better. So Ross and I worked to build out an "error log" in the trading department. From then on, anytime there was any kind of bad outcome (a trade wasn't executed, we paid significantly higher transaction costs than expected, etc.), the traders would make a record of it and we would follow up. As we consistently tracked and addressed those issues, our trade execution machine continually improved.

Having a process that ensures problems are brought to the surface, and their root causes diagnosed, assures that continual improvements occur.

For that reason I insisted that an issue log be adopted throughout Bridgewater. My rule was simple: If something went badly, you had to put it in the log, characterize its severity, and make clear who was responsible for it. If a mistake happened and you logged it, you were okay. If you didn't log it, you would be in deep trouble. This way managers had problems brought to them, which was worlds better than having to seek them out. The error log (which we now call the issue log) was our first management tool. I learned subsequently how important tools are in helping to reinforce desired behaviors, which led us to create a number of tools I will describe later.

This culture of bringing problems and disagreements to the surface generated a lot of discomfort and conflict, especially when it came to exploring people's weaknesses. Before long, things came to a boil.

MY "INTRACTABLE" PEOPLE PROBLEM

One winter day in 1993, Bob, Giselle, and Dan proposed taking me out to dinner with the stated purpose of "giving Ray feedback about how he affects people and company morale." They sent me a memo first, the gist of which was that my way of operating was having a negative effect on everyone in the company. Here's how they put it:

What does Ray do well?
He is very bright and innovative. He understands markets and money management. He is intense and energetic. He has very high standards and passes these to others around him. He has good intentions about teamwork, building group ownership, providing flexible work conditions to employees, and compensating people well.

What Ray doesn't do as well:
Ray sometimes says or does things to employees which makes them feel incompetent, unnecessary, humiliated, overwhelmed, belittled,

oppressed, or otherwise bad. The odds of this happening rise when Ray is under stress. At these times, his words and actions toward others create animosity toward him and leave a lasting impression. The impact of this is that people are demotivated rather than motivated. This reduces productivity and the quality of the environment. The effect reaches far beyond the single employee. The smallness of the company and the openness of communication means that everyone is affected when one person is demotivated, treated badly, not given due respect. The future success of the company is highly dependent on Ray's ability to manage people as well as money. If he doesn't manage people well, growth will be stunted and we will all be affected.

Ugh. That hurt and surprised me. I never imagined that I was having that sort of effect. These people were my extended family. I didn't want them to feel "incompetent, unnecessary, humiliated, overwhelmed, belittled, oppressed, or otherwise bad." Why didn't they tell me directly? What was I doing wrong? Were my standards too high? For Bridgewater to continue to be a one-in-ten-thousand–type company we had to have exceptional people and hold them to extremely high standards. Was I demanding too much?

This looked to me like another one of those fork-in-the-road cases in which I had to choose between one of two seemingly essential but mutually exclusive options: 1) being radically truthful with each other including probing to bring our problems and weaknesses to the surface so we could deal with them forthrightly and 2) having happy and satisfied employees. And it reminded me that when faced with the choice between two things you need that are seemingly at odds, go slowly to figure out how you can have as much of both as possible. There is almost always a good path that you just haven't figured out yet, so look for it until you find it rather than settle for the choice that is then apparent to you.

My first step was to make sure I knew exactly what the problems were and how to handle them. So I asked Bob, Giselle, and Dan what they thought was going on. I learned that they personally, and many others who knew me well, weren't as demoralized by me as some others because they understood my heart was in a good place. If they hadn't known that they would have quit, because, as they put it, "I wasn't paying them enough money to put up with my crap."

They knew that I wanted the best for them and Bridgewater, and to get that I needed to be radically truthful with them and I needed them to be radically truthful with me. This wasn't only because it produced better results, but also because being truthful with each other was fundamental to how I believed we should be with each other. We agreed that being this way was essential, but since it was making some people feel bad, something had to change.

While those people I had contact with understood me, liked me, and in some cases even loved me, those who had less contact with me were offended by my directness. It was clear that I needed to be better understood and to understand others better. I realized then how essential it is that people in relationships must be crystal clear about their principles for dealing with each other.

That began our decades-long process of putting our principles into writing, which evolved into the Work Principles. Those principles were both agreements for how we would be with each other and my reflections on how we should handle every situation that came up. Since most types of situations arose repeatedly with slight variations, these principles were continually refined. As for our agreements with each other, the most important one was our need to do three things:

1. Put our honest thoughts out on the table,
2. Have thoughtful disagreements in which people are willing to shift their opinions as they learn, and
3. Have agreed-upon ways of deciding (e.g., voting, having clear authorities) if disagreements remain so that we can move beyond them without resentments.

I believe that for any organization or for any relationship to be great, these things are required. I also believe that for a group decision-making system to be effective, the people using it have to believe that it's fair.

Having our work principles written out and getting in sync about them in the same way we had with our investment principles were essential for our understanding each other, especially since our unique way of operating—this radical truth and radical transparency—that led to our unique results is counterintuitive and emotionally challenging for some.

Trying to understand how we could get our meaningful work and meaningful relationships through this straightforwardness led me to speak with neuroscientists, psychologists, and educators over the decades that followed. I learned a lot, which I can summarize as follows. There are two parts of each person's brain: the upper-level logical part and the lower-level emotional part. I call these the "two yous." They fight for control of each person. How that conflict is managed is the most important driver of our behaviors. That fighting was the biggest reason for the problems Bob, Giselle, and Dan raised. While the logical part of people's brains could easily understand that knowing one's weaknesses is a good thing (because it's the first step toward getting around them), the emotional part typically hates it.

CHAPTER 5

THE ULTIMATE BOON:

1995–2010

By 1995, Bridgewater had grown to forty-two employees and $4.1 billion under management, which was more than I'd ever hoped for, especially considering that Bridgewater had been down to just me only a dozen years before. While things were much better and more stable, we were still doing basically the same things I'd been doing from the start—wrestling with the markets, thinking independently and creatively about how to make our bets, making mistakes, bringing those mistakes to the surface, diagnosing them to get at their root causes, designing new and better ways of doing things, systematically implementing the changes, making new mistakes, and so on.[4] This iterative, evolutionary approach allowed us to continually refine the investment systems that I'd begun building in 1982. Back then, we showed that a few bright guys with computers could beat the big, well-equipped establishment players. Now we were becoming the well-equipped establishment ourselves.

As the number of decision rules and the amount of data in our

---

[4] This approach is what I call the "5-Step Process." I'll dive into it in more detail later on.

systems grew more complex, we hired young programmers who were better than us in converting our instructions into code and smart new grads right out of college to help with our investment research. One of these new whiz kids, Greg Jensen, joined Bridgewater as a college intern in 1996. Because he shined, I grabbed him as my research assistant. Over the decades that followed, he contributed a lot, grew into the co-chief investment officer role with Bob Prince and me, and became a co-CEO. He also became like a godson to me.

We also invested in more and more powerful computers.[5] Having our systems running through these machines freed us to get above the daily movements of the markets and consider things from a higher level, where we could make novel, creative connections that produced innovations for our clients.

DISCOVERING INFLATION-INDEXED BONDS

Around this time, I had dinner with David White, the man in charge of the Rockefeller Foundation's money. David asked me how I would engineer the foundation's portfolio to produce a return that was 5 percent above the U.S. inflation rate. I answered that a portfolio of leveraged foreign inflation-indexed bonds with the currency hedged back to U.S. dollars should deliver exactly that. (The bonds needed to be foreign because there were no U.S. inflation-indexed bonds at the time, and they needed to be hedged to the dollar so there would be no currency risk.)

Thinking about this later, I realized that we could create an entirely new and radically different asset class, so Dan Bernstein and I researched such a portfolio more closely. According to our analysis, this new asset class would perform even better than we'd thought. In fact, it would be uniquely effective because we could engineer it to have the same expected return as equities but with less risk and with

---

[5] I'll explore more on the topic of working with computer-aided decision-making systems in Chapter Five of Life Principles, Learn How to Make Decisions Effectively.

a negative correlation with bonds and equities over long time frames. We showed this research to our clients and they loved it. Before long, we became the first global inflation-indexed bond manager in the world. In 1996, U.S. Treasury deputy secretary Larry Summers began looking into whether the U.S. should issue its own inflation-indexed bonds, and because we were the only manager with a portfolio of such bonds, he called us in as experts.

Dan and I traveled down to Washington to meet with Summers, his Treasury colleagues, and a number of representatives from well-known Wall Street firms. We were late (punctuality isn't one of my strengths) and the doors to the big meeting room at Treasury were locked. I wasn't going to let that stop me, so I knocked until someone opened it. It was a large room with a table in the middle and a press gallery off to the side. There was only one seat open at the table and it had Dan's nameplate in front of it—we'd agreed that he'd be our one allowed representative since he'd done a lot of the prep work. I had forgotten that, so I walked over to the press gallery, grabbed a chair, and carried it next to Dan's so I had a seat at the table too. Dan describes that meeting as an analogy for what it was like for us in the 1990s in general: We had to barge our way into things. Larry Summers has since said that the advice he got from us was the most important in shaping this market. When the Treasury did create the bonds, they followed the structure we recommended.

DISCOVERING RISK PARITY

By the mid-1990s, I had enough money to set up a trust for my family, so I began to think about what the best asset allocation mix for preserving wealth over generations would look like. In my years as an investor, I had seen all sorts of economic and market environments and all kinds of ways that wealth could be created and destroyed. I knew what drove asset returns, but I also knew that no matter what asset class one held, there would come a time when it would lose most of its value. This included cash, which is the worst investment over time because it loses value after adjusting for inflation and taxes. I also knew how difficult it was to anticipate the swings that cause those losses. I've devoted my life to it and I've made my share of bad calls; anticipating these swings wasn't something I'd bet on others doing well when I wasn't around. Finding investors who have done well in all economic environments—when inflation rises and when it falls, when there are booms and when there are busts—is like finding needles in a haystack, and they don't live forever so that's not a viable path. I didn't want the wealth I had created to protect my family to be wiped out after I was gone. That meant I had to create a mix of assets that could be good in all economic environments.

I knew which shifts in the economic environment caused asset classes to move around, and I knew that those relationships had remained essentially the same for hundreds of years. There were only two big forces to worry about: growth and inflation. Each could either be rising or falling, so I saw that by finding four different investment strategies—each one of which would do well in a particular environment (rising growth with rising inflation, rising growth with falling inflation, and so on)—I could construct an asset-allocation mix that was balanced to do well over time while being protected against unacceptable losses. Since that strategy would never change, practically anyone could implement it. And so, with help from Bob and Dan, I created a portfolio mix that I could comfortably put my trust money in for the next hundred or more years. I called it the "All Weather Portfolio" because it could perform well in all environments.

Between 1996 and 2003 I was the only "client" investing in it because we didn't sell it as a product. But in 2003, the head of Verizon's pension fund, a longtime client, told us he was looking for an approach to investing that would do well across all environments. After Verizon made its investment, others quickly followed, and a dozen years later we were managing nearly $80 billion. It was another industry-shaping concept. Seeing its success, other investment managers followed with their own versions. It is now generically called "risk parity" investing.

TO REMAIN A BEAUTIFUL BOUTIQUE
OR BECOME A GREAT INSTITUTION?

With our people and culture producing these industry-shaping investment products, Bridgewater really took off. By 2000, we were managing more than $32 billion, almost eight times what we had been managing just five years before. Our head count had doubled, so we moved out of our strip mall office into a larger space situated in a nature preserve on the banks of the Saugatuck River. But while we continued to grow, it was never clear sailing. Building the business while managing investments required me to do two challenging jobs simultaneously and develop two distinct skill sets, while being a good father, husband, and friend. The demands of these roles changed over time, so the skills and abilities I needed changed as well.

Most people assume that the challenges that go along with growing a large business are greater than those of growing a smaller one. That is not true. Going from a five-person organization to a sixty-person organization was just as challenging as going from a sixty-person organization to a seven-hundred-person organization—and from a seven-hundred-person organization to a 1,500-person one. Looking back, I can't say that the challenges were easier or harder at any of the various phases we went through. They were just different. For example, when I had no one to manage, I had the challenge of having to do almost everything myself. When I learned and earned enough to pay others, I had the challenge of managing them. Similarly, the challenges of wrestling with market and economic swings were constantly changing. I didn't think about it then, but it's obvious to me now that while one gets better at things over time, it doesn't become any easier if one is also progressing to higher levels—the Olympic athlete finds his sport to be every bit as challenging as the novice does.

Very soon we faced another critical choice: What kind of company did we want to have? Should we continue to grow or stay about the same size?

By 2003, I had come to believe that we needed to grow Bridgewater into a real institution instead of remaining a typical boutique-sized investment manager. Doing this would make us better in many ways— better technology, better security controls, a deeper talent pool—all of which would make us more stable and permanent. This meant hiring more people in technology, infrastructure, and other areas, as well as additional HR and IT staff to train and support them.

Giselle argued strongly that we should not grow. She believed that introducing a lot of new people would threaten our culture, and that the time and attention that hiring, training, and managing them required would dilute our focus. While I agreed with her points, I didn't like the alternative of not allowing ourselves to become all we could be. I felt about this fork-in-the-road choice the way I felt about most others—that whether or not we could have our cake and eat it too was merely a test of our creativity and character. For example, I could envision ways in which technology would help us get the most out of people. After a fair amount of wrestling with these questions, we decided to go ahead.

FLESHING OUT PRINCIPLES

Ever since Bob, Giselle, and Dan had presented me with the "Ray Feedback Memo" in the 1990s, I had been much more explicit in writing down and sharing my work principles in the same way I had written down my investment principles. At first, this took the form of shared philosophy statements and emails to the entire company. Then, whenever something new came along that required me to make a decision, I would reflect on my criteria for making that decision and write it down as a principle so people could make the connections between the situation, my principle for handling these situations, and my actions. More and more, we saw everything as "another one of those"—another of a certain type of situation like hiring, firing, determining compensation, dealing with dishonesty—that had principles for handling them. By having them explicitly written out, I could foster the idea meritocracy by having us together reflect on and refine those principles—and then adhere to them.

The number of principles started small and grew over time. By the mid-2000s, Bridgewater was beginning to grow rapidly, and we had a number of new managers trying to learn and adapt to our unique culture—and who were increasingly asking me for advice. I was also beginning to have people from outside Bridgewater ask me how they could create idea meritocracies of their own. So in 2006, I prepared a rough list of about sixty Work Principles and distributed them to Bridgewater's managers so they could begin to evaluate them, debate them, and make sense of them for themselves. "It's a rough draft," I wrote in the covering memo, "but it is being put out now for comments."

This began an ongoing evolutionary process of encountering many situations, forming principles about how to deal with them, and getting in sync with other Bridgewater leaders and managers about them. Over time, I encountered most everything there is to encounter in running a company, so I had a few hundred principles that covered most everything. That collection of principles, like our collection of investment principles, became a kind of decision-making library. Those principles are the basis of what you'll find in Work Principles.

But it wasn't enough to codify and teach our philosophy; we had to live it. As the company grew bigger, how that happened evolved. In Bridgewater's early days, everyone knew each other, so being radically transparent was easy—people could attend the meetings they wanted to and communicate with each other informally. But as we grew, that became logistically impossible, which was a real problem. How could people engage productively with the idea meritocracy if they didn't know everything that was going on? Without transparency, people would spin whatever happened to suit their own interests, sometimes behind closed doors. Problems would be hidden instead of brought to the surface where they could be resolved. To have a real idea meritocracy, there must be transparency so that people can see things for themselves.

To make sure this happened, I required that virtually all our meetings be recorded and made available to everyone, with extremely rare exceptions such as when we were discussing very private matters like personal health or proprietary information about a trade or decision rule. At first I sent these tapes of management meetings unedited to the entire company, but that was a huge burden on people's time. So I built a small team to edit the tapes, focusing on the most important moments, and over time we added questions to create "virtual reality" case studies that could be used for training.[6] Over time, these tapes became part of a "boot camp" for new employees as well as a window into an ongoing stream of situations connected to the principles for handling them.

All this openness led to some very frank discussions about who did what and why, and as a result we were able to deepen our understanding of our different ways of thinking. This was enlightening to all of us in showing how differently people's brains worked. If nothing else, I could better appreciate people I'd once wanted to strangle! Moreover, I recognized that managers who do not understand people's different thinking styles cannot understand how the people working for them will handle different situations, which is like a foreman not understanding how his equipment will behave. That insight led us to explore psychometric testing as a way of learning how people think differently.

DISCOVERING PSYCHOMETRIC TESTING

Early in my kids' lives, I'd had them tested by a brilliant psychologist named Sue Quinlan. Her assessments proved spot-on and provided a great road map for how they would develop over the years. Because that testing process had been so successful, I worked with her and others to try to identify the best tests for determining what the people I worked with were like. In 2006, I took the Myers-Briggs Type Indicator (MBTI) assessment for the first time and found its description of my preferences to be remarkably accurate.

Many of the differences it described, such as those between "intuiting people," who tend to focus on big-picture concepts, and "sensing

---

[6] With advances in digital technology, we continue to innovate our methods for recording and distributing this content.

people," who pay more attention to specific facts and details, were highly relevant to the conflicts and disagreements we were having at Bridgewater. I began to look for other tests that could help us deepen our understanding of each other. This was slow going at first, largely because most of the psychologists I met were surprisingly squeamish about exploring differences. But eventually I found a few great people, especially a psychologist named Bob Eichinger, who pointed me to a number of other very useful tests.

In early 2008, I had most of Bridgewater's managers take the Myers-Briggs assessment. The results astounded me. I couldn't believe that some of them actually thought in the ways the test described, yet when I asked them to rate how well it described them on a scale of one to five, more than 80 percent of them gave it a four or five.

CREATING BASEBALL CARDS

Even after we were armed with the Myers-Briggs data and other tests we'd taken, I found that we were still having a hard time connecting the dots between the outcomes that we were seeing and what we knew about the people producing them. Over and over again, the same people would walk into the same meetings, do things the same ways, and get the same results without seeking to understand why. (Recently I came across a study that revealed a cognitive bias in which people consistently overlook the evidence of one person being better than another at something and assume that both are equally good at a task. This was exactly what we were seeing.) For example, people who were known not to be creative were being assigned tasks that required creativity; people who didn't pay attention to details were being assigned to detail-oriented jobs, and so on. We needed a way to make the data that showed what people were like even clearer and more explicit, so I began making "Baseball Cards" for employees that listed their "stats." The idea was that they could be passed around and referred to when assigning responsibilities. Just as you wouldn't have a great fielder with a .160 batting average bat third, you wouldn't assign a big-picture person a task requiring attention to details.

At first, this idea met a lot of resistance. People were concerned that the Baseball Cards wouldn't be accurate, that producing them would be too time-consuming, and that they would only succeed in pigeonholing people unfairly. But over time, everyone's attitudes toward this approach of openly exploring what people are like shifted 180 degrees. Most people found that having this information out in the open for everyone to see was more liberating than constraining because when it became the norm, people gained the sort of comfort that comes with just being themselves at work that family members have with each other at home.

Because this way of operating was so unusual, a number of behavioral psychologists came to Bridgewater to evaluate it. I urge you to read their assessments, which were overwhelmingly favorable.[7] The Harvard psychologist Bob Kegan called Bridgewater "a form of proof that the quest for business excellence and the search for personal realization need not be mutually exclusive—and can, in fact, be essential to each other."

I should also explain that my personal circumstances at the time also drew me to psychology and neurology. While for the most part I am keeping my family members' lives out of this book to protect their privacy, I will tell you this one story about my son Paul as it is relevant and he is open about it.

After graduating from NYU's Tisch film school, Paul headed out to Los Angeles to take a job. One day he went to the front desk of the hotel where he was staying while he looked for an apartment and smashed their computer. He was arrested and thrown in jail, where he was beaten up by guards. Ultimately, he was diagnosed with bipolar disorder, released into my custody, and admitted to the psychiatric ward of a hospital.

That was the beginning of a three-year roller-coaster ride that took Paul, Barbara, and me to the peaks of his manias and the depths of his depressions, through the twists and turns of the health care system,

---

[7] You can find the references to books by Robert Kegan, Edward Hess, and Adam Grant in the bibliography.

and into discussions with some of the most brilliant and caring psychologists, psychiatrists, and neuroscientists at work today. There is nothing to prompt learning like pain and necessity, and this gave me plenty of both. At times I felt as though I was holding Paul by the hand as he was dangling over a cliff—from one day to the next, I never knew whether I could hold on or if he would slip from my grip. I worked intensely with his caregivers to understand what was going on and what to do about it. Thanks both to the help he received and his own great character, Paul worked through this and is now better off than if he hadn't fallen into his abyss, because he developed strengths he didn't have but needed. Paul was once wild—staying out till all hours, disorganized, smoking marijuana and drinking—but he now faithfully takes his meds, meditates, goes to bed early, and avoids drugs and alcohol. He had loads of creativity but lacked discipline. Now he has plenty of both. As a result, he is more creative now than he was before and is happily married, the father of two boys, an accomplished filmmaker, and a crusader helping those who struggle with bipolar disorder.

His radical transparency about being bipolar and his commitment to helping others with it inspires me. His first feature film, *Touched with Fire*, which received lots of acclaim, gave many people who might have lost their lives to bipolar disorder both the hope and the path forward they needed. I remember watching him shoot one scene based on a real conversation between us in which he was manic and I was struggling to reason with him. I could simultaneously see the actor playing Paul at his worst while the real Paul was at his best, directing the scene. As I watched, my mind flashed over his whole journey—from the depths of his abyss, through his metamorphosis into the strong hero standing in front of me, someone on a mission to help others going through what he had gone through.

That journey through hell gave me a much deeper understanding of how and why we see things differently. I learned that much of how we think is physiological and can be changed. For example, Paul's wild swings were due to the inconsistent secretions of dopamine and other chemicals in his brain, so he could change by controlling those chemicals and the activities and stimuli affecting them. I learned that creative genius and insanity can be quite close to each other, that the same chemistry that creates insights can cause distortions, and that being stuck in one's own head is terribly dangerous. When Paul was "crazy," he always believed his own illogical arguments, no matter how strange they sounded to others. While more extreme in the case of someone with bipolar disorder, this is something I've seen most everyone do. I also learned how people can control how their brains work to produce dramatically better effects. These insights helped me to deal with people more effectively, as I will explain in detail in Chapter Four, Understand That People Are Wired Very Differently.

MAKING BRIDGEWATER ROCK-SOLID AND CUTTING-EDGE

At our annual town hall meeting in June 2008, I said that seen through my eyes Bridgewater was then, and always had been, "both terrible and terrific at the same time." After about five years of rapid growth toward building Bridgewater as an institution, we had encountered our newest set of problems. This was nothing new. Since I started Bridgewater we always had some problems because we were always doing bold new things, making mistakes, and evolving quickly. For example, technology had changed so quickly during the years we'd built the company that we had literally switched from using slide rules to spreadsheet software to advanced artificial intelligence. With so much changing so fast, it had seemed pointless to focus on getting everything "just right" when something newer and better was sure to come along. So we built our technology in a light and flexible way, which made sense at the time but also created a number of hairballs that badly needed untangling. That same approach of moving quickly and flexibly had been true throughout the company, so several departments had become overstretched as we grew. It had always been fun being cutting-edge, but we were having a hard time becoming rock-solid, especially in the noninvestment side of the business. The organization needed to be renovated in several ways—but it wasn't going to be easy.

In 2008 I was working about eighty hours a week doing my two full-time jobs (overseeing our investments and overseeing the company), and in my opinion not doing well enough at either. I felt that I, and the company more broadly, were slipping from being pervasively excellent. From the get-go I had toggled acceptably between investment management and business management. But now that we were a bigger company, the business management side was demanding much more time than I had to give it. I conducted a time-and-motion study of all of my investment and management responsibilities; it showed it would take me about 165 hours a week to achieve the level of excellence that I would be satisfied with in overseeing both our investments and management. That was obviously impossible. Since I wanted to delegate as much as possible, I asked whether the things I was doing could be done excellently by others, and if so, who those others were. Everyone agreed that most of those areas couldn't adequately be delegated. I clearly hadn't done a good enough job of finding and training others to whom I could delegate my responsibilities.

To me, the greatest success you can have as the person in charge is to orchestrate others to do things well without you. A step below that is doing things well yourself, and worst of all is doing things poorly yourself. As I reflected on my position, I could see that despite all of my and Bridgewater's amazing achievements, I had not achieved this highest level of success. In fact, I was still struggling to achieve the second-highest level (doing things well myself), even though Bridgewater was extremely successful.

At the time, there were 738 people working at Bridgewater, with fourteen department heads. I oversaw the department heads, along with a Management Committee I'd created because I knew I couldn't trust myself to know what was best without others probing me. I had structured the reporting lines so that I both reported to the Management Committee and held its members accountable for their oversight of the company. I wanted them to also own the responsibility of producing pervasive excellence and I wanted to be at their service in helping them achieve it.

In May 2008, I wrote an email to the five members of the Management Committee, copying the company, telling them that "I am escalating to let you know that I have reached my limits and that the quality of my work, and my work-life balance, are both suffering unacceptably."

THE FINANCIAL AND ECONOMIC CRISIS OF 2008

Recognizing that I was stretched wouldn't by itself be enough to slow the flow of things coming at me, especially in the investment area at what proved to be a time of historic turbulence.

Because too often I had been painfully surprised by different types of events that hadn't happened to me before but happened in other times or other places—like the currency devaluation of 1971, or the debt crisis in the early 1980s—I'd developed our economic and market principles to be timeless and universal. In other words, I knew that we needed to understand all important economic and market movements, not just those that happened to me, and to make sure the principles we were using to position ourselves would have worked in all past times and all other countries.

As a result, back in the early 2000s, we had included a "depression gauge" in our systems that specified the actions we should take if a certain configuration of events began to play out in a way indicating a heightened risk of a debt crisis and depression. In 2007, this gauge indicated that a bubble of debt was nearing its bursting point because the costs of debt service were outpacing projected cash flows. Because interest rates were so close to 0 percent, I knew that central banks could not ease monetary policy enough to reverse the downturn the way they had in prior recessions. This was the exact configuration that had led to past depressions.

My mind and gut flashed back to my 1979–82 experience. I was now both thirty years more knowledgeable and a whole lot less confident. While the dynamic in the economy seemed clear to me, I was much less sure I was right. I remembered how clearly it had seemed to me that the debt bust I'd been expecting in 1982 would sink the economy—and how painfully wrong I had turned out to be.

That experience also drove me to learn a lot more about debt crises and their effects on the markets, and I researched and traded through a number of them, including the Latin American debt crisis in the 1980s, the Japanese debt crisis of the 1990s, the blowup of Long-Term Capital Management in 1998, the bursting of the dot-com bubble in 2000, and the fallout from the attacks on the World Trade Center and Pentagon in 2001. With the help of my teammates at Bridgewater, I took history books and old newspapers and went day by day through the Great Depression and the Weimar Republic, comparing what happened then with what was happening in the present. The exercise only confirmed my worst fears: It seemed inevitable to me that large numbers of individuals, companies, and banks were about to have serious debt problems and that the Federal Reserve couldn't lower interest rates to cushion the blow, as was the case in 1930–32.

My fear of being wrong pushed me to seek out other smart folks to poke holes in my view. I also wanted to walk key policymakers through my thinking, both to stress-test it and to make them aware of the situation as I saw it, so I went to Washington to speak with people in both the U.S. Treasury and the White House. Though they were polite, what I was presenting seemed too far-fetched to them, especially when by all outward indications the economy seemed to be booming. Most of them didn't go very deep into our reasoning or calculations before they dismissed them, with one exception: Ramsen Betfarhad, Vice President Dick Cheney's deputy assistant of domestic policy. He worked through all our numbers and was concerned by them.

Because everything we saw lined up and we couldn't find anyone who could refute our views, we prepared our clients' portfolios by balancing our positions in a way that there would be considerable upside and limited downside in the portfolios if we were right and putting in a backup plan in case we were wrong. Though we thought we were well prepared, we were as worried about being right as we were about being wrong. The prospect of the world economy going over a waterfall was scary to all of us because of what it might mean to those who weren't protected.

As in 1982, when conditions deteriorated and circumstances increasingly transpired as we'd predicted, policymakers began to pay more attention to us. Betfarhad had me come to the White House to meet with him. Tim Geithner, president of the New York Fed, asked to see me as well. I brought Bob, Greg, and a young analyst named Bob Elliott to a lunch meeting with Geithner. We walked him through the numbers and he literally turned white. When he asked me where we'd gotten them from, I told him they were publicly available. We'd just put them together and looked at them in a different way.

Two days after our meeting with Geithner, Bear Stearns collapsed. That didn't trigger much worry for most people or for the markets, though it was a sign of what was to come. It wasn't until six months later in September, when Lehman Brothers collapsed, that everyone else connected the dots. At that point the dominoes fell fast, and though they couldn't contain all the damage, policymakers, most importantly Fed chairman Ben Bernanke, reacted brilliantly to create "a beautiful deleveraging" (i.e., a way of lowering debt burdens while keeping economic growth positive and inflation low).[8]

To make this long story short, we navigated this period well for our clients, anticipating market moves and avoiding losses. Our flagship fund made over 14 percent in 2008, a year when many other investors recorded losses of more than 30 percent. We would have done even better had we not feared being wrong, which led us to balance our bets instead of arrogantly and foolishly putting more chips at stake. But I had no regrets because I had learned that it wasn't smart to bet that way. While in this case we would have made more money if we were less balanced, we certainly wouldn't have survived and succeeded long enough to be in such a position if we'd approached our investments in that way.

The 2008 debt crisis was another one of those like the one in 1982, which were both like many more before them and many more that

---

[8] Treasury secretary Hank Paulson's moves, especially putting government money into systemically important banks, were also crucial.

will come. I enjoyed reflecting back on my painful mistakes and the value of the principles they gave me. When the next big one comes along in twenty-five years or so, or who knows when, it will probably come as a surprise and cause a lot of pain unless those principles are properly encoded in algorithms put into our computers.

HELPING POLICYMAKERS

Our economic and market principles were very different from most others, which accounted for our different results. I will explain these differences in *Economic and Investment Principles* and won't digress into them now.

As former Fed chairman Alan Greenspan put it, "The models failed at a time when we needed them most . . . JP Morgan had the American economy accelerating three days before [the Lehman Brothers' collapse]—their model failed. The Fed model failed. The IMF model failed . . . So that left me asking myself: What happened?" Bill Dudley, president of the New York Fed, homed in on the problem when he said, "I think there's a fundamental problem in terms of how macroeconomists look at the economic outlook, growth, and inflation . . . If you look at the big macro models, they don't have a financial sector typically in them. They don't admit the possibility that the financial sector could essentially melt down, and therefore the monetary policy impulse could be completely impaired. So I think the lesson of the crisis is to do a lot more work to make sure that the finance people are talking to the macroeconomist people and building models that are more robust." He was right. We "finance people" see the world very differently from the way economists do. As a result of our success, policymakers reached out to us more, which led me to have a lot more contact with senior economic policymakers in the U.S. and around the world. Out of respect for the privacy of our conversations, I won't say much about them except to note that they became much more open to our nontraditional ways of looking at economies and markets, and more skeptical about traditional economic thinking, which had failed to either signal or avert the crisis.

Most of our exchanges were one-sided; I generally answered their questions and didn't ask any that would put them in the awkward position of having to avoid answering for fear of compromising confidential information. I met with these leaders without making judgments and without regard for their particular ideologies. I approached them like a doctor, just wanting to make the most beneficial impact.

They wanted my help because my global macroeconomic perspective as an investor was very different from theirs as policymakers. We were both products of our environments. Investors think independently, anticipate things that haven't happened yet, and put real money at stake with their bets. Policymakers come from environments that nurture consensus, not dissent, that train them to react to things that have already occurred, and that prepare them for negotiations, not placing bets. Because they don't benefit from the constant feedback about the quality of their decisions that investors get, it's not clear who the good and bad decision makers among them are. They also have to be politicians. Even the most clear-sighted and capable policymakers must constantly divert their attention from the immediate problems they are dealing with to fight the objections of other policymakers, and the political systems they must navigate are often dysfunctional.

While the economic machine is more powerful than any political system in the long run (ineffective politicians will be replaced and incapable political systems will change), the interaction between the two is what drives economic cycles in the here and now—and it's often not pretty to watch.

MAKING GREAT RETURNS

Our returns in 2010 were the best ever—nearly 45 and 28 percent in our two Pure Alpha funds and close to 18 percent in All Weather— almost exclusively because the systems we had programmed to take in information and process it were doing it superbly. These systems worked far better than we could with just our brains. Without them, we would have had to manage money the old and painful way: by trying to weigh in our heads all the markets and all the influences on them and then bring them together into a portfolio of bets. We would have had to hire and supervise a bunch of different investment managers, and because we couldn't have blind faith in them, we'd have had to understand how each one made their decisions, which would mean watching what they were doing and why so we could know what to expect from them, while dealing with all their different personality issues. Why would I want to do that? It seemed to me that that way of investing or managing an organization was obsolete, like reading a map instead of following a GPS. Of course, building our system was hard work—it had taken us over thirty years to do it.

Having too much money to manage can hurt performance, since the costs of getting in and out of positions can be high because being too big can push the markets. Making over 40 percent in 2010 had put us in the position of having to return a lot of money to clients who actually wanted to give us more to manage. We were always careful to stay safely short of being too big, lest we kill the goose that lays the golden eggs.

Our clients didn't want their money back—they wanted us to grow it. So we were presented with the puzzle of how to maximize our capacity without hurting our performance. We hadn't looked at that before, because we'd never had that much money. We quickly discovered that if we just tweaked what we did and created a new fund that managed money the same way as Pure Alpha but invested it solely in the most liquid markets, our expected returns would be the same and the expected risk (i.e., volatility) only slightly higher.

We programmed this new approach into our computers, backtested it to see how it worked in all countries and time frames, and explained it to our clients in detail so they could thoroughly understand the logic behind it. As much as I love and have benefited from artificial intelligence, I believe that only people can discover such things and then program computers to do them. That's why I believe that the right people, working with each other and with computers, are the key to success.

Toward the end of the year, we opened "Pure Alpha Major Markets" and clients invested $15 billion in it. Since then its returns have been as expected—that is, about the same as Pure Alpha's (actually better, but only slightly). Our clients were delighted. In fact, this new option was so popular that by 2011 we had to close it to new investment too.

GOING FROM BELOW THE RADAR TO ABOVE IT

Success is a double-edged sword—as I learned after we anticipated the financial crisis and Bridgewater and I began to receive unwanted public attention. Our unusual performance, our unusual way of looking at economics and markets, and our unusual culture made us a continuing subject of interest. I wanted to stay under the radar so I avoided interacting with the press. That didn't stop the press from writing about me and Bridgewater, which they typically did in a sensationalistic way—either painting me as a superhero investor who walked on water or as a leader of a cult, and sometimes both.

Getting a lot of attention for being successful is a bad position to be in. Australians call it the "tall poppy syndrome," because the tallest poppies in a field are the ones most likely to have their heads whacked off. I didn't like the attention and I especially didn't like the mischaracterizations of Bridgewater as a cult, because I felt it was hurting our ability to recruit great people. At the same time, I realized that because we didn't let the media see how we truly operated inside Bridgewater, those sensational portrayals were unavoidable.

So I decided in late 2010 to make public my *Principles*—which explained exactly what we were doing and why. I put it on our website so it could be read freely and understood by people outside the company.

Doing that was a hard decision, but it turned out to be a great one. Most people got it and many beyond Bridgewater benefited from reading them. More than three million people have downloaded *Principles*; some even had it translated into their own languages at their own expense. I've received a large number of thank-you notes from people who said that reading *Principles* had changed their lives.

PREPARING BRIDGEWATER
TO SUCCEED WITHOUT ME

Since I was a kid, I've learned by doing. I'd just dive in after things I wanted and try to survive long enough to learn from my mistakes and improve. If I changed fast enough to become sustainable at whatever I was doing, then I would build on that to flourish. I've always had great faith in my ability to figure things out, and over time my need to figure things out made me better at doing so. As a result, I tended to hire people who were the same way—who would dive right into challenges, figure out what to do about them, and then do it. I figured that if they had great character, common sense, and creativity, and were driven to achieve our shared mission, they would discover what it took to be successful if I gave them the freedom to figure out how to make the right decisions. I knew that micromanaging and handcuffing them wouldn't work because neither of us would like it. If I was the one telling them what to do, I wouldn't be getting any leverage from them. Besides, I didn't want to work with people who needed that.

But starting in the 1990s, I began to recognize the emotional barriers most people had to looking at their problems and weaknesses forthrightly. Rather than embracing ambiguous situations and difficult challenges, they tended to get uncomfortable when facing them. It is the rare bird who has the right mix of common sense, creativity, and character to shape change. Almost everyone needs help before they can get there. So I wrote down my principles and the logic behind them and shared them, hoping they could be used by those who thought they were good and debated openly by those who didn't. I figured that over time we would all get in sync about how particular situations should be handled.

But while almost all of us quickly agreed on the principles intellectually, many still struggled to convert what they had agreed to intellectually into effective action. This was because their habits and emotional barriers remained stronger than their reasoning. The training and the virtual-reality tapes helped a lot, but they still weren't enough.

No matter how much effort we put into screening new hires and training them to work in our idea meritocracy, it was inevitable that many of them would fall short. My approach was to hire, train, test, and then fire or promote quickly, so that we could rapidly identify the excellent hires and get rid of the ordinary ones, repeating the process again and again until the percentage of those who were truly great was high enough to meet our needs.

But for this to work, we needed people with high standards who wouldn't hesitate to eliminate people who couldn't cut it. Many new employees (and some older ones) still were reluctant to probe hard at what people were like, which made things worse. It's tough to be tough on people.

Of course, most of the people who come to Bridgewater are adventurous types; they know what they're getting into. They understand that the chances their job will not work out are higher than normal, but they embrace the risk because the upside of succeeding is huge relative to the downside of having it not work out. In the worst case they learn a lot about themselves, have an interesting experience, and leave for other jobs; in the best case, they become a part of an exceptional team achieving exceptional things.

New hires typically go through an acclimation period of about eighteen to twenty-four months before becoming comfortable with the truthfulness and transparency that is such an essential part of the Bridgewater culture—especially accepting one's mistakes and figuring out how to deal with them. But some people never adapt to it. I've been told that joining Bridgewater is a bit like joining an intellectual Navy SEALs; others describe it as going to a school of self-discovery run by someone like the Dalai Lama. The people who thrive say that while the period of adjustment is difficult, it is also joyous because of the excellence they achieve and the extraordinary relationships they make. And the ones who can't or won't adapt must be cut; this is essential to keeping Bridgewater excellent.

For a long time, I had been the one responsible for establishing the culture and upholding its high standards. But in 2010, I was sixty years old and had been running Bridgewater for thirty-five years. Though I expected to be good for another ten years or so, I was ready to put my energy into other things. While I always wanted to be deep into the markets, I wanted to spend more time with my family and friends, to help policymakers, and to pursue a few growing passions (like ocean exploration and philanthropy) as well as whatever else interested me. My plan was to step out as CEO while helping my replacements as a mentor, remain in my investment role, and take the time I gained from no longer managing the company to suck the marrow out of life while I still could.

As with all organizations, whether Bridgewater would succeed would come down to the people and the culture. People who run companies are faced with important choices every day. How they make those choices determines the character of the company, the quality of its relationships, and the outcomes it produces. When the buck stopped with me, I was responsible for most of the important decisions. Now those decisions would be in the hands of others. While they would have a well-established culture and agreed-upon principles that had worked for decades, the proof would be in the pudding.

CHAPTER 6

RETURNING THE BOON:

2011–2015

It seems to me that life consists of three phases. In the first, we are dependent on others and we learn. In the second, others depend on us and we work. And in the third and last, when others no longer depend on us and we no longer have to work, we are free to savor life.

I was beginning my transition from my second to my third phase. Both intellectually and emotionally, I was no longer as excited about being successful as I was excited about having the people I cared about be successful without me.

I had two jobs at Bridgewater to transition out of: overseeing the management of the company as chief executive officer, and overseeing the management of our investments as a chief investment officer. I wasn't going to stop playing the markets, because that's a game I've loved playing since I was twelve and I will keep playing until I die. But I didn't want to be *needed* in either role, because of the key-man risk that would create for the company.

My partners and I understood that transitioning from the first generation of leadership to the next in a founder-led organization with a unique culture is difficult, especially if the leader has been in place for a long time. Bill Gates's transition out of the CEO role at Microsoft in 2008 was the most recent example of that but there have been many others.

The biggest question I wrestled with was whether I should leave management completely or stay involved as a mentor. On the one hand, I liked the idea of stepping out completely because it would give the new leadership the freedom to find their own ways of succeeding without me looking over their shoulder. My friends urged me to do that—to "declare victory," collect my chips, and move on. But I wasn't confident that the transition would go well, as I hadn't done such a thing before. I do things through trial and error—making mistakes, figuring out what I did wrong, coming up with new principles, and finally succeeding—and I didn't see why my transition should be any different. I also didn't believe that it would be fair for me to dump the heavy workload I was carrying on those I was passing my CEO responsibilities to. I knew that Lee Kuan Yew, the wise founder and leader of Singapore for forty-one years, had transitioned out of his leadership responsibilities to be a mentor, and I had seen how well that went. For all those reasons, I decided I would stay on as a mentor. That meant I would either not speak at all or speak last, but always be available to provide advice. My partners liked the idea.

We agreed we should begin as soon as possible, so those replacing me could gain experience and we could make adjustments as needed. Since what we didn't know about transitioning was greater than what we did know about it, we knew we would need to be careful. We expected that transitioning well would take a number of years— perhaps two or three, perhaps as many as ten. Since we had worked together for many years, we were optimistic that it would be on the shorter end of that range.

On the first day of 2011 I announced to the company that I would be stepping down as CEO, with Greg Jensen and David McCormick replacing me. On July 1, I handed over my management responsibilities to Greg, David, and the rest of the Management Committee. Simultaneously, we explained our "up-to-ten-year transition plan" to our clients.

LEARNING WHAT SHAPERS ARE LIKE

Naturally the new management team struggled over the next eighteen months or so. We diagnosed why in the same way an engineer would diagnose why a machine is operating suboptimally so it could be reengineered to perform better. Since different people produce different outcomes based on differences in what they are like, whenever we create a team we seek to "engineer" the right mix of attributes and people to achieve our goals. So we looked at my attributes relative to others to see what was missing, which we called the "Ray gap." To be clear, we were looking at the "Ray gap" because I was the one leaving—had Bob, David, or Greg been the ones stepping back, we would have been studying the gaps they left.

Greg and David created a log of my various responsibilities and the differences between the qualities they and I brought to handling them. Everyone agreed the gap was in what we called "shaping."

To visualize what I mean by "shaping" and "shapers," think of Steve Jobs, who was probably the greatest and most iconic shaper of our time, as measured by the size and success of his shaping. A shaper is someone who comes up with unique and valuable visions and builds them out beautifully, typically over the doubts and opposition of others. Jobs built the world's largest and most successful company by revolutionizing computing, music, communications, animation, and photography with beautifully designed products. Elon Musk (of Tesla, SpaceX, and SolarCity), Jeff Bezos (of Amazon), and Reed Hastings (of Netflix) are other great shapers from the business world. In philanthropy, Muhammad Yunus (of Grameen), Geoffrey Canada (of Harlem Children's Zone), and Wendy Kopp (of Teach for America) come to mind; and in government, Winston Churchill, Dr. Martin Luther King, Jr., Lee Kuan Yew, and Deng Xiaoping. Bill Gates has been a shaper in both business and philanthropy, as was Andrew Carnegie. Mike Bloomberg has been a shaper in business, philanthropy, and government. Einstein, Freud, Darwin, and Newton were giant shapers in the sciences. Christ, Muhammad, and the Buddha were religious shapers. They all had original visions and successfully built them out.

While these are the biggest shapers, I saw that shapers come in varying sizes. You probably know a few personally. They might be your local business, nonprofit, or community leaders—the people who drive change and build lasting organizations. My objective was to identify who the future shapers of Bridgewater would be—either by helping the people who were replacing me in the CEO job become them or by finding shapers on the outside and bringing them in.

On October 5, 2011, a few months after I began to think about what makes a shaper, Steve Jobs died. I wrote about him in our *Daily Observations*, one of the very few times I used the space to address noninvestment-related content, because I admired him as a man who could visualize and execute in breathtakingly wonderful ways. Soon after, Walter Isaacson published his biography of Jobs. I noticed a number of similarities between us, especially when he quoted Jobs's own words. Soon after that, an article titled "Is Ray Dalio the Steve Jobs of Investing?" came out in *aiCIO*, a prominent investment-industry publication. It also pointed out a number of similarities between us—that I, like Jobs, started my businesses from scratch (his from a garage, mine from the second bedroom of my apartment), that we both came up with innovative products that reshaped how our industries did things, and that we had unique management styles. Bridgewater has often been called the Apple of the investment world—but to be clear, I didn't think that Bridgewater or I held a candle to Apple and Jobs.

Isaacson's book and the article pointed to other parallels in our backgrounds, goals, and approaches to shaping—for example, we were both rebellious, independent thinkers who worked relentlessly for innovation and excellence; we were both meditators who wanted to "put a dent in the universe"; and we were both notoriously tough on people. Of course, there were important differences too. I wished Jobs had shared the principles he had used to achieve his goals.

I wasn't just interested in Jobs and his principles; I wanted to know about the qualities and principles of all shapers, so I could better understand the likenesses and differences between them and form an archetype of the typical shaper. I had followed that approach for understanding everything; for example, I had made an exhaustive study of recessions so that I could form a timeless picture of an archetypal recession and then understand the differences among them. I did that for all economic and market movements and was inclined to do it for just about everything, because this approach helps me understand how things work. So it made sense I'd do that to understand shapers too.

I started by exploring the qualities of Jobs and other shapers with Isaacson, at first in a private conversation in his office, and later at a public forum at Bridgewater. Since Isaacson had also written biographies of Albert Einstein and Ben Franklin—two other great shapers—I read them and probed him about them to try to glean what characteristics they had in common.

Then I spoke with proven shapers I knew—Bill Gates, Elon Musk, Reed Hastings, Muhammad Yunus, Geoffrey Canada, Jack Dorsey (of Twitter), David Kelley (of IDEO), and more. They had all visualized remarkable concepts and built organizations to actualize them, and done that repeatedly and over long periods of time. I asked them to take an hour's worth of personality assessments to discover their values, abilities, and approaches. While not perfect, these assessments have been invaluable. (In fact, I have been adapting and refining them to help us in our recruiting and management.) The answers these shapers provided to the standardized questions gave me objective and statistically measurable evidence about their similarities and differences.

It turns out they have a lot in common. They are all independent thinkers who do not let anything or anyone stand in the way of achieving their audacious goals. They have very strong mental maps of how things should be done, and at the same time a willingness to test those mental maps in the world of reality and change the ways they do things to make them work better. They are extremely resilient, because their need to achieve what they envision is stronger than the pain they experience as they struggle to achieve it. Perhaps most interesting, they have a wider range of vision than most people, either because they have that vision themselves or because they know how to get it from others who can see what they can't. All are able to see both big pictures and granular details (and levels in between) and synthesize the perspectives they gain at those different levels, whereas most people see just one or the other. They are simultaneously creative, systematic, and practical. They are assertive and open-minded at the same time. Above all, they are passionate about what they are doing, intolerant of people who work for them who aren't excellent at what they do, and want to have a big, beneficial impact on the world.

Take Elon Musk. When he had just come out with the Tesla and showed me his own car for the first time, he had as much to say about the key fob that opened the doors as he did about his overarching vision for how Tesla fits into the broader future of transportation and how important that is to our planet. Later on, when I asked him how he came to start his company SpaceX, the audacity of his answer startled me.

"For a long time," he answered, "I've thought that it's inevitable that something bad is going to happen on a planetary scale—a plague, a meteor—that will require humanity to start over somewhere else, like Mars. One day I went to the NASA website to see what progress they were making on their Mars program, and I realized that they weren't even thinking about going there anytime soon.

"I had gotten $180 million when my partners and I sold PayPal," he continued, "and it occurred to me that if I spent $90 million and used it to acquire some ICBMs from the former USSR and sent one to Mars, I could inspire the exploration of Mars."

When I asked him about his background in rocketry, he told me he didn't have one. "I just started reading books," he said. That's how shapers think and act.

At times, their extreme determination to achieve their goals can make them appear abrasive or inconsiderate, which was reflected in their test results. Nothing is ever good enough, and they experience the gap between what is and what could be as both a tragedy and a source of unending motivation. No one can stand in the way of their achieving what they're going after. On one of the personality assessments there is a category they all ranked low on called "Concern for Others." But that doesn't mean quite what it sounds like.

Consider Muhammad Yunus, for example. A great philanthropist, he has devoted his life to helping others. He received the Nobel Peace Prize for pioneering the ideas of microcredit and microfinance and has won the Congressional Gold Medal, the Presidential Medal of Freedom, the Gandhi Peace Prize, and more. Yet he tested low on "Concern for Others." Geoffrey Canada, who has devoted most of his adult life to taking care of all the disadvantaged children in a hundred-square-block area of New York's Harlem, also tested low on "Concern for Others." Bill Gates, who is devoting most of his wealth and energy to saving and improving lives, tested low as well. Obviously Yunus, Canada, and Gates care deeply about other people, yet the personality tests they took rated them low. Why was that? In speaking with them and reviewing the questions that led to these ratings, it became clear: When faced with a choice between achieving their goal or pleasing (or not disappointing) others, they would choose achieving their goal every time.

Through this investigative process, I learned that there are distinctly different types of shapers. The most important difference lies in whether their shaping comes in the form of inventing, managing, or both. For example, while Einstein shaped by inventing, he didn't have to manage, and while Jack Welch (who ran GE) and Lou Gerstner (who ran IBM) were great managers/leaders of people, they didn't have to be as inventive. The rarest cases were people like Jobs, Musk, Gates, and Bezos, who were inventive visionaries and managed big organizations to build those visions out.

There are a lot of people who look like shapers, in that they came up with a great idea and got it to the point where they could sell it for a lot of money, but did not shape consistently. Silicon Valley has many of these types; perhaps they should be called "inventors." I also saw that there were wonderful leaders of organizations who weren't classic shapers, in that they didn't come up with the original visions and build them out; rather, they entered existing organizations and led them well. Only true shapers consistently move from one success to another and sustain success over decades, and those are the people I want to bring to Bridgewater.

My examination of shapers and my reflections on my own qualities made clear to me that nobody sees the full range of what they need to see in order to be exceptionally successful, though some see a wider range than others. Those that do best both see a wide range themselves while triangulating well with other brilliant people who see things in different, complementary ways.

This realization has been important in making my transition out of management go well. While in the past I would encounter problems, figure out their causes, and design my own ways to get around them, others who think differently than I do will make different diagnoses and designs. My job as mentor was to help them be successful at that.

This exercise reminded me that there are far fewer types of people in the world than there are people and far fewer different types of situations than there are situations, so matching the right types of people to the right types of situations is key.

Because Gates and Jobs had recently left Microsoft and Apple, I watched their former organizations closely to help me better understand how I could help prepare Bridgewater to thrive without me. Certainly the most notable difference between them and Bridgewater was in our cultures—how we use the idea meritocracy of radical truth and radical transparency to bring problems and weaknesses to the surface to prompt forthright dealing with them.

SYSTEMIZING OUR IDEA MERITOCRACY

The more I did the research on people, the clearer it became that there are different types of people and that, by and large, the same types of people in the same types of circumstances are going to produce the same types of results. Said differently, by knowing what someone is like we can have a pretty good idea of what we can expect from them. So I was more motivated than ever to continue gathering lots of data on what people are like to build pointillist pictures of them to help us match people to responsibilities well. Doing this in an evidence-based way would enhance the idea-meritocratic process of aligning people's responsibilities with their merits.

While this all seemed so clear and commonsensical to me, it was much harder to achieve in practice. About a year into my transition, I saw that many new managers (and some older ones) still couldn't see the patterns of people's behaviors through time (in other words, they couldn't connect the dots between what people are like and the outcomes they produce). Their reluctance to probe hard to get at what people are like was making things more difficult.

But then I had a breakthrough, which grew out of an observation that the challenges we were having with making management decisions didn't exist in our investment decision making. I realized that, by using big data analytics and other algorithms, our computers could connect those dots more efficiently than any of us could, just as they had helped us make connections in the markets. These systems also didn't have personal biases and emotional barriers to overcome, so those being analyzed couldn't be offended by the data-driven conclusions the computers were coming up with. In fact, they could look at the data and algorithms, assess them for themselves, and suggest changes if they wanted. We were like scientists trying to develop tests and algorithms for analyzing ourselves objectively.

On November 10, 2012, I shared my thoughts with the Management Committee in an email. Its subject line was "The Path Out: Systemizing Good Management":

> *It is now clear to me that the main difference behind why the investment management part of Bridgewater is likely to continue to do well and most of the other parts of Bridgewater are unlikely to do as well (if we don't change how we are operating) is that the decision-making processes for investment management have been so systemized that it's hard for people to screw them up (because they are largely following the systems' instructions) while the other areas of Bridgewater are much more dependent on the quality of the people and their decision making.*

Think about that. Imagine how Bridgewater's investment decision making would work if it operated the same as Bridgewater's management decision making (i.e., dependent on the people we hired and how they collectively made decisions in their own ways). It would be a mess.

The way the investment decision-making process works is that a small group of investment managers who created these systems see the systems' conclusions and the reasoning of the systems while we make our own conclusions and explore our reasoning on our own. . . . The machine does most of the work and we interact with it in a quality way. . . . [And] we are not dependent on much more faulty people.

Think about how different management is. While we have principles, we don't have decision-making systems.

In other words, I believe that the investment decision-making process is effective because the investment principles have been put into decision rules that make decisions that people then follow while the management decision-making process is less effective because the management principles have not been put into decision rules that people can follow to make management decisions.

It doesn't have to be that way. Having built the investment systems (with the help of others) and knowing about both investment decision making and management decision making, I am confident that it can be the same. The only questions are whether it can happen fast enough and what will happen in the meantime.

I am working with Greg (and others) to develop these management systems in the same way I worked with Greg and others (Bob, etc.) on the investment systems. You are seeing this happen via the development of the Baseball Cards, Dot Collector, Pain Button, testing, job specing, etc. Because I have a limited time to do this, we need to move fast. At the same time we will have to fight the battles in the trenches, with hand-to-hand combat, to clean out those who are incapable and bring in or promote those who are excellent.

One of the great things about algorithmic decision making is that it focuses people on cause-effect relationships and, in that way, helps foster a real idea meritocracy. When everyone can see the criteria the algorithms use and have a hand in developing them, they can all agree that the system is fair and trust the computer to look at the evidence, make the right assessments about people, and assign them the right authorities. The algorithms are essentially principles in action on a continuous basis.

While our management system has a long way to go before it is as well automated as our investment system, the tools it has made possible, especially the "Dot Collector" (an app that gathers information about people in real time described in detail in the Work Principles), have already made an incredible difference in the way we work.

All these tools reinforce good habits and good thinking. The good habits come from thinking repeatedly in a principled way, like learning to speak a language. The good thinking comes from exploring the reasoning behind the principles.

The ultimate goal of all this was to help the people I cared about be more successful without me, which was becoming increasingly pressing as life's milestones continued to remind me of my stage in life. For example, I became a grandfather with the birth of Christopher Dalio on May 31, 2013. And in the summer of 2013, I had a serious health scare that turned out to be nothing but reminded me of my mortality. At the same time, I still loved playing the markets, which I plan to do until I die, making me even more eager to speed the transition from the second to the third phase of my life.

ANTICIPATING THE EUROPEAN DEBT CRISIS

Beginning in 2010, my Bridgewater colleagues and I began to see the emergence of a debt crisis in Europe. We had looked at how much debt had to be sold and how much could be bought for a number of countries and determined that many Southern European nations were likely to come up short. The resulting crisis could be as bad as or worse than the one in 2008–09.

As in 1980 and 2008, while our calculations clearly pointed to a debt crisis ahead, I knew that I could be wrong. Because it would be a big deal if I was right, I wanted to discuss what I was seeing with top policymakers both to alert them and to have them correct me if they saw things differently. I encountered the same sort of resistance without good explanations that I had encountered in Washington in 2008, only this time in Europe. Things were stable at the time, and though I knew there was no reason to believe they would stay that way, most of the people I spoke to weren't ready to listen to my reasoning. I remember a meeting I had with the head of the International Monetary Fund when we were still in the calm before the storm. He doubted my seemingly crazy conclusions, and he wasn't interested in going through the numbers.

Just as U.S. policymakers had before 2008, the Europeans did not fear what they hadn't experienced before. Because things were good at the time and the picture I was painting was worse than anything they'd experienced in their lifetimes, they found what I was saying implausible. They also didn't possess a granular understanding of who the borrowers and lenders were and how their abilities to borrow and lend would change with changing market conditions. Their understandings of how markets and economies work were oversimplified, like those of academics. For example, they looked at investors as a single thing they called "the market," rather than an amalgam of different players who bought and sold for different reasons. When the markets did badly, they wanted to do things that increased confidence, figuring that if they built confidence the money would come and the problems would disappear. They didn't see that whether they were confident or not, specific buyers didn't have enough money and credit to buy all the debt that had to be sold.

Just as all human bodies work in essentially the same way, so do the economic machines in different countries. And just as physical diseases infect people without regard to nationality, so do economic diseases. So, while the policymakers were at first skeptical, I approached my conversations with them by looking at the physiology of the case at hand. I would diagnose the economic disease they were suffering from, and show them how its symptoms progress by referencing prior analogous cases. Then I'd explain the best practices for treating the disease at its different stages. We would have high-quality back-and-forths about the linkages and the evidence.

Yet even when I did succeed in helping them see the linkages, the political decision-making systems they had to work within were dysfunctional. Not only did they have to decide what they would do as individual countries, the nineteen countries of the European Union had to agree with each other before they could act—in many cases unanimously. There was often no clear way of resolving disagreements, which was a big problem because what needed to be done (printing money) was objectionable to German economic conservatives. As a result, crises would intensify to breaking points while Europe's leaders grappled in long closed-door meetings. Those power struggles tested the nerves of everyone involved. I can't possibly convey the amount of bad behavior these policymakers had to endure for the benefit of the people they represented.

For example, in January 2012, a few weeks after he'd been appointed minister of economy and competitiveness by Spain's new president, I met Luis de Guindos, a man I learned to admire for his forthrightness, intelligence, and heroic willingness to sacrifice himself for his country's well-being. The old government in Spain had been thrown out and the new government took office as Spanish banks were about to collapse. The new Spanish policymakers were immediately forced to haggle with representatives from the IMF, the European Union, and the European Central Bank (the "Troika" as it was called). They did this into the wee hours of the morning and at the end were required to sign a loan agreement that essentially handed over control of their banking system to the Troika in exchange for the financial support they desperately needed.

My meeting with Minister de Guindos took place the morning after the first and most difficult of these negotiations. With bloodshot eyes but a very alert mind, he patiently and forthrightly answered all my difficult questions and shared his thoughts about what reforms Spain should undertake to deal with their problems. During the next couple of years, over considerable objections, he and his government pushed these controversial reforms through. He never got the praise he deserved, but he didn't care because his satisfaction came from seeing the results he produced. To me, that is a hero.

As time passed, the European debtor countries fell into deeper depressions. This led Mario Draghi, the president of the European Central Bank, to make the bold decision to buy bonds in September 2012. This move averted the imminent debt crisis, saved the euro, and, as it would turn out, made a lot of money for the ECB. But it failed to immediately stimulate credit and economic growth in the countries that were in depression. Inflation, which the ECB was mandated to get to about 2 percent, was below that target and falling. While the ECB had offered loans on attractive terms to banks in an attempt to solve this issue, banks weren't taking them up on the offer sufficiently to make a difference. I believed that things would continue to worsen unless the ECB "printed money" and pushed it into the system by buying more bonds. The move toward quantitative easing appeared obvious and necessary to me, so I visited Draghi and the ECB's executive board to share my concerns.

At the meeting, I told them why this approach would not be inflationary (because it is the level of spending, which is money plus credit, and not just the amount of money, that drives spending and inflation). I focused on how the economic machine works because I felt that if we could agree on that—most importantly, how buying bonds moves money through the system—we could agree on its impacts on inflation and economic growth. In that meeting, and in all such meetings, I shared our calculations as well as the important cause-effect relationships as I saw them, so that together we could assess whether the conclusions made sense.

A major impediment to this action was that there is no single bond market for the entire Eurozone, and the ECB, like most central banks, isn't supposed to favor one area/country over another. Given those conditions, I shared my theory for how the ECB could do quantitative easing without breaking its rules by buying bonds proportionately across every member country, even though Germany didn't need or want the easing that such purchases would bring them. (The German economy was doing relatively well and inflation fears were beginning to emerge there.)

In the course of those eighteen months, I met with several top European economic policymakers, perhaps most importantly German finance minister Wolfgang Schäuble, whom I judged to be exceptionally thoughtful and selfless. I also saw how politics within Germany and Europe worked.[9] When push came to shove, the ECB would have to do what was best for Europe, which was to print the money and buy the bonds in the way I had suggested. Doing that was consistent with the ECB's mandate, and the Southern European debtor countries had the votes to allow it to do that, so I figured that it would be the Germans who would get overruled and face the decision to leave the Eurozone, which they would ultimately not do because their leaders had a strong commitment to the Eurozone with Germany as part of it.

Draghi finally announced the move in January 2015. It had a great effect and created a precedent that would allow more quantitative easings in the future if they were needed. The market reaction was very positive. On the day of Draghi's announcement European equities were up a percent and a half, government bond yields fell across the major European economies, and the euro fell 2 percent against the dollar (which helped stimulate the economy). These moves continued over the following months, stimulating European economies, supporting a pickup in growth, and reversing the decline in inflation.

The ECB's decision was obviously the right thing to do, for reasons that were relatively simple. But seeing how controversial its move was, it occurred to me that the world needed a simple explanation of how the economic machine works, because if everyone understood the basics, then economic policymakers would be able to do the right things a lot faster and with less angst in the future. That led me to make a thirty-minute video, *How the Economic Machine Works*, which

---

[9] In Germany politics are like everywhere else in that there are opposing forces that struggle with each other and decisions are made via a mix of power and negotiation. This makes it desirable to know who has what power and is willing to negotiate what. What makes Germany different is the amount of attention it pays to legal technicalities.

I released in 2013. Besides explaining how the economy works it provides a template that helps people assess their economies and gives them guidance about what to do and what to expect during a crisis. It had a much bigger impact than I expected, as it was watched by more than five million people in eight languages. A number of policymakers told me in private that they found it helpful for their own understanding, for dealing with their constituents, and for finding better paths forward. This was very rewarding to me.

From my contacts with policymakers in a number of countries I learned quite a bit about how international relations really works. It is quite different from what most people imagine. Countries behave in a more self-interested and less considerate way than what most of us would consider appropriate for individuals. When countries negotiate with one another, they typically operate as if they are opponents in a chess match or merchants in a bazaar in which maximizing one's own benefit is the sole objective. Smart leaders know their own countries' vulnerabilities, take advantage of others' vulnerabilities, and expect the other countries' leaders to do the same.

Most people who haven't had direct contact with the leadership of their own and other countries form their views based on what they learn in the media, and become quite naive and inappropriately opinionated as a result. That's because dramatic stories and gossip draw more readers and viewers than does clinical objectivity. Also, in some cases "journalists" have their own ideological biases that they are trying to advance. As a result, most people who see the world through the lens of the media tend to look for who is good and who is evil rather than what the vested interests and relative powers are and how they are being played out. For example, people tend to embrace stories about how their own country is moral and the rival country is not, when most of the time these countries have different interests that they are trying to maximize. The best behaviors one can hope for come from leaders who can weigh the benefits of cooperation, and who have long enough time frames that they can see how the gifts they give this year may bring them benefits in the future.

These conflicts of vested interests don't just play out internationally; it can also be nasty within countries. Finding out what's true and trying to do what's in everyone's best interests is rare, though most policymakers pretend that's what they're doing. More typically, they act in support of their constituents' interests. For example, representatives of those with greater income will say higher taxes stifle growth while representatives of those with less income will say the opposite. It's hard to get everyone to even try to look at the whole picture objectively, let alone to operate in the interests of the whole.

Nonetheless, I came to respect most of the policymakers I worked with and to feel sorry for them because of the terrible positions they were in. Most are highly principled people who are forced to operate in unprincipled environments. The job of a policymaker is challenging under the best of circumstances, and it's almost impossible during a crisis. The politics are horrendous and distortions and outright misinformation from the media make things worse. A number of the policymakers I met—including Draghi, de Guindos, Schäuble, Bernanke, Geithner, Summers, and many others—were real heroes, meaning that they put others and the mission they committed to above themselves. Unfortunately, most policymakers enter their careers as idealists and leave disillusioned.

One of those heroes I have been fortunate enough to learn from and, I hope, help is China's Wang Qishan, who has been a remarkable force for good for decades. To explain what he is like and the journey that took him to the top of China's leadership would take more of this book than I can spare. In brief, Wang is a historian, a very high-level thinker, and a very practical man. I have rarely known a person to be both extremely wise and extremely practical. A leading shaper of the Chinese economy for decades who is also responsible for eliminating corruption, he is known to be a no-nonsense man who can be trusted to get stuff done.

Every time I go to China, we meet for sixty to ninety minutes. We talk about what's happening in the world, and how that relates to thousands of years of history and the never-changing nature of mankind. We discuss a wide range of other topics as well, ranging from physics to artificial intelligence. We are both keenly interested in how most everything happens over and over again, the forces behind those patterns, and the principles that work and don't work in dealing with them.

I gave Wang a copy of Joseph Campbell's great book *The Hero with a Thousand Faces*, because he is a classic hero and I thought it might help him. I also gave him *The Lessons of History*, a 104-page distillation of the major forces through history by Will and Ariel Durant, and *River Out of Eden* by the insightful Richard Dawkins, which explains how evolution works. He gave me Georgi Plekhanov's classic *On the Role of the Individual in History*. All these books showed how the same things happened over and over again throughout history.

Most of my conversations with Wang are at the principle level; he sees the rhyme of history and puts the particulars we speak of in that context. "Unattainable goals appeal to heroes," he once told me. "Capable people are those who sit there worrying about the future. The unwise are those who worry about nothing. If conflicts got resolved before they became acute, there wouldn't be any heroes." His advice has helped me in my planning for Bridgewater's future. For example, when I asked him about checks and balances of power, he pointed to Julius Caesar's overthrow of the Roman Senate and Republic as an illustration of how important it is to make sure no one person is more powerful than the system. I took his advice to heart as I set out to improve Bridgewater's governance model.

Every time I speak with Wang, I feel like I get closer to cracking the unifying code that unlocks the laws of the universe. He uses his timeless perspective to see the present and the likely future more clearly.

Being around such people, especially if I can help them, is thrilling to me.

RETURNING THE BOON

Joseph Campbell's *The Hero with a Thousand Faces*, one of the books I gave to Wang as well as a number of other heroes I know, was introduced to me by my son Paul in 2014. While I had seen Campbell on television nearly thirty years earlier and remembered being impressed by him, I hadn't read his book. In it, Campbell looks at large numbers of "heroes" from different cultures—some real and some mythical—and describes their archetypal journeys through life. Campbell's description of how heroes become heroes aligned with my thinking about shapers. And it gave me powerful insights about the heroes I know and the patterns of my own life.

For Campbell, a "hero" isn't a perfect person who always gets things right. Far from it. A hero is someone who "found or achieved or [did] something beyond the normal range of achievement," and who "has given his life to something bigger than himself or other than himself." I had met a number of such people throughout my life. What was most interesting about Campbell's work was his description of how they got that way. Heroes don't begin as heroes; they just become them because of the way one thing leads to another. The diagram on the following page shows the archetypal hero's journey.

They typically start out leading ordinary lives in an ordinary world and are drawn by a "call to adventure." This leads them down a "road of trials" filled with battles, temptations, successes, and failures. Along the way, they are helped by others, often by those who are further along the journey and serve as mentors, though those who are less far along also help in various ways. They also gain allies and enemies and learn how to fight, often against convention. Along the way, they encounter temptations and have clashes and reconciliations with their fathers and their sons. They overcome their fear of fighting because of their great determination to achieve what they want, and they gain their "special powers" (i.e., skills) from both "battles" that test and teach them, and from gifts (such as advice) that they receive from others. Over time, they both succeed and fail, but they increasingly succeed more than they fail as they grow stronger and keep striving for more, which leads to ever-bigger and more challenging battles.

Heroes inevitably experience at least one very big failure (which Campbell calls an "abyss" or the "belly of the whale" experience) that tests whether they have the resilience to come back and fight smarter and with more determination. If they do, they undergo a change (have

THE HERO'S JOURNEY

ADVENTURE

RETURNING THE BOON

CALL TO ADVENTURE

CROSSING THE THRESHOLD

THE ROAD OF TRIALS

THE ULTIMATE BOON

METAMORPHOSIS

ABYSS

a "metamorphosis") in which they experience the fear that protects them, without losing the aggressiveness that propels them forward. With triumphs come rewards. Though they don't realize it when they are in their battles, the hero's biggest reward is what Campbell calls the "boon," which is the special knowledge about how to succeed that the hero has earned through his journey.

Late in life, winning more battles and acquiring more rewards typically becomes less exciting to heroes than passing along that knowledge to others—"returning the boon" as Campbell called it. Once the boon is returned, the hero is free to live and then free to die, or, as I see it, to transition from the second phase in life to the third phase (in which one is free to savor life until one passes away).

Reading Campbell, I saw that heroes, like shapers, come in varying sizes—there are big ones and small ones—that they are real people, and that we all know some. I also saw that being a hero is typically not all it's cracked up to be—they get beat up a lot, and many are attacked, humiliated, or killed even after they triumph. In fact, it's hard to see the logic for choosing this hero role, if one were to choose. But I could see and relate to how a certain type of person would start and stay on that path.

While Campbell's description of the hero's journey captured the essence of my own journey through life and the journeys of many of the people I call shapers, "hero" is not a word that I would use to describe myself and I certainly would not put my own accomplishments on the level of the heroes Campbell wrote about.[10] But learning about the hero's journey did help me crystallize my understanding of where I was in my own journey, and what I should do next. The section on returning the boon spoke to me in a personal way, as though Campbell knew exactly what I was wrestling with. With the reflections it prompted, I could see that my life would be over in a relatively short time and that what I'd leave behind could be more important,

---

[10] I want to be clear that I don't believe that those who are "heroes" or "shapers" are either better people or are on better paths. It's perfectly sensible to not have any desire to go on such a journey. I believe that what's most important is to know one's own nature and operate consistently with it.

last longer, and affect many more people than just those at Bridgewater and my family. That helped make clear that I needed to pass along the things I had that could help others beyond me, most importantly the principles in this book, but also my money.

As the saying goes, "You can't take it with you." My need to start thinking about who should get what wasn't just because of my age and the time it would take to do it well; it was also instinctive. Over time, the circle of people and things I cared about had broadened from just me when I was young, to me and my family when I became a parent, to my community when I was a bit more mature, to people beyond my community and the whole environment now.

WRESTLING WITH THE QUESTIONS OF PHILANTHROPY

My first exposure to "philanthropy"[11] occurred back in the late 1990s when I was approaching fifty. At that time, Matt was sixteen, spoke Mandarin, and visited a Chinese orphanage to help someone, where he learned that a $500 surgery could save or radically improve some lives. We and our friends gave him money to help. Then, my friend Paul Tudor Jones taught Matt how to create a 501(c)(3) foundation and Matt, just a junior in high school, created the China Care Foundation in 2000. Matt brought our family to the orphanages, so we had close contact with these special-needs children and fell in love with them. We also watched Matt struggle to decide which children would live and which would die because there wasn't enough money to save them all. Imagine being faced with the choice between a big night out on the town or saving a child's life. That was essentially the choice we constantly faced. This experience led us to become more involved with philanthropy, so in 2003 we set up our own foundation

---

[11] The word "philanthropy" doesn't sit well with me in describing what we are doing. What we are doing is helping out with what we care about because of the joy it gives us—like the joy one gets from helping a friend. To my ear, "philanthropy" has taken on a meaning that sounds more official. For example, some people have come to judge whether something is philanthropic by whether it is consistent with what tax law determines is philanthropic. When we approach our philanthropy, we just see people and things that we are excited about helping.

to provide support in more organized ways. We wanted to do our philanthropy together, as a family activity, which has proven to be fabulous.

Figuring out how to best give away money is as complex an undertaking as figuring out how to make it. Though we now know a lot more about it than we did when we started, we still don't always feel capable to make the best decisions possible, so my family and I are still feeling our way through it. I will give you a few examples of the questions we have been wrestling with and how our thinking about them has evolved, starting with the question of how much money should be saved for my family relative to how much should go to people and causes that are more distant, yet more desperately in need.

Long before I had a lot of money, I had determined that I wanted my sons to have only enough to afford excellent health care, excellent education, and an initial boost to help their careers get started. My perspective was influenced by my own journey through life, which took me from having nothing to having a lot. That taught me to struggle well and made me strong. I wanted the same for the people I loved. So, when I had earned a lot of money, I felt I had plenty of money to give away to others.

Over time, as we gained experience in trying to help in a number of areas, I learned how fast money goes and that we didn't have nearly enough to take care of everything we cared about. Additionally, when my first grandchild was born, it prompted me to wonder how many generations I should budget to protect. Speaking to others in comparable positions, I discovered that even the richest people feel short of the money they need to do the things they want to do. So I studied how other families approach the question of how much to set aside for family and how much to give away at what pace. While our family still has not answered these questions definitely, I know that I personally will give more than half of my money to those beyond my family.

Which causes we should donate to was another big question. Barbara's biggest passion has been helping students in the most stressed public school districts in Connecticut, especially those students who are called "disengaged and disconnected."[12] A study she funded showed that 22 percent of high school students fall into one of these two categories, which was shocking because most will probably become adults who will suffer and be burdens on society rather than flourishing contributors to it. Because she has a lot of direct contact with these children and their teachers, she understands their needs. When she learned that 10,000 of them didn't have winter coats, she felt compelled to provide them. What she showed me opened my eyes. How can clothing and nutrition be so severely deficient in this "land of opportunity"? Everyone in our family believes that equal opportunity, which is one of the most fundamental human rights, requires equal educational opportunity—and that educational opportunities are terribly unequal. The economic costs—in the forms of crime and incarceration—as well as the social costs of not investing in improving these conditions are immense. While we have felt compelled to help, we've discovered it is very difficult to have a significant impact relative to the size of the problem.

I feel deeply connected to nature, especially the oceans. The oceans are our world's greatest asset, covering 72 percent of its surface and comprising 99 percent of its livable space. It thrills me to support scientists who are exploring the oceans and media showing them in the incredible environments they visit. I'm on a mission to make clear that ocean exploration is even more important and exciting than space exploration so that our oceans get more support and will be more sensibly managed. To add to my excitement, my son Mark is a wildlife filmmaker who shares my passion, so we get to pursue it together.

Matt's passion is to bring inexpensive, effective computing to the developing world as a way of expanding and improving education and health care. Paul's passion is mental health and his wife's is fighting climate change. Devon is more focused on his career than on philanthropy now, but his wife cares deeply about animal welfare. Our family continues to support special-needs children in China, as well as an

---

[12] A disengaged student is one who attends school but doesn't engage in doing the work. A disconnected student is one who doesn't attend school and the system has lost track of.

institute that teaches best practices to Chinese philanthropists. We also support the teaching of meditation to children in stressful environments and to veterans with PTSD, cutting-edge heart research, microfinance and other social enterprises, and much more.

We view our donations as investments and want to make sure that we have high philanthropic returns on our money. So another big question we wrestle with is how to measure those returns. It's much easier to measure efficiency in a business by seeing how much its revenue exceeds its cost. Because of this, we developed an attraction to sustainable social enterprises. Still, I saw that so many philanthropic investments could pay off economically as well as socially, and it tormented me that our society passes them up.

We also wrestled with how big our organization should be and what governance controls we should have in order to ensure the quality of our philanthropic decision making. I approached these decisions the same way I explain in Work Principles—by creating formalized principles and policies for our decision making. For example, because we are bombarded with more requests for grants than we can intelligently look at, I mandated a policy not to review unsolicited requests so our staff has the time to sort through the areas we want to be focused on. We are continuously improving all our principles and policies, and I dream about building decision-making algorithms for our philanthropic efforts, though that's beyond my reach at the moment.

As you might have guessed, we also seek advice from the most experienced and respected people possible. Bill Gates and the people we met through our participation in his, Melinda Gates's, and Warren Buffett's Giving Pledge have been enlightening. Others such as Muhammad Yunus, Paul Jones, Jeff Skoll, the Omidyar folks, and the people at TED have been very helpful. The most important thing we've learned is that there's no one right way to do philanthropy, though there are plenty of wrong ways.

Giving away the money that I acquired during my lifetime—and doing that well—has been a joy, a challenge, and the appropriate thing to do at this stage in my life.

BRIDGEWATER TURNS FORTY

In June 2015, Bridgewater marked its fortieth anniversary, an amazing milestone we celebrated by throwing a big party. We had a lot to celebrate, since by most measures no firm in our industry had been as successful.[13] Key people who had been a part of our journey from its outset and throughout our forty years got up to speak. Each of them described the evolution of the company through their eyes—how some things had changed over the years while others had stayed the same, most importantly, our culture of striving for excellence in work and excellence in relationships by being radically truthful and radically transparent with each other. They recounted how we uniquely and repeatedly tried new things, failed, learned from our failures, improved, and tried again, doing that over and over in an upward spiral. When it was my turn to speak, I wanted to convey what I had always tried to give the people at Bridgewater, and what I wanted them to have in the future without me:

A community in which you always have the right and obligation to make sense of things and a process for working yourselves through disagreements— i.e., a real, functioning idea meritocracy. I want you to think, not follow—while recognizing that you can be wrong and that you have weaknesses—and I want to help you get the most likely best answers, even if you personally don't believe that they're the best answers. I want to give you radical open-mindedness and an idea meritocracy that will take you from being trapped in your own heads to having access to the best minds in the world to help you make the best decisions for you and for our community. I want to help you all struggle well and evolve to get the most out of life.

Though there were still important things that had to be done, at the time I thought that we were wrapping up my transition nicely. I had no idea how difficult the next year would be.

---

[13] That January, we'd launched our first new product in more than a decade, a fund we called "Optimal Porfolio," which combined alphas and betas in ways uniquely suited for a global macro environment in which interest rates were near zero. The launch was a big success, the largest in the history of the hedge fund industry.

CHAPTER 7

MY LAST YEAR AND MY GREATEST CHALLENGE:

2016–2017

While even before that fortieth anniversary we had all been aware that our transition wasn't going as smoothly as we'd hoped, in the months that followed our problems came to a head in ways that caught us off guard. While the investment part of Bridgewater was better than ever, other parts of the business, like the technology and recruiting areas, were slipping.

I was no longer CEO, so it was not my job to manage the company. As chairman, my job was to oversee the CEOs, to make sure that they were managing it well. And Greg Jensen and Eileen Murray, the CEOs at the time, were clearly overstretched. We all agreed that the company wasn't being managed adequately, but we disagreed on what to do about it. Disagreements like these were expected, as we always want everyone to think independently and argue for what they view as best. That is why we have principles and processes for resolving them.

So, over a period of several weeks, we exchanged our views. Then key parties presented their perspectives and recommendations to members of our Management Committee and our Stakeholders Committee (which is essentially the Bridgewater board), who considered the alternative paths and ultimately voted on them. The most important decision that came out of that process was announced in

March 2016: Greg would step out of his co-CEO role so that he could focus all his attention on his co-chief investment officer role (which he handled with Bob Prince and me), and I would temporarily join Eileen as co-CEO while we implemented the structural changes needed to allow Bridgewater to work well without me.

While that wasn't the outcome any of us had hoped for when I first stepped out as CEO and passed it on to others, it wasn't entirely unexpected. Our struggles had been apparent for some time, and we'd tried different iterations. We knew that leadership transitions are never easy, and our modus operandi has always been to try, fail, diagnose, redesign, and try again. That's what we were doing. Now was the time for a leadership change.

Still, this particular failure was painful, especially for Greg and me. I realized that I had handed Greg too heavy a load in expecting him to carry out both the co-CEO and co-CIO roles. I regret that mistake more than any other I made in running Bridgewater because it hurt both of us and the company. I had not only mentored Greg, but he had been like a son to me for nearly twenty years. He and I both wanted and expected him to run the company. The pain of this failure was made worse, especially for Greg, by the sensational and inaccurate accounts that appeared in the media. Story after story portrayed it as a bitter death-match between two titans rather than what it really was, which was people who loved Bridgewater working through their disagreements in an idea-meritocratic way. This was Greg's going-into-the-abyss experience on his own hero's journey—and it was also that for me, and for a number of other leaders of the company—and not just because it was so painful, but because it led us to a metamorphosis that improved us a lot.

Greg is twenty-five years younger than me. I often think about where I was at his age, and how much I've learned in the years since. I know Greg will go on to succeed remarkably in his own way. I was pleased that we both came through this stronger, and especially pleased that our systems for identifying and resolving problems had worked as well as they had. While we all had different perspectives, this case reaffirmed our belief that our collective idea-meritocratic decision-making process would produce better results than any one of us could have done alone. It was having such a process, along with our deep relationships, that kept us together.

I realized again that what I didn't know was much greater than what I did, in this case not knowing how to transition out of the founder-leader role. So I reached out to some of the greatest experts I could speak with for advice. Perhaps the best advice we received came from management expert Jim Collins, who told us that "to transition well, there are only two things that you need to do: Put capable CEOs in place and have a capable governance system to replace the CEOs if they're not capable." That was what I had failed to do and what I now had a second shot at doing right. So I began to think about governance in a way that I never had before.

Simply put, governance is the system of checks and balances ensuring that an organization will be stronger than whoever happens to be leading it at any one time. Because I was a founder-entrepreneur, I had run Bridgewater for thirty-five years with no formal rules to check and balance me (though I had created an informal governance system by having me report to our Management Committee as a check on my decision making).

While that informal system had worked for me, it could not work well without me. Clearly, we needed to build a new governance system that would allow Bridgewater to retain its unique way of being and its uncompromising standards no matter who was in charge—and build it to be resilient enough to change the company's management if that was required. I went on to do that with the help of others, and we are doing that still.

I had learned that it's wrong to assume either that a person in one role will be successful in another role or that the ways one person operates will work well for another. This difficult year also taught me a lot about the people around me, especially David McCormick and Eileen Murray, who showed their commitments to our shared mission, as numerous other people did. There were some failures that we would have rather not had, but that was to be expected, given our unique culture of trial and error and learning from mistakes. Thanks to the changes we put into place, I was able to step out of my temporary stint as CEO after one year, in April 2017.

As I write these words in 2017, I view this year as the final one in my transition from the second phase of my life to the third, when I will have finished passing along the knowledge I have gathered along the way, and, as Joseph Campbell described it, I will be free to live and free to die. But right now I'm not thinking about the dying part; I'm thinking about how to live freely, and I'm excited about it.

CHAPTER 8

LOOKING BACK FROM
A HIGHER LEVEL

A s I look back on my experiences, it's interesting to reflect on how my perspectives have changed.

When I started out, each and every twist and turn I encountered, whether in the markets or in my life in general, looked really big and dramatic up close, like unique life-or-death experiences that were coming at me fast.

With time and experience, I came to see each encounter as "another one of those" that I could approach more calmly and analytically, like a biologist might approach an encounter with a threatening creature in the jungle: first identifying its species and then, drawing on his prior knowledge about its expected behaviors, reacting appropriately. When I was faced with types of situations I had encountered before, I drew on the principles I had learned for dealing with them. But when I ran into ones I hadn't seen before, I would be painfully surprised. Studying all those painful first-time encounters, I learned that even if they hadn't happened to me, most of them had happened to other people in other times and places, which gave me a healthy respect for history, a hunger to have a universal understanding of how reality works, and the desire to build timeless and universal principles for dealing with it.

Watching the same things happen again and again, I began to see reality as a gorgeous perpetual motion machine, in which causes become effects that become causes of new effects, and so on. I realized that reality was, if not perfect, at least what we are given to deal with, so that any problems or frustrations I had with it were more productively directed to dealing with them effectively than complaining about them. I came to understand that my encounters were tests of my character and creativity. Over time, I came to appreciate what a tiny and short-lived part of that remarkable system I am, and how it's both good for me and good for the system for me to know how to interact with it well.

In gaining this perspective, I began to experience painful moments in a radically different way. Instead of feeling frustrated or overwhelmed, I saw pain as nature's reminder that there is something important for me to learn. Encountering pains and figuring out the lessons they were trying to give me became sort of a game to me. The more I played it, the better I got at it, the less painful those situations became, and the more rewarding the process of reflecting, developing principles, and then getting rewards for using those principles became. I learned to love my struggles, which I suppose is a healthy perspective to have, like learning to love exercising (which I haven't managed to do yet).

In my early years, I looked up to extraordinarily successful people, thinking that they were successful because they were extraordinary. After I got to know such people personally, I realized that all of them—like me, like everyone—make mistakes, struggle with their weaknesses, and don't feel that they are particularly special or great. They are no happier than the rest of us, and they struggle just as much or more than average folks. Even after they surpass their wildest dreams, they still experience more struggle than glory. This has certainly been true for me. While I surpassed my wildest dreams decades ago, I am still struggling today. In time, I realized that the satisfaction of success doesn't come from achieving your goals, but from struggling well. To understand what I mean, imagine your greatest goal, whatever it is—making a ton of money, winning an Academy Award, running a great organization, being great at a sport. Now imagine instantaneously achieving it. You'd be happy at first, but not for long. You would soon find yourself needing something else to struggle for. Just look at people who attain their dreams early—the child star, the lottery winner, the professional athlete who peaks early. They typically don't end up happy unless they get excited about something else bigger and better to struggle for. Since life brings both ups and downs, struggling well doesn't just make your ups better; it makes your downs less bad. I'm still struggling and I will until I die, because even if I try to avoid the struggles, they will find me.

Thanks to all that struggling and learning, I have done everything I wanted to do, gone everywhere I wanted to go, met whomever I wanted to meet, gotten everything I wanted to own, had a career that has been enthralling, and, most rewardingly, had many wonderful relationships. I have experienced the full range, from having nothing to having an enormous amount, and from being a nobody to being a somebody, so I know the differences. While I experienced them going from the bottom up rather than from the top down (which was preferable and probably influenced my perspective), my assessment is that the incremental benefits of having a lot and being on top are not nearly as great as most people think. Having the basics—a good bed to sleep in, good relationships, good food, and good sex—is most important, and those things don't get much better when you have a lot of money or much worse when you have less. And the people one meets at the top aren't necessarily more special than those one meets at the bottom or in between.

The marginal benefits of having more fall off pretty quickly. In fact, having a lot more is worse than having a moderate amount more because it comes with heavy burdens. Being on top gives you a wider range of options, but it also requires more of you. Being well-known is probably worse than being anonymous, all things considered. And while the beneficial impact one can have on others is great, when you put it in perspective, it is still infinitesimally small. For all those reasons, I cannot say that having an intense life filled with accomplishments is better than having a relaxed life filled with savoring, though

I can say that being strong is better than being weak, and that struggling gives one strength. My nature being what it is, I would not have changed my life, but I can't tell you what is best for you. That is for you to choose. What I have seen is that the happiest people discover their own nature and match their life to it.

Now that my desire to succeed has given way to a desire to help others succeed, that's become my current struggle. It's now clear to me that my purpose, your purpose, and the purpose of everything else is to evolve and to contribute to evolution in some small way. I didn't think about that at the start; I just went after the things I wanted. But along the way I evolved, and now I am sharing these principles with you to help you evolve too. I realized that passing on knowledge is like passing on DNA—it is more important than the individual, because it lives way beyond the individual's life. This is my attempt to help you succeed by passing along to you what I learned about how to struggle well—or, at the very least, to help you get the most out of each unit of effort you put in.

PRINCIPLES

Good principles are effective ways of dealing with reality. To learn my own, I spend a lot of time reflecting. So rather than just giving you my principles, I will share the reflections behind them.

I believe that everything that happens comes about because of cause-effect relationships that repeat and evolve over time. At the big bang, all the laws and forces of the universe were created and propelled forward, interacting with each other over time like a complex series of machines that work together: the structure of galaxies, the makeup of Earth's geography and ecosystems, our economies and markets, and each one of us. Individually, we are machines made up of different machines—our circulatory systems, our nervous systems, and so on—that produce our thoughts, our dreams, our emotions, and every other aspect of our distinct personalities. All these machines are evolving together to produce the reality we encounter every day.

● **Look to the patterns of those things that affect you in order to understand the cause-effect relationships that drive them and to learn principles for dealing with them effectively.**

By doing this, you will begin to understand how the machinery underlying any "another one of those" works and develop a mental map for dealing with it. As your understanding of these relationships grows, the essentials stand out from the blizzard of things coming at you; you will notice which "one of those" you are facing and instinctually apply the right principles to help you through it. Reality, in turn, will send you loud signals about how well your principles are working by rewarding or punishing you, so you will learn to fine-tune them accordingly.

Having good principles for dealing with the realities we encounter is the most important driver of how well we handle them. I'm not saying that all people have the same encounters. It is certainly the case that different people in different parts of the world face different challenges. Still, most of our encounters with reality fall under one category or another and the number of those categories is not enormous. If you were to write down what type of encounter you have every time you have one (e.g., the birth of a child, the loss of a job, a personal disagreement) and compile them in a list, it would probably total just a few hundred items and only a few of them would be unique to you. You might want to try this. Not only will you see for yourself if what I'm saying is true, but you will also start to build a list of the things you need to think about and have principles for.

Whatever success I've had is because of the principles I followed and not because of anything unique about me, so anyone following these principles can expect to produce broadly similar results. That said, I don't want you to follow my (or anyone's) principles blindly. I suggest that you think through all the principles available to you from different sources and put together a collection of your own that you can turn to whenever reality sends "another one of those" your way.

Life Principles and Work Principles are organized in outline form at three different levels so you can skim along the surface or dive in depending on the amount of time and interest you have.

1 Higher-level principles, which are also the chapter titles, are preceded by single numbers.

1.1 Mid-level principles are contained within each chapter and are designated by two numbers: one indicating the higher-level principle it is under and the other showing the order in which it appears in the chapter.

a. Sub-principles fall under the mid-level principles and are marked with letters.

All three levels of principles have explanations following them. To give you a quick overview, I've included summaries of principles at the end of Life Principles and the beginning of Work Principles. I suggest you start with the higher-level principles and the text explaining them, plus the headings for both the principles and subprinciples. Life Principles is intended to be read in its entirety, while Work Principles is meant as more of a reference book.

PART II

LIFE
PRINCIPLES

1 Embrace Reality and Deal with It

There is nothing more important than understanding how reality works and how to deal with it. The state of mind you bring to this process makes all the difference. I have found it helpful to think of my life as if it were a game in which each problem I face is a puzzle I need to solve. By solving the puzzle, I get a gem in the form of a principle that helps me avoid the same sort of problem in the future. Collecting these gems continually improves my decision making, so I am able to ascend to higher and higher levels of play in which the game gets harder and the stakes become ever greater.

All sorts of emotions come to me while I am playing and those emotions can either help me or hurt me. If I can reconcile my emotions with my logic and only act when they are aligned, I make better decisions.

Learning how reality works, visualizing the things I want to create, and then building them out is incredibly exciting to me. Stretching for big goals puts me in the position of failing and needing to learn and come up with new inventions in order to move forward. I find it exhilarating being caught up in the feedback loop of rapid learning—just as a surfer loves riding a wave, even though it sometimes leads to crashes. Don't get me wrong, I'm still scared of the crashes and I still find them painful. But I keep that pain in perspective, knowing that I will get through these setbacks and that most of my learning will come from reflecting on them.[14] Just as long-distance runners push through pain to experience the pleasure of "runner's high," I have largely gotten past the pain of my mistake making and instead enjoy the pleasure that comes with learning from it. I believe that with practice you can change your habits and experience the same "mistake learner's high."

1.1 Be a hyperrealist.

Understanding, accepting, and working with reality is both practical and beautiful. I have become so much of a hyperrealist that I've learned to appreciate the beauty of all realities, even harsh ones, and have come to despise impractical idealism.

Don't get me wrong: I believe in making dreams happen. To me, there's nothing better in life than doing that. The pursuit of dreams is what gives life its flavor. My point is that people who create great things aren't idle dreamers: They are totally grounded in reality. Being hyperrealistic will help you choose your dreams wisely and then achieve them. I have found the following to be almost always true:

a. **Dreams + Reality + Determination = A Successful Life.** People who achieve success and drive progress deeply understand the cause-effect relationships that govern reality and have principles for using them to get what they want. The converse is also true: Idealists who are not well grounded in reality create problems, not progress.

What does a successful life look like? We all have our own deep-seated needs, so we each have to decide for ourselves what success is. I don't care whether you want to be a master of the universe, a couch potato, or anything else—I really don't. Some people want to change the world and others want to operate in simple harmony with it and

---

[14] I'm sure Transcendental Meditation, which I have been practicing regularly for nearly half a century, helped provide me with the equanimity I needed to approach my challenges this way.

savor life. Neither is better. Each of us needs to decide what we value most and choose the paths we take to achieve it.

Take a moment to reflect on where you are on the following scale, which illustrates an overly simplified choice you should think about. Where would you put yourself on it?

SAVOR   MAKE AN

LIFE   IMPACT

The question isn't just how much of each to go after, but how hard to work to get as much as possible. I wanted crazy amounts of each, was thrilled to work hard to get as much of them as possible, and found that they could largely be one and the same and mutually reinforcing. Over time I learned that getting more out of life wasn't just a matter of working harder at it. It was much more a matter of working effectively, because working effectively could increase my capacity by hundreds of times. I don't care what you want or how hard you want to work for it. That's for you to decide. I'm just trying to pass along to you what has helped me get the most out of each hour of time and each unit of effort.

Most importantly, I've learned that there is no escaping the fact that:

1.2 Truth—or, more precisely, an accurate understanding of reality —is the essential foundation for any good outcome.

Most people fight seeing what's true when it's not what they want it to be. That's bad, because it is more important to understand and deal with the bad stuff since the good stuff will take care of itself.

Do you agree with that? If not, you are unlikely to benefit from what follows. If you do agree, let's build on it.

1.3 Be radically open-minded and radically transparent.

None of us is born knowing what is true; we either have to discover what's true for ourselves or believe and follow others. The key is to know which path will yield better results.[15] I believe that:

a. Radical open-mindedness and radical transparency are invaluable for rapid learning and effective change. Learning is the product of a continuous real-time feedback loop in which we make decisions, see their outcomes, and improve our understanding of reality as a result. Being radically open-minded enhances the efficiency of those feedback loops, because it makes what you are doing, and why, so clear to yourself and others that there can't be any misunderstandings. The more open-minded you are, the less likely you are to deceive your-self—and the more likely it is that others will give you honest feed-back. If they are "believable" people (and it's very important to know who is "believable"[16]), you will learn a lot from them.

Being radically transparent and radically open-minded accelerates this learning process. It can also be difficult because being radically transparent rather than more guarded exposes one to criticism. It's

---

[15] You shouldn't assume that you are always the best person to make decisions for yourself because often you aren't. While it is up to us to know what we want, others may know how to get it better than we do because they have strengths where we have weaknesses, or more relevant knowledge and experience. For example, it's probably better for you to follow your doctor's advice than your own if you have a medical condition. Later in this book, we will look at some of the different ways people's brains are wired and how our understanding of our own wiring should influence which choices we make for ourselves and which we should delegate to others. Knowing when not to make your own decisions is one of the most important skills you can develop.

[16] I'll explain the concept of believability in more detail in later chapters, but to cover it quickly: Believable parties are those who have repeatedly and successfully accomplished something— and have great explanations for how they did it.

natural to fear that. Yet if you don't put yourself out there with your radical transparency, you won't learn.

b. **Don't let fears of what others think of you stand in your way.** You must be willing to do things in the unique ways you think are best—and to open-mindedly reflect on the feedback that comes inevitably as a result of being that way.

Learning to be radically transparent is like learning to speak in public: While it's initially awkward, the more you do it, the more comfortable you will be with it. This has been true for me. For example, I still instinctively find being as radically transparent in the ways that I am in this book uncomfortable because I am exposing personal material to the public that will attract attention and criticism. Yet I am doing it because I've learned that it's best, and I wouldn't feel good about myself if I let my fears stand in the way. In other words, I have experienced the positive effects of radical transparency for so long that it's now uncomfortable for me not to be that way.

Besides giving me the freedom to be me, it has allowed me to understand others and for them to understand me, which is much more efficient and much more enjoyable than not having this under-standing. Imagine how many fewer misunderstandings we would have and how much more efficient the world would be—and how much closer we all would be to knowing what's true—if instead of hiding what they think, people shared it openly. I'm not talking about every-one's very personal inner secrets; I'm talking about people's opinions of each other and of how the world works. As you'll see, I've learned firsthand how powerful this kind of radical truth and transparency is in improving my decision making and my relationships. So whenever I'm faced with the choice, my instinct is to be transparent. I practice it as a discipline and I recommend you do the same.

c. **Embracing radical truth and radical transparency will bring more meaningful work and more meaningful relationships.** My experience, based on watching thousands of people try this approach, is that with practice the vast majority find it so rewarding and pleasurable that they have a hard time operating any other way.

This takes practice and changing one's habits. I have found that it typically takes about eighteen months, which is how long it takes to change most habits.

1.4 Look to nature to learn how reality works.

All the laws of reality were given to us by nature. Man didn't create these laws, but by understanding them we can use them to foster our own evolution and achieve our goals. For example, our ability to fly or to send cell phone signals around the world came from understanding and applying the existing rules of reality—the physical laws or principles that govern the natural world.

While I spend most of my time studying the realities that affect me most directly—those that drive economies, the markets, and the people I deal with—I also spend time in nature and can't help reflecting on how it works by observing, reading, and speaking with some of the greatest specialists on the subject. I've found it both interesting and valuable to observe which laws we humans have in common with the rest of nature and which differentiate us. Doing that has had a big impact on my approach to life.

First of all, I see how cool it is that the brain's evolution gave us the ability to reflect on how reality works in this way. Man's most distinctive quality is our singular ability to look down on reality from a higher perspective and synthesize an understanding of it. While other species operate by following their instincts, man alone can go above himself and look at himself within his circumstances and within time (including before and after his existence). For example, we can ponder the ways that nature's flying machines, swimming machines, and billions of other machines, from the microscopic to the cosmic, interact with one another to make up a working whole that evolves through time. This is because the evolution of the brain gave man a much more developed neocortex, which gives us the power to think abstractly and logically.

While our higher-level thinking makes us unique among species, it can also make us uniquely confused. Other species have much simpler and more straightforward lives, without any of man's wrestling with what's good and what's bad. In contrast with animals, most people struggle to reconcile their emotions and their instincts (which come from the animal parts of their brains) with their reasoning (which comes from parts of the brain more developed in humans). This struggle causes people to confuse what they want to be true with what actually is true. Let's look at this dilemma to try to understand how reality works.

When trying to understand anything—economies, markets, the weather, whatever—one can approach the subject with two perspectives:

1. **Top down:** By trying to find the one code/law that drives them all. For example, in the case of markets, one could study universal laws like supply and demand that affect all economies and markets. In the case of species, one could focus on learning how the genetic code (DNA) works for all species.
2. **Bottom up:** By studying each specific case and the codes/laws that are true for them, for example, the codes or laws particular to the market for wheat or the DNA sequences that make ducks different from other species.

Seeing things from the top down is the best way to understand ourselves and the laws of reality within the context of overarching universal laws. That's not to say it's not worth having a bottom-up perspective. In fact, to understand the world accurately you need both. By taking a bottom-up perspective that looks at each individual case, we can see how it lines up with our theories about the laws that we expect to govern it. When they line up, we're good.

By looking at nature from the top down, we can see that much of what we call human nature is really animal nature. That's because the human brain is programmed with millions of years of genetic learning that we share with other species. Because we share common roots and common laws, we and other animals have similar attributes and constraints. For example, the male/female sexual reproduction process, using two eyes to provide depth perception, and many other systems are shared by many species in the animal kingdom. Similarly, our brains have some "animal" parts that are much older in evolutionary terms than humanity is. These laws that we have in common are the most overarching ones. They wouldn't be apparent to us if we just looked at ourselves.

If you just looked at one species—ducks, for example—to try to understand the universal laws, you'd fail. Similarly, if you just looked at mankind to understand the universal laws, you'd fail. Man is just one of ten million species and just one of the billions of manifestations of the forces that bring together and take apart atoms through time. Yet most people are like ants focused only on themselves and their own anthill; they believe the universe revolves around people and don't pay attention to the universal laws that are true for all species.

To try to figure out the universal laws of reality and principles for dealing with it, I've found it helpful to try to look at things from nature's perspective. While mankind is very intelligent in relation to other species, we have the intelligence of moss growing on a rock compared to nature as a whole. We are incapable of designing and building a mosquito, let alone all the species and most of the other things in the universe. So I start from the premise that nature is smarter than I am and try to let nature teach me how reality works.

a. Don't get hung up on your views of how things "should" be because you will miss out on learning how they really are. It's important not to let our biases stand in the way of our objectivity. To get good results, we need to be analytical rather than emotional.

Whenever I observe something in nature that I (or mankind) think is wrong, I assume that *I'm* wrong and try to figure out why what nature is doing makes sense. That has taught me a lot. It has changed my thinking about 1) what's good and what's bad, 2) what my purpose in life is, and 3) what I should do when faced with my most important choices. To help explain why, I will give you a simple example.

When I went to Africa a number of years ago, I saw a pack of hyenas take down a young wildebeest. My reaction was visceral. I felt empathy for the wildebeest and thought that what I had witnessed was horrible. But was that because it *was* horrible or was it because I am biased to believe it's horrible when it is actually wonderful? That got me thinking. Would the world be a better or worse place if what I'd seen hadn't occurred? That perspective drove me to consider the second- and third-order consequences so that I could see that the world would be worse. I now realize that nature optimizes for the whole, not for the individual, but most people judge good and bad based only on how it affects them. What I had seen was the process of nature at work, which is much more effective at furthering the improvement of the whole than any process man has ever invented.

Most people call something bad if it is bad for them or bad for those they empathize with, ignoring the greater good. This tendency extends to groups: One religion will consider its beliefs good and another religion's beliefs bad to such an extent that their members might kill each other in the mutual conviction that each is doing what's right. Typically, people's conflicting beliefs or conflicting interests make them unable to see things through another's eyes. That's not good and it doesn't make sense. While I could understand people liking something that helps them and disliking things that hurt them, it doesn't make sense to call something good or bad in an absolute sense based only on how it affects individuals. To do so would presume that what the individual wants is more important than the good of the whole. To me, nature seems to define good as what's good for the whole and optimizes for it, which is preferable. So I have come to believe that as a general rule:

b. To be "good" something must operate consistently with the laws of reality and contribute to the evolution of the whole; that is what is most rewarded. For example, if you come up with something the world values, you almost can't help but be rewarded. Conversely, reality tends to penalize those people, species, and things that don't work well and detract from evolution.[17]

In looking at what is true for everything, I have come to believe that:

c. Evolution is the single greatest force in the universe; it is the only thing that is permanent and it drives everything.[18] Everything from the smallest subatomic particle to the entire galaxy is evolving. While everything apparently dies or disappears in time, the truth is that it all just gets reconfigured in evolving forms. Remember that energy can't be destroyed—it can only be reconfigured. So the same stuff is continuously falling apart and coalescing in different forms. The force behind that is evolution.

For example, the primary purpose of every living thing is to act as a vessel for the DNA that evolves life through time. The DNA that exists within each individual came from an eternity ago and will continue to live long after its individual carriers pass away, in increasingly evolved forms.[19]

As I thought about evolution, I realized that it exists in other forms than life and is carried out through other transmission mechanisms than DNA. Technologies, languages, and everything else evolves. Knowledge, for example, is like DNA in that it is passed from generation to generation and evolves; its impact on people over many generations can be as great or greater than that of the genetic code.

Evolution is good because it is the process of adaptation that generally moves things toward improvement. All things such as products, organizations, and human capabilities evolve through time in a similar way. It is simply the process by which things either adapt and improve or die. To me this evolutionary process looks like what you see on the right:

---

[17] There are many things people consider "good" in the sense that they are kind or considerate but fail to deliver what's desired (like communism's "from each according to his ability, to each according to his needs"). Nature would appear to consider them "bad," and I'd agree with nature.
[18] Everything other than evolution eventually disintegrates; we all are, and everything else is, vehicles for evolution. For example, while we see ourselves as individuals, we are essentially vessels for our genes that have lived millions of years and continuously use and shed bodies like ours.
[19] I recommend Richard Dawkins's and E. O. Wilson's books on evolution. If I had to pick just one, it would be Dawkins's *River Out of Eden*.

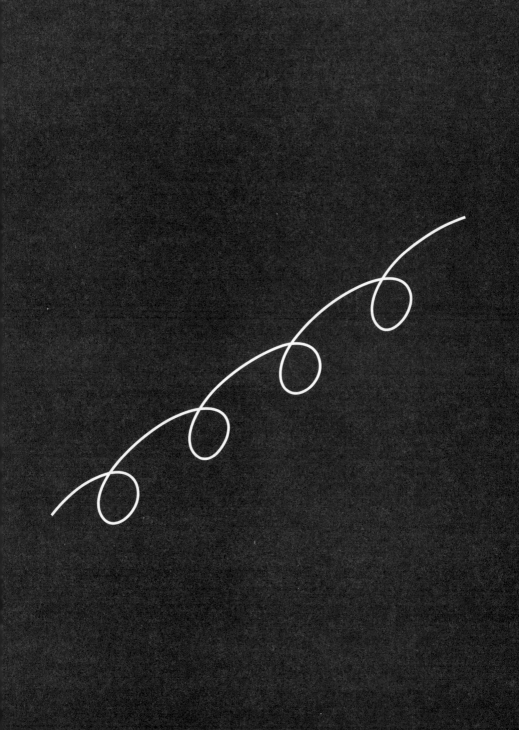

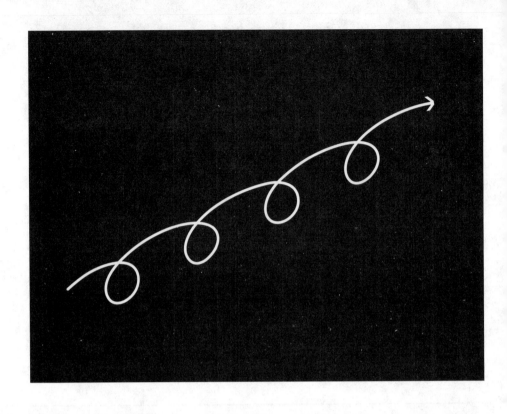

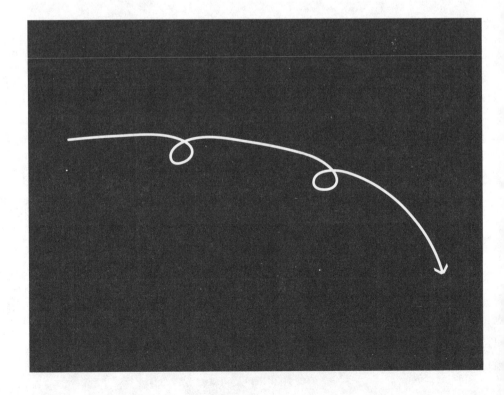

Evolution consists of adaptations/inventions that provide spurts of benefits that decline in value. That painful decline leads either to new adaptations and new inventions that bring new products, organizations, and human capabilities to new and higher levels of development (as shown in the top diagram on the facing page); or decline and death, which looks like the diagram at bottom left.

Think of any product, organization, or person you know and you will see that this is true. The world is littered with once-great things that deteriorated and failed; only a rare few have kept reinventing themselves to go on to new heights of greatness. All machines eventually break down, decompose, and have their parts recycled to create new machines. That includes us. Sometimes this makes us sad because we've become attached to our machines, but if you look at it from the higher level, it's really beautiful to observe how the machine of evolution works.

From this perspective, we can see that perfection doesn't exist; it is a goal that fuels a never-ending process of adaptation. If nature, or anything, were perfect it wouldn't be evolving. Organisms, organizations, and individual people are always highly imperfect but capable of improving. So rather than getting stuck hiding our mistakes and pretending we're perfect, it makes sense to find our imperfections and deal with them. You will either learn valuable lessons from your mistakes and press on, better equipped to succeed—or you won't and you will fail.

As the saying goes:

d. Evolve or die. This evolutionary cycle is not just for people but for countries, companies, economies—for everything. And it is naturally self-correcting as a whole, though not necessarily for its parts. For example, if there is too much supply and waste in a market, prices will go down, companies will go out of business, and capacity will be reduced until the supply falls in line with the demand, at which time the cycle will start to move in the opposite direction. Similarly, if an economy turns bad enough, those responsible for running it will make the political and policy changes that are needed—or they will not survive, making room for their replacements to come along. These

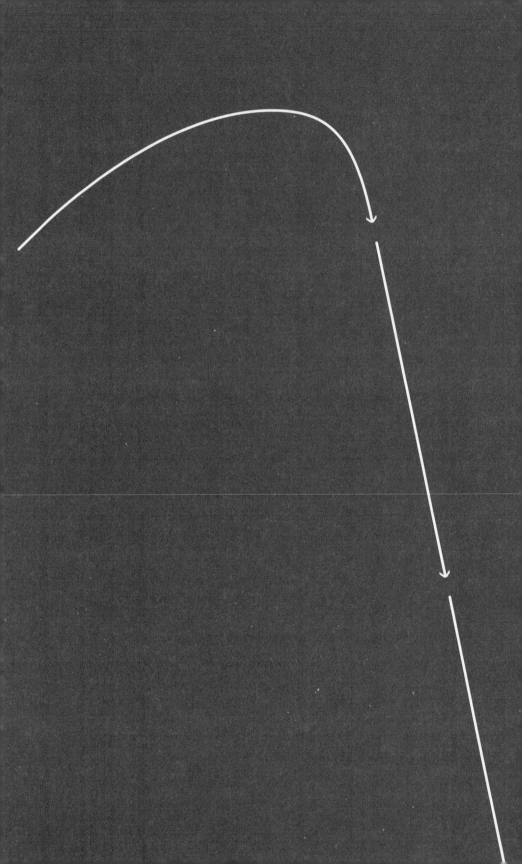

cycles are continuous and play out in logical ways—and they tend to be self-reinforcing.

The key is to fail, learn, and improve quickly. If you're constantly learning and improving, your evolutionary process will look like the one that's ascending. Do it poorly and it will look like what you see on the left, or worse.

I believe that:

1.5 Evolving is life's greatest accomplishment and its greatest reward.

It is instinctually that way, which is why most of us feel the pull of it— in other words, we instinctively want to get better at things and have created and evolved technology to help us. History has shown that all species will either go extinct or evolve into other species, though with our limited time window that is hard for us to see. But we do know that what we call mankind was simply the result of DNA evolving into a new form about two hundred thousand years ago, and we know that mankind will certainly either go extinct or evolve into a higher state. I personally believe there is a good chance man will begin to evolve at an accelerating pace with the help of man-made technologies that can analyze vast amounts of data and "think" faster and better than we can. I wonder how many centuries it will take for us to evolve into a higher-level species that will be much closer to omniscience than we are now—if we don't destroy ourselves first.

One of the great marvels of nature is how the whole system, which is full of individual organisms acting in their own self-interest and without understanding or guiding what's going on, can create a beautifully operating and evolving whole. While I'm not an expert at this, it seems that it's because evolution has produced a) incentives and interactions that lead to individuals pursuing their own interests and resulting in the advancement of the whole, b) the natural selection process, and c) rapid experimentation and adaptation.

a. The individual's incentives must be aligned with the group's goals. To give you a quick example of nature creating incentives that lead to individuals pursuing their own interests that result in the advancement of the whole, look at sex and natural selection. Nature gave us one hell of an incentive to have sex in the form of the great pleasure it provides, even though the purpose of having sex is to contribute to the advancement of the DNA. That way, we individually get what we want while contributing to the evolution of the whole.

b. Reality is optimizing for the whole—not for you. Contribute to the whole and you will likely be rewarded. Natural selection leads to better qualities being retained and passed along (e.g., in better genes, better abilities to nurture others, better products, etc.). The result is a constant cycle of improvement for the whole.

c. Adaptation through rapid trial and error is invaluable. Natural selection's trial-and-error process allows improvement without anyone understanding or guiding it. The same can apply to how we learn. There are at least three kinds of learning that foster evolution: memory-based learning (storing the information that comes in through one's conscious mind so that we can recall it later); subconscious learning (the knowledge we take away from our experiences that never enters our conscious minds, though it affects our decision making); and "learning" that occurs without thinking at all, such as the changes in DNA that encode a species' adaptations. I used to think that memory-based, conscious learning was the most powerful, but I've since come to understand that it produces less rapid progress than experimentation and adaptation. To give you an example of how nature improves without thinking, just look at the struggle that mankind (with all its thinking) has experienced in trying to outsmart viruses (which don't even have brains). Viruses are like brilliant chess opponents. By evolving quickly (combining different genetic material across different strains), they keep the smartest minds in the global health community busy thinking up countermoves to hold them off. Understanding that is especially helpful in an era when computers can run large numbers of simulations replicating the evolutionary process to help us see what works and what doesn't.

In the next chapter I will describe a process that has helped me, and I believe can help you, evolve quickly. But first I want to emphasize how important your perspective is in trying to decide what is important to you and what to go after.

d. Realize that you are simultaneously everything and nothing—and decide what you want to be. It is a great paradox that individually we are simultaneously everything and nothing. Through our own eyes, we are everything—e.g., when we die, the whole world disappears. So to most people (and to other species) dying is the worst thing possible, and it is of paramount importance that we have the best life possible. However, when we look down on ourselves through the eyes of nature we are of absolutely no significance. It is a reality that each one of us is only one of about seven billion of our species alive today and that our species is only one of about ten million species on our planet. Earth is just one of about 100 billion planets in our galaxy, which is just one of about two trillion galaxies in the universe. And our lifetimes are only about 1/3,000 of humanity's existence, which itself is only 1/20,000 of the Earth's existence. In other words, we are unbelievably tiny and short-lived and no matter what we accomplish, our impact will be insignificant. At the same time, we instinctually want to matter and to evolve, and we *can* matter a tiny bit—and it's all those tiny bits that add up to drive the evolution of the universe.

The question is *how* we matter and evolve. Do we matter to others (who also don't matter in the grand scope of things) or in some greater sense that we will never actually achieve? Or does it not matter if we matter so we should forget about the question and just enjoy our lives while they last?

e. What you will be will depend on the perspective you have. Where you go in life will depend on how you see things and who and what you feel connected to (your family, your community, your country, mankind, the whole ecosystem, everything). You will have to decide to what extent you will put the interests of others above your own, and which others you will choose to do so for. That's because you will regularly encounter situations that will force you to make such choices.

While such decisions might seem too erudite for your taste, you will make them either consciously or subliminally, and they will be very important.

For me personally, I now find it thrilling to embrace reality, to look down on myself through nature's perspective, and to be an infinitesimally small part of the whole. My instinctual and intellectual goal is simply to evolve and contribute to evolution in some tiny way while I'm here and while I am what I am. At the same time, the things I love most—my work and my relationships—are what motivate me. So, I find how reality and nature work, including how I and everything will decompose and recompose, beautiful—though emotionally I find the separation from those I care about difficult to appreciate.

1.6 Understand nature's practical lessons.

I have found understanding how nature and evolution work helpful in a number of ways. Most importantly, it has helped me deal with my realities more effectively and make difficult choices. When I began to look at reality through the perspective of figuring out how it really works, instead of thinking things should be different, I realized that most everything that at first seemed "bad" to me—like rainy days, weaknesses, and even death—was because I held preconceived notions of what I personally wanted. With time, I learned that my initial reaction was because I hadn't put whatever I was reacting to in the context of the fact that reality is built to optimize for the whole rather than for me.

a. **Maximize your evolution.** Earlier, I mentioned that the unique abilities of thinking logically, abstractly, and from a higher level are carried out in structures located in the neocortex. These parts of the brain are more developed in humans and allow us to reflect on ourselves and direct our own evolution. Because we are capable of conscious, memory-based learning, we can evolve further and faster than any other species, changing not just across generations but within our own lifetimes.

This constant drive toward learning and improvement makes getting better innately enjoyable and getting better fast exhilarating. Though most people think that they are striving to get the things (toys, bigger houses, money, status, etc.) that will make them happy, for most people those things don't supply anywhere near the long-term satisfaction that getting better at something does.[20] Once we get the things we are striving for, we rarely remain satisfied with them. The things are just the bait. Chasing after them forces us to evolve, and it is the evolution and not the rewards themselves that matters to us and to those around us. This means that for most people success is struggling and evolving as effectively as possible, i.e., learning rapidly about oneself and one's environment, and then changing to improve.

It is natural that it should be this way because of the law of diminishing returns.[21] Consider what acquiring money is like. People who earn so much that they derive little or no marginal gains from it will experience negative consequences, as with any other form of excess, like gluttony. If they are intellectually healthy, they will begin seeking something new or seeking new depths in something old—and they will get stronger in the process. As Freud put it, "Love and work are the cornerstones of our humanness."

The work doesn't necessarily have to be a job, though I believe it's generally better if it is a job. It can be any kind of long-term challenge that leads to personal improvement. As you might have guessed, I believe that the need to have meaningful work is connected to man's innate desire to improve. And relationships are the

---

[20] Of course, we are often satisfied with the same things—relationships, careers, etc.—but when that is the case, it is typically because we are getting new enjoyments from the changing dimensions of those things.

[21] The marginal benefits of moving from a shortage to an abundance of anything decline.

natural connections to others that make us relevant to each other and to society more broadly.

b. Remember "no pain, no gain." Realizing that we innately want to evolve—and that the other stuff we are going after, while nice, won't sustain our happiness—has helped me focus on my goals of evolving and contributing to evolution in my own infinitely small way. While we don't like pain, everything that nature made has a purpose, so nature gave us pain for a purpose. So what is its purpose? It alerts us and helps direct us.

c. It is a fundamental law of nature that in order to gain strength one has to push one's limits, which is painful. As Carl Jung put it, "Man needs difficulties. They are necessary for health." Yet most people instinctually avoid pain. This is true whether we are talking about building the body (e.g., weight lifting) or the mind (e.g., frustration, mental struggle, embarrassment, shame)—and especially true when people confront the harsh reality of their own imperfections.

1.7 Pain + Reflection = Progress.

There is no avoiding pain, especially if you're going after ambitious goals. Believe it or not, you are lucky to feel that kind of pain if you approach it correctly, because it is a signal that you need to find solutions so you can progress. If you can develop a reflexive reaction to psychic pain that causes you to reflect on it rather than avoid it, it will lead to your rapid learning/evolving.[22] After seeing how much more effective it is to face the painful realities that are caused by your prob-

---

[22] Your unique power of reflectiveness—your ability to look at yourself, the world around you, and the relationship between you and the world—means that you can think deeply and weigh subtle things to come up with learning and wise choices. Asking other believable people about the root causes of your pain in order to enhance your reflections is also typically very helpful—especially others who have opposing views but who share your interest in finding the truth rather than being proven right. If you can reflect deeply about your problems, they almost always shrink or disappear, because you almost always find a better way of dealing with them than if you don't face them head-on.

lems, mistakes, and weaknesses, I believe you won't want to operate any other way. It's just a matter of getting in the habit of doing it.

Most people have a tough time reflecting when they are in pain and they pay attention to other things when the pain passes, so they miss out on the reflections that provide the lessons. If you can reflect well while you're in pain (which is probably too much to ask), great. But if you can remember to reflect after it passes, that's valuable too. (I created a Pain Button app to help people do this, which I describe in the appendix.)

The challenges you face will test and strengthen you. If you're not failing, you're not pushing your limits, and if you're not pushing your limits, you're not maximizing your potential. Though this process of pushing your limits, of sometimes failing and sometimes breaking through—and deriving benefits from both your failures and your successes—is not for everyone, if it is for you, it can be so thrilling that it becomes addictive. Life will inevitably bring you such moments, and it'll be up to you to decide whether you want to go back for more.

If you choose to push through this often painful process of personal evolution, you will naturally "ascend" to higher and higher levels. As you climb above the blizzard of things that surrounds you, you will realize that they seem bigger than they really are when you are seeing them up close; that most things in life are just "another one of those." The higher you ascend, the more effective you become at working with reality to shape outcomes toward your goals. What once seemed impossibly complex becomes simple.

a. Go to the pain rather than avoid it. If you don't let up on yourself and instead become comfortable always operating with some level of pain, you will evolve at a faster pace. That's just the way it is.

Every time you confront something painful, you are at a potentially important juncture in your life—you have the opportunity to choose healthy and painful truth or unhealthy but comfortable delusion. The irony is that if you choose the healthy route, the pain will soon turn into pleasure. The pain is the signal! Like switching from not exercising to exercising, developing the habit of embrac-

ing the pain and learning from it will "get you to the other side."
By "getting to the other side," I mean that you will become hooked on:

- Identifying, accepting, and learning how to deal with your weaknesses,
- Preferring that the people around you be honest with you rather than keep their negative thoughts about you to themselves, and
- Being yourself rather than having to pretend to be strong where you are weak.

b. Embrace tough love. In my own life, what I want to give to people, most importantly to people I love, is the power to deal with reality to get what they want. In pursuit of my goal to give them strength, I will often deny them what they "want" because that will give them the opportunity to struggle so that they can develop the strength to get what they want on their own. This can be difficult for people emotionally, even if they understand intellectually that having difficulties is the exercise they need to grow strong and that just giving them what they want will weaken them and ultimately lead to them needing more help.[23]

Of course most people would prefer not to have weaknesses. Our upbringings and our experiences in the world have conditioned us to be embarrassed by our weaknesses and hide them. But people are happiest when they can be themselves. If you can be open with your weaknesses it will make you freer and will help you deal with them better. I urge you to not be embarrassed about your problems, recognizing that everyone has them. Bringing them to the surface will help you break your bad habits and develop good ones, and you will acquire real strengths and justifiable optimism.

---

[23] To be clear, I am not saying people should not be helped. I believe that people should be helped by giving them opportunities and the coaching they need to become strong enough to take advantage of their opportunities. As the saying goes, "God helps those who help themselves." But this isn't easy, especially with people you care about. To be effective in helping people learn from painful experiences, you must explain the logic and caring behind what you're doing clearly and repeatedly. As you read in "Where I'm Coming From," this was a large part of what compelled me to explain my principles.

This evolutionary process of productive adaptation and ascent—the process of seeking, obtaining, and pursuing more and more ambitious goals—does not just pertain to how individuals and society move forward. It is equally relevant when dealing with setbacks, which are inevitable. At some point in your life you will crash in a big way. You might fail at your job or with your family, lose a loved one, suffer a serious accident or illness, or discover the life you imagined is out of reach forever. There are a whole host of ways that something will get you. At such times, you will be in pain and might think that you don't have the strength to go on. You almost always do, however; your ultimate success will depend on you realizing that fact, even though it might not seem that way at the moment.

This is why many people who have endured setbacks that seemed devastating at the time ended up as happy as (or even happier than) they originally were after they successfully adapted to them. The quality of your life will depend on the choices you make at those painful moments. The faster one appropriately adapts, the better.[24] No matter what you want out of life, your ability to adapt and move quickly and efficiently through the process of personal evolution will determine your success and your happiness. If you do it well, you can change your psychological reaction to it so that what was painful can become something you crave.

1.8 Weigh second- and third-order consequences.

By recognizing the higher-level consequences nature optimizes for, I've come to see that people who overweigh the first-order consequences of their decisions and ignore the effects of second- and subsequent-order consequences rarely reach their goals. This is because first-order consequences often have opposite desirabilities from second-order conse-

---

[24] Your ability to see the changing landscape and adapt is more a function of your perception and reasoning than your ability to learn and process quickly.

quences, resulting in big mistakes in decision making. For example, the first-order consequences of exercise (pain and time spent) are commonly considered undesirable, while the second-order consequences (better health and more attractive appearance) are desirable. Similarly, food that tastes good is often bad for you and vice versa.

Quite often the first-order consequences are the temptations that cost us what we really want, and sometimes they are the barriers that stand in our way. It's almost as though nature sorts us by throwing us trick choices that have both types of consequences and penalizing those who make their decisions on the basis of the first-order consequences alone.

By contrast, people who choose what they really want, and avoid the temptations and get over the pains that drive them away from what they really want, are much more likely to have successful lives.

1.9 Own your outcomes.

For the most part, life gives you so many decisions to make and so many opportunities to recover from your mistakes that, if you handle them well, you can have a terrific life. Of course, sometimes there are major influences on the quality of our lives that come from things beyond our control—the circumstances we are born into, accidents and illnesses, and so forth—but for the most part even the worst circumstances can be made better with the right approach. For example, a friend of mine dove into a swimming pool, hit his head, and became a quadriplegic. But he approached his situation well and became as happy as anybody else, because there are many paths to happiness.

My point is simply this: Whatever circumstances life brings you, you will be more likely to succeed and find happiness if you take responsibility for making your decisions well instead of complaining about things being beyond your control. Psychologists call this having an "internal locus of control," and studies consistently show that people who have it outperform those who don't.

So don't worry about whether you like your situation or not. Life doesn't give a damn about what you like. It's up to you to connect what you want with what you need to do to get it and then find the courage to carry it through. In the next chapter I will show you the 5-Step Process that helped me learn about reality and evolve.

1.10 Look at the machine from the higher level.

Our uniquely human ability to look down from a higher level doesn't apply just to understanding reality and the cause-effect relationships underlying it; it also applies to looking down on yourself and those around you. I call this ability to rise above your own and others' circumstances and objectively look down on them "higher-level thinking." Higher-level thinking gives you the ability to study and influence the cause-effect relationships at play in your life and use them to get the outcomes you want.

a. Think of yourself as a machine operating within a machine and know that you have the ability to alter your machines to produce better outcomes. You have your goals. I call the way you will operate to achieve your goals your machine. It consists of a design (the things that have to get done) and the people (who will do the things that need getting done). Those people include you and those who help you. For example, imagine that your goal is a military one: to take a hill from an enemy. Your design for your "machine" might include two scouts, two snipers, four infantrymen, and so on. While the right design is essential, it is only half the battle. It is equally important to put the right people in each of those positions. They need different qualities to do their jobs well—the scouts must be fast runners, the snipers must be good marksmen—so that the machine will produce the outcomes you seek.

b. By comparing your outcomes with your goals, you can determine how to modify your machine. This evaluation and improvement process exactly mirrors the evolutionary process I described earlier. It means

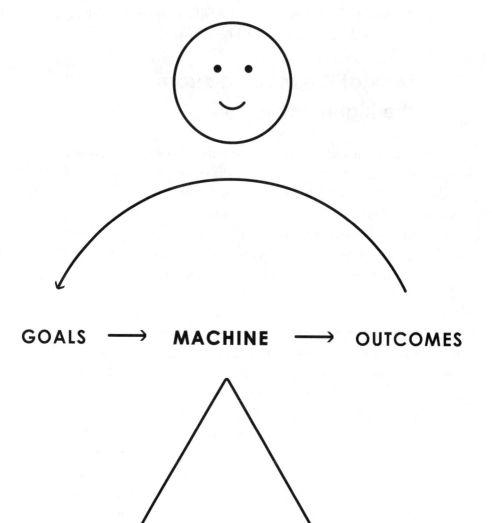

looking at how to improve or change the design or people to achieve your goals. Schematically, the process is a feedback loop, as shown in the diagram on the opposite page.

c. Distinguish between you as the designer of your machine and you as a worker with your machine. One of the hardest things for people to do is to objectively look down on themselves within their circumstances (i.e., their machine) so that they can act as the machine's designer and manager. Most people remain stuck in the perspective of being a worker within the machine. If you can recognize the differences between those roles and that it is much more important that you are a good designer/manager of your life than a good worker in it, you will be on the right path. To be successful, the "designer/manager you" has to be objective about what the "worker you" is really like, not believing in him more than he deserves, or putting him in jobs he shouldn't be in. Instead of having this strategic perspective, most people operate emotionally and in the moment; their lives are a series of undirected emotional experiences, going from one thing to the next. If you want to look back on your life and feel you've achieved what you wanted to, you can't operate that way.

d. The biggest mistake most people make is to not see themselves and others objectively, which leads them to bump into their own and others' weaknesses again and again. People who do this fail because they are stubbornly stuck in their own heads. If they could just get around this, they could live up to their potential.

This is why higher-level thinking is essential for success.

e. Successful people are those who can go above themselves to see things objectively and manage those things to shape change. They can take in the perspectives of others instead of being trapped in their own heads with their own biases. They are able to look objectively at what they are like—their strengths and weaknesses—and what others are like to put the right people in the right roles to achieve their goals. Once you understand how to do this you'll see that there's virtually nothing you can't accomplish. You will just have to learn how to face your realities and use the full range of resources at your disposal. For example, if you as the designer/manager discover that you as the worker can't do something well, you need to fire yourself as the worker and get a good replacement, while staying in the role of designer/manager of your own life. You shouldn't be upset if you find out that you're bad at something—you should be happy that you found out, because knowing that and dealing with it will improve your chances of getting what you want.

If you are disappointed because you can't be the best person to do everything yourself, you are terribly naive. Nobody can do everything well. Would you want to have Einstein on your basketball team? When he fails to dribble and shoot well, would you think badly of him? Should he feel humiliated? Imagine all the areas in which Einstein was incompetent, and imagine how hard he struggled to excel even in the areas in which he was the best in the world.

Watching people struggle and having others watch you struggle can elicit all kinds of ego-driven emotions such as sympathy, pity, embarrassment, anger, or defensiveness. You need to get over all that and stop seeing struggling as something negative. Most of life's greatest opportunities come out of moments of struggle; it's up to you to make the most of these tests of creativity and character.

When encountering your weaknesses you have four choices:

1. You can deny them (which is what most people do).
2. You can accept them and work at them in order to try to convert them into strengths (which might or might not work depending on your ability to change).
3. You can accept your weaknesses and find ways around them.
4. Or, you can change what you are going after.

Which solution you choose will be critically important to the direction of your life. The worst path you can take is the first. Denial can only lead to your constantly banging up against your weaknesses, having pain, and not getting anywhere. The second—accepting your weaknesses while trying to turn them into strengths—is probably the best path if it works. But some things you will never be good at and it takes a lot of time and effort to change. The best single clue as to whether you should go down this path is whether the thing you are trying to do is consistent with your nature (i.e., your natural abilities). The third path—accepting your weaknesses while trying to find ways around them—is the easiest and typically the most viable path, yet it is the one least followed. The fourth path, changing what you are going after, is also a great path, though it requires flexibility on your part to get past your preconceptions and enjoy the good fit when you find it.

f. Asking others who are strong in areas where you are weak to help you is a great skill that you should develop no matter what, as it will help you develop guardrails that will prevent you from doing what you shouldn't be doing. All successful people are good at this.

g. Because it is difficult to see oneself objectively, you need to rely on the input of others and the whole body of evidence. I know that my own life has been full of mistakes and lots of great feedback. It was only by looking down on this body of evidence from a higher level that I was able to get around my mistakes and go after what I wanted. For as long as I have been practicing this, I still know I can't see myself objectively, which is why I continue to rely so much on the input of others.

h. If you are open-minded enough and determined, you can get virtually anything you want. So I certainly don't want to dissuade you from going after whatever you want. At the same time, I urge you to reflect on whether what you are going after is consistent with your nature. Whatever your nature is, there are many paths that will suit you, so don't fixate on just one. Should a particular path close, all you have to do is find another good one consistent with what you're like. (You'll learn a lot about how to determine what you're like later, in Understand That People Are Wired Very Differently.)

But most people lack the courage to confront their own weaknesses and make the hard choices that this process requires. Ultimately, it comes down to the following five decisions:

1. **Don't confuse what you wish were true with what is really true.**

2. **Don't worry about looking good—worry instead about achieving your goals.**

3. **Don't overweight first-order consequences relative to second- and third-order ones.**

4. **Don't let pain stand in the way of progress.**

5. **Don't blame bad outcomes on anyone but yourself.**

BAD
Avoid facing "harsh realities."

GOOD
Face "harsh realities."

BAD
Worry about
appearing good.

GOOD
Worry about
achieving the goal.

BAD
Make your decisions on the basis of first-order consequences.

GOOD
Make your decisions on the basis of first-, second-, and third-order consequences.

BAD
Allow pain to
stand in the way
of progress.

GOOD
Understand how
to manage pain
to produce progress.

BAD
Don't hold yourself and others accountable.

GOOD
Hold yourself and others accountable.

2 Use the 5-Step Process to Get What You Want Out of Life

t seems to me that the personal evolutionary process—the looping I described in the last chapter—takes place in five distinct steps. If you can do those five things well, you will almost certainly be successful. Here they are in a nutshell:

1. **Have clear goals.**

2. **Identify and don't tolerate the problems that stand in the way of your achieving those goals.**

3. **Accurately diagnose the problems to get at their root causes.**

4. **Design plans that will get you around them.**

5. **Do what's necessary to push these designs through to results.**

Together, these five steps make up a loop, like the one on the facing page. Let's look at this process more granularly.

First you have to pick what you are going after—your **goals**. Your choice of goals will determine your direction. As you move toward them, you will encounter **problems**. Some of those problems will bring you up against your own weaknesses. How you react to the pain that causes is up to you. If you want to reach your goals, you must be calm and analytical so that you can accurately **diagnose** your problems, **design** a plan that will get you around them, and **do** what's necessary to push through to results. Then you will look at the new results you achieve and go through the process again. To evolve quickly, you will have to do this fast and continuously, setting your goals successively higher.

You will need to do all five steps well to be successful and you must do them one at a time and in order. For example, when setting goals, just set goals. Don't think about how you will achieve them or what you will do if something goes wrong. When you are diagnosing problems, don't think about how you will solve them—just diagnose them. Blurring the steps leads to suboptimal outcomes because it interferes with uncovering the true problems. The process is iterative: Doing each step thoroughly will provide you with the information you need to move on to the next step and do it well.

It is essential that you approach this process in a clearheaded, rational way, looking down on yourself from a higher level and being ruthlessly honest. If your emotions are getting the better of you, step back and take time out until you can reflect clearly. If necessary, seek guidance from calm, thoughtful people.

To help you stay centered and effective, pretend that your life is a martial art or a game, the object of which is to get around a challenge and reach a goal. Once you accept its rules, you'll get used to the discomfort that comes with the constant frustration. You will never handle everything perfectly: Mistakes are inevitable and it's important to recognize and accept this fact of life. The good news is that every mistake you make can teach you something, so there's no end to learning. You'll soon realize that excuses like "that's not easy" or "it

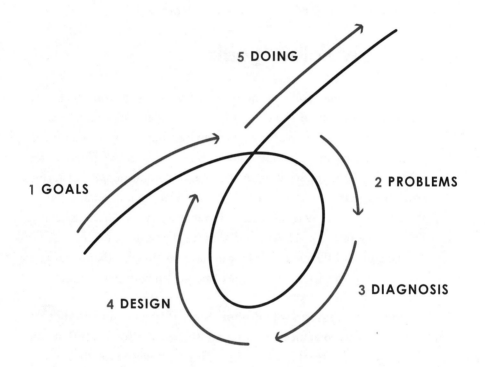

doesn't seem fair" or even "I can't do that" are of no value and that it pays to push through.

So what if you don't have all the skills you need to succeed? Don't worry about it because that's true for everyone. You just have to know when they are needed and where you can go to get them. With practice, you will eventually play this game with a calm unstoppable centeredness in the face of adversity. Your ability to get what you want will thrill you.

Now let's look at how to approach each of the five steps.

2.1 Have clear goals.

a. Prioritize: While you can have virtually anything you want, you can't have everything you want. Life is like a giant smorgasbord with more delicious alternatives than you can ever hope to taste. Choosing a goal often means rejecting some things you want in order to get other things that you want or need even more. Some people fail at this point, before they've even started. Afraid to reject a good alternative for a better one, they try to pursue too many goals at once, achieving few or none of them. Don't get discouraged and don't let yourself be paralyzed by all the choices. You can have much more than what you need to be happy. Make your choice and get on with it.

b. Don't confuse goals with desires. A proper goal is something that you really need to achieve. Desires are things that you want that can prevent you from reaching your goals. Typically, desires are first-order consequences. For example, your goal might be physical fitness, while your desire is to eat good-tasting but unhealthy food. Don't get me wrong, if you want to be a couch potato, that's fine with me. You can pursue whatever goals you want. But if you don't want to be a couch potato, then you better not open that bag of chips.

c. Decide what you really want in life by reconciling your goals and your desires. Take passion, for example. Without passion, life would be dull; you wouldn't want to live without it. But what's key is what you do with your passion. Do you let it consume you and drive you to irrational acts, or do you harness it to motivate and drive you while you pursue your real goals? What will ultimately fulfill you are things that feel right at both levels, as both desires *and* goals.

d. Don't mistake the trappings of success for success itself. Achievement orientation is important, but people who obsess over a $1,200 pair of shoes or a fancy car are very rarely happy because they don't know what it is that they really want and hence what will satisfy them.

e. Never rule out a goal because you think it's unattainable. Be audacious. There is always a best possible path. Your job is to find it and have the courage to follow it. What you think is attainable is just a function of what you know at the moment. Once you start your pursuit you will learn a lot, especially if you triangulate with others; paths you never saw before will emerge. Of course there are some impossibilities or near-impossibilities, such as playing center on a professional basketball team if you're short, or running a four-minute mile at age seventy.

f. Remember that great expectations create great capabilities. If you limit your goals to what you *know* you can achieve, you are setting the bar way too low.

g. Almost nothing can stop you from succeeding if you have a) flexibility and b) self-accountability. Flexibility is what allows you to accept what reality (or knowledgeable people) teaches you; self-accountability is essential because if you really believe that failing to achieve a goal is your personal failure, you will see your failing to achieve it as indicative that you haven't been creative or flexible or determined enough to do what it takes. And you will be that much more motivated to find the way.

h. Knowing how to deal well with your setbacks is as important as knowing how to move forward. Sometimes you know that you are going over a waterfall and there is no way to avoid it. Life will throw you such challenges, some of which will seem devastating at the time. In bad times, your goal might be to keep what you have, to minimize your rate of loss, or simply to deal with a loss that is irrevocable. Your mission is to always make the best possible choices, knowing that you will be rewarded if you do.

2.2 Identify and don't tolerate problems.

a. View painful problems as potential improvements that are screaming at you. Though it won't feel that way at first, each and every problem you encounter is an opportunity; for that reason, it is essential that you bring them to the surface. Most people don't like to do this, especially if it exposes their own weaknesses or the weaknesses of someone they care about, but successful people know they have to.

b. Don't avoid confronting problems because they are rooted in harsh realities that are unpleasant to look at. Thinking about problems that are difficult to solve may make you anxious, but *not* thinking about them (and hence not dealing with them) should make you more anxious still. When a problem stems from your own lack of talent or skill, most people feel shame. Get over it. I cannot emphasize this enough: Acknowledging your weaknesses is not the same as surrendering to them. It's the first step toward overcoming them. The pains you are feeling are "growing pains" that will test your character and reward you as you push through them.

c. Be specific in identifying your problems. You need to be precise, because different problems have different solutions. If a problem is due to inadequate skill, additional training may be called for; if it arises from an innate weakness, you may need to seek assistance from someone else or change the role you play. In other words, if you're bad at accounting, hire an accountant. If a problem stems from someone else's weaknesses, replace them with someone who is strong where it's needed. That's just the way it is.

d. Don't mistake a cause of a problem with the real problem. "I can't get enough sleep" is not a problem; it is a potential cause (or perhaps the result) of a problem. To clarify your thinking, try to identify the bad outcome first; e.g., "I am performing poorly in my job." Not sleeping enough may be the cause of that problem, or the cause may be something else—but in order to determine that, you need to know exactly what the problem is.

e. Distinguish big problems from small ones. You only have so much time and energy; make sure you are investing them in exploring the problems that, if fixed, will yield you the biggest returns. But at the same time, make sure you spend enough time with the small problems to make sure they're not symptoms of larger ones.

f. Once you identify a problem, don't tolerate it. Tolerating a problem has the same consequences as failing to identify it. Whether you tolerate it because you believe it cannot be solved, because you don't care enough to solve it, or because you can't muster enough of whatever it takes to solve it, if you don't have the will to succeed, then your situation is hopeless. You need to develop a fierce intolerance of badness of any kind, regardless of its severity.

2.3 Diagnose problems to get at their root causes.

a. Focus on the "what is" before deciding "what to do about it." It is a common mistake to move in a nanosecond from identifying a tough problem to proposing a solution for it. Strategic thinking requires both diagnosis and design. A good diagnosis typically takes between fifteen minutes and an hour, depending on how well it's done and how complex the issue is. It involves speaking with the relevant people and looking at the evidence together to determine the root causes. Like principles, root causes manifest themselves over and over again in seemingly different situations. Finding them and dealing with them pays dividends again and again.

b. Distinguish proximate causes from root causes. Proximate causes are typically the actions (or lack of actions) that lead to problems, so they are described with verbs (*I missed the train because I didn't check the train schedule*). Root causes run much deeper and they are typically described with adjectives (*I didn't check the train schedule because I am forgetful*). You can only truly solve your problems by removing their root causes, and to do that, you must distinguish the symptoms from the disease.

c. Recognize that knowing what someone (including you) is like will tell you what you can expect from them. You will have to get over your reluctance to assess what people are like if you want to surround your-self with people who have the qualities you need. That goes for yourself too. People almost always find it difficult to identify and accept their own mistakes and weaknesses. Sometimes it's because they're blind to them, but more often it's because their egos get in the way. Most likely your associates are equally reluctant to point out your mistakes, because they don't want to hurt you. You all need to get over this. More than anything else, what differentiates people who live up to their potential from those who don't is their willingness to look at themselves and others objectively and understand the root causes standing in their way.

2.4 Design a plan.

a. Go back before you go forward. Replay the story of where you have been (or what you have done) that led up to where you are now, and then visualize what you and others must do in the future so you will reach your goals.

b. Think about your problem as a set of outcomes produced by a machine. Practice higher-level thinking by looking down on your machine and thinking about how it can be changed to produce better outcomes.

c. Remember that there are typically many paths to achieving your goals. You only need to find one that works.

d. Think of your plan as being like a movie script in that you visualize who will do what through time. Sketch out the plan broadly at first (e.g., "hire great people") and then refine it. You should go from the big picture and drill down to specific tasks and estimated time lines (e.g., "In the next two weeks, choose the headhunters who will find those great people"). The real-world issues of costs, time, and personnel will undoubtedly surface as you do this, and that will lead you to further refine your design until all the gears in the machine are meshing smoothly.

e. Write down your plan for everyone to see and to measure your progress against. This includes all the granular details about who needs to do what tasks and when. The tasks, the narrative, and the goals are different, so don't mix them up. Remember, the tasks are what connect the narrative to your goals.

f. Recognize that it doesn't take a lot of time to design a good plan. A plan can be sketched out and refined in just hours or spread out over days or weeks. But the process is essential because it determines what you will have to do to be effective. Too many people make the mistake of spending virtually no time on designing because they are preoccupied with execution. Remember: Designing precedes doing!

2.5 Push through to completion.

a. Great planners who don't execute their plans go nowhere. You need to push through and that requires self-discipline to follow your script. It's important to remember the connections between your tasks and the goals that they are meant to achieve. When you feel yourself losing sight of that, stop and ask yourself "why?" Lose sight of the why and you will surely lose sight of your goals.

b. Good work habits are vastly underrated. People who push through successfully have to-do lists that are reasonably prioritized, and they make certain each item is ticked off in order.

c. Establish clear metrics to make certain that you are following your plan. Ideally, someone other than you should be objectively measuring and reporting on your progress. If you're not hitting your targets, that's another problem that needs to be diagnosed and solved. There are many successful, creative people who aren't good at execution. They succeed because they forge symbiotic relationships with highly reliable task-doers.

That's all there is to it!

Remember that all 5 Steps proceed from your values. Your values determine what you want, i.e., your goals. Also keep in mind that the 5 Steps are iterative. When you complete one step, you will have acquired information that will most likely lead you to modify the other steps. When you've completed all five, you'll start again with a new goal. If the process is working, your goals will change more slowly than your designs, which will change more slowly than your tasks.

One last important point: You will need to synthesize and shape well. The first three steps—setting goals, identifying problems, and then diagnosing them—are synthesizing (by which I mean knowing where you want to go and what's really going on). Designing solutions and making sure that the designs are implemented are shaping.

2.6 Remember that weaknesses don't matter if you find solutions.

You almost certainly can't do all these steps well, because each requires different types of thinking and virtually nobody can think well in all these ways. For example, goal setting (such as determining what you want your life to be) requires you to be good at higher-level thinking like visualization and prioritization. Identifying and not tolerating problems requires you to be perceptive and good at synthesis and maintaining high standards; diagnosis requires you to be logical, able to see multiple possibilities, and willing to have hard conversations with others; designing requires visualization and practicality; doing what you set out to do requires self-discipline, good work habits, and a results orientation. Who do you know who has all those qualities? Probably no one. Yet doing all 5 Steps well is required for being really successful. So what do you do? First and foremost, *have humility so you can get what you need from others!*

Everyone has weaknesses. They are generally revealed in the patterns of mistakes they make. Knowing what your weaknesses are and staring hard at them is the first step on the path to success.

a. Look at the patterns of your mistakes and identify at which step in the 5-Step Process you typically fail. Ask others for their input too, as nobody can be fully objective about themselves.

b. Everyone has at least one big thing that stands in the way of their success; find yours and deal with it. Write down what your one big thing is (such as identifying problems, designing solutions, pushing through to results) and why it exists (your emotions trip you up, you can't visualize adequate possibilities). While you and most people probably have more than one major impediment, if you can remove or get around that one really big one, you will hugely improve your life. If you work on it, you will almost certainly be able to deal successfully with your one big thing.

You can either fix it or you can get the help of others to deal with it well. There are two paths to success: 1) to have what you need yourself or 2) to get it from others. The second path requires you to have humility. Humility is as important, or even more important, as having the strengths yourself. Having both is best. On the following page is a template that some people find helpful.

2.7 Understand your own and others' mental maps and humility.

Some people are good at knowing what to do on their own; they have good mental maps. Maybe they acquired them from being taught; maybe they were blessed with an especially large dose of common sense. Whatever the case, they have more answers inside themselves than others do. Similarly, some people are more humble and open-minded than others. Humility can be even more valuable than having good mental maps if it leads you to seek out better answers than you could come up with on your own. Having both open-mindedness and good mental maps is most powerful of all.

To convey this simple concept, imagine rating from one to ten how good someone's mental map is (in other words, what they know) on the Y-axis and how humble/open-minded they are on the X-axis, as shown on the opposite page.

Everyone starts out in the lower left area, with poor mental maps and little open-mindedness, and most people remain tragically and arrogantly stuck in that position. You can improve by either going up on the mental-maps axis (by learning how to do things better) or out on the open-mindedness axis. Either will provide you with better knowledge of what to do. If you have good mental maps and low open mindedness, that will be good but not great. You will still miss a lot that is of value. Similarly, if you have high open-mindedness but bad mental maps, you will probably have challenges picking the right people and points of view to follow. The person who has good mental maps and a lot of open-mindedness will always beat out the person who doesn't have both.

Now take a minute to think about your path to becoming more effective. Where would you place yourself on this chart? Ask others where they'd place you.

Once you understand what you're missing and gain open-mindedness

that will allow you to get help from others, you'll see that there's virtually nothing you can't accomplish.

Most people fail to do this most of the time. In the next chapters, I'll explore why and how to rectify that.

3 Be Radically Open-Minded

his is probably the most important chapter because it explains how to get around the two things standing in most people's way of getting what they want out of life. These barriers exist because of the way that our brains work, so nearly everyone encounters them.

3.1 Recognize your two barriers.

The two biggest barriers to good decision making are your ego and your blind spots. Together, they make it difficult for you to objectively see what is true about you and your circumstances and to make the best possible decisions by getting the most out of others. If you can understand how the machine that is the human brain works, you can understand why these barriers exist and how to adjust your behavior to make yourself happier, more effective, and better at interacting with others.

a. Understand your ego barrier. When I refer to your "ego barrier," I'm referring to your subliminal defense mechanisms that make it hard for you to accept your mistakes and weaknesses. Your deepest-seated needs and fears—such as the need to be loved and the fear of losing love, the need to survive and the fear of not surviving, the need to be important and the fear of not mattering—reside in primitive parts of your brain such as the amygdala, which are structures in your temporal lobe that process emotions. Because these areas of your brain are not accessible to your conscious awareness, it is virtually impossible for you to understand what they want and how they control you. They oversimplify things and react instinctively. They crave praise and respond to criticism as an attack, even when the higher-level parts of the brain understand that constructive criticism is good for you. They make you defensive, especially when it comes to the subject of how good you are.

At the same time, higher-level consciousness resides in your neocortex, more specifically in the part called the prefrontal cortex. This is the most distinctively human feature of your brain; relative to the rest of the brain, it's larger in humans than in most other species. This is where you experience the conscious awareness of decision making (the so-called "executive function"), as well as the application of logic and reasoning.

b. Your two "yous" fight to control you. It's like Dr. Jekyll and Mr. Hyde, though your higher-level you is not aware of your lower-level you. This conflict is universal; if you pay close enough attention, you can actually see when the different parts of a person's brain are arguing with one another. For example, when someone gets "angry with himself," his prefrontal cortex is sparring with his amygdala (or other lower-level parts of his brain[25]). When someone asks, "Why did I let myself eat all that cake?" the answer is "Because the lower-level you won out over the thoughtful, higher-level you."

---

[25] The brain is a highly interconnected organ with many different structures responsible for producing our thoughts, feelings, and actions. When explaining these things, I've adopted some conventions, such as describing the amygdala as the sole cause of emotional flight-or-fight reactions, even though the exact neuroanatomy is more complex. I'll cover this in more detail in the following chapter.

Once you understand how your a) logical/conscious you and b) emotional/subconscious you fight with each other, you can imagine what it's like when your two yous deal with other people and their own two "thems." It's a mess. Those lower-level selves are like attack dogs—they want to fight even when their higher-level selves want to figure things out. This is very confusing because you and the people you are dealing with typically don't even know that these lower-level beasts exist, never mind that they are trying to hijack everyone's behavior.

Let's look at what tends to happen when someone disagrees with you and asks you to explain your thinking. Because you are programmed to view such challenges as attacks, you get angry, even though it would be more logical for you to be interested in the other person's perspective, especially if they are intelligent. When you try to explain your behavior, your explanations don't make any sense. That's because your lower-level you is trying to speak through your upper-level you. Your deep-seated, hidden motivations are in control, so it is impossible for you to logically explain what "you" are doing.

Even the most intelligent people generally behave this way, and it's tragic. To be effective you must not let your need to be right be more important than your need to find out what's true. If you are too proud of what you know or of how good you are at something you will learn less, make inferior decisions, and fall short of your potential.

c. Understand your blind spot barrier. In addition to your ego barrier, you (and everyone else) also have blind spots—areas where your way of thinking prevents you from seeing things accurately. Just as we all have different ranges for hearing pitch and seeing colors, we have different ranges for seeing and understanding things. We each see things in our own way. For example, some people naturally see big pictures and miss small details while others naturally see details and miss big pictures; some people are linear thinkers while others think laterally, and so on.

Naturally, people can't appreciate what they can't see. A person who can't identify patterns and synthesize doesn't know what it's like to see patterns and synthesize any more than a color-blind person knows what it's like to see color. These differences in how our brains work are much less apparent than the differences in how our bodies work. Color-blind people eventually find out that they are color-blind, whereas most people never see or understand the ways in which their ways of thinking make them blind. To make it even harder, we don't like to see ourselves or others as having blind spots, even though we all have them. When you point out someone's psychological weakness, it's generally about as well received as if you pointed out a physical weakness.

If you're like most people, you have no clue how other people see things and aren't good at seeking to understand what they are thinking, because you're too preoccupied with telling them what you yourself think is correct. In other words, you are closed-minded; you presume too much. This closed-mindedness is terribly costly; it causes you to miss out on all sorts of wonderful possibilities and dangerous threats that other people might be showing you—and it blocks criticism that could be constructive and even lifesaving.

The end result of these two barriers is that parties in disagreements typically remain convinced that they're right—and often end up angry at each other. This is illogical and leads to suboptimal decision making. After all, when two people reach opposite conclusions, someone must be wrong. Shouldn't you want to make sure that someone isn't you?

This failure to benefit from others' thinking doesn't just occur when disagreements arise; it occurs when people encounter problems that they are trying to solve. When trying to figure things out, most people spin in their own heads instead of taking in all the wonderful thinking available to them. As a result, they continually run toward what they see and keep crashing into what they are blind to until the crashing leads them to adapt. Those who adapt do so by a) teaching their brains to work in a way that doesn't come naturally (the creative person learns to become organized through discipline and practice, for instance), b) using compensating mechanisms (such as programmed reminders), and/or c) relying on the help of others who are strong where they are weak.

Differences in thinking can be symbiotic and complementary instead of disruptive. For example, the lateral approach to thinking common among creative people can lead them to be unreliable, while more linear thinkers are often more dependable; some people are more emotional while others are more logical, and so on. None of these individuals would be able to succeed at any kind of complex project without the help of others who have complementary strengths.

Aristotle defined tragedy as a terrible outcome arising from a person's fatal flaw—a flaw that, had it been fixed, instead would have led to a wonderful outcome. In my opinion, these two barriers—ego and blind spots—are the fatal flaws that keep intelligent, hardworking people from living up to their potential.

Would you like to learn how to get past them? You can do it; everybody can. Here's how.

3.2 Practice radical open-mindedness.

If you know that you are blind, you can figure out a way to see, whereas if you don't know that you're blind, you will continue to bump into your problems. In other words, if you can recognize that you have blind spots and open-mindedly consider the possibility that others might see something better than you—and that the threats and opportunities they are trying to point out really exist—you are more likely to make good decisions.

Radical open-mindedness is motivated by the genuine worry that you might not be seeing your choices optimally. It is the ability to effectively explore different points of view and different possibilities without letting your ego or your blind spots get in your way. It requires you to replace your attachment to always being right with the joy of learning what's true. Radical open-mindedness allows you to escape from the control of your lower-level you and ensures your upper-level you sees and considers all the good choices and makes the best possible decisions. If you can acquire this ability—and with practice you can—you'll be able to deal with your realities more effectively and radically improve your life.

Most people don't understand what it means to be radically open-minded. They describe open-mindedness as being "open to being wrong," but stubbornly cling to whatever opinion is in their head and fail to seek an understanding of the reasoning behind alternative points of view. To be radically open-minded you must:

a. Sincerely believe that you might not know the best possible path and recognize that your ability to deal well with "not knowing" is more important than whatever it is you do know. Most people make bad decisions because they are so certain that they're right that they don't allow themselves to see the better alternatives that exist. Radically open-minded people know that coming up with the right questions and asking other smart people what they think is as important as having all the answers. They understand that you can't make a great decision without swimming for a while in a state of "not knowing." That is because what exists within the area of "not knowing" is so much greater and more exciting than anything any one of us knows.

b. Recognize that decision making is a two-step process: First take in all the relevant information, then decide. Most people are reluctant to take in information that is inconsistent with what they have already concluded. When I ask why, a common answer is: "I want to make up my own mind." These people seem to think that considering opposing views will somehow threaten their ability to decide what they want to do. Nothing could be further from the truth. Taking in others' perspectives in order to consider them in no way reduces your freedom to think independently and make your own decisions. It will just broaden your perspective as you make them.

c. Don't worry about looking good; worry about achieving your goal. People typically try to prove that they have the answer even when they don't. Why do they behave in this unproductive way? It's generally because they believe the senseless but common view that great people have all the answers and don't have any weaknesses. Not only does this view not square with reality, it stands in the way of their progress. People interested in making the best possible decisions are rarely confident that they have the best answers. They recognize that they have weaknesses and blind spots, and they always seek to learn more so that they can get around them.

d. Realize that you can't put out without taking in. Most people seem much more eager to put out (convey their thinking and be productive) than to take in (learn). That's a mistake even if one's primary goal is to put out, because what one puts out won't be good unless one takes in as well.

e. Recognize that to gain the perspective that comes from seeing things through another's eyes, you must suspend judgment for a time—only by empathizing can you properly evaluate another point of view. Open-mindedness doesn't mean going along with what you don't believe in; it means considering the reasoning of others instead of stubbornly and illogically holding on to your own point of view. To be radically open-minded, you need to be so open to the possibility that you could be wrong that you encourage others to tell you so.

f. Remember that you're looking for the best answer, not simply the best answer that you can come up with yourself. The answer doesn't have to be in your head; you can look outside yourself. If you're truly looking at things objectively, you must recognize that the probability of you always having the best answer is small and that, even if you have it, you can't be confident that you do before others test you. So it is invaluable to know what you don't know. Ask yourself: Am I seeing this just through my own eyes? If so, then you should know that you're terribly handicapped.

g. Be clear on whether you are arguing or seeking to understand, and think about which is most appropriate based on your and others' believability. If both parties are peers, it's appropriate to argue. But if one person is clearly more knowledgeable than the other, it is preferable for the less knowledgeable person to approach the more knowledgeable one as a student and for the more knowledgeable one to act as a teacher. Doing this well requires you to understand the concept of **believability**. I define believable people as those who have repeatedly and successfully accomplished the thing in question—who have a strong track record with at least three successes—and have great explanations of their approach when probed.

If you have a different view than someone who is believable on the topic at hand—or at least more believable than you are (if, say, you are in a discussion with your doctor about your health)—you should make it clear that you are asking questions because you are seeking to understand their perspective. Conversely, if you are clearly the more believable person, you might politely remind the other of that and suggest that they ask you questions.

All these strategies come together in two practices that, if you seek to become radically open-minded, you must master.

3.3 Appreciate the art of thoughtful disagreement.

When two people believe opposite things, chances are that one of them is wrong. It pays to find out if that someone is you. That's why I believe you must appreciate and develop the art of thoughtful disagreement. In thoughtful disagreement, your goal is not to convince the other party that you are right—it is to find out which view is true and decide what to do about it. In thoughtful disagreement, both parties are motivated by the genuine fear of missing important perspectives. Exchanges in which you really see what the other person is seeing and they really see what you are seeing—with both your "higher-level yous" trying to get to the truth—are immensely helpful and a giant source of untapped potential.

To do this well, approach the conversation in a way that conveys that you're just trying to understand.[26] Use questions rather than make statements. Conduct the discussion in a calm and dispassionate manner, and encourage the other person to do that as well. Remember, you are not arguing; you are openly exploring what's true. Be reasonable and expect others to be reasonable. If you're calm, collegial, and respectful you will do a lot better than if you are not. You'll get better at this with practice.

To me, it's pointless when people get angry with each other when they disagree because most disagreements aren't threats as much as opportunities for learning. People who change their minds because they learned something are the winners, whereas those who stubbornly refuse to learn are the losers. That doesn't mean that you should blindly accept others' conclusions. You should be what I call open-minded and assertive at the same time—you should hold and explore conflicting possibilities in your mind while moving fluidly toward whatever is likely to be true based on what you learn. Some people can do this easily while others can't. A good exercise to make sure that you are doing this well is to describe back to the person you are disagreeing with their own perspective. If they agree that you've got it, then you're in good shape. I also recommend that both parties observe a "two-minute rule" in which neither interrupts the other, so they both have time to get all their thoughts out.

Some people worry that operating this way is time consuming. Working through disagreements does take time but it's just about the best way you can spend it. What's important is that you prioritize what you spend time on and who you spend it with. There are lots of

---

[26] One way to do this is by asking questions like "Would you rather I be open with my thoughts and questions or keep them to myself?"; "Are we going to try to convince each other that we are right or are we going to open-mindedly hear each other's perspectives to try to figure out what's true and what to do about it?"; or "Are you arguing with me or seeking to understand my perspective?"

people who will disagree with you, and it would be unproductive to consider all their views. It doesn't pay to be open-minded with everyone. Instead, spend your time exploring ideas with the most believable people you have access to.

If you find you're at an impasse, agree on a person you both respect and enlist them to help moderate the discussion. What's really counterproductive is spinning in your own head about what's going on, which most people are prone to do—or wasting time disagreeing past the point of diminishing returns. When that happens, move on to a more productive way of getting to a mutual understanding, which isn't necessarily the same thing as agreement. For example, you might agree to disagree.

Why doesn't thoughtful disagreement like this typically occur? Because most people are instinctively reluctant to disagree. For example, if two people go to a restaurant and one says he likes the food, the other is more likely to say "I like it too" or not say anything at all, even if that's not true. The reluctance to disagree is the "lower-level you's" mistaken interpretation of disagreement as conflict. That's why radical open-mindedness isn't easy: You need to teach yourself the art of having exchanges in ways that don't trigger such reactions in yourself or others. This was what I had to learn back when Bob, Giselle, and Dan told me I made people feel belittled.

Holding wrong opinions in one's head and making bad decisions based on them instead of having thoughtful disagreements is one of the greatest tragedies of mankind. Being able to thoughtfully disagree would so easily lead to radically improved decision making in all areas—public policy, politics, medicine, science, philanthropy, personal relationships, and more.

3.4 Triangulate your view with believable people who are willing to disagree.

By questioning experts individually and encouraging them to have thoughtful disagreement with each other that I can listen to and ask questions about, I both raise my probability of being right and become much better educated. This is most true when the experts disagree with me or with each other. Smart people who can thoughtfully disagree are the greatest teachers, far better than a professor assigned to stand in front of a board and lecture at you. The knowledge I acquire usually leads to principles that I develop and refine for similar cases that arise in the future.

In some cases in which the subjects are just too complex for me to understand in the time required, I will turn over the decision making to knowledgeable others who are more believable than me, but I still want to listen in on their thoughtful disagreement. I find that most people don't do that—they prefer to make their own decisions, even when they're not qualified to make the kinds of judgments required. In doing so, they're giving in to their lower-level selves.

This approach of triangulating the views of believable people can have a profound effect on your life. I know it has made the difference between life and death for me. In June 2013, I went to Johns Hopkins for an annual physical, where I was told that I had a precancerous condition called Barrett's esophagus with high-grade dysplasia. Dysplasia is an early stage in the development of cancer, and the probability that it will turn into esophageal cancer is relatively high—about 15 percent of cases per year. Cancer of the esophagus is deadly, so if left untreated, the odds were that in something like three to five years I'd develop cancer and die. The standard protocol for cases like mine is to remove the esophagus, but I wasn't a candidate for that because of something specific to my condition. The doctor advised that I wait and see how things progressed.

In the weeks that followed, I started to plan for my eventual death, while also fighting to live. I like to:

a. Plan for the worst-case scenario to make it as good as possible. I felt fortunate because this prognosis gave me enough time to ensure that the people I cared most about would be okay without me, and to savor life with them in the years I had left. I would have time to get to know my first grandson, who had just been born, but not so much time that I could take it for granted.

But as you know by now, rather than following what I am told is best, even by an expert, I like to triangulate opinions with believable people. So I also had my personal physician, Dr. Glazer, set up visits with four other experts on this particular disease.

The first call was with the head of thoracic surgery at a major cancer hospital. She explained that my condition had advanced quickly and that, contrary to what the first physician said, there was a surgery that could cure me. It would involve removing both my esophagus and my stomach and attaching my intestines to the remaining little bit of my esophagus I'd have left. She estimated I'd have a 10 percent chance of dying on the operating table and a 70 percent chance of a crippling outcome. But the odds were in favor of my living, so her recommendation was clearly worth taking seriously. Naturally I wanted her to speak with the doctor from Johns Hopkins who originally diagnosed me and recommended a watch-and-wait approach, so right then and there I called the other doctor to see what each would say about the other's views. This was eye-opening. While the two doctors had told me completely different things when I met with them in person, when they were on the phone together, they sought to minimize their disagreement and make the other look good, putting professional courtesy ahead of thrashing things out to get at the best answer. Still, the differences in their views were clear, and listening to them deepened my understanding.

The next day I met with a third doctor who was a world-renowned specialist and researcher at another esteemed hospital. He told me that my condition would basically cause me no problems so long as I came in for an endoscopic examination every three months. He explained that it was like skin cancer but on the inside—if it was watched and any new growth was clipped before it metastasized into the bloodstream, I'd be okay. According to him, the results for patients monitored in this way were no different than for those who had their esophagus removed. To put that plainly: They didn't die from cancer. Life went on as normal for them except for those occasional examinations and procedures.

To recap: Over the course of forty-eight hours, I had gone from a likely death sentence to a likely cure that would essentially involve disemboweling me, and then finally to a simple, and only slightly inconvenient, way of watching for abnormalities and removing them before they could cause any harm. Was this doctor wrong?

Dr. Glazer and I went on to meet two other world-class specialists and they both agreed that undergoing the scoping procedure would do no harm, so I decided to go ahead with it. During the procedure, they clipped some tissue from my esophagus and sent it to the laboratory for testing. A few days after the procedure, exactly a week before my sixty-fourth birthday, I got the results. They were shocking to say the least. After analyzing the tissue, it turned out there wasn't any high-grade dysplasia at all!

Even experts can make mistakes; my point is simply that it pays to be radically open-minded and triangulate with smart people. Had I not pushed for other opinions, my life would have taken a very different course. My point is that you can significantly raise your probabilities of making the right decisions by open-mindedly triangulating with believable people.

3.5 Recognize the signs of closed-mindedness and open-mindedness that you should watch out for.

It's easy to tell an open-minded person from a closed-minded person because they act very differently. Here are some cues to tell you whether you or others are being closed-minded:

1. **Closed-minded people don't want their ideas challenged.** They are typically frustrated that they can't get the other person to agree with them instead of curious as to why the other person disagrees. They feel bad about getting something wrong and are more interested in being proven right than in asking questions and learning others' perspectives.

   Open-minded people are more curious about why there is disagreement. They are not angry when someone disagrees. They understand that there is always the possibility that they might be wrong and that it's worth the little bit of time it takes to consider the other person's views in order to be sure they aren't missing something or making a mistake.

2. **Closed-minded people are more likely to make statements than ask questions.** While believability entitles you to make statements in certain circumstances, truly open-minded people, even the most believable people I know, always ask a lot of questions. Nonbelievable people often tell me that their statements are actually implicit questions, though they're phrased as low-confidence statements. While that's sometimes true, in my experience it's more often not.

   Open-minded people genuinely believe they could be wrong; the questions that they ask are genuine. They also assess their relative believability to determine whether their primary role should be as a student, a teacher, or a peer.

3. **Closed-minded people focus much more on being understood than on understanding others.** When people disagree, they tend to be quicker to assume that they aren't being understood than to consider whether they're the ones who are not understanding the other person's perspective.
Open-minded people always feel compelled to see things through others' eyes.

4. **Closed-minded people say things like "I could be wrong . . . but here's my opinion."** This is a classic cue I hear all the time. It's often a perfunctory gesture that allows people to hold their own opinion while convincing themselves that they are being open-minded. If your statement starts with "I could be wrong" or "I'm not believable," you should probably follow it with a question and not an assertion.
Open-minded people know when to make statements and when to ask questions.

5. **Closed-minded people block others from speaking.** If it seems like someone isn't leaving space for the other person in a conversation, it's possible they are blocking. To get around blocking, enforce the "two-minute rule" I mentioned earlier.
Open-minded people are always more interested in listening than in speaking; they encourage others to voice their views.

6. **Closed-minded people have trouble holding two thoughts simultaneously in their minds.** They allow their own view to crowd out those of others.
Open-minded people can take in the thoughts of others without losing their ability to think well—they can hold two or more conflicting concepts in their mind and go back and forth between them to assess their relative merits.

7. **Closed-minded people lack a deep sense of humility.** Humility typically comes from an experience of crashing, which leads to an enlightened focus on knowing what one doesn't know.
Open-minded people approach everything with a deep-seated fear that they may be wrong.

Once you can sort out open-minded from closed-minded people, you'll find that you want to surround yourself with open-minded ones. Doing so will not only make your decision making more effective but you'll also learn a tremendous amount. A few good decision makers working effectively together can significantly outperform a good decision maker working alone—and even the best decision maker can significantly improve his or her decision making with the help of other excellent decision makers.

3.6 Understand how you can become radically open-minded.

No matter how open-minded you are now, it is something you can learn. To practice open-mindedness:

a. Regularly use pain as your guide toward quality reflection. Mental pain often comes from being too attached to an idea when a person or an event comes along to challenge it. This is especially true when what is being pointed out to you involves a weakness on your part. This kind of mental pain is a clue that you are potentially wrong and that you need to think about the question in a quality way. To do this, first calm yourself down. This can be difficult: You will probably feel your amygdala kicking in through a tightening in your head, tension in your body, or an emerging sense of annoyance, anger, or irritability. Note these feelings when they arise in you. By being aware of such signals of closed-mindedness, you can use them as cues to control your behavior and guide yourself toward open-mindedness. Doing this regularly will strengthen your ability to keep your "higher-level you" in control. The more you do it, the stronger you will become.

b. Make being open-minded a habit. The life that you will live is most simply the result of habits you develop. If you consistently use feelings of anger/frustration as cues to calm down, slow down, and approach the subject at hand thoughtfully, over time you'll experience negative emotions much less frequently and go directly to the open-minded practices I just described.

Of course, this can be very hard for people to do in the moment because your "lower-level you" emotions are so powerful. The good news is that these "amygdala hijackings"[27] don't last long so even if you're having trouble controlling yourself in the moment, you can also allow a little time to pass to give your higher-level you space to reflect in a quality way. Have others whom you respect help you too.

c. Get to know your blind spots. When you are closed-minded and form an opinion in an area where you have a blind spot, it can be deadly. So take some time to record the circumstances in which you've consistently made bad decisions because you failed to see what others saw. Ask others—especially those who've seen what you've missed—to help you with this. Write a list, tack it up on the wall, and stare at it. If ever you find yourself about to make a decision (especially a big decision) in one of these areas without consulting others, understand that you're taking a big risk and that it would be illogical to expect that you'll get the results you think you will.

d. If a number of different believable people say you are doing something wrong and you are the only one who doesn't see it that way, assume that you are probably biased. Be objective! While it is possible that you are right and they are wrong, you should switch from a fighting mode to an "asking questions" mode, compare your believability with theirs, and if necessary agree to bring in a neutral party you all respect to break the deadlock.

e. Meditate. I practice Transcendental Meditation and believe that it has enhanced my open-mindedness, higher-level perspective, equa-

---

[27] Psychologist and science journalist Daniel Goleman originally coined this term in *Emotional Intelligence*.

nimity, and creativity. It helps slow things down so that I can act calmly even in the face of chaos, just like a ninja in a street fight. I'm not saying that you have to meditate in order to develop this perspective; I'm just passing along that it has helped me and many other people and I recommend that you seriously consider exploring it.

f. Be evidence-based and encourage others to be the same. Most people do not look thoughtfully at the facts and draw their conclusions by objectively weighing the evidence. Instead, they make their decisions based on what their deep-seated subconscious mind wants and then they filter the evidence to make it consistent with those desires. It is possible to become aware of this subconscious process happening and to catch yourself, or to allow others to catch you going down this path. When you're approaching a decision, ask yourself: Can you point to clear facts (i.e., facts believable people wouldn't dispute) leading to your view? If not, chances are you're not being evidence-based.

g. Do everything in your power to help others also be open-minded. Being calm and reasonable in how you present your view will help prevent the "flight-or-fight" animal/amygdala reaction in others. Be reasonable and expect others to be reasonable. Ask them to point to the evidence that supports their point of view. Remember, it is not an argument; it is an open exploration of what's true. Demonstrating that you are taking in what they are telling you can be helpful.

h. Use evidence-based decision-making tools. These principles were designed to help you get control over your lower-level/animal you and put your better, higher-level decision-making brain in charge.

What if you could unplug that lower part of your brain entirely and instead connect with a decision-making computer that gives you logically derived instructions, as we do with our investment systems? Suppose this computer-based decision-making machine has a much better track record than you because it captures more logic, processes more information more quickly, and makes decisions without being emotionally hijacked. Would you use it? In confronting the challenges I've faced in the course of my career I've created exactly such tools, and I am convinced that I would not have been nearly as successful without them. I have no doubt that in the years ahead such "machine-thinking" tools will continue to develop and that smart decision makers will learn how to integrate them into their thinking. I urge you to learn about them and consider using them.

i. Know when it's best to stop fighting and have faith in your decision-making process. It's important that you think independently and fight for what you believe in, but there comes a time when it's wiser to stop fighting for your view and move on to accepting what believable others think is best. This can be extremely difficult. But it's smarter and ultimately better for you to be open-minded and have faith that the consensus of believable others is better than whatever you think. If you can't understand their view, you're probably just blind to their way of thinking. If you continue doing what you think is best when all the evidence and believable people are against you, you're being dangerously arrogant.

The truth is that while most people can become radically open-minded, some can't, even after they have repeatedly encountered lots of pain from betting that they were right when they were not.[28] People who don't learn radical open-mindedness don't experience the metamorphosis that allows them to do much better. I myself had to have that humility beaten into me by my crashes, especially my big one in 1982. Gaining open-mindedness doesn't mean losing assertiveness. In fact, because it increases one's odds of being right, it should increase one's confidence. That has been true for me since my big crash, which is why I've been able to have more success with less risk.

Becoming truly open-minded takes time. Like all real learning, doing this is largely a matter of habit; once you do it so many times it

---

[28] Some of this may be a result of what is called the Dunning-Kruger effect, a cognitive bias in which low-ability individuals believe that they are in fact superior.

is almost instinctive, you'll find it intolerable to be any other way. As noted earlier, this typically takes about eighteen months, which in the course of a lifetime is nothing.

ARE YOU UP FOR THE CHALLENGE?

For me, there is really only one big choice to make in life: Are you willing to fight to find out what's true? Do you deeply believe that finding out what is true is essential to your well-being? Do you have a genuine need to find out if you or others are doing something wrong that is standing in the way of achieving your goals? If your answer to any of these questions is no, accept that you will never live up to your potential. If, on the other hand, you are up for the challenge of becoming radically open-minded, the first step in doing so is to look at yourself objectively. In the next chapter, Understand That People Are Wired Very Differently, you'll have a chance to do just that.

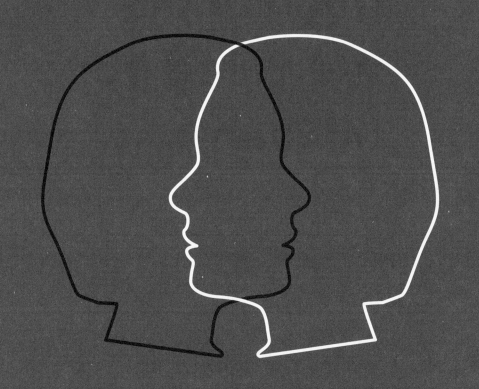

4 Understand That People Are Wired Very Differently

Because of the different ways that our brains are wired, we all experience reality in different ways and any single way is essentially distorted. This is something that we need to acknowledge and deal with. So if you want to know what is true and what to do about it, you must understand your own brain.

That insight led me to talk with many psychologists, psychiatrists, neuroscientists, personality testers, and other believable people in the field, and it led me to read many books. I discovered that though it is obvious to all of us that we are born with different strengths and weaknesses in areas such as common sense, creativity, memory, synthesis, attention to detail, and so forth, examining these differences objectively makes even most scientists uncomfortable. But that doesn't make it any less necessary, so I pushed forward with these explorations over several decades.

As a result, I have learned a lot that helped me and that I believe can help you. In fact, I attribute as much of my success to what I've learned about the brain as I do to my understanding of economics and investing. In this chapter, I will share some of the amazing things I've learned.

WHY I TURNED TO NEUROSCIENCE

When I started Bridgewater two years out of business school, I had to manage people for the first time. At first I thought that hiring smart people—for instance, the top students out of the top schools—should get me capable employees, but as often as not, those people didn't turn out well. "Book smarts" didn't typically equate to the type of smarts I needed.

I wanted to work with independent thinkers who were creative, conceptual, and had a lot of common sense. But I had a hard time finding those sorts of people and even when I did, I was shocked at how differently their brains seemed to work. It was as though we were speaking different languages. For example, those who were "conceptual" and imprecise spoke one language while those who were literal and precise spoke another. At the time, we chalked this up to "communication problems," but the differences were much deeper than that—and they were painful for all of us, particularly when we were trying to achieve big things together.

I remember one research project—an ambitious attempt to systemize our global understanding of the bond markets—that took place years ago. Bob Prince was running it, and while we agreed conceptually on what we were trying to do, the project didn't get pushed through to results. We'd meet with Bob and his team to agree on the goal and lay out how to get there. But when they'd go off to work on it, they'd make no progress. The problem was that conceptual people who visualized what should be done in vague ways expected more literal people to figure out for themselves how to do it. When they didn't, the more conceptual people thought the more literal people had no imagination, and the more literal people thought the more conceptual people had their heads in the clouds. To make matters worse, none of them knew which were which—the more literal people thought that they were as conceptual as the conceptual people and vice versa. In short, we were gridlocked, and everyone thought it was someone else's fault—that the people they were locking horns with were blind, stubborn, or just plain stupid.

Those meetings were painful for everyone. Because no one was clear about what they were good or bad at, everybody expressed opinions about everything and there wasn't any sensible way of sorting through them. We discussed why the group was failing, which led us to see that the individuals Bob had chosen for his team reflected his own strengths and weaknesses in their own roles. While that took frankness and open-mindedness and was a big step forward, it wasn't recorded and systematically converted into adequate changes, so the same people kept making the same sort of mistakes, over and over again.

Isn't it obvious that our different ways of thinking, our emotional responses, and our not having ways of dealing with them is crippling us? What are we supposed to do, not deal with them?

I'm sure you've been in contentious disagreements before—ones where people have different points of view and can't agree on what's right. Good people with good intentions get angry and emotional; it is frustrating and often becomes personal. Most companies avoid this by suppressing open debate and having those with the most authority simply make the calls. I didn't want that kind of company. I knew we needed to dig more deeply into what was preventing us from working together more effectively, bring those things to the surface, and explore them.

Bridgewater's roughly 1,500 employees do many different things— some strive to understand the global markets; others develop technologies; still others serve clients, manage health insurance and other benefits for employees, provide legal guidance, manage IT and facilities, and so on. All these activities require different types of people to work together in ways that harvest the best ideas and throw away the worst. Organizing people to complement their strengths and compensate for their weaknesses is like conducting an orchestra. It can be magnificent if done well and terrible if done poorly.

While "know thyself" and "to thine own self be true" are fundamental tenets I had heard long before I began looking into the brain, I had no idea how to go about getting that knowledge or how to act on it until we made these discoveries about how people think differently. The better we know ourselves, the better we can recognize both what can be changed and how to change it, and what *can't* be changed and what we can do about that. So no matter what you set out to do—whether on your own, as a member of an organization, or as its director—you need to understand how you and other people are wired.

4.1 Understand the power that comes from knowing how you and others are wired.

As I related in the first part of this book, my first breakthrough in understanding how people think differently occurred when I was a young father and had my kids tested by Dr. Sue Quinlan. I found the results remarkable, because she not only confirmed my own observations of the ways that their minds were working at the time but also predicted how they would develop in the future. For example, one of my kids was struggling with arithmetic. Because he tested well in mathematical reasoning, she correctly told him that if he pushed through the boredom of rote memorization required in elementary school, he would love the higher-level concepts he would be exposed to when he got older. These insights opened my eyes to new possibilities. I turned to her and others years later when I was trying to figure out the different thinking styles of my employees and colleagues.

At first, the experts gave me both bad and good advice. Many seemed as if they were more interested in making people feel good (or not feel bad) than they were at getting at the truth. Even more startling, I found that most psychologists didn't know much about neuroscience and most neuroscientists didn't know much about psychology—and both were reluctant to connect the physiological differences in people's brains to the differences in their aptitudes and behaviors. But eventually I found Dr. Bob Eichinger, who opened the world of psychometric testing to me. Using Myers-Briggs and other assessments, we evolved a much clearer and more data-driven way of understanding our different types of thinking.

Our differences weren't a product of poor communication; it was the other way around. Our different ways of thinking led to our poor communications.

From conversations with experts and my own observations, I learned that many of our mental differences are physiological. Just as our physical attributes determine the limits of what we are able to do physically—some people are tall and others are short, some muscular and others weak—our brains are innately different in ways that set the parameters of what we are able to do mentally. As with our bodies, some parts of our brains cannot be materially affected by external experience (in the same way that your skeleton isn't changed much through working out), while other parts can be strengthened through exercise (I will have more to say about brain plasticity later in this chapter).

This was driven home to me by my son Paul's three-year struggle with bipolar disorder. As terrifying and frustrating as his behavior was, I came to realize that it was due to his brain's chemistry (specifically, its secreting serotonin and dopamine in spurts and sputters). As I went through that terrible journey with him, I experienced the frustration and anger of trying to reason with someone who wasn't thinking well. I constantly had to remind myself that there was no basis for my anger because his distorted logic was a product of his physiology—and I saw for myself how the doctors who approached it that way brought him to a state of crystal clarity. The experience not only taught me a lot about how brains work but why creative genius often exists at the edge of insanity. Many highly productive and creative people have suffered from bipolar disorder, among them Ernest Hemingway, Beethoven, Tchaikovsky, Vincent van Gogh, Jackson Pollock, Virginia Woolf, Winston Churchill, and the psychologist Kay Redfield Jamison (who has written frankly about her own experiences with the disease in her book *An Unquiet Mind*). I learned that we are all different because of the different ways that the machine that is our brain works—and that nearly one in five Americans are clinically mentally ill in one way or another.

Once I understood that it's all physiological, many things became clearer to me. While I used to get angry and frustrated at people because of the choices they made, I came to realize that they weren't intentionally acting in a way that seemed counterproductive; they were just living out things as they saw them, based on how their brains worked. I also realized that as off-base as they seemed to me, they saw me the same way. The only sensible way of behaving with each other was to look down upon ourselves with mutual understanding so we could make objective sense of things. Not only did this make our disagreements less frustrating, it also allowed us to maximize our effectiveness.

Everyone is like a Lego set of attributes, with each piece reflecting the workings of a different part of their brain. All these pieces come together to determine what each person is like, and if you know what a person is like, you'll have a pretty good idea of what you can expect from them.

a. We are born with attributes that can both help us and hurt us, depending on their application. Most attributes are a double-edged sword that bring potential benefits and potential harm. The more extreme the attribute, the more extreme the potential good or bad outcomes it is likely to produce. For example, a highly creative, goal-oriented person good at imagining new ideas might undervalue the minutiae of daily life, which is also important; he might be so driven in his pursuit of long-term goals that he might have disdain for people who focus on the details of daily life. Similarly, a task oriented person who is great with details might undervalue creativity—and worse still, may squelch it in the interests of efficiency. These two people might make a great team, but are likely to have trouble taking advantage of the ways they're complementary, because the ways their minds work make it difficult for them to see the value of each other's ways of thinking.

Having expectations for people (including yourself) without knowing what they are like is a sure way to get in trouble. I learned this the hard way, through years of frustrating conversations and the pain of expecting things from people who were constitutionally incapable of delivering them. I'm sure that I caused them plenty of pain too. Over time, I realized that I needed a systematic approach to capturing and recording our differences so that we could actively take them into consideration when putting people into different roles at Bridgewater.

This led to one of my most valuable management tools: Baseball Cards, which I mentioned in the first part of this book. Just as a baseball card compiles the relevant data on a baseball player, helping fans know what that player is good and bad at, I decided that it would be similarly helpful for us to have cards for all of our players at Bridgewater.

In creating the attributes for our baseball cards, I used a combination of adjectives we already used to describe people, like "conceptual," "reliable," "creative," and "determined"; the actions people took or didn't take such as "holding others accountable" and "pushing through to results"; and terms from personality tests such as "extroverted" or "judging." Once the cards were established, I created a process to have people evaluate each other, with the people rated highest in each dimension (e.g., "most creative") having more weight on the ratings of other people in that dimension. People with proven track records in a certain area would get more believability, or decision-making weight, within that area. By recording these qualities in people's Baseball Cards, others who'd never worked with them before could know what to expect from them. When people changed, their rating would change. And when they didn't change, we were even more sure of what we could expect of them.

Naturally when I introduced this tool, people were skeptical or scared of it for various reasons. Some were afraid that the cards would be inaccurate; others thought it would be uncomfortable to have their weaknesses made so apparent, or that it would lead to their being pigeonholed, inhibiting their growth; still others thought it would be too complex to be practical. Imagine how you would feel if you were asked to force-rank all your colleagues on creativity, determination, or reliability. Most people at first find that prospect frightening.

Still, I knew that we needed to be radically open in recording and considering what people were like, and that things would eventually evolve to address people's concerns if we were sensible about how we approached the process. Today, most everyone at Bridgewater finds these Baseball Cards to be essential, and we have built a whole suite of other tools, which will be further described in Work Principles, to support our drive to understand what people are like and who is believable at what.

I've already noted that our unique way of operating and the treasure trove of data we accumulated brought us to the attention of some world-renowned organizational psychologists and researchers. Bob Kegan of Harvard University, Adam Grant of the Wharton School, and Ed Hess of the University of Virginia have written about us extensively, and I have learned a great deal from them in turn. In a way I never intended, our trial-and-error discovery process has put us at the cutting edge of academic thinking about personal development within organizations. As Kegan wrote in his book *An Everyone Culture*, "from the individual experience of probing in every one-on-one meeting, to the technologically integrated processes for discussing . . . issues and baseball cards, to the company-wide practices of daily updates and cases, Bridgewater has built an ecosystem to support personal development. The system helps everyone in the company confront the truth about what everyone is like."

Our journey of discovery has coincided with an incredibly fertile epoch in neuroscience, when, thanks to rapid advances in brain imaging and the ability to gather and process big data, our understanding has accelerated dramatically. As with all sciences on the cusp of breakthroughs, I am sure that much of what is thought to be true today will soon be radically improved. But what I do know is how incredibly beautiful and useful it is to understand how the thinking machine between our ears works.

Here's some of what I've learned:

The brain is even more complex than we can imagine. It has an estimated eighty-nine billion tiny computers (called neurons) that are connected to each other through many trillions of "wires" called axons and chemical synapses. As David Eagleman describes it in his wonderful book *Incognito*:

Your brain is built of cells called neurons and glia—hundreds of billions of them. Each one of them is as complex as a city. . . . The cells [neurons] are connected in a network of such staggering complexity that it bankrupts human language and necessitates new strains of mathematics. A typical neuron makes about ten thousand connections to neighboring neurons. Given billions of neurons, this means that there are as many connections in a single cubic centimeter of brain tissue as there are stars in the Milky Way galaxy.

When we are born our brains are preprogrammed with learning accumulated over hundreds of millions of years. For example, researchers at the University of Virginia have shown that while many people have an instinctual fear of snakes, no one has an instinctual fear of flowers. The brains that we were born with had learned that snakes are dangerous and flowers are not. There's a reason for that.

There is one grand design for the brains of all mammals, fish, birds, amphibians, and reptiles, which was established nearly 300 million years ago and has been evolving ever since. Just as cars have evolved into different versions—sedans, SUVs, sports cars, etc.—that rely on many of the same underlying parts, all vertebrate brains have similar parts that do similar things but that are well adapted to the needs of their own particular species. For example, birds have superior occipital lobes because they need to spot prey (and predators) from great heights. While we humans think of ourselves as superior overall because we overemphasize the importance of our own advantages, other species could justifiably make the same claims on their own behalf—birds for flight, eyesight, and instinctual magnetic navigation; most animals for smell; and several for appearing to have particularly enjoyable sex.

This "universal brain" has evolved from the bottom up, meaning that its lower parts are evolutionarily the oldest and the top parts are the newest. The brainstem controls the subconscious processes that keep us and other species alive—heartbeat, breathing, nervous system, and our degree of arousal and alertness. The next layer up, the cerebellum, gives us the ability to control our limb movements by

FRONT

BACK

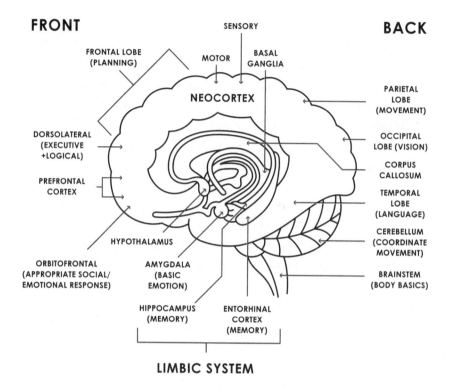

SENSORY

FRONTAL LOBE (PLANNING)

MOTOR

BASAL GANGLIA

NEOCORTEX

PARIETAL LOBE (MOVEMENT)

DORSOLATERAL (EXECUTIVE +LOGICAL)

OCCIPITAL LOBE (VISION)

CORPUS CALLOSUM

PREFRONTAL CORTEX

TEMPORAL LOBE (LANGUAGE)

CEREBELLUM (COORDINATE MOVEMENT)

HYPOTHALAMUS

ORBITOFRONTAL (APPROPRIATE SOCIAL/ EMOTIONAL RESPONSE)

AMYGDALA (BASIC EMOTION)

BRAINSTEM (BODY BASICS)

HIPPOCAMPUS (MEMORY)

ENTORHINAL CORTEX (MEMORY)

LIMBIC SYSTEM

coordinating sensory input with our muscles. Then comes the cerebrum, which includes the basal ganglia (which controls habit) and other parts of the limbic system (which controls emotional responses and some movement) and the cerebral cortex (which is where our memories, thoughts, and sense of consciousness reside). The newest and most advanced part of the cortex, that wrinkled mass of gray matter that looks like a bunch of intestines, is called the neocortex, which is where learning, planning, imagination, and other higher-level thoughts come from. It accounts for a significantly higher ratio of the brain's gray matter than is found in the brains of other species.

4.2 Meaningful work and meaningful relationships aren't just nice things we chose for ourselves—they are genetically programmed into us.

Neuroscientists, psychologists, and evolutionists agree the human brain comes pre-programmed with the need for and enjoyment of social cooperation. Our brains want it and develop better when we have it. The meaningful relationships we get from social cooperation make us happier, healthier, and more productive; social cooperation is also integral to effective work. It is one of the defining characteristics of being human.[29]

Leonard Mlodinow, in his excellent book *Subliminal,* writes, "We usually assume that what distinguishes us [from other species] is IQ. But it is our social IQ that ought to be the principal quality that differentiates us." He points out that humans have a unique ability to understand what other people are like and how they are likely to behave. The brain comes programmed to develop this ability; by the time they are four years old, most children are able to read others' mental states. This sort of human understanding and cooperation is what makes us so accomplished as a species. As Mlodinow explains, "Building a car for example requires the participation of thousands of people with diverse skills, in diverse lands, performing diverse tasks. Metals like iron must be extracted from the ground and processed; glass, rubber, and plastics must be created from numerous chemical precursors and molded; batteries, radiators and countless other parts must be produced; electronic and mechanical systems must be designed; and it all must come together, coordinated from far and wide, in one factory so

---

[29] Lots of data show that relationships are the greatest reward—that they're more important to your health and happiness than anything else. For example, as Robert Waldinger, director of Harvard's seventy-five-year Grant and Glueck study of adult males from a variety of socioeconomic backgrounds, puts it, "You could have all the money you've ever wanted, a successful career, and be in good physical health, but without loving relationships, you won't be happy . . . The good life is built with good relationships."

that the car can be assembled. Today, even the coffee and bagel you might consume while driving to work in the morning is the result of the activities of people all over the world."

In his book *The Meaning of Human Existence*, Pulitzer Prize-winning author Edward O. Wilson surmises that between one million and two million years ago, when our ancestors were somewhere between chimpanzees and modern homo sapiens, the brain evolved in ways supporting cooperation so man could hunt and do other activities. This led the centers of memory and reasoning in the prefrontal cortex to develop beyond those of our primate relatives. As groups became more powerful than individuals and our brains evolved in ways that made larger groups manageable, competition between groups became more important than competition between individuals and groups that had more cooperative individuals did better than those without them. This evolution led to the development of altruism, morality, and the sense of conscience and honor. Wilson explains that man is perpetually suspended between the two extreme forces that created us: "Individual selection [which] prompted sin and group selection [which] promoted virtue."

Which of these forces (self-interest or collective interest) wins out in any organization is a function of that organization's culture, which is a function of the people who shape it. But it's clear that collective interest is what's best, not just for the organization but for the individuals who make it up. As I'll explain in Work Principles, the rewards of working together to make the pie bigger are greater than the rewards of self-interest, not only in terms of how much "pie" one gets but also in the psychic rewards wired into our brains that make us happier and healthier.

Knowing how the brain has evolved thus far, we might extrapolate the past into the future to imagine where it will go. Clearly the evolution of the brain has moved from being nonthinking and self-focused toward being more abstract and more universally focused. For example, the brain evolution that I described has given us (some people more than others) the ability to see ourselves and our circumstances from a higher holistic level and, in some cases, to value the whole that we are part of even more than ourselves.

A few years ago, I had a conversation with the Dalai Lama in which I explained to him the contemporary neuroscience view that all of our thinking and feeling is due to physiology (in other words, the chemicals, electricity, and biology in our brains working like a machine). This implied that spirituality is due to these physiological mechanics rather than something coming from above, so I asked him what he thought about that. Without hesitation, he responded "Absolutely!" and told me that the next day he was meeting with the University of Wisconsin professor of neuroscience who had helped him learn about this, and he asked me if I wanted to join him. Regrettably, I couldn't but I recommended to him a book I'd read on the subject called *The Spiritual Brain* (which I also recommend to you). In our conversation, we went on to discuss the similarities and differences between spirituality and religion. His view was that prayer and meditation seemed to have similar effects on the brain in producing feelings of spirituality (the rising above oneself to feel a greater connection to the whole) but that each religion adds its own different superstitions on top of that common feeling of spirituality. Rather than trying to squeeze my own summary of his thinking in here, I'll simply recommend the Dalai Lama's book, *Beyond Religion*, if you're interested in learning more.

In imagining what the future of our thinking will be like, it's also interesting to consider how man himself might change how the brain works. We are certainly doing that with drugs and technology. Given advances in genetic engineering, it's reasonable to expect that someday genetic engineers might mix and match features of different species' brains for different purposes—if you want to have a heightened sense of sight, say, genetic engineers might be able to manipulate the human brain so it grows optic lobes more like those of birds. But since such things won't happen anytime soon, let's get back to the practical question of how all this can help us better deal with ourselves and each other.

4.3 Understand the great brain battles and how to control them to get what "you" want.

The following sections explore the different ways your brain fights for control of "you." While I will refer to the specific parts of the brain that neurophysiologists believe are responsible for specific types of thinking and emotions, the actual physiology is much more complex—and scientists are only beginning to understand it.

a. Realize that the conscious mind is in a battle with the subconscious mind. Earlier in the book, I introduced the concept of the "two yous" and explained how your higher-level you can look down on your lower-level you to make sure that your lower-level you isn't sabotaging what your higher-level you wants. Though I've often seen these two yous in action in myself and others, it wasn't until I learned why they exist that I really understood them.

As with animals, many of our decision-making drivers are below the surface. An animal doesn't "decide" to fly or hunt or sleep or fight in the way that we go about making many of our own choices of what to do—it simply follows the instructions that come from the subconscious parts of its brain. These same sorts of instructions come to us from the same parts of our brains, sometimes for good evolutionary reasons and sometimes to our detriment. Our subconscious fears and desires drive our motivations and actions through emotions such as love, fear, and inspiration. It's physiological. Love, for example, is a cocktail of chemicals (such as oxytocin) secreted by the pituitary gland.

While I had always assumed that logical conversation is the best way for people to get at what is true, armed with this new knowledge about the brain, I came to understand that there are large parts of our brains that don't do what is logical. For example, I learned that when people refer to their "feelings"—such as saying "I feel that you were unfair with me"—they are typically referring to messages that originate in the emotional, subconscious parts of their brains. I also came to understand that while some subconscious parts of our brains are dangerously animalistic, others are smarter and quicker than our conscious minds. Our greatest moments of inspiration often "pop" up from our subconscious. We experience these creative breakthroughs when we are relaxed and not trying to access the part of the brain in which they reside, which is generally the neocortex. When you say, "I just thought of something," you noticed your subconscious mind telling your conscious mind something. With training, it's possible to open this stream of communication.

Many people only see the conscious mind and aren't aware of the benefits of connecting it to the subconscious. They believe that the way to accomplish more is to cram more into the conscious mind and make it work harder, but this is often counterproductive. While it may seem counterintuitive, clearing your head can be the best way to make progress.

Knowing this, I now understand why creativity comes to me when I relax (like when I'm in the shower) and how meditation helps open this connection. Because it is physiological, I can actually feel the creative thoughts coming from elsewhere and flowing into my conscious mind. It's a kick to understand how that works.

But a note of caution is in order too: When thoughts and instructions come to me from my subconscious, rather than acting on them immediately, I have gotten into the habit of examining them with my conscious, logical mind. I have found that in addition to helping me figure out which thoughts are valid and why I am reacting to them as I do, doing this opens further communication between my conscious and subconscious minds. It's helpful to write down the results of this process. In fact that's how my Principles came about.

If you take nothing else away from this chapter, be aware of your subconscious—of how it can both harm you and help you, and how by consciously reflecting on what comes out of it, perhaps with the help of others, you can become happier and more effective.

b. Know that the most constant struggle is between feeling and thinking. There are no greater battles than those between our feelings (most importantly controlled by our amygdala, which operates subconsciously) and our rational thinking (most importantly controlled by our prefrontal cortex, which operates consciously). If you understand how those battles occur you will understand why it is so important to reconcile what you get from your subconscious with what you get from your conscious mind.

That damned amygdala, which is a little almond-shaped structure that lies deeply embedded in the cerebrum, is one of the most powerful parts of your brain. It controls your behavior, even though you're not conscious of it. How does it work? When something upsets us—and that something could be a sound, a sight, or just a gut feeling—the amygdala sends notice to our bodies to prepare to fight or flee: the heartbeat speeds up, the blood pressure rises, and breathing quickens. During an argument, you'll often notice a physical response similar to how you react to fear (for instance, rapid heartbeats and tensing muscles). Recognizing that, your conscious mind (which resides in the prefrontal cortex) can refuse to obey its instructions. Typically, these amygdala hijackings come on fast and dissipate quickly, except in rare cases, such as when a person develops post-traumatic stress disorder from a particularly horrible event or series of events. Knowing how these hijackings work, you know that if you allow yourself to react spontaneously, you will be prone to overreact. You can also comfort yourself with the knowledge that whatever psychological pain you are experiencing will go away before very long.

c. Reconcile your feelings and your thinking. For most people, life is a never-ending battle between these two parts of the brain. While the amygdala's reactions come in spurts and then subside, reactions from the prefrontal cortex are more gradual and constant. The biggest difference between people who guide their own personal evolution and achieve their goals and those who don't is that those who make progress reflect on what causes their amygdala hijackings.

d. Choose your habits well. Habit is probably the most powerful tool in your brain's toolbox. It is driven by a golf-ball-sized lump of tissue called the basal ganglia at the base of the cerebrum. It is so deep-seated and instinctual that we are not conscious of it, though it controls our actions.

If you do just about anything frequently enough over time, you will form a habit that will control you. Good habits are those that get you to do what your "upper-level you" wants, and bad habits are those that are controlled by your "lower-level you" and stand in the way of your getting what your "upper-level you" wants. You can create a better set of habits if you understand how this part of your brain works. For example, you can develop a habit that will make you "need" to work out at the gym.

Developing this skill takes some work. The first step is recognizing how habits develop in the first place. Habit is essentially inertia, the strong tendency to keep doing what you have been doing (or not doing what you have not been doing). Research suggests that if you stick with a behavior for approximately eighteen months, you will build a strong tendency to stick to it nearly forever.

For a long time, I didn't appreciate the extent to which habits control people's behavior. I experienced this at Bridgewater in the form of people who agreed with our work principles in the abstract but had trouble living by them; I also observed it with friends and family members who wanted to achieve something but constantly found themselves working against their own best interests.

Then I read Charles Duhigg's best-selling book *The Power of Habit*, which really opened my eyes. I recommend that you read it yourself if your interest in this subject goes deeper than what I'm able to cover here. Duhigg's core idea is the role of the three-step "habit loop." The first step is a cue—some "trigger that tells your brain to go into automatic mode and which habit to use," according to Duhigg. Step two is the routine, "which can be physical or mental or emotional." Finally, there is a reward, which helps your brain figure out if this particular loop is "worth remembering for the future." Repetition reinforces this loop until over time it becomes automatic. This anticipation and craving is the key to what animal trainers call operant conditioning, which is a method of training that uses positive reinforcement. For example, dog trainers use a sound (typically a clicker) to reinforce behavior by pairing that sound with a more desirable reward (typically food) until

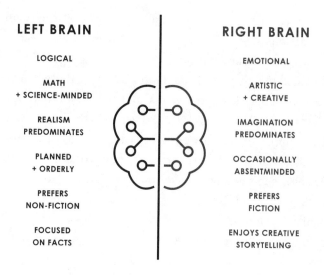

LEFT BRAIN	RIGHT BRAIN
LOGICAL	EMOTIONAL
MATH + SCIENCE-MINDED	ARTISTIC + CREATIVE
REALISM PREDOMINATES	IMAGINATION PREDOMINATES
PLANNED + ORDERLY	OCCASIONALLY ABSENTMINDED
PREFERS NON-FICTION	PREFERS FICTION
FOCUSED ON FACTS	ENJOYS CREATIVE STORYTELLING

the dog will perform the desired behavior when it merely hears the click. In humans, Duhigg says, rewards can be just about anything, ranging "from food or drugs that cause physical sensations, to emotional payoffs, such as the feelings of pride that accompany praise or self-congratulation."

Habits put your brain on "automatic pilot." In neuroscientific terms, the basal ganglia takes over from your cortex, so that you can execute activities without even thinking about them.

Reading Duhigg's book taught me that if you really want to change, the best thing you can do is choose which habits to acquire and which to get rid of and then go about doing that. To help you, I recommend that you write down your three most harmful habits. Do that right now. Now pick one of those habits and be committed to breaking it. Can you do that? That would be extraordinarily impactful. If you break all three, you will radically improve the trajectory of your life. Or you can pick habits that you want to acquire and then acquire them.

The most valuable habit I've acquired is using pain to trigger quality reflections. If you can acquire this habit yourself, you will learn what causes your pain and what you can do about it, and it will have an enormous impact on your effectiveness.

e. Train your "lower-level you" with kindness and persistence to build the right habits. I used to think that the upper-level you needed to fight with the lower-level you to gain control, but over time I've learned that it is more effective to train that subconscious, emotional you the same way you would teach a child to behave the way you would like him or her to behave—with loving kindness and persistence so that the right habits are acquired.

f. Understand the differences between right-brained and left-brained thinking. Just as your brain has its conscious upper part and its subconscious lower part, it also has two halves called hemispheres.[30] You might have heard it said that some people are more left-brained while others are more right-brained. That's not just a saying—Caltech professor Roger Sperry won the Nobel Prize in medicine for discovering it. In a nutshell:

1. The left hemisphere reasons sequentially, analyzes details, and excels at linear analysis. "Left-brained" or "linear" thinkers who are analytically strong are often called "bright."
2. The right hemisphere thinks across categories, recognizes themes, and synthesizes the big picture. "Right-brained" or "lateral" thinkers with more street smarts are often called "smart."

The diagram on the left summarizes the qualities of "right-brained" and "left-brained" thinking types.

Most people tend to get more of their instructions from one side than the other and they have trouble understanding people who get theirs from the opposite side. Our experience has been that left-brained folks tend to see right-brained folks as "spacey" or "abstract," while right-brained thinkers tend to find left-brained thinkers "literal"

---

[30] A good book on this is *A Whole New Mind* by Daniel H. Pink, and a good article on the science of this is "A Wandering Mind Heads Straight Toward Insight" by Robert Lee Hotz from *The Wall Street Journal*. While many parts of the brain come in two halves, it's only the more recently developed cortex, which accounts for three-quarters of the brain, that has been shown to have functional differences between the right and left sides.

or "narrow." I have seen wonderful results occur when people know where their own and others' inclinations lie, realize that both ways of thinking are invaluable, and assign responsibilities accordingly.

g. Understand how much the brain can and cannot change. This brings us to an important question: Can we change?[31] We can all learn new facts and skills, but can we also learn to change how we are inclined to think? The answer is a qualified yes.

Brain plasticity is what allows your brain to change its "softwiring." For a long time, scientists believed that after a certain critical period in childhood, most of our brain's neurological connections were fixed and highly unlikely to change. But recent research has suggested that a wide variety of practices—from physical exercise to studying to meditation—can lead to physical and physiological changes in our brains that affect our abilities to think and form memories. In a study of Buddhist monks who had practiced more than ten thousand hours of meditation, researchers at the University of Wisconsin measured significantly higher levels of gamma waves in their brains; these waves are associated with perception and problem solving.[32]

That doesn't mean the brain is infinitely flexible. If you have a preference for a certain way of thinking, you might be able to train yourself to operate another way and find that easier to do over time, but you're very unlikely to change your underlying preference. Likewise, you may be able to train yourself to be more creative, but if you're not naturally creative, there's likely a limit to what you can do. That is simply reality, so we all might as well accept it and learn how to deal

---

[31] That's a big question. Entire specialties are dedicated to this question alone, and no one answer is authoritative, certainly not mine. However, because knowing what can change is important for people trying to manage themselves and others, I have looked fairly deeply into the issue of brain plasticity. What I learned coincided with my own experiences, and I will pass that along to you.

[32] A brain-imaging study by Harvard-affiliated researchers at Massachusetts General Hospital found physical changes in the brain after an eight-week meditation course. Researchers identified increased activity in parts of the brain associated with learning, memory, self-awareness, compassion, and introspection, as well as decreased activity in the amygdala.

with it. There are coping techniques that we can use—for example, the creative, disorganized person who is likely to lose track of time can develop the habit of using alarms; the person who isn't good at some type of thinking can train himself to rely on the thinking of others who are better at it. The best way to change is through doing mental exercises. As with physical exercise, this can be painful unless you enlist the habit loop discussed earlier to connect the rewards to the actions, "rewiring" your brain to love learning and beneficial change.

Remember that accepting your weaknesses is contrary to the instincts of those parts of your brain that want to hold on to the illusion that you are perfect. Doing the things that will reduce your instinctual defensiveness takes practice, and requires operating in an environment that reinforces open-mindedness.

As you'll see when we get into Work Principles, I've developed a number of tools and techniques that help overcome that resistance, individually and across organizations. Instead of expecting yourself or others to change, I've found that it's often most effective to acknowledge one's weaknesses and create explicit guardrails against them. This is typically a faster and higher-probability path to success.

4.4 Find out what you and others are like.

Because of the biases with which we are wired, our self-assessments (and our assessments of others) tend to be highly inaccurate. Psychometric assessments are much more reliable. They are important in helping explore how people think during the hiring process and throughout employment. Though psychometric assessments cannot fully replace speaking with people and looking at their backgrounds and histories, they are far more powerful than traditional interviewing and screening methods. If I had to choose between just the assessments or just traditional job interviews to get at what people are like, I would choose the assessments. Fortunately, we don't have to make that choice.

The four main assessments we use are the Myers-Briggs Type Indicator (MBTI), the Workplace Personality Inventory, the Team Dimensions Profile, and Stratified Systems Theory.[33] But we are constantly experimenting (for example, with the Big Five) so our mix will certainly change. Whatever the mix, they all convey people's preferences for thinking and action. They also provide us with new attributes and terminologies that clarify and amplify those we had identified on our own. I will describe a few of them below. These descriptions are based on my own experiences and learnings, which are in many ways different from the official descriptions used by the assessment companies.[34]

a. **Introversion vs. extroversion.** Introverts focus on the inner world and get their energy from ideas, memories, and experiences while extroverts are externally focused and get their energy from being with people. Introversion and extroversion are also linked to differences in communication styles. If you have a friend who loves to "talk out" ideas (and even has trouble thinking through something if there isn't someone around to work it through with), he or she is likely an extrovert. Introverts will usually find such conversations painful, preferring to think privately and share only after they've worked things out on their own. I've found that it is important to help each communicate in the way that they feel most comfortable. For example, introverts often prefer communicating in writing (such as email) rather than speaking in group settings and tend to be less open with their critical thoughts.

b. **Intuiting vs. sensing.** Some people see big pictures (forests) and others see details (trees). In the Myers-Briggs framework, these ways of seeing are best represented by the continuum from intuiting to sensing. You can get an idea of people's preferences by observing what they focus on. For example, when reading, a sensing person who focuses on details can be thrown off by typos such as "there" instead of "their," while intuitive thinkers won't even notice the mistake. That is

---

[33] This test is helpful for seeing how people navigate levels and which levels they naturally go to.
[34] If you'd like to experience some of these assessments for yourself and see your own results, visit assessments.principles.com.

because the intuitive thinker's attention is focused on the context first and the details second. Naturally, you'd rather have a sensing person than an intuitor preparing your legal documents, where every "i" must be properly dotted and every "t" crossed just so.

c. Thinking vs. feeling. Some people make decisions based on logical analysis of objective facts, considering all the known, provable factors important to a given situation and using logic to determine the best course of action. This approach is an indicator of a preference for thinking and is how you'd hope your doctor thinks when he makes a diagnosis. Other people—who prefer feeling—focus on harmony between people. They are better suited to roles that require lots of empathy, interpersonal contact, and relationship building, for example HR and customer service. Before we had assessments to identify these differences, conversations between "Ts" and "Fs" were really frustrating. Now we laugh as we bump up against our differences, because we know what they are and can see them playing out in classic ways.

d. Planning vs. perceiving. Some people like to live in a planned, orderly way and others prefer flexibility and spontaneity.[35] Planners (or "Judgers" in Myers-Briggs terms) like to focus on a plan and stick with it, while perceivers are prone to focus on what's happening around them and adapt to it. Perceivers work from the outside in; they see things happening and work backward to understand the cause and how to respond; they also see many possibilities that they compare and choose from—often so many that they are confused by them. In contrast, planners work from the inside out, first figuring out what they want to achieve and then how things should unfold. Planners and perceivers have trouble appreciating each other. Perceivers see new things and change direction often. This is discomforting to planners, who weigh precedent much more heavily in their decision making, and assume if it was done in a certain way before, it should

---

[35] On the MBTI scale, this continuum is described as "Judging" vs. "Perceiving" though I prefer to use "Planning" as judging has other connotations. In MBTI language, judging does not mean judgmental and perceiving does not mean perceptive.

be done in the same way again. Similarly, planners can discomfort perceivers by being seemingly rigid and slow to adapt.

e. Creators vs. refiners vs. advancers vs. executors vs. flexors. By identifying talents and preferences that lead people to feel a particular way, you can place them in jobs at which they will likely excel. At Bridgewater, we use a test called the "Team Dimensions Profile" (TDP) to connect people with their preferred role. The five types identified by the TDP are Creators, Refiners, Advancers, Executors, and Flexors.

- **Creators** generate new ideas and original concepts. They prefer unstructured and abstract activities and thrive on innovation and unconventional practices.
- **Advancers** communicate these new ideas and carry them forward. They relish feelings and relationships and manage the human factors. They are excellent at generating enthusiasm for work.
- **Refiners** challenge ideas. They analyze projects for flaws, then refine them with a focus on objectivity and analysis. They love facts and theories and working with a systematic approach.
- **Executors** can also be thought of as **Implementers**. They ensure that important activities are carried out and goals accomplished; they are focused on details and the bottom line.
- **Flexors** are a combination of all four types. They can adapt their styles to fit certain needs and are able to look at a problem from a variety of perspectives.

Triangulating what I learn from each test reinforces or raises questions about the pictures of people I'm forming in my head. For example, when people's MBTI results suggest a preference for "S" (focus on details) and "J" (planful), and they come out as executors on the Team Dimension assessment, there is a very good chance that they are more detail-focused than right-brained and imaginative, which means that they would likely fit better in jobs that have less ambiguity and more structure and clarity.

f. Focusing on tasks vs. focusing on goals. Some people are focused on daily tasks while others are focused on their goals and how to achieve them. I've found these differences to be quite similar to the differences between people who are intuitive vs. sensing. Those who tend to focus on goals and "visualize" best can see the big pictures over time and are also more likely to make meaningful changes and anticipate future events. These goal-oriented people can step back from the day-to-day and reflect on what and how they're doing. They are the most suitable for creating new things (organizations, projects, etc.) and managing organizations that have lots of change. They typically make the most visionary leaders because of their ability to take a broad view and see the whole picture.

In contrast, those who tend to focus on daily tasks are better at managing things that don't change much or that require processes to be completed reliably. Task-oriented people tend to make incremental changes that reference what already exists. They are slower to depart from the status quo and more likely to be blindsided by sudden events. On the other hand, they're typically more reliable. Although it may seem that their focus is narrower than higher-level thinkers, the roles they play are no less critical. I would never have gotten this book out or accomplished hardly anything else worthwhile if I didn't work with people who are wonderful at taking care of details.

g. Workplace Personality Inventory. Another assessment we use is the Workplace Personality Inventory, a test based on data from the U.S. Department of Labor. It anticipates behavior and predicts job fit and satisfaction, singling out certain key characteristics/qualities, including persistence, independence, stress tolerance, and analytical thinking. This test helps us understand what people value and how they will make trade-offs between their values. For example, someone with low Achievement Orientation and high Concern for Others might be unwilling to step on others' toes in order to accomplish their goals. Likewise, someone who is bad at Rule Following may be more likely to think independently.

We have found that something like twenty-five to fifty attributes can pretty well describe what a person is like. Each one comes in varying degrees of strength (like color tones). If you know what they are and put them together correctly, they will paint a pretty complete picture of a person. Our objective is to use test results and other information to try to do just that. We prefer to do it in partnership with the person being looked at, because it helps us be more accurate and at the same time it's very helpful to them to see themselves objectively.

Certain attributes combine frequently to produce recognizable archetypes. If you think about it, you can probably come up with a handful of archetypal people you meet over and over again in life: the spacey, impractical Artist; the tidy Perfectionist; the Crusher who runs through brick walls to get things done; the Visionary who pulls amazing big ideas seemingly out of the air. Over time I came up with a list of others, including Shaper, Chirper, Tweaker, and Open-Minded Learner, as well as Advancer, Creator, Cat-Herder, Gossiper, Loyal Doer, Wise Judge, and others.

To be clear, archetypes are less useful than the better fleshed-out pictures created through the assessments. They are not precise; they are more like simple caricatures, but they can be useful when it comes to assembling teams. Individual people will always be more complex than the archetypes that describe them, and they may well match up with more than one. For example, the Spacey Artist may or may not also be a Perfectionist or may be a Crusher too. While I won't go over all of them, I will describe Shapers—the one that best represents me—in some depth.

h. Shapers are people who can go from visualization to actualization. I wrote a lot about the people I call "shapers" in the first part of this book. I use the word to mean someone who comes up with unique and valuable visions and builds them out beautifully, typically over the doubts of others. Shapers get both the big picture and the details right. To me, it seems that Shaper = Visionary + Practical Thinker + Determined.

I've found that shapers tend to share attributes such as intense curiosity and a compulsive need to make sense of things, independent thinking that verges on rebelliousness, a need to dream big and unconventionally, a practicality and determination to push through all obstacles to achieve their goals, and a knowledge of their own and others' weaknesses and strengths so they can orchestrate teams to achieve them. Perhaps even more importantly, they can hold conflicting thoughts simultaneously and look at them from different angles. They typically love to knock things around with other really smart people and can easily navigate back and forth between the big picture and the granular details, counting both as equally important.

People wired with enough of these ways of thinking that they can operate in the world as shapers are very rare. But they could never succeed without working with others who are more naturally suited for other things and whose ways of thinking and acting are also essential.

Knowing how one is wired is a necessary first step on any life journey. It doesn't matter what you do with your life, as long as you are doing what is consistent with your nature and your aspirations. Having spent time with some of the richest, most powerful, most admired people in the world, as well as some of the poorest, most disadvantaged people in the most obscure corners of the globe, I can assure you that, beyond a basic level, there is no correlation between happiness levels and conventional markers of success. A carpenter who derives his deepest satisfaction from working with wood can easily have a life as good or better than the president of the United States. If you've learned anything from this book I hope it's that everyone has strengths and weaknesses, and everyone has an important role to play in life. Nature made everything and everyone for a purpose. The courage that's needed the most isn't the kind that drives you to prevail over others, but the kind that allows you to be true to your truest self, no matter what other people want you to be.

4.5 Getting the right people in the right roles in support of your goal is the key to succeeding at whatever you choose to accomplish.

Whether it's in your private life or your work life, it is best for you to work with others in such a way that each person is matched up with other complementary people to create the best mix of attributes for their tasks.

a. Manage yourself and orchestrate others to get what you want. Your greatest challenge will be having your thoughtful higher-level you manage your emotional lower-level you. The best way to do that is to consciously develop habits that will make doing the things that are good for you habitual. In managing others, the analogy that comes to mind is a great orchestra. The person in charge is the shaper-conductor who doesn't "do" (e.g., doesn't play an instrument, though he or she knows a lot about instruments) as much as visualize the outcome and sees to it that each member of the orchestra helps achieve it. The conductor makes sure each member of the orchestra knows what he or she is good at and what they're not good at, and what their responsibilities are. Each must not only perform at their personal best but work together so the orchestra becomes more than the sum of its parts. One of the conductor's hardest and most thankless jobs is getting rid of people who consistently don't play well individually or with others. Most importantly, the conductor ensures that the score is executed exactly as he or she hears it in his or her head. "The music needs to sound this way," she says, and then she makes sure it does. "Bass players, bring out the structure. Here are the connections, here's the spirit." Each section of the orchestra has its own leaders—the concertmaster, the first chairs—who also help bring out the composer's and the conductor's visions.

Approaching things in this way has helped me a lot. For example, with the bond systemization project I mentioned earlier, having this new perspective allowed us to better see the gaps between what we had and what we needed. While Bob was a great intellectual partner to me in understanding the big-picture problem we wanted to solve, he was much weaker at visualizing the process required to get us from where we were to the solution. He also wasn't surrounding himself with the right people. He tended to want to work with people who were like him, so his main deputy on the project was a great sparring partner for mapping out big ideas on a whiteboard but a lousy one for fleshing out the who, what, and when needed to bring those ideas to life. This deputy tested as a "Flexor," meaning that he was great at going in whatever direction Bob wanted to but lacked the clear, independent view needed to keep Bob on track.

After a few rounds of not making progress, we used our new tools for understanding people and acted on them, pushing Bob to transition to a new deputy who was especially skilled at navigating the levels between the big-picture ideas and the discrete, smaller projects required to bring them about. Comparing the new deputy's Baseball Card to the original deputy's, she excelled in independent and systematic thinking, which were essential for having a clear picture of what to do with Bob's big ideas. This new deputy brought on other layers of support, including a project manager who was less engaged with the concepts and much more focused on the details of specific tasks and deadlines. When we looked at the new team members' Baseball Cards, we could quickly see them lighting up in some of the areas around being planful, concrete, and driving things to completion, which were areas of weakness for Bob. With this new team in place, things really started to hum. It was only by looking hard at the complete "Lego set" required to achieve our goal—and then going out and finding the missing pieces—that we were able to do it.

Bond systemization is just one of countless projects that have benefited from our frank and open approach to understanding what people are like. And to be clear, I have just scratched the surface of what there is to know about mental wiring.

In the next chapter, I'll bring everything you've read about up to now together and break down the essentials of decision making. Some decisions you should make yourself and some you should delegate to someone more believable. Using self-knowledge to know which are which is the key to success—no matter what it is you are trying to do.

5 Learn How to Make Decisions Effectively

As a professional decision maker, I have spent my life studying how to make decisions effectively and have constantly looked for rules and systems that will improve my odds of being right and ending up with more of whatever it is that I am after.

One of the most important things I've come to understand is that most of the processes that go into everyday decision making are subconscious and more complex than is widely understood. For example, think about how you choose and maintain a safe distance behind the car in front of you when you are driving. Now describe the process in enough detail that someone who has never driven a car before can do it as well as you can, or so that it can be programmed into the computer that controls an autonomous car. I bet you can't.

Now think about the challenge of making all of your decisions well, in a systematic, repeatable way, and then being able to describe the processes so clearly and precisely that anyone else can make the same quality decisions under the same circumstances. That is what I aspire to do and have found to be invaluable, even when highly imperfect.

While there is no one best way to make decisions, there are some universal rules for good decision making. They start with:

5.1 Recognize that 1) the biggest threat to good decision making is harmful emotions, and 2) decision making is a two-step process (first learning and then deciding).

Learning must come before deciding. As explained in Chapter One, your brain stores different types of learning in your subconscious, your rote memory bank, and your habits. But no matter how you acquire your knowledge or where you store it, what's most important is that what you know paints a true and rich picture of the realities that will affect your decision. That's why it always pays to be radically open-minded and seek out believable others as you do your learning. Many people have emotional trouble doing this and block the learning that could help them make better decisions. Remind yourself that it's never harmful to at least hear an opposing point of view.

Deciding is the process of choosing which knowledge should be drawn upon—both the facts of this particular "what is" and your broader understanding of the cause-effect machinery that underlies it—and then weighing them to determine a course of action, the "what to do about it." This involves playing different scenarios through time to visualize how to get an outcome consistent with what you want. To do this well, you need to weigh first-order consequences against second- and third-order consequences, and base your decisions not just on near-term results but on results over time.

Failing to consider second- and third-order consequences is the cause of a lot of painfully bad decisions, and it is especially deadly when the first inferior option confirms your own biases. Never seize on the first available option, no matter how good it seems, before you've asked questions and explored. To prevent myself from falling into this trap, I used to literally ask myself questions: Am I learning? Have I learned enough yet that it's time for deciding? After a while, you will just naturally and open-mindedly gather all the relevant info, but in doing so you will have avoided the first pitfall of bad decision making, which is to subconsciously make the decision first and then cherry-pick the data that supports it.

But how does one learn well?

LEARNING WELL

For me, getting an accurate picture of reality ultimately comes down to two things: being able to synthesize accurately and knowing how to navigate levels.

Synthesis is the process of converting a lot of data into an accurate picture. The quality of your synthesis will determine the quality of your decision making. This is why it always pays to triangulate your views with people who you know synthesize well. This raises your chances of having a good synthesis, even if you feel like you've already done it yourself. No sensible person should reject a believable person's views without great fear of being wrong.

To synthesize well, you must 1) synthesize the situation at hand, 2) synthesize the situation through time, and 3) navigate levels effectively.

5.2 Synthesize the situation at hand.

Every day you are faced with an infinite number of things that come at you. Let's call them "dots." To be effective, you need to be able to tell which dots are important and which dots are not. Some people go through life collecting all kinds of observations and opinions like pocket lint, instead of just keeping what they need. They have "detail anxiety," worrying about unimportant things.

Sometimes small things can be important—for example, that little rattle in your car's engine could just be a loose piece of plastic or it could be a sign your timing belt is about to snap. The key is having the higher-level perspective to make fast and accurate judgments on what the real risks are without getting bogged down in details.

Remember:

a. One of the most important decisions you can make is who you ask questions of. Make sure they're fully informed and believable. Find out who is responsible for whatever you are seeking to understand and then ask them. Listening to uninformed people is worse than having no answers at all.

b. Don't believe everything you hear. Opinions are a dime a dozen and nearly everyone will share theirs with you. Many will state them as if they are facts. Don't mistake opinions for facts.

c. Everything looks bigger up close. In all aspects of life, what's happening today seems like a much bigger deal than it will appear in retrospect. That's why it helps to step back to gain perspective and sometimes defer a decision until some time passes.

d. New is overvalued relative to great. For example, when choosing which movie to watch or what book to read, are you drawn to proven classics or the newest big thing? In my opinion, it is smarter to choose the great over the new.

e. Don't oversqueeze dots. A dot is just one piece of data from one moment in time; keep that in perspective as you synthesize. Just as you need to sort big from small, and what's happening in the moment from overall patterns, you need to know how much learning you can get out of any one dot without overweighing it.

5.3 Synthesize the situation through time.

To see how the dots connect through time you must collect, analyze, and sort different types of information, which isn't easy. For example, let's imagine a day in which eight outcomes occur. Some are good, some bad. Let's illustrate this day as shown, with each type of event represented by a letter and the quality of the outcome represented by its height.

In order to see the day this way, you must categorize outcomes by type (signified by letters) and quality (the higher up the graph, the better), which will require synthesizing a by-and-large assessment of each. (To make the example more concrete, imagine you're running an ice cream shop and the W's represent sales, the X's represent customer experience ratings, the Y's represent press and reviews, the Z's represent staff engagement, etc.) Keep in mind that our example is a relatively simple one: just eight occurrences over one day.

From the chart on the right, you can see that it was a great day for sales (because the W's are at the top) and a bad day for customer experience (the X's). You might conjecture why—maybe a crowd generated sales but produced long lines.

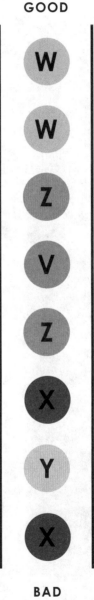

GOOD

BAD

Now let's look at what a month of workdays looks like. Confusing, eh?

GOOD

GOODNESS
OF OUTCOME

BAD

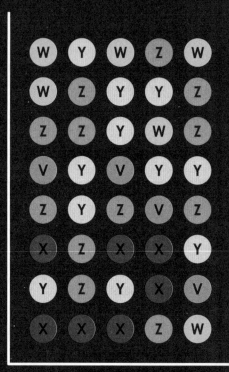

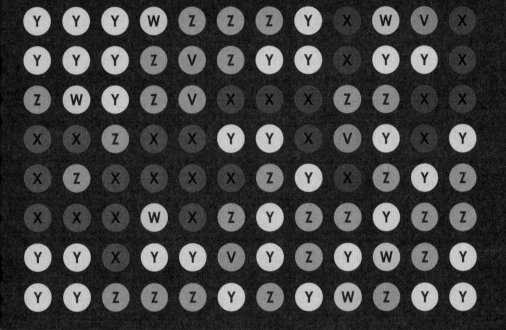

TIME

The chart below plots just the type X dots,
which you can see are improving.

GOOD

GOODNESS
OF OUTCOME

BAD

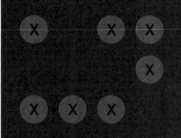

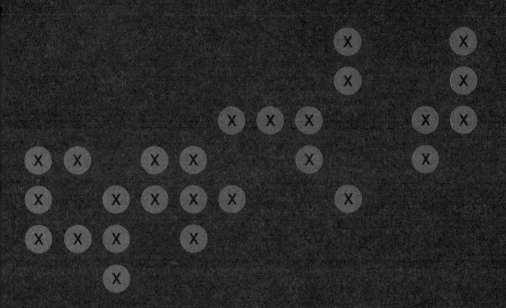

TIME

People who are good at pulling out such patterns of events are rare and essential, but as with most abilities, synthesizing through time is only partially innate; even if you're not good at it, you can get better through practice. You'll increase your chances of succeeding at it if you follow the next principle.

a. Keep in mind both the rates of change and the levels of things, and the relationships between them. When determining an acceptable rate of improvement for something, it is its level in relation to the rate of change that matters. I often see people lose sight of this. They say "it's getting better" without noticing how far below the bar it is and whether the rate of change will get it above the bar in an acceptable amount of time. If someone who has been getting grades of 30s and 40s on their tests raised their scores to 50s over the course of a few months it would be accurate to say that they are getting better, but they would still be woefully inadequate. Everything important in your life needs to be on a trajectory to be above the bar and headed toward excellent at an appropriate pace. The lines in the chart on the next page show how the dots connect through time. A's trajectory gets you above the bar in an appropriate amount of time; B's does not. To make good decisions, you need to understand the reality of which of these two cases is happening.

b. Be imprecise. Understand the concept of "by-and-large" and use approximations. Because our educational system is hung up on precision, the art of being good at approximations is insufficiently valued. This impedes conceptual thinking. For example, when asked to multiply 38 by 12, most people do it the slow and hard way rather than simply rounding 38 up to 40, rounding 12 down to 10, and quickly determining that the answer is about 400. Look at the ice cream shop example and imagine the value of quickly seeing the approximate relationships between the dots versus taking the time to see all the edges precisely. It would be silly to spend time doing that, yet that's exactly what most people do. "By-and-large" is the level at which you need to understand most things in order to make effec-

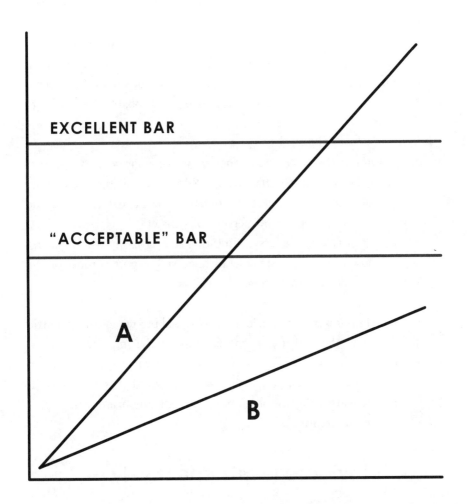

tive decisions. Whenever a big-picture "by-and-large" statement is made and someone replies "Not always," my instinctual reaction is that we are probably about to dive into the weeds—i.e., into a discussion of the exceptions rather than the rule, and in the process we will lose sight of the rule. To help people at Bridgewater avoid this time waster, one of our just-out-of-college associates coined a saying I often repeat: "When you ask someone whether something is true and they tell you that it's not totally true, it's probably by-and-large true."

c. Remember the 80/20 Rule and know what the key 20 percent is. The 80/20 Rule states that you get 80 percent of the value out of something from 20 percent of the information or effort. (It's also true that you're likely to exert 80 percent of your effort getting the final 20 percent of value.) Understanding this rule saves you from getting bogged down in unnecessary detail once you've gotten most of the learning you need to make a good decision.

d. Be an imperfectionist. Perfectionists spend too much time on little differences at the margins at the expense of the important things. There are typically just five to ten important factors to consider when making a decision. It is important to understand these really well, though the marginal gains of studying even the important things past a certain point are limited.

5.4 Navigate levels effectively.

Reality exists at different levels and each of them gives you different but valuable perspectives. It's important to keep all of them in mind as you synthesize and make decisions, and to know how to navigate between them.

Let's say you're looking at your hometown on Google Maps. Zoom in close enough to see the buildings and you won't be able to see the region surrounding your town, which can tell you important things. Maybe your town sits next to a body of water. Zoom in too close and you won't be able to tell if the shoreline is along a river, a lake, or an ocean. You need to know which level is appropriate to your decision.

We are constantly seeing things at different levels and navigating between them, whether we know it or not, whether we do it well or not, and whether our objects are physical things, ideas, or goals. For example, you can navigate levels to move from your values to what you do to realize them on a day-to-day basis. This is what that looks like in outline:

1 The High-Level Big Picture: I want meaningful work that's full of learning.

  1.1 Subordinate Concept: I want to be a doctor.

    • **Sub-Point:** I need to go to medical school.

      • **Sub-Sub Point:** I need to get good grades in the sciences.

        • **Sub-Sub-Sub Point:** I need to stay home tonight and study.

To observe how well you do this in your own life, pay attention to your conversations. We tend to move between levels when we talk.

a. Use the terms "above the line" and "below the line" to establish which level a conversation is on. An above-the-line conversation addresses the main points and a below-the-line conversation focuses on the sub-points. When a line of reasoning is jumbled and confusing, it's often because the speaker has gotten caught up in below-the-line details without connecting them back to the major points. An above-the-line discourse should progress in an orderly and accurate way to its conclusion, only going below the line when it's necessary to illustrate something about one of the major points.

b. Remember that decisions need to be made at the appropriate level, but they should also be consistent across levels. For instance,

GOOD

A → B → C → D → E → F → G → SYNTHESIS

1	1	1	1	1	1	1
2	2	2	2	2	2	2
3	3	3	3	3	3	3
4	4	4	4	4	4	4
5	5	5	5	5	5	5

A BIGGER SEQUENCE THAT WORKS

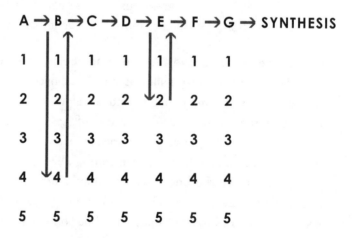

A LOGICAL SEQUENCE THAT EXPLORES
SPECIFICS AND WORKS

BAD

A RANDOM STORY THAT GETS DERAILED

NO SYNTHESIS

A STORY THAT PLUNGES INTO THE WEEDS

if you want to have a healthy life, you shouldn't have twelve sausage links and a beer every day for breakfast. In other words, you need to constantly connect and reconcile the data you're gathering at different levels in order to draw a complete picture of what's going on. Like synthesizing in general, some people are naturally better at this than others, but anyone can learn to do this to one degree or another. To do it well, it's necessary to:

1. Remember that multiple levels exist for all subjects.
2. Be aware on what level you're examining a given subject.
3. Consciously navigate levels rather than see subjects as undifferentiated piles of facts that can be browsed randomly.
4. Diagram the flow of your thought processes using the outline template shown on the previous page.

When you do all this with radical open-mindedness, you will become more aware not just of what you're seeing, but what you're not seeing and what others, perhaps, are. It's a little like when jazz musicians jam; knowing what level you're on allows everyone to play in the same key. When you know your own way of seeing and are open to others' ways too, you can create good conceptual jazz together rather than just screech at each other. Now let's go up a level and examine deciding.

DECIDE WELL

Using decision-making logic to produce the best long-term outcomes has become its own science—one that employs probabilities and statistics, game theory, and other tools. While many of these tools are helpful, the fundamentals of effective decision making are relatively simple and timeless—in fact they are genetically encoded in our brains to varying degrees. Watch animals in the wild and you'll see that they instinctively make expected value calculations to optimize the energy they expend to find food. Those that did this well prospered and passed on their genes through the process of natural selection; those that did it poorly perished. While most humans who do this badly won't perish, they will certainly be penalized by the process of economic selection.

As previously explained, there are two broad approaches to decision making: evidence/logic-based (which comes from the higher-level brain) and subconscious/emotion-based (which comes from the lower-level animal brain).

5.5 Logic, reason, and common sense are your best tools for synthesizing reality and understanding what to do about it.

Be wary of relying on anything else. Unfortunately, numerous tests by psychologists show that the majority of people follow the lower-level path most of the time, which leads to inferior decisions without their realizing it. As Carl Jung put it, "Until you make the unconscious conscious, it will direct your life and you will call it fate." It's even more important that decision making be evidence-based and logical when groups of people are working together. If it's not, the process will inevitably be dominated by the most powerful rather than the most insightful participants, which is not only unfair but suboptimal. Successful organizations have cultures in which evidence-based decision making is the norm rather than the exception.

5.6 Make your decisions as expected value calculations.

Think of every decision as a bet with a probability and a reward for being right and a probability and a penalty for being wrong. Normally a winning decision is one with a positive expected value, meaning that the reward times its probability of occurring is greater than the penalty times its probability of occurring, with the best decision being the one with the highest expected value.

Let's say the reward for being right is $100 and its probability is 60 percent, while the penalty for being wrong is also $100. If you multiply the reward by the probability of being right you get $60 and if you multiply the penalty by the probability of being wrong (40 percent) you get $40. If you subtract the penalty from the reward, the difference is the expected value, which in this case is positive (+$20). Once you understand expected value, you also understand that it's not always best to bet on what's most probable. For example, suppose something that has only a one-in-five chance (20 percent) of succeeding will return ten times (e.g., $1,000) the amount that it will cost you if it fails ($100). Its expected value is positive ($120), so it's probably a smart decision, even though the odds are against you, as long as you can also cover the loss. Play these probabilities over and over again and they will surely give you winning results over time.

Though we mostly don't carry out these calculations explicitly, we constantly make them intuitively. For example, when you decide to take an umbrella to the store even though there's just a 40 percent chance of rain, or you check your phone to confirm the directions somewhere, even though you're almost certain you know the way, you're making expected value calculations.

Sometimes it's smart to take a chance even when the odds are overwhelmingly against you if the cost of being wrong is negligible relative to the reward that comes with the slim chance of being right. As the saying goes, "It never hurts to ask."

This principle made a big difference in my own life. Years ago, when I was just starting my family, I saw a house that was perfect for us in every way. The problem was that it wasn't on the market and everyone I asked told me the owner wasn't interested in selling. To make matters worse, I was pretty sure I would be turned down for an adequate mortgage. But I figured that it wouldn't cost me anything to call the owner to see if we could work something out.

As it turned out, not only was he willing to sell, he was willing to give me a loan!

The same principle applies when the downside is terrible. For example, even if the probability of your having cancer is low, it might pay to get yourself tested when you have a symptom just to make sure.

To help you make expected value calculations well, remember that:

a. Raising the probability of being right is valuable no matter what your probability of being right already is. I often observe people making decisions if their odds of being right are greater than 50 percent. What they fail to see is how much better off they'd be if they raised their chances even more (you can almost always improve your odds of being right by doing things that will give you more information). The expected value gain from raising the probability of being right from 51 percent to 85 percent (i.e., by 34 percentage points) is seventeen times more than raising the odds of being right from 49 percent (which is probably wrong) to 51 percent (which is only a little more likely to be right). Think of the probability as a measure of how often you're likely to be wrong. Raising the probability of being right by 34 percentage points means that a third of your bets will switch from losses to wins. That's why it pays to stress-test your thinking, even when you're pretty sure you're right.

b. Knowing when not to bet is as important as knowing what bets are probably worth making. You can significantly improve your track record if you only make the bets that you are most confident will pay off.

c. The best choices are the ones that have more pros than cons, not those that don't have any cons at all. Watch out for people who argue against something whenever they can find something—anything—wrong with it, without properly weighing all the pluses and minuses. Such people tend to be poor decision makers.

5.7 Prioritize by weighing the value of additional information against the cost of not deciding.

Some decisions are best made after acquiring more information; some are best made immediately. Just as you need to constantly sort the big from the small when you are synthesizing what's going on, you need to constantly evaluate the marginal benefit of gathering more information against the marginal cost of waiting to decide. People who prioritize well understand the following:

a. All of your "must-dos" must be above the bar before you do your "like-to-dos." Separate your "must-dos" from your "like-to-dos" and don't mistakenly slip any "like-to-dos" onto the first list.

b. Chances are you won't have time to deal with the unimportant things, which is better than not having time to deal with the important things. I often hear people say, "Wouldn't it be good to do this or that?" It's likely they are being distracted from far more important things that need to be done well.

c. Don't mistake possibilities for probabilities. Anything is possible. It's the probabilities that matter. Everything must be weighed in terms of its likelihood and prioritized. People who can accurately sort probabilities from possibilities are generally strong at "practical thinking"; they're the opposite of the "philosopher" types who tend to get lost in clouds of possibilities.

SHORTCUTS FOR BECOMING A GREAT DECISION MAKER

Great decision makers don't remember all of these steps in a rote way and carry them out mechanically, yet they do follow them. That's because through time and experience they've learned to do most of them reflexively, just as a baseball player catches a fly ball without thinking about how he's going to do it. If they had to call each of the principles up from their memory and then run them through their slow conscious minds, they couldn't possibly handle all the things that are coming at them well. But there are a couple of things that they do carry out consciously and you should do them too.

5.8 Simplify!

Get rid of irrelevant details so that the essential things and the relationships between them stand out. As the saying goes, "Any damn fool can make it complex. It takes a genius to make it simple." Think of Picasso. He could paint beautiful representational paintings from an early age, but he continually pared down and simplified as his career progressed. Not everyone has a mind that works that way, but just because you can't do something naturally doesn't mean you can't do it—you just have to have creativity and determination. If necessary, you can seek the help of others.

5.9 Use principles.

Using principles is a way of both simplifying and improving your decision making. While it might seem obvious to you by now, it's worth repeating that realizing that almost all "cases at hand" are just "another one of those," identifying which "one of those" it is, and then applying well-thought-out principles for dealing with it will allow you to massively reduce the number of decisions you have to make (I estimate by a factor of something like 100,000) and will lead you to make much better ones. The key to doing this well is to:

1. Slow down your thinking so you can note the criteria you are using to make your decision.

2. Write the criteria down as a principle.

3. Think about those criteria when you have an outcome to assess, and refine them before the next "one of those" comes along.

Identifying which "one of those" each thing is is like identifying which species an animal is. Doing that for each thing and then matching it up with the appropriate principles will become like playing a game, so it will be fun as well as helpful. Of course it can also be challenging. Many "cases at hand," as I call them, are hybrids. When a case at hand contains a few "another ones of those," one must weigh different principles against each other, using mental maps of how the different types of things I encounter should be handled. To help people do that, I created a tool called a Coach, which is explained in the Appendix.

You can use your own principles, or you can use others'; you just want to use the best ones possible well. If you think that way constantly, you will become an excellent principled thinker.

5.10 Believability weight your decision making.

I have found triangulating with highly believable people who are willing to have thoughtful disagreements has never failed to enhance my learning and sharpen the quality of my decision making. It typically leads me to make better decisions than I could have otherwise and it typically provides me with thrilling learning. I urge you to do it.

To do it well, be sure to avoid the common perils of: 1) valuing your own believability more than is logical and 2) not distinguishing between who is more or less credible.

In case of a disagreement with others, start by seeing if you can agree on the principles that should be used to make that decision. This discussion should include exploring the merits of the reasoning behind the different principles. If you agree on them, apply them to the case at hand and you'll arrive at a conclusion everyone agrees on. If you disagree on the principles, try to work through your disagreement based on your respective believabilities. I will explain how we do this in more detail in Work Principles.

This sort of principled and believability-weighted decision making is fascinating and leads to much different and much better decision making than is typical. For example, imagine if we used this approach to choose the president. It would be fascinating to see which principles we would come up with both for determining what makes a good president as well as for deciding who is most believable in making such determinations. Would we wind up with something like one person one vote, or something different? And if different, in what ways? It certainly would lead to very different outcomes. During the next election, let's do this in parallel with our ordinary electoral process so we can see the difference.

While believability-weighted decision making can sound complicated, chances are you do it all the time—pretty much whenever you ask yourself, "Who should I listen to?" But it's almost certainly true that you'd do it a lot better if you gave more thought to it.

5.11 Convert your principles into algorithms and have the computer make decisions alongside you.

If you can do that, you will take the power of your decision making to a whole other level. In many cases, you will be able to test how that principle would have worked in the past or in various situations that will help you refine it, and in all cases, it will allow you to compound your understanding to a degree that would otherwise be impossible. It will also take emotion out of the equation. Algorithms work just like words in describing what you would like to have done, but they are written in a language that the computer can understand. If you don't know how to speak this language, you should either learn it or have someone close to you who can translate for you. Your children and their peers must learn to speak this language because it will soon be as important or more important than any other language.

By developing a partnership with your computer alter ego in which you teach each other and each do what you do best, you will be much more powerful than if you went about your decision making alone. The computer will also be your link to great collective decision making, which is far more powerful than individual decision making, and will almost certainly advance the evolution of our species.

SYSTEMIZED AND COMPUTERIZED DECISION MAKING

In the future, artificial intelligence will have a profound impact on how we make decisions in every aspect of our lives—especially when combined with the new era of radical transparency about people that's already upon us. Right now, whether you like it or not, it is easy for anyone to access your digital data to learn a tremendous amount about what you're like, and this data can be fed into computers that do everything from predict what you're likely to buy to what you value in life. While this sounds scary to many people, at Bridgewater we have been combining radical transparency with algorithmic decision making for more than thirty years and have found that it produces remarkable results. In fact, I believe that it won't be long before this kind of computerized decision making guides us nearly as much as our brains do now.

The concept of artificial intelligence is not new. Even back in the 1970s, when I first started experimenting with computerized decision making, it had already been around for nearly twenty years (the term "artificial intelligence" was first introduced in 1956 at a conference at Dartmouth College). While a lot has changed since then, the basic concepts remain the same.

To give you just one ultrasimple example of how computerized decision making works, let's say you have two principles for heating

THINKING

↓

PRINCIPLES

↓

ALGORITHMS

↓

GREAT DECISIONS

your home: You want to turn the heat on when the temperature falls below 68 and you want to turn the heat off between midnight and 5:00 a.m. You can express the relationship between these criteria in a simple decision-making formula: *If* the temperature is less than 68 degrees *and* the time is not between 5:00 a.m. and midnight, *then* turn on the heat. By gathering many such formulas, it's possible to create a decision-making system that takes in data, applies and weighs the relevant criteria, and recommends a decision.

Specifying our investment decision-making criteria in algorithms and running historical data through them, or specifying our work principles in algorithms and using them to aid in management decision making, are just bigger and more complicated versions of that smart thermostat. They allow us to make more informed and less emotional decisions much faster than we could on our own.

I believe that people will increasingly do this and that computer coding will become as essential as writing. In time, we will use machine assistants as much for decision making as we do for information gathering today. As these machines help us, they will learn about what we are like—what we value, what our strengths and weaknesses are—and they will be able to tailor the advice they give us by automatically seeking out the help of others who are strong where we are weak. It won't be long before our machine assistants are speaking to others' machine assistants and collaborating in this way. In fact, that's beginning to happen already.

Imagine a world in which you can use technology to connect to a system in which you can input the issue you're dealing with and have exchanges about what you should do and why with the highest-rated thinkers in the world. We'll soon be able to do this. Before too long, you will be able to tap the highest-quality thinking on nearly every issue you face and get the guidance of a computerized system that weighs different points of view. For example, you will be able to ask what lifestyle or career you should choose given what you're like, or how to best interact with specific people based on what they're like. These innovations will help people get out of their own heads and unlock an incredibly powerful form of collective thinking. We are doing this now and have found it way better than traditional thinking.

While this kind of view often leads to talk of artificial intelligence competing with human intelligence, in my opinion human and artificial intelligence are far more likely to work together because that will produce the best results. It'll be decades—and maybe never—before the computer can replicate many of the things that the brain can do in terms of imagination, synthesis, and creativity. That's because the brain comes genetically programmed with millions of years of abilities honed through evolution. The "science" of decision making that underlies many computer systems remains much less valuable than the "art." People still make the most important decisions better than computers do. To see this, you need look no further than at the kinds of people who are uniquely successful. Software developers, mathematicians, and game-theory modelers aren't running away with all the rewards; it is the people who have the most common sense, imagination, and determination.

Only human intelligence can apply the interpretations that are required to provide computer models with appropriate input. For example, a computer can't tell you how to weigh the value of the time you spend with your loved ones against the time you spend at work or the optimal mix of hours that will provide you with the best marginal utilities for each activity. Only you know what you value most, who you want to share your life with, what kind of environment you want to be in, and ultimately how to make the best choices to bring those things about. What's more, so much of our thinking comes from the subconscious in ways we don't understand, that thinking we can model it fully is as unlikely as an animal that has never experienced abstract thinking attempting to define and replicate it.

Yet at the same time, the brain cannot compete with the computer in many ways. Computers have much greater "determination" than any person, as they will work 24/7 for you. They can process vastly more information, and they can do it much faster, more reliably, and more objectively than you could ever hope to. They can bring millions of possibilities that you never thought of to your attention.

Perhaps most important of all, they are immune to the biases and consensus-driven thinking of crowds; they don't care if what they see is unpopular, and they never panic. During those terrible days after 9/11, when the whole country was being whipsawed by emotion, or the weeks between September 19 and October 10, 2008, when the Dow fell 3,600 points, there were times I felt like hugging our computers. They kept their cool no matter what.

This combination of man and machine is wonderful. The process of man's mind working with technology is what elevates us—it's what has taken us from an economy where most people dig in the dirt to today's Information Age. It's for that reason that people who have common sense, imagination, and determination, who know what they value and what they want, and who *also* use computers, math, and game theory, are the best decision makers there are. At Bridgewater, we use our systems much as a driver uses a GPS in a car: not to substitute for our navigational abilities but to supplement them.

5.12 Be cautious about trusting AI without having deep understanding.

I worry about the dangers of AI in cases where users accept—or, worse, act upon—the cause-effect relationships presumed in algorithms produced by machine learning without understanding them deeply.

Before I explain why, I want to clarify my terms. "Artificial intelligence" and "machine learning" are words that are thrown around casually and often used as synonyms, even though they are quite different. I categorize what is going on in the world of computer-aided decision making under three broad types: expert systems, mimicking, and data mining (these categories are mine and not the ones in common use in the technology world).

Expert systems are what we use at Bridgewater, where designers specify criteria based on their logical understandings of a set of cause-effect relationships, and then see how different scenarios would emerge under different circumstances.

But computers can also observe patterns and apply them in their decision making without having any understanding of the logic behind them. I call such an approach "mimicking." This can be effective when the same things happen reliably over and over again and are not subject to change, such as in a game bounded by hard-and-fast rules. But in the real world things do change, so a system can easily fall out of sync with reality.

The main thrust of machine learning in recent years has gone in the direction of data mining, in which powerful computers ingest massive amounts of data and look for patterns. While this approach is popular, it's risky in cases when the future might be different from the past. Investment systems built on machine learning that is not accompanied by deep understanding are dangerous because when some decision rule is widely believed, it becomes widely used, which affects the price. In other words, the value of a widely known insight disappears over time. Without deep understanding, you won't know if what happened in the past is genuinely of value and, even if it was, you will not be able to know whether or not its value has disappeared—or worse. It's common for some decision rules to become so popular that they push the price far enough that it becomes smarter to do the opposite.

Remember that computers have no common sense. For example, a computer could easily misconstrue the fact that people wake up in the morning and then eat breakfast to indicate that waking up makes people hungry. I'd rather have fewer bets (ideally uncorrelated ones) in which I am highly confident than more bets I'm less confident in, and would consider it intolerable if I couldn't argue the logic behind any of my decisions. A lot of people vest their blind faith in machine learning because they find it much easier than developing deep understanding. For me, that deep understanding is essential, especially for what I do.

I don't mean to imply that these mimicking or data-mining systems, as I call them, are useless. In fact, I believe that they can be extremely useful in making decisions in which the future range and configuration of events are the same as they've been in the past.

Given enough computing power, all possible variables can be taken into consideration. For example, by analyzing data about the moves that great chess players have made under certain circumstances, or the procedures great surgeons have used during certain types of operations, valuable programs can be created for chess playing or surgery. Back in 1997, the computer program Deep Blue beat Garry Kasparov, the world's highest-ranked chess player, using just this approach. But this approach fails in cases where the future is different from the past and you don't know the cause-effect relationships well enough to recognize them all. Understanding these relationships as I do has saved me from making mistakes when others did, most obviously in the 2008 financial crisis. Nearly everyone else assumed that the future would be similar to the past. Focusing strictly on the logical cause-effect relationships was what allowed us to see what was really going on.

When you get down to it, our brains are essentially computers that are programmed in certain ways, take in data, and spit out instructions. We can program the logic in both the computer that is our mind and the computer that is our tool so that they can work together and even double-check each other. Doing that is fabulous.

For example, suppose we were trying to derive the universal laws that explain species change over time. Theoretically, with enough processing power and time, this should be possible. We would need to make sense of the formulas the computer produces, of course, to make sure that they are not data-mined gibberish, by which I mean based on correlations that are not causal in any way. We would do this by constantly simplifying these rules until their elegance is unmistakable.

Of course, given our brain's limited capacity and processing speed, it could take us forever to achieve a rich understanding of all the variables that go into evolution. Is all the simplifying and understanding that we employ in our expert systems truly required? Maybe not. There is certainly a risk that changes not in the tested data might still occur. But one might argue that if our data-mining-based formulas *seem* able to account for the evolution of all species through all time, then the risks of relying on them for just the next ten, twenty, or fifty years is relatively low compared to the benefits of having a formula that appears to work but is not fully understandable (and that, at the very least, might prove useful in helping scientists cure genetic diseases).

In fact, we may be too hung up on understanding; conscious thinking is only one part of understanding. Maybe it's enough that we derive a formula for change and use it to anticipate what is yet to come. I myself find the excitement, lower risk, and educational value of achieving a deep understanding of cause-effect relationships much more appealing than a reliance on algorithms I don't understand, so I am drawn to that path. But is it my lower-level preferences and habits that are pulling me in this direction or is it my logic and reason? I'm not sure. I look forward to probing the best minds in artificial intelligence on this (and having them probe me).

Most likely, our competitive natures will compel us to place bigger and bigger bets on relationships computers find that are beyond our understanding. Some of those bets will pay off, while others will backfire. I suspect that AI will lead to incredibly fast and remarkable advances, but I also fear that it could lead to our demise.

We are headed for an exciting and perilous new world. That's our reality. And as always, I believe that we are much better off preparing to deal with it than wishing it weren't true.

In order to have
the best life possible,
you have to:

1) know what the best
decisions are and

2) have the courage
to make them.

LIFE PRINCIPLES:
PUTTING IT ALL TOGETHER

I n Life Principles, I've explained some principles that helped me do both of these things. I believe that because the same kinds of things happen over and over again, a relatively few well-thought-out principles will allow you to deal with just about anything that reality throws at you. Where you get these principles from doesn't matter as much as having them and using them consistently—and that you never stop refining and improving them.

To acquire principles that work, it's essential that you **embrace reality and deal with it well**. Don't fall into the common trap of wishing that reality worked differently than it does or that your own realities were different. Instead, embrace your realities and deal with them effectively. After all, making the most of your circumstances is what life is all about. This includes being transparent with your thoughts and open-mindedly accepting the feedback of others. Doing so will dramatically increase your learning.

Along your journey you will inevitably experience painful failures. It is important to realize that they can either be the impetus that fuels your personal evolution or they can ruin you, depending on how you react to them. I believe that evolution is the greatest force in the universe and that we all evolve in basically the same way. Conceptually, it looks like a series of loops that either lead upward toward constant improvement or remain flat or even trend downward toward ruin. You will determine what your own loops look like.

Your evolutionary process can be described as a **5-Step Process for getting what you want**. It consists of setting goals, identifying and not tolerating problems, diagnosing problems, coming up with designs to get around them, and then doing the tasks required. The important thing to remember is that no one can do all the steps well, but that it's possible to rely on others to help. Different people with different abilities working well together create the most powerful machines to produce achievements.

If you're willing to confront reality, accept the pain that comes with doing so, and follow the 5-Step Process to drive yourself toward your goals, you're on the path to success. Yet most people fail to do this because they hold on to bad opinions that could easily be rectified by going above themselves to objectively look down at their situation and weigh what they and others think about it. It's for that reason I believe you must be **radically open-minded**.

Our biggest barriers for doing this well are our ego barrier and our blind spot barrier. The ego barrier is our innate desire to be capable and have others recognize us as such. The blind spot barrier is the result of our seeing things through our own subjective lenses; both barriers can prevent us from seeing how things really are. The most important antidote for them is radical open-mindedness, which is motivated by the genuine worry that one might not be seeing one's choices optimally. It is the ability to effectively explore different points of view and different possibilities without letting your ego or your blind spots get in your way.

Doing this well requires practicing thoughtful disagreement, which is the process of seeking out brilliant people who disagree with you in order to see things through their eyes and gain a deeper understanding. Doing this will raise your probability of making good decisions and will also give you a fabulous education. If you can learn radical open-mindedness and practice thoughtful disagreement, you'll radically increase your learning.

Finally, being radically open-minded requires you to have an accurate self-assessment of your own and others' strengths and weaknesses. This is where understanding something about how the brain works and the different psychometric assessments that can help you discover what your own brain is like comes in. To get the best results out of yourself and others, you must **understand that people are wired very differently.**

In a nutshell, learning how to make decisions in the best possible way and learning to have the courage to make them comes from a) going after what you want, b) failing and reflecting well through radical open-mindedness, and c) changing/evolving to become ever more capable and less fearful. In the final chapter of this section, Learn How to Make Decisions Effectively, I shared some more granular principles for how to do all of the above and weigh your options in specific situations to determine the right path to follow.

You can of course do all of these things alone, but if you've understood anything about the concept of radical open-mindedness, it should be obvious that going it alone will only take you so far. We all need others to help us triangulate and get to the best possible decisions—and to help us see our weaknesses objectively and compensate for them. More than anything else, your life is affected by the people around you and how you interact with each other.

Your ability to get what you want when working with others who want the same things is much greater than your ability to get these things by yourself. Yet we haven't talked about how groups should operate to be most effective. That's what we'll do in Work Principles.

Work Principles is about people working together. Because the power of a group is so much greater than the power of an individual, the principles that follow are likely even more important than those we covered up to this point. In fact, I wrote them first and then wrote Life Principles in order to help others make sense of the approach I was implicitly applying in running Bridgewater. My Work

Principles are basically the Life Principles you just read, applied to groups. I will show you, principle by principle, how an actual, practical, believability-weighted decision-making system converts independent thinking into effective group decision making. I believe that such a system can work to make any kind of organization—business, government, philanthropic—both more effective and more satisfying to belong to.

I hope these principles will help you struggle well and get all the joy you can out of life.

SUMMARY AND TABLE
OF LIFE PRINCIPLES

- Think for yourself to decide 1) what you want,   xi
2) what is true, and 3) what you should do to
achieve #1 in light of #2, and do that with humility
and open-mindedness so that you consider the
best thinking available to you.

LIFE PRINCIPLES INTRODUCTION
126

- Look to the patterns of those things that affect you   127
in order to understand the cause-effect relationships
that drive them and to learn principles for dealing
with them effectively.

PART II: LIFE PRINCIPLES
131

1	**Embrace Reality and Deal with It**	132
	1.1 **Be a hyperrealist.**	134
	a. Dreams + Reality + Determination = A Successful Life.	134
	1.2 **Truth—or, more precisely, an accurate understanding of reality —is the essential foundation for any good outcome.**	135
	1.3 **Be radically open-minded and radically transparent.**	136
	a. Radical open-mindedness and radical transparency are invaluable for rapid learning and effective change.	136
	b. Don't let fears of what others think of you stand in your way.	137
	c. Embracing radical truth and radical transparency will bring more meaningful work and more meaningful relationships.	137
	1.4 **Look to nature to learn how reality works.**	138
	a. Don't get hung up on your views of how things "should" be because you will miss out on learning how they really are.	140
	b. To be "good," something must operate consistently with the laws of reality and contribute to the evolution of the whole; that is what is most rewarded.	141
	c. Evolution is the single greatest force in the universe; it is the only thing that is permanent and it drives everything.	142
	d. Evolve or die.	145

1.5 Evolving is life's greatest accomplishment and its greatest   147
reward.
    a. The individual's incentives must be aligned with the group's   148
      goals.
    b. Reality is optimizing for the whole—not for you.   148
    c. Adaptation through rapid trial and error is invaluable.   148
    d. Realize that you are simultaneously everything and nothing   149
      —and decide what you want to be.
    e. What you will be will depend on the perspective you have.   149

1.6 Understand nature's practical lessons.   150
    a. Maximize your evolution.   150
    b. Remember "no pain, no gain."   152
    c. It is a fundamental law of nature that in order to gain   152
      strength one has to push one's limits, which is painful.

1.7 Pain + Reflection = Progress.   152
    a. Go to the pain rather than avoid it.   153
    b. Embrace tough love.   154

1.8 Weigh second- and third-order consequences.   155

1.9 Own your outcomes.   156

1.10 Look at the machine from the higher level.   157
    a. Think of yourself as a machine operating within a machine   157
      and know that you have the ability to alter your machines to
      produce better outcomes.
    b. By comparing your outcomes with your goals, you can   157
      determine how to modify your machine.
    c. Distinguish between you as the designer of your machine   159
      and you as a worker with your machine.
    d. The biggest mistake most people make is to not see   159
      themselves and others objectively, which leads them to
      bump into their own and others' weaknesses again and again.
    e. Successful people are those who can go above themselves to   159
      see things objectively and manage those things to shape change.
    f. Asking others who are strong in areas where you are weak   161
      to help you is a great skill that you should develop no matter
      what, as it will help you develop guardrails that will
      prevent you from doing what you shouldn't be doing.
    g. Because it is difficult to see oneself objectively, you need to   161
      rely on the input of others and the whole body of evidence.
    h. If you are open-minded enough and determined, you can   161
      get virtually anything you want.

2 Use the 5-Step Process to Get What You Want Out of Life
168

2.1 Have clear goals. 172
  a. Prioritize: While you can have virtually anything you want, you can't have everything you want. 172
  b. Don't confuse goals with desires. 172
  c. Decide what you really want in life by reconciling your goals and your desires. 172
  d. Don't mistake the trappings of success for success itself. 173
  e. Never rule out a goal because you think it's unattainable. 173
  f. Remember that great expectations create great capabilities. 173
  g. Almost nothing can stop you from succeeding if you have a) flexibility and b) self-accountability. 173
  h. Knowing how to deal well with your setbacks is as important as knowing how to move forward. 173

2.2 Identify and don't tolerate problems. 174
  a. View painful problems as potential improvements that are screaming at you. 174
  b. Don't avoid confronting problems because they are rooted in harsh realities that are unpleasant to look at. 174
  c. Be specific in identifying your problems. 174
  d. Don't mistake a cause of a problem with the real problem. 175
  e. Distinguish big problems from small ones. 175
  f. Once you identify a problem, don't tolerate it. 175

2.3 Diagnose problems to get at their root causes. 175
  a. Focus on the "what is" before deciding "what to do about it." 175
  b. Distinguish proximate causes from root causes. 176
  c. Recognize that knowing what someone (including you) is like will tell you what you can expect from them. 176

2.4 Design a plan. 176
  a. Go back before you go forward. 176
  b. Think about your problem as a set of outcomes produced by a machine. 176
  c. Remember that there are typically many paths to achieving your goals. 177
  d. Think of your plan as being like a movie script in that you visualize who will do what through time. 177
  e. Write down your plan for everyone to see and to measure your progress against. 177
  f. Recognize that it doesn't take a lot of time to design a good plan. 177

2.5 Push through to completion. 177
  a. Great planners who don't execute their plans go nowhere. 177
  b. Good work habits are vastly underrated. 178
  c. Establish clear metrics to make certain that you are following your plan. 178

2.6 **Remember that weaknesses don't matter if you find solutions.**   178
  a. Look at the patterns of your mistakes and identify at which   179
  step in the 5-Step Process you typically fail.
  b. Everyone has at least one big thing that stands in the way   179
  of their success; find yours and deal with it.

2.7 **Understand your own and others' mental maps and humility.**   180

3 Be Radically Open-Minded   182

3.1 **Recognize your two barriers.**   183
  a. Understand your ego barrier.   183
  b. Your two "yous" fight to control you.   184
  c. Understand your blind spot barrier.   185

3.2 **Practice radical open-mindedness.**   187
  a. Sincerely believe that you might not know the best possible   188
  path and recognize that your ability to deal well with "not
  knowing" is more important than whatever it is you do know.
  b. Recognize that decision making is a two-step process: 188
  First take in all the relevant information, then decide.
  c. Don't worry about looking good; worry about achieving   188
  your goal.
  d. Realize that you can't put out without taking in.   189
  e. Recognize that to gain the perspective that comes from   189
  seeing things through another's eyes, you must suspend
  judgment for a time—only by empathizing can you properly
  evaluate another point of view.
  f. Remember that you're looking for the best answer, not   189
  simply the best answer that you can come up with yourself.
  g. Be clear on whether you are arguing or seeking to understand,   190
  and think about which is most appropriate based on your and
  others' believability.

3.3 **Appreciate the art of thoughtful disagreement.**   190

3.4 **Triangulate your view with believable people who are willing**   193
  to disagree.
  a. Plan for the worst-case scenario to make it as good as   194
  possible.

3.5 **Recognize the signs of closed-mindedness and**   196
  open-mindedness that you should watch out for.

3.6 **Understand how you can become radically open-minded.**   198
  a. Regularly use pain as your guide toward quality reflection.   198
  b. Make being open-minded a habit.   198
  c. Get to know your blind spots.   199
  d. If a number of different believable people say you are doing   199
  something wrong and you are the only one who doesn't see
  it that way, assume that you are probably biased.
  e. Meditate.   199
  f. Be evidence-based and encourage others to be the same.   200

g. Do everything in your power to help others also be open-minded. — 200

h. Use evidence-based decision-making tools. — 200

i. Know when it's best to stop fighting and have faith in your decision-making process. — 201

4 Understand That People Are Wired Very Differently — 204

4.1 Understand the power that comes from knowing how you and others are wired. — 208

a. We are born with attributes that can both help us and hurt us, depending on their application. — 210

4.2 Meaningful work and meaningful relationships aren't just nice things we chose for ourselves—they are genetically programmed into us. — 215

4.3 Understand the great brain battles and how to control them to get what "you" want. — 218

a. Realize that the conscious mind is in a battle with the subconscious mind. — 218

b. Know that the most constant struggle is between feeling and thinking. — 219

c. Reconcile your feelings and your thinking. — 220

d. Choose your habits well. — 220

e. Train your "lower-level you" with kindness and persistence to build the right habits. — 223

f. Understand the differences between right-brained and left-brained thinking. — 223

g. Understand how much the brain can and cannot change. — 224

4.4 Find out what you and others are like. — 225

a. Introversion vs. extroversion. — 226

b. Intuiting vs. sensing. — 226

c. Thinking vs. feeling. — 227

d. Planning vs. perceiving. — 227

e. Creators vs. refiners vs. advancers vs. executors vs. flexors. — 228

f. Focusing on tasks vs. focusing on goals. — 229

g. Workplace Personality Inventory. — 229

h. Shapers are people who can go from visualization to actualization. — 230

4.5 Getting the right people in the right roles in support of your goal is the key to succeeding at whatever you choose to accomplish. — 231

a. Manage yourself and orchestrate others to get what you want. — 232

5 Learn How to Make Decisions Effectively — 234

5.1 Recognize that 1) the biggest threat to good decision making is harmful emotions, and 2) decision making is a two-step process (first learning and then deciding). — 236

5.2 **Synthesize the situation at hand.**   237

    a. One of the most important decisions you can make is   238
who you ask questions of.

    b. Don't believe everything you hear.   238

    c. Everything looks bigger up close.   238

    d. New is overvalued relative to great.   238

    e. Don't oversqueeze dots.   238

5.3 **Synthesize the situation through time.**   239

    a. Keep in mind both the rates of change and the levels of   244
things, and the relationships between them.

    b. Be imprecise.   244

    c. Remember the 80/20 Rule and know what the key   246
20 percent is.

    d. Be an imperfectionist.   246

5.4 **Navigate levels effectively.**   246

    a. Use the terms "above the line" and "below the line" to   247
establish which level a conversation is on.

    b. Remember that decisions need to be made at the   247
appropriate level, but they should also be consistent
across levels.

5.5 **Logic, reason, and common sense are your best tools for   251
synthesizing reality and understanding what to do about it.**

5.6 **Make your decisions as expected value calculations.**   251

    a. Raising the probability of being right is valuable no matter 253
what your probability of being right already is.

    b. Knowing when not to bet is as important as knowing what   253
bets are probably worth making.

    c. The best choices are the ones that have more pros than cons, 253
not those that don't have any cons at all.

5.7 **Prioritize by weighing the value of additional information   254
against the cost of not deciding.**

    a. All of your "must-dos" must be above the bar before you   254
do your "like-to-dos."

    b. Chances are you won't have time to deal with the   254
unimportant things, which is better than not having
time to deal with the important things.

    c. Don't mistake possibilities for probabilities.   254

5.8 **Simplify!**   255

5.9 **Use principles.**   255

5.10 **Believability weight your decision making.**   256

5.11 **Convert your principles into algorithms and have the   257
computer make decisions alongside you.**

5.12 **Be cautious about trusting AI without having
deep understanding.**   262

PART III

WORK

PRINCIPLES

SUMMARY AND TABLE OF WORK PRINCIPLES

I'm including this summary and table of Work Principles here so that you have the choice of skimming them all, finding the ones you're most interested in, or skipping this section and continuing your reading on page 296.

PART III: WORK PRINCIPLES
279

- **An organization is a machine consisting of two major parts: culture and people.** — 299
  - a. A great organization has both great people and a great culture. — 299
  - b. Great people have both great character and great capabilities. — 299
  - c. Great cultures bring problems and disagreements to the surface and solve them well, and they love imagining and building great things that haven't been built before. — 299

- **Tough love is effective for achieving both great work and great relationships.** — 305
  - a. In order to be great, one can't compromise the uncompromisable. — 305

- **A believability-weighted idea meritocracy is the best system for making effective decisions.** — 307

- **Make your passion and your work one and the same and do it with people you want to be with.** — 317

TO GET THE CULTURE RIGHT . . .
318

1 Trust in Radical Truth and Radical Transparency — 322

1.1 Realize that you have nothing to fear from knowing the truth. — 326

1.2 Have integrity and demand it from others. — 327
  - a. Never say anything about someone that you wouldn't say to them directly and don't try people without accusing them to their faces. — 327
  - b. Don't let loyalty to people stand in the way of truth and the well-being of the organization. — 328

1.3 Create an environment in which everyone has the right to   329
understand what makes sense and no one has the right
to hold a critical opinion without speaking up.

    a. Speak up, own it, or get out.   329
    b. Be extremely open.   329
    c. Don't be naive about dishonesty.   329

1.4 Be radically transparent.   330
    a. Use transparency to help enforce justice.   332
    b. Share the things that are hardest to share.   333
    c. Keep exceptions to radical transparency very rare.   333
    d. Make sure those who are given radical transparency   334
       recognize their responsibilities to handle it well and to
       weigh things intelligently.
    e. Provide transparency to people who handle it well and   335
       either deny it to people who don't handle it well or remove
       those people from the organization.
    f. Don't share sensitive information with the organization's   335
       enemies.

1.5 Meaningful relationships and meaningful work are mutually   336
reinforcing, especially when supported by radical truth and
radical transparency.

2 Cultivate Meaningful Work and Meaningful   338
Relationships

2.1 Be loyal to the common mission and not to anyone who is not   342
operating consistently with it.

2.2 Be crystal clear on what the deal is.   342
    a. Make sure people give more consideration to others than   343
       they demand for themselves.
    b. Make sure that people understand the difference between   344
       fairness and generosity.
    c. Know where the line is and be on the far side of fair.   345
    d. Pay for work.   345

2.3 Recognize that the size of the organization can pose a threat   346
to meaningful relationships.

2.4 Remember that most people will pretend to operate in your   346
interest while operating in their own.

2.5 Treasure honorable people who are capable and will treat   347
you well even when you're not looking.

3 Create a Culture in Which It Is Okay to Make   348
Mistakes and Unacceptable Not to Learn from
Them

3.1 Recognize that mistakes are a natural part of the evolutionary   351
process.
    a. Fail well.   351

    b. Don't feel bad about your mistakes or those of others.   **351**
    Love them!

3.2 Don't worry about looking good—worry about achieving   **352**
your goals.
    a. Get over "blame" and "credit" and get on with "accurate"   **352**
    and "inaccurate."

3.3 Observe the patterns of mistakes to see if they are products   **352**
of weaknesses.

3.4 Remember to reflect when you experience pain.   **353**
    a. Be self-reflective and make sure your people are   **353**
    self-reflective.
    b. Know that nobody can see themselves objectively.   **354**
    c. Teach and reinforce the merits of mistake-based learning.   **354**

3.5 Know what types of mistakes are acceptable and what types   **354**
are unacceptable, and don't allow the people who work for
you to make the unacceptable ones.

4 Get and Stay in Sync   **356**

4.1 Recognize that conflicts are essential for great relationships   **360**
because they are how people determine whether their
principles are aligned and resolve their differences.
    a. Spend lavishly on the time and energy you devote to getting   **360**
    in sync, because it's the best investment you can make.

4.2 Know how to get in sync and disagree well.   **361**
    a. Surface areas of possible out-of-syncness.   **361**
    b. Distinguish between idle complaints and complaints meant   **362**
    to lead to improvement.
    c. Remember that every story has another side.   **362**

4.3 Be open-minded and assertive at the same time.   **362**
    a. Distinguish open-minded people from closed-minded   **362**
    people.
    b. Don't have anything to do with closed-minded people.   **363**
    c. Watch out for people who think it's embarrassing not to know.   **363**
    d. Make sure that those in charge are open-minded about the   **363**
    questions and comments of others.
    e. Recognize that getting in sync is a two-way responsibility.   **363**
    f. Worry more about substance than style.   **364**
    g. Be reasonable and expect others to be reasonable.   **364**
    h. Making suggestions and questioning are not the same as   **364**
    criticizing, so don't treat them as if they are.

4.4 If it is your meeting to run, manage the conversation.   **364**
    a. Make it clear who is directing the meeting and whom it is   **365**
    meant to serve.
    b. Be precise in what you're talking about to avoid confusion.   **365**
    c. Make clear what type of communication you are going to   **365**
    have in light of the objectives and priorities.

d. Lead the discussion by being assertive and open-minded. 365
e. Navigate between the different levels of the conversation. 366
f. Watch out for "topic slip." 366
g. Enforce the logic of conversations. 366
h. Be careful not to lose personal responsibility via group decision making. 366
i. Utilize the "two-minute rule" to avoid persistent interruptions. 367
j. Watch out for assertive "fast talkers." 367
k. Achieve completion in conversations. 367
l. Leverage your communication. 367

4.5 Great collaboration feels like playing jazz. 368
a. 1+1=3. 368
b. 3 to 5 is more than 20. 368

4.6 When you have alignment, cherish it. 369

4.7 If you find you can't reconcile major differences—especially in values—consider whether the relationship is worth preserving. 369

5 Believability Weight Your Decision Making 370

5.1 Recognize that having an effective idea meritocracy requires that you understand the merit of each person's ideas. 374
a. If you can't successfully do something, don't think you can tell others how it should be done. 374
b. Remember that everyone has opinions and they are often bad. 375

5.2 Find the most believable people possible who disagree with you and try to understand their reasoning. 375
a. Think about people's believability in order to assess the likelihood that their opinions are good. 375
b. Remember that believable opinions are most likely to come from people 1) who have successfully accomplished the thing in question at least three times, and 2) who have great explanations of the cause-effect relationships that lead them to their conclusions. 376
c. If someone hasn't done something but has a theory that seems logical and can be stress-tested, then by all means test it. 376
d. Don't pay as much attention to people's conclusions as to the reasoning that led them to their conclusions. 376
e. Inexperienced people can have great ideas too, sometimes far better ones than more experienced people. 376
f. Everyone should be up-front in expressing how confident they are in their thoughts. 376

5.3 Think about whether you are playing the role of a teacher, a student, or a peer and whether you should be teaching, asking questions, or debating. 377

    a. It's more important that the student understand the teacher   **377**
than that the teacher understand the student, though both
are important.

    b. Recognize that while everyone has the right and responsibility **378**
to try to make sense of important things, they must do so with
humility and radical open-mindedness.

5.4 Understand how people came by their opinions.   **379**

    a. If you ask someone a question, they will probably give   **379**
you an answer, so think through to whom you should
address your questions.

    b. Having everyone randomly probe everyone else is an   **379**
unproductive waste of time.

    c. Beware of statements that begin with "I think that . . ."   **380**

    d. Assess believability by systematically capturing people's   **380**
track records over time.

5.5 Disagreeing must be done efficiently.   **380**

    a. Know when to stop debating and move on to agreeing   **380**
about what should be done.

    b. Use believability weighting as a tool rather than a substitute   **381**
for decision making by Responsible Parties.

    c. Since you don't have the time to thoroughly examine   **381**
everyone's thinking yourself, choose your believable
people wisely.

    d. When you're responsible for a decision, compare the   **381**
believability-weighted decision making of the crowd to
what you believe.

5.6 Recognize that everyone has the right and responsibility to try   **382**
to make sense of important things.

    a. Communications aimed at getting the best answer should   **382**
involve the most relevant people.

    b. Communication aimed at educating or boosting cohesion   **383**
should involve a broader set of people than would be needed
if the aim were just getting the best answer.

    c. Recognize that you don't need to make judgments about   **383**
everything.

5.7 Pay more attention to whether the decision-making system is   **383**
fair than whether you get your way.

6 Recognize How to Get Beyond Disagreements   **384**

6.1 Remember: Principles can't be ignored by mutual agreement.   **386**

    a. The same standards of behavior apply to everyone.   **386**

6.2 Make sure people don't confuse the right to complain, give   **387**
advice, and openly debate with the right to make decisions.

    a. When challenging a decision and/or a decision maker,   **387**
consider the broader context.

6.3 Don't leave important conflicts unresolved.   **388**

a. Don't let the little things divide you when your agreement on the big things should bind you. 388

b. Don't get stuck in disagreement—escalate or vote! 388

6.4 Once a decision is made, everyone should get behind it even though individuals may still disagree. 389

a. See things from the higher level. 389

b. Never allow the idea meritocracy to slip into anarchy. 390

c. Don't allow lynch mobs or mob rule. 390

6.5 Remember that if the idea meritocracy comes into conflict with the well-being of the organization, it will inevitably suffer. 391

a. Declare "martial law" only in rare or extreme circumstances when the principles need to be suspended. 391

b. Be wary of people who argue for the suspension of the idea meritocracy for the "good of the organization." 391

6.6 Recognize that if the people who have the power don't want to operate by principles, the principled way of operating will fail. 392

TO GET THE PEOPLE RIGHT . . .

394

7 Remember That the WHO Is More Important than the WHAT 398

7.1 Recognize that the most important decision for you to make is who you choose as your Responsible Parties. 401

a. Understand that the most important RPs are those responsible for the goals, outcomes, and machines at the highest levels. 401

7.2 Know that the ultimate Responsible Party will be the person who bears the consequences of what is done. 402

a. Make sure that everyone has someone they report to. 402

7.3 Remember the force behind the thing. 403

8 Hire Right, Because the Penalties for Hiring Wrong Are Huge 404

8.1 Match the person to the design. 407

a. Think through which values, abilities, and skills you are looking for (in that order). 407

b. Make finding the right people systematic and scientific. 408

c. Hear the click: Find the right fit between the role and the person. 409

d. Look for people who sparkle, not just "any ol' one of those." 409

e. Don't use your pull to get someone a job. 409

8.2 Remember that people are built very differently and that different ways of seeing and thinking make people suitable for different jobs. 410

    a. Understand how to use and interpret personality assessments.   **411**

    b. Remember that people tend to pick people like themselves,   **411**
       so choose interviewers who can identify what you are looking
       for.

    c. Look for people who are willing to look at themselves   **411**
       objectively.

    d. Remember that people typically don't change all that much.   **411**

8.3 Think of your teams the way that sports managers do: No one   **412**
person possesses everything required to produce success,
yet everyone must excel.

8.4 Pay attention to people's track records.   **412**

    a. Check references.   **412**

    b. Recognize that performance in school doesn't tell you   **413**
       much about whether a person has the values and abilities
       you are looking for.

    c. While it's best to have great conceptual thinkers, understand   **413**
       that great experience and a great track record also count for
       a lot.

    d. Beware of the impractical idealist.   **414**

    e. Don't assume that a person who has been successful   **414**
       elsewhere will be successful in the job you're giving them.

    f. Make sure your people have character and are capable.   **414**

8.5 Don't hire people just to fit the first job they will do; hire people   **415**
you want to share your life with.

    a. Look for people who have lots of great questions.   **415**

    b. Show candidates your warts.   **415**

    c. Play jazz with people with whom you are compatible but   **415**
       who will also challenge you.

8.6 When considering compensation, provide both stability and   **416**
opportunity.

    a. Pay for the person, not the job.   **416**

    b. Have performance metrics tied at least loosely to   **416**
       compensation.

    c. Pay north of fair.   **416**

    d. Focus more on making the pie bigger than on exactly how   **416**
       to slice it so that you or anyone else gets the biggest piece.

8.7 Remember that in great partnerships, consideration and   **417**
generosity are more important than money.

    a. Be generous and expect generosity from others.   **417**

8.8 Great people are hard to find so make sure you think about   **418**
how to keep them.

9 Constantly Train, Test, Evaluate, and Sort People   **420**

9.1 Understand that you and the people you manage will go   **423**
through a process of personal evolution.

a. Recognize that personal evolution should be relatively rapid 423
and a natural consequence of discovering one's strengths and
weaknesses; as a result, career paths are not planned at the
outset.

b. Understand that training guides the process of personal 424
evolution.

c. Teach your people to fish rather than give them fish, even if 424
that means letting them make some mistakes.

d. Recognize that experience creates internalized learning that 425
book learning can't replace.

9.2 **Provide constant feedback.** 425

9.3 **Evaluate accurately, not kindly.** 426

a. In the end, accuracy and kindness are the same thing. 426

b. Put your compliments and criticisms in perspective. 426

c. Think about accuracy, not implications. 426

d. Make accurate assessments. 426

e. Learn from success as well as from failure. 427

f. Know that most everyone thinks that what they did, and 427
what they are doing, is much more important than it really is.

9.4 **Recognize that tough love is both the hardest and the most** 427
important type of love to give (because it is so rarely
welcomed).

a. Recognize that while most people prefer compliments, 428
accurate criticism is more valuable.

9.5 **Don't hide your observations about people.** 428

a. Build your synthesis from the specifics up. 428

b. Squeeze the dots. 429

c. Don't oversqueeze a dot. 429

d. Use evaluation tools such as performance surveys, metrics, 429
and formal reviews to document all aspects of a person's
performance.

9.6 **Make the process of learning what someone is like open,** 430
evolutionary, and iterative.

a. Make your metrics clear and impartial. 430

b. Encourage people to be objectively reflective about their 431
performance.

c. Look at the whole picture. 431

d. For performance reviews, start from specific cases, look 432
for patterns, and get in sync with the person being reviewed
by looking at the evidence together.

e. Remember that when it comes to assessing people, the two 433
biggest mistakes you can make are being overconfident in
your assessment and failing to get in sync on it.

f. Get in sync on assessments in a nonhierarchical way. 433

g. Learn about your people and have them learn about you 433
through frank conversations about mistakes and their root
causes.

h. Understand that making sure people are doing a good job
doesn't require watching everything that everybody is doing
at all times.   434

i. Recognize that change is difficult.   434

j. Help people through the pain that comes with exploring
their weaknesses.   434

9.7 Knowing how people operate and being able to judge whether
that way of operating will lead to good results is more important
than knowing what they did.   435

a. If someone is doing their job poorly, consider whether it is
due to inadequate learning or inadequate ability.   435

b. Training and testing a poor performer to see if he or she can
acquire the required skills without simultaneously trying to
assess their abilities is a common mistake.   436

9.8 Recognize that when you are really in sync with someone
about their weaknesses, the weaknesses are probably true.   436

a. When judging people, remember that you don't have to get
to the point of "beyond a shadow of a doubt."   436

b. It should take you no more than a year to learn what a
person is like and whether they are a click for their job.   438

c. Continue assessing people throughout their tenure.   438

d. Evaluate employees with the same rigor as you evaluate
job candidates.   438

9.9 Train, guardrail, or remove people; don't rehabilitate them.   438

a. Don't collect people.   439

b. Be willing to "shoot the people you love."   439

c. When someone is "without a box," consider whether there
is an open box that would be a better fit or whether you need
to get them out of the company.   440

d. Be cautious about allowing people to step back to another
role after failing.   440

9.10 Remember that the goal of a transfer is the best, highest use of
the person in a way that benefits the community as a whole.   441

a. Have people "complete their swings" before moving on to
new roles.   441

9.11 Don't lower the bar.   442

TO BUILD AND EVOLVE YOUR MACHINE . . .

444

10 Manage as Someone Operating a Machine to Achieve a Goal   **448**

10.1 Look down on your machine and yourself within it from the higher level.   **450**

    a. Constantly compare your outcomes to your goals.   **450**

    b. Understand that a great manager is essentially an organizational engineer.   **451**

    c. Build great metrics.   **452**

    d. Beware of paying too much attention to what is coming at you and not enough attention to your machine.   **452**

    e. Don't get distracted by shiny objects.   **452**

10.2 Remember that for every case you deal with, your approach should have two purposes: 1) to move you closer to your goal, and 2) to train and test your machine (i.e., your people and your design).   **453**

    a. Everything is a case study.   **453**

    b. When a problem occurs, conduct the discussion at two levels: 1) the machine level (why that outcome was produced) and 2) the case-at-hand level (what to do about it).   **453**

    c. When making rules, explain the principles behind them.   **453**

    d. Your policies should be natural extensions of your principles.   **454**

    e. While good principles and policies almost always provide good guidance, remember that there are exceptions to every rule.   **454**

10.3 Understand the differences between managing, micromanaging, and not managing.   **455**

    a. Managers must make sure that what they are responsible for works well.   **455**

    b. Managing the people who report to you should feel like skiing together.   **455**

    c. An excellent skier is probably going to be a better ski coach than a novice skier.   **455**

    d. You should be able to delegate the details.   **456**

10.4 Know what your people are like and what makes them tick, because your people are your most important resource.   **456**

    a. Regularly take the temperature of each person who is important to you and to the organization.   **456**

    b. Learn how much confidence to have in your people—don't assume it.   **457**

    c. Vary your involvement based on your confidence.   **457**

10.5 Clearly assign responsibilities. 457
    a. Remember who has what responsibilities. 457
    b. Watch out for "job slip." 458

10.6 Probe deep and hard to learn what you can expect from your machine. 458
    a. Get a threshold level of understanding. 458
    b. Avoid staying too distant. 458
    c. Use daily updates as a tool for staying on top of what your people are doing and thinking. 459
    d. Probe so you know whether problems are likely to occur before they actually do. 459
    e. Probe to the level below the people who report to you. 459
    f. Have the people who report to the people who report to you feel free to escalate their problems to you. 459
    g. Don't assume that people's answers are correct. 459
    h. Train your ear. 460
    i. Make your probing transparent rather than private. 460
    j. Welcome probing. 460
    k. Remember that people who see things and think one way often have difficulty communicating with and relating to people who see things and think another way. 460
    l. Pull all suspicious threads. 461
    m. Recognize that there are many ways to skin a cat. 461

10.7 Think like an owner, and expect the people you work with to do the same. 462
    a. Going on vacation doesn't mean one can neglect one's responsibilities. 462
    b. Force yourself and the people who work for you to do difficult things. 462

10.8 Recognize and deal with key-man risk. 463

10.9 Don't treat everyone the same—treat them appropriately. 463
    a. Don't let yourself get squeezed. 463
    b. Care about the people who work for you. 464

10.10 Know that great leadership is generally not what it's made out to be. 464
    a. Be weak and strong at the same time. 465
    b. Don't worry about whether or not your people like you and don't look to them to tell you what you should do. 465
    c. Don't give orders and try to be followed; try to be understood and to understand others by getting in sync. 466

10.11 Hold yourself and your people accountable and appreciate them for holding you accountable. 468
    a. If you've agreed with someone that something is supposed to go a certain way, make sure it goes that way—unless you get in sync about doing it differently. 468

    b. Distinguish between a failure in which someone broke their   **468**
"contract" and a failure in which there was no contract to
begin with.

    c. Avoid getting sucked down.   **469**

    d. Watch out for people who confuse goals and tasks, because   **469**
if they can't make that distinction, you can't trust them with
responsibilities.

    e. Watch out for the unfocused and unproductive "theoretical   **469**
should."

10.12 Communicate the plan clearly and have clear metrics   **470**
conveying whether you are progressing according to it.

    a. Put things in perspective by going back before going   **470**
forward.

10.13 Escalate when you can't adequately handle your   **471**
responsibilities and make sure that the people who
work for you are proactive about doing the same.

11 Perceive and Don't Tolerate Problems   **472**

11.1 If you're not worried, you need to worry—and if you're worried,   **476**
you don't need to worry.

11.2 Design and oversee a machine to perceive whether things are   **476**
good enough or not good enough, or do it yourself.

    a. Assign people the job of perceiving problems, give them   **476**
time to investigate, and make sure they have independent
reporting lines so that they can convey problems without
any fear of recrimination.

    b. Watch out for the "Frog in the Boiling Water Syndrome."   **476**

    c. Beware of group-think: The fact that no one seems   **477**
concerned doesn't mean nothing is wrong.

    d. To perceive problems, compare how the outcomes are   **477**
lining up with your goals.

    e. "Taste the soup."   **478**

    f. Have as many eyes looking for problems as possible.   **478**

    g. "Pop the cork."   **479**

    h. Realize that the people closest to certain jobs probably   **479**
know them best.

11.3 Be very specific about problems; don't start with generalizations.   **479**

    a. Avoid the anonymous "we" and "they," because they mask   **479**
personal responsibility.

11.4 Don't be afraid to fix the difficult things.   **480**

    a. Understand that problems with good, planned solutions   **480**
in place are completely different from those without such
solutions.

    b. Think of the problems you perceive in a machinelike way.   **480**

12 Diagnose Problems to Get at Their Root Causes 482

12.1 **To diagnose well, ask the following questions: 1. Is the** 485
outcome good or bad? 2. Who is responsible for the
outcome? 3. If the outcome is bad, is the Responsible
Party incapable and/or is the design bad?
   a. Ask yourself: "Who should do what differently?" 488
   b. Identify at which step in the 5-Step Process the failure 488
      occurred.
   c. Identify the principles that were violated. 488
   d. Avoid Monday morning quarterbacking. 488
   e. Don't confuse the quality of someone's circumstances 489
      with the quality of their approach to dealing with the
      circumstances.
   f. Identifying the fact that someone else doesn't know what 489
      to do doesn't mean that you know what to do.
   g. Remember that a root cause is not an action but a reason. 489
   h. To distinguish between a capacity issue and a capability 490
      issue, imagine how the person would perform at that
      particular function if they had ample capacity.
   i. Keep in mind that managers usually fail or fall short of 491
      their goals for one (or more) of five reasons.

12.2 **Maintain an emerging synthesis by diagnosing continuously.** 491

12.3 **Keep in mind that diagnoses should produce outcomes.** 491
   a. Remember that if you have the same people doing the same 491
      things, you should expect the same results.

12.4 **Use the following "drill-down" technique to gain an 80/20** 492
understanding of a department or sub-department that is
having problems.

12.5 **Understand that diagnosis is foundational to both progress** 495
and quality relationships.

13 Design Improvements to Your Machine to Get 496
Around Your Problems

13.1 **Build your machine.** 499

13.2 **Systemize your principles and how they will be implemented.** 499
   a. Create great decision-making machines by thinking through 499
      the criteria you are using to make decisions while you are
      making them.

13.3 **Remember that a good plan should resemble a movie script.** 500
   a. Put yourself in the position of pain for a while so that you 500
      gain a richer understanding of what you're designing for.
   b. Visualize alternative machines and their outcomes, and then 500
      choose.

c. Consider second- and third-order consequences, not just   **501**
first-order ones.

d. Use standing meetings to help your organization run like   **501**
a Swiss clock.

e. Remember that a good machine takes into account the fact   **501**
that people are imperfect.

13.4 Recognize that design is an iterative process. Between a bad   **501**
"now" and a good "then" is a "working through it" period.

a. Understand the power of the "cleansing storm."   **502**

13.5 Build the organization around goals rather than tasks.   **502**

a. Build your organization from the top down.   **503**

b. Remember that everyone must be overseen by a believable   **503**
person who has high standards.

c. Make sure the people at the top of each pyramid have the   **503**
skills and focus to manage their direct reports and a deep
understanding of their jobs.

d. In designing your organization, remember that the 5-Step   **504**
Process is the path to success and that different people
are good at different steps.

e. Don't build the organization to fit the people.   **504**

f. Keep scale in mind.   **504**

g. Organize departments and sub-departments around the   **505**
most logical groupings based on "gravitational pull."

h. Make departments as self-sufficient as possible so that they   **505**
have control over the resources they need to achieve their
goals.

i. Ensure that the ratios of senior managers to junior managers   **505**
and of junior managers to their reports are limited to preserve
quality communication and mutual understanding.

j. Consider succession and training in your design.   **505**

k. Don't just pay attention to your job; pay attention to how   **506**
your job will be done if you are no longer around.

l. Use "double-do" rather than "double-check" to make sure   **506**
mission-critical tasks are done correctly.

m. Use consultants wisely and watch out for consultant   **507**
addiction.

13.6 Create an organizational chart to look like a pyramid, with   **508**
straight lines down that don't cross.

a. Involve the person who is the point of the pyramid when   **508**
encountering cross-departmental or cross-sub-departmental
issues.

b. Don't do work for people in another department or grab   **508**
people from another department to do work for you unless
you speak to the person responsible for overseeing the other
department.

c. Watch out for "department slip."   **510**

13.7 **Create guardrails when needed—and remember it's better**   510
not to guardrail at all.
     a. Don't expect people to recognize and compensate for their   511
        own blind spots.
     b. Consider the clover-leaf design.   511
13.8 **Keep your strategic vision the same while making appropriate**   511
tactical changes as circumstances dictate.
     a. Don't put the expedient ahead of the strategic.   512
     b. Think about both the big picture and the granular details,   512
        and understand the connections between them.
13.9 **Have good controls so that you are not exposed to the**   513
dishonesty of others.
     a. Investigate and let people know you are going to investigate.   513
     b. Remember that there is no sense in having laws unless you   513
        have policemen (auditors).
     c. Beware of rubber-stamping.   513
     d. Recognize that people who make purchases on your behalf   514
        probably will not spend your money wisely.
     e. Use "public hangings" to deter bad behavior.   514
13.10 **Have the clearest possible reporting lines and delineations**   514
of responsibilities.
     a. Assign responsibilities based on workflow design and   515
        people's abilities, not job titles.
     b. Constantly think about how to produce leverage.   515
     c. Recognize that it is far better to find a few smart people   516
        and give them the best technology than to have a greater
        number of ordinary people who are less well equipped.
     d. Use leveragers.   516
13.11 **Remember that almost everything will take more time and**   516
cost more money than you expect.

14 **Do What You Set Out to Do**   518

14.1 **Work for goals that you and your organization are excited**   520
about and think about how your tasks connect to those goals.
     a. Be coordinated and consistent in motivating others.   521
     b. Don't act before thinking. Take the time to come up with   521
        a game plan.
     c. Look for creative, cut-through solutions.   521
14.2 **Recognize that everyone has too much to do.**   522
     a. Don't get frustrated.   522
14.3 **Use checklists.**   523
     a. Don't confuse checklists with personal responsibility.   523
14.4 **Allow time for rest and renovation.**   523
14.5 **Ring the bell.**   523

15 Use Tools and Protocols to Shape How Work Is Done   524

15.1 Having systemized principles embedded in tools is especially   526
valuable for an idea meritocracy.

    a. To produce real behavioral change, understand that there   526
    must be internalized or habitualized learning.

    b. Use tools to collect data and process it into conclusions   527
    and actions.

    c. Foster an environment of confidence and fairness by having   527
    clearly-stated principles that are implemented in tools and
    protocols so that the conclusions reached can be assessed
    by tracking the logic and data behind them.

16 And for Heaven's Sake, Don't Overlook Governance!   530

16.1 To be successful, all organizations must have checks and   532
balances.

    a. Even in an idea meritocracy, merit cannot be the only   532
    determining factor in assigning responsibility and
    authority.

    b. Make sure that no one is more powerful than the system   533
    or so important that they are irreplaceable.

    c. Beware of fiefdoms.   533

    d. Make clear that the organization's structure and rules   533
    are designed to ensure that its checks-and-balances system
    functions well.

    e. Make sure reporting lines are clear.   535

    f. Make sure decision rights are clear.   535

    g. Make sure that the people doing the assessing 1) have the   535
    time to be fully informed about how the person they are
    checking on is doing, 2) have the ability to make the
    assessments, and 3) are not in a conflict of interest that
    stands in the way of carrying out oversight effectively.

    h. Recognize that decision makers must have access to the   536
    information necessary to make decisions and must be
    trustworthy enough to handle that information safely.

16.2 Remember that in an idea meritocracy a single CEO is not   536
as good as a great group of leaders.

16.3 No governance system of principles, rules, and checks and   537
balances can substitute for a great partnership.

For any group or organization to function well, its work principles must be aligned with its members' life principles.

don't mean that they must be aligned on everything, but I do mean that they have to be aligned on the most important things, like the mission they're on and how they will be with each other.

If people in an organization feel that alignment, they will treasure their relationships and work together harmoniously; its culture will permeate everything they do. If they don't, they will work for different, often conflicting, goals and will be confused about how they should be with each other. For that reason, it pays for all organizations—companies, governments, foundations, schools, hospitals, and so on—to spell out their principles and values clearly and explicitly and to operate by them consistently.

Those principles and values aren't vague slogans, like "the customer always comes first" or "we should strive to be the best in our industry," but a set of concrete directives anyone can understand, get aligned on, and carry out. As we shift our attention from Life Principles to Work Principles, I will explain how we went about achieving these alignments at Bridgewater and how that affected our results. But first, I want to explain how I think about organizations.

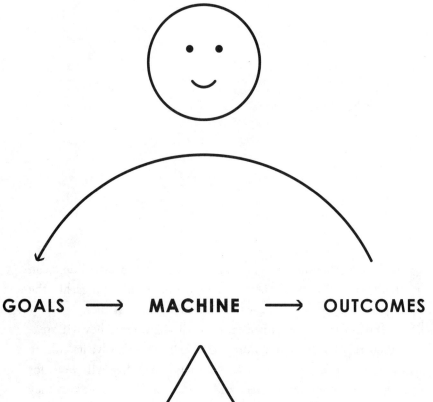

GOALS → **MACHINE** → OUTCOMES

CULTURE ⟷ **PEOPLE**

● An organization is a machine consisting of two major parts: culture and people.

Each influences the other, because the people who make up an organization determine the kind of culture it has, and the culture of the organization determines the kinds of people who fit in.

a. A great organization has both great people and a great culture.
Companies that get progressively better over time have both. Nothing is more important or more difficult than to get the culture and people right.

b. Great people have both great character and great capabilities.
By great character, I mean they are radically truthful, radically transparent, and deeply committed to the mission of the organization. By great capabilities, I mean they have the abilities and skills to do their jobs excellently. People who have one without the other are dangerous and should be removed from the organization. People who have both are rare and should be treasured.

c. Great cultures bring problems and disagreements to the surface and solve them well, and they love imagining and building great things that haven't been built before. Doing that sustains their evolution. In our case, we do that by having an idea meritocracy that strives for meaningful work and meaningful relationships through radical truth and radical transparency. By meaningful work, I mean work that people are excited to get their heads into, and by meaningful relationships I mean those in which there is genuine caring for each other (like an extended family). I find that these reinforce each other and that being radically truthful and radically transparent with each other makes both the work and the relationships go better.

By constantly looking down on the machine, its managers can objectively compare the outcomes it produces with their goals. If those outcomes are consistent with those goals, then the machine is working effectively; if the outcomes are inconsistent with the goals, then something is wrong with either the design of the machine or the people who are a part of it and the problem needs to be diagnosed so the machine can be modified. As laid out in Chapter Two of Life Principles, this ideally happens in a 5-Step Process: 1) having clear goals, 2) identifying the problems preventing the goals from being achieved, 3) diagnosing what parts of the machine (i.e., which people or which designs) are not working well, 4) designing changes, and 5) doing what is needed. This is the fastest and most efficient way that an organization improves.

I call this process of converting problems into progress "looping," and how it happens through time is visualized in the diagrams to the right. In the first, a problem occurs that takes you off track from your goals and makes things worse than you planned.

If you identify the decline, diagnose the problems that caused it so as to get at their root causes, come up with new designs, and then push them through, the trajectory will loop back on itself and continue its upward ascent, like in the second diagram.

If you don't identify the problem, design a suboptimal solution, or fail to push it through effectively, the decline will continue as shown in the diagram at the bottom.

A manager's ability to recognize when outcomes are inconsistent with goals and then modify designs and assemble people to rectify them makes all the difference in the world. The more often and more effectively a manager does this, the steeper the upward trajectory.

As I explained in Life Principles, this is what I believe evolution looks like for all organisms and organizations. Having a culture and people that will evolve in this way is critical because the world changes quickly and in ways that can't possibly be anticipated. I'm sure you can think of a number of companies that failed to identify and address their problems on time and ended up in a terminal decline (see: BlackBerry and Palm) and a rare few that have consistently looped well. Most don't. For example, only six of the companies that forty years ago made up the Dow Jones 30, which is about

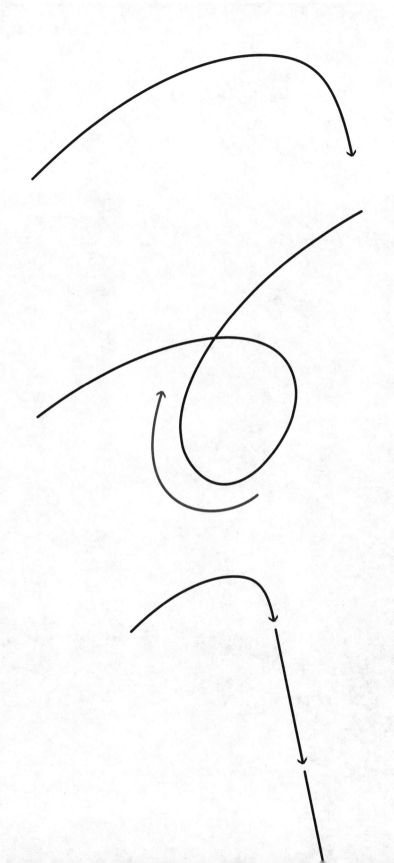

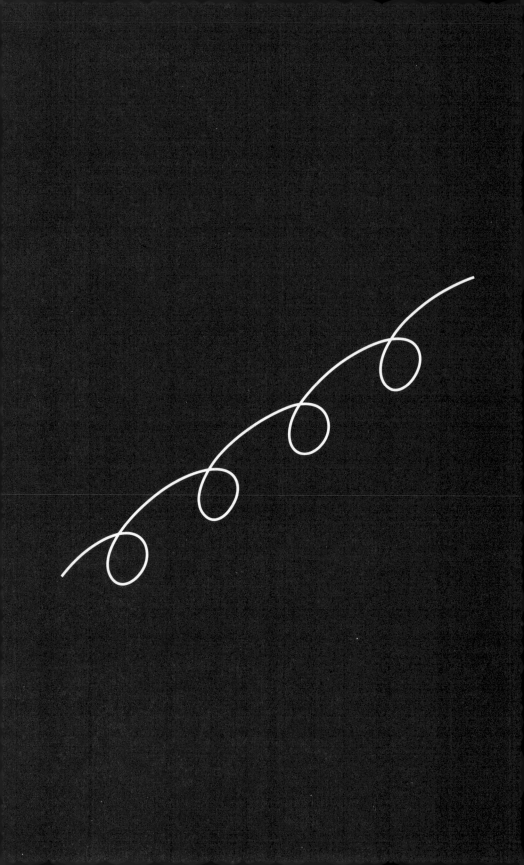

when Bridgewater got started, are still in the Dow 30 today. Many of them—American Can, American Tobacco, Bethlehem Steel, General Foods, Inco, F. W. Woolworth—don't even exist; some (Sears Roebuck, Johns-Manville, Eastman Kodak) are so different as to be almost unrecognizable. And many of the standouts on the list today—Apple, Cisco—were yet to be founded.

The rare few that have been able to evolve well over the decades have been successful at that evolutionary/looping process, which also is the process that has made Bridgewater progressively more successful for forty years. That is the process I want to pass along to you.

As I mentioned earlier, nothing is more important or more difficult than to get the culture and the people right. Whatever successes we've had at Bridgewater were the result of doing that well—and whatever failures were due to our not doing it adequately. That might seem odd because, as a global macroeconomic investor, one might think that, above all else, I had to get the economics and investments right, which is true. But to do that, I needed to get the people and culture right first. And, to inspire me to do what I did, I needed to have meaningful work and meaningful relationships.

As the entrepreneur/builder of Bridgewater, I naturally shaped the organization to be consistent with my values and principles. I went after what I wanted most, in the way that seemed most natural to me with the people I chose to be with, and we and Bridgewater evolved together.

If you had asked me what my objective was when I started out, I would've said it was to have fun working with people I like. Work was a game I played with passion and I wanted to have a blast playing it with people I enjoyed and respected. I started Bridgewater out of my apartment with a pal I played rugby with who had no experience in the markets and a friend we hired as our assistant. I certainly wasn't thinking about management at the time. Management seemed to me like something people in gray suits with slide presentations did. I never set out to manage, let alone to have principles about work and management.

From reading Life Principles, you know that I liked to imagine and build out new, practical concepts that never existed before. I especially loved doing these things with people who were on the same mission with me. I treasured thoughtful disagreement with them as a way of learning and raising our odds of making good decisions, and I wanted *all* the people I worked with to be my "partners" rather than my "employees." In a nutshell, I was looking for meaningful work and meaningful relationships. I quickly learned that the best way to do that was to have great partnerships with great people.

To me, great partnerships come from sharing common values and interests, having similar approaches to pursuing them, and being reasonable with, and having consideration for, each other. At the same time, partners must be willing to hold each other to high standards and work through their disagreements. The main test of a great partnership is not whether the partners ever disagree—people in all healthy relationships disagree—but whether they can bring their disagreements to the surface and get through them well. Having clear processes for resolving disagreements efficiently and clearly is essential for business partnerships, marriages, and all other forms of partnership.

My wanting these things attracted others who wanted the same things, which drove how we shaped Bridgewater together.[36] When there were five of us it was totally different than when there were fifty of us, which was totally different than it was when we were five hundred, a thousand, and so on. As we grew, most everything changed beyond recognition, except for our core values and principles.

When Bridgewater was still a small company, the principles by which we operated were more implicit than explicit. But as more and more new people came in, I couldn't take for granted that they would understand and preserve them. I realized that I needed to write our principles out explicitly and explain the logic behind them. I remember the precise moment when this shift occurred—it was when the number of people at Bridgewater passed sixty-seven. Up until then, I had personally chosen each employee's holiday gift and written them

---

[36] We applied these ways of operating to the businesses of investing and managing. In the process of investing I developed a practical understanding of what makes businesses and economies succeed, and in the process of managing my company I had to develop a practical understanding of how to manage businesses well. And I liked that my understanding of these subjects could be objectively measured via our investment performance as well as our business performance.

a lengthy personalized card, but trying to do it that year broke my back. From that point on, an increasing number of people came in who didn't work closely with me, so I couldn't assume they would understand where I was coming from or what I was striving to create, which was an idea meritocracy built on tough love.

● Tough love is effective for achieving both great work and great relationships.

To give you an idea of what I mean by tough love, think of Vince Lombardi, who for me personified it. From when I was ten years old until I was eighteen, Lombardi was head coach of the Green Bay Packers. With limited resources, he led his team to five NFL championships. He won two NFL Coach of the Year awards and many still call him the best coach of all time. Lombardi loved his players and he pushed them to be great. I admired, and still admire, how uncompromising his standards were. His players, their fans, and he himself all benefited from his approach. I wish Lombardi had written out his principles for me to read.

a. In order to be great, one can't compromise the uncompromisable. Yet I see people doing it all the time, usually to avoid making others or themselves feel uncomfortable, which is not just backward but counterproductive. Putting comfort ahead of success produces worse results for everyone. I both loved the people I worked with and pushed them to be great, and I expected them to do the same with me.

From the very beginning, I felt that the people I worked with at Bridgewater were a part of my extended family. When they or members of their families got sick, I put them in touch with my personal doctor to make sure that they were well taken care of. I invited all of them to stay at my house in Vermont on weekends and loved it when they took me up on it. I celebrated their marriages and the births of their children with them and mourned the losses of their loved ones.

But to be clear, this was no lovefest. We were tough on each other too, so we could all be as great as we could be. I learned that the more caring we gave each other, the tougher we could be on each other, and the tougher we were on each other, the better we performed and the more rewards there were for us to share. This cycle was self-reinforcing. I found that operating this way made the lows less low and the highs higher. It even made the bad times better than the good ones in some important ways.

Think about some of your toughest experiences in life. I bet it is as true for you as it has been for me that going through them with people you cared about, who cared about you, and who were working as hard as you were for the same mission, was incredibly rewarding. As hard as they were, we look back on some of these challenging times as our finest moments. For most people, being part of a great community on a shared mission is even more rewarding than money. Numerous studies have shown there is little to no correlation between one's happiness and the amount of money one accumulates, yet there is a strong correlation between one's happiness and the quality of one's relationships.

I laid this out in a memo to Bridgewater in 1996:

Bridgewater is not about plodding along at some kind of moderate standard, it is about working like hell to achieve a standard that is extraordinarily high, and then getting the satisfaction that comes along with that sort of super-achievement.

Our overriding objective is excellence, or more precisely, constant improvement, a superb and constantly improving company in all respects.

Conflict in the pursuit of excellence is a terrific thing. There should be no hierarchy based on age or seniority. Power should lie in the reasoning, not the position, of the individual. The best ideas win no matter who they come from.

Criticism (by oneself and by others) is an essential ingredient in the improvement process, yet, if handled incorrectly, can be destructive. It should be handled objectively. There should be no hierarchy in the giving or receiving of criticism.

Teamwork and team spirit are essential, including intolerance of substandard performance. This is referring to 1) one's recognition of the responsibilities one has to help the team achieve its common goals and 2) the willingness to help others (work within a group) toward these common goals. Our fates are intertwined. One should know that others can be relied upon to help. As a corollary, substandard performance cannot be tolerated anywhere because it would hurt everyone.

Long-term relationships are both a) intrinsically gratifying and b) efficient, and should be intentionally built. Turnover requires re-training and therefore creates setbacks.

Money is a byproduct of excellence, not a goal. Our overriding objective is excellence and constant improvement at Bridgewater. To be clear, it is not to make lots of money. The natural extension of this is not that you should be happy with little money. On the contrary— you should expect to make a lot. If we operate consistently with this philosophy we should be productive and the company should do well financially. There is comparatively little age- and seniority-based hierarchy.

Each person at Bridgewater should act like an owner, responsible for operating in this way and for holding others accountable to operate in this way.

● A believability-weighted idea meritocracy is the best system for making effective decisions.

Unlike Lombardi, whose success depended on having his players follow his instructions, I needed my players to be independent thinkers who could bang around their different points of view and reach better conclusions than any one of us could come up with on our own. I needed to create an environment in which everyone had the right and the responsibility to make sense of things for themselves and to fight openly for what they think is best—and where the best thinking won out. I needed a *real* idea meritocracy, not some theoretical version of one. That's because an idea meritocracy—i.e., a system that brings together smart, independent thinkers and has them productively disagree to come up with the best possible collective thinking and resolve their disagreements in a believability-weighted way—will outperform any other decision-making system.

Our idea-meritocratic system evolved over the decades. At first, we just argued like hell with each other about what was best and by thrashing through our disagreements came up with better paths than if we had made our decisions individually. But as Bridgewater grew and our range of disagreements and needs to resolve them changed, we became more explicit in how this idea meritocracy would work. We needed a system that could both effectively weigh the believability of different people to come to the best decisions and do that in a way that was so obviously fair everyone would recognize it as such. I knew that without such a system, we would lose both the best thinking and the best thinkers, and I'd be stuck with either kiss-asses or subversives who kept their disagreements and hidden resentments to themselves.

For this all to work, I believed and still believe that we need to be radically truthful and radically transparent with each other.

RADICAL TRUTH AND RADICAL TRANSPARENCY

By radical truth, I mean not filtering one's thoughts and one's questions, especially the critical ones. If we don't talk openly about our issues and have paths for working through them, we won't have partners who collectively own our outcomes.

By radical transparency, I mean giving most everyone the ability to see most everything. To give people anything less than total transparency would make them vulnerable to others' spin and deny them the ability to figure things out for themselves. Radical transparency reduces harmful office politics and the risks of bad behavior because bad behavior is more likely to take place behind closed doors than out in the open.

Some people have called this way of operating radical straightforwardness.

I knew that if radical truth and radical transparency didn't apply across the board, we would develop two classes of people at the company—those with power who are in the know, and those who aren't—so I pushed them both to their limits. To me, a pervasive **Idea Meritocracy = Radical Truth + Radical Transparency + Believability-Weighted Decision Making.**

From a small group of people arguing informally about what's true and what to do about it, we developed approaches, technologies, and tools over the last forty years that have taken us to a whole other level, which has been eye-opening and invaluable in ways that you can read about in the tools chapter at the end of this book. We have always been unwavering in providing this environment, and we let the people who didn't like it self-select themselves out of the company.

By being radically truthful and radically transparent, we could see that we all have terribly incomplete and/or distorted perspectives. This isn't unique to Bridgewater—you would recognize the same thing if you could see into the heads of the people around you. As explained in Understand That People Are Wired Very Differently, people tend to see the same situations in dramatically different ways, depending on how their brains are wired.

Seeing this will help you evolve. At first most people remain stuck in their own heads, stubbornly clinging to the idea that their views are best and that something is wrong with other people who don't see things their way. But when they repeatedly face the questions "How do you know that you're not the wrong one?" and "What process would you use to draw upon these different perspectives to make the best decisions?" they are forced to confront their own believability and see things through others' eyes as well as their own. This shift in perspective is what produces great collective decision making. Ideally, this takes place in an "open-source" way, with the best ideas flowing freely, living, dying, and producing rapid evolution based on their merits.

Most people initially find this process very uncomfortable. While most appreciate it intellectually, they typically are challenged by it emotionally because it requires them to separate themselves from

IDEA MERITOCRACY

=

RADICAL TRUTH

+

RADICAL TRANSPARENCY

+

BELIEVABILITY-WEIGHTED DECISION MAKING

their ego's attachment to being right and try to see what they have a hard time seeing. A small minority get it and love it from the start, a slightly larger minority can't stand it and leave the company, and the majority stick with it, get better at it with time, and eventually wouldn't want to operate any other way.

While operating this way might sound difficult and inefficient, it is actually extremely efficient. In fact, it is much harder and much less efficient to work in an organization in which most people don't know what their colleagues are really thinking. Also, when people can't be totally open, they can't be themselves. As Harvard developmental psychologist Bob Kegan, who has studied Bridgewater, likes to say, in most companies people are doing two jobs: their actual job and the job of managing others' impressions of how they're doing their job. For us, that's terrible. We've found that bringing everything to the surface 1) removes the need to try to look good and 2) eliminates time required to guess what people are thinking. In doing so, it creates more meaningful work and more meaningful relationships.

Here are the forces behind Bridgewater's self-reinforcing evolutionary spiral:

1. We went from one independent thinker who wanted to achieve audacious goals to a group of independent thinkers who wanted to achieve audacious goals.
2. To enable these independent thinkers to have effective collective decision making, we created an idea meritocracy based on principles that ensured we would be radically honest and transparent with each other, have thoughtful disagreements, and have idea-meritocratic ways of getting past our disagreements to make decisions.
3. We recorded these decision-making principles on paper and later encoded them into computers and made our decisions based on them.
4. This produced our successes and failures, which produced more learnings, which were written into more principles that were systemized and acted upon.

5. This process resulted in excellent work and excellent relationships that led us to having well-rewarded and happy employees and clients.

6. That led us to be able to bring in more audacious independent thinkers with more audacious goals to strengthen this self-reinforcing upward spiral.

We did that over and over again, which produced the evolutionary looping behind Bridgewater's forty-plus years of success. It's shown in the diagram on the facing page.

This really works! You don't have to take my word for it. There are two ways you can evaluate the likelihood that this approach and the principles that follow from it are as powerful as I believe they are. You can 1) look at the results they produced and 2) look at the logic behind them.

As for the results, like Lombardi's and the Packers', our track record speaks for itself. We consistently got better over forty years, going from my two-bedroom apartment to become the fifth most important private company in the U.S., according to *Fortune,* and the world's largest hedge fund, making more total money for our clients than any other hedge fund in history. We have received over one hundred industry awards and I've earned three lifetime achievement awards—not to mention remarkable financial and psychological rewards, and most importantly, amazing relationships.

But even more important than these results is the underlying cause-effect logic behind these principles, which came before the results. Over forty years ago, this way of being was a controversial, untested theory that nevertheless seemed logical to me. I will explain this logic to you in the pages that follow. That way, you can assess it for yourself.

There's no doubt that our approach is very different. Some people have even described Bridgewater as a cult. The truth is that Bridgewater succeeds because it is the opposite of a cult. The essential difference between a culture of people with shared values (which is a great thing) and a cult (which is a terrible thing) is the extent to which

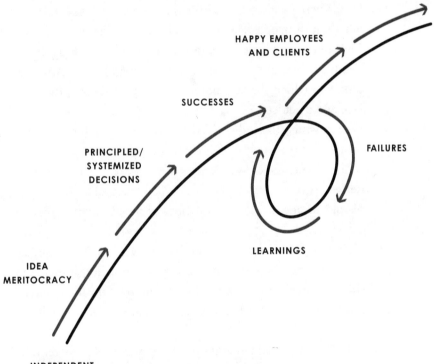

MORE INDEPENDENT
THINKERS AND MORE
AUDACIOUS GOALS

HAPPY EMPLOYEES
AND CLIENTS

SUCCESSES

FAILURES

PRINCIPLED/
SYSTEMIZED
DECISIONS

LEARNINGS

IDEA
MERITOCRACY

INDEPENDENT
THINKERS WITH
AUDACIOUS GOALS

there is independent thinking. Cults demand unquestioning obedience. Thinking for yourself and challenging each other's ideas is anticult behavior, and that is the essence of what we do at Bridgewater.

WHO'S CRAZY?

Some people say that our approach is crazy, but think about it: Which approach do you think is crazy and which one is sensible?

- One where people are truthful and transparent, or one in which most people keep their real thoughts hidden?
- One where problems, mistakes, weaknesses, and disagreements are brought to the surface and thoughtfully discussed, or one in which they are not forthrightly brought to the surface and discussed?
- One in which the right to criticize is nonhierarchical, or one in which it primarily comes from the top down?
- One in which objective pictures of what people are like are derived through lots of data and broad triangulations of people, or one in which evaluations of people are more arbitrary?
- One in which the organization pursues very high standards for achieving both meaningful work and meaningful relationships, or one in which work quality and relationship quality are not equally valued and/or the standards aren't as high?

Which kind of organization do you think will enable better development for the people who work there, foster deeper relationships between them, and produce better results? Which approach would you prefer to see the leaders and organizations that you deal with follow? Which way of being would you prefer the people who run our government to follow?

My bet is that after reading this book, you will agree that our way of operating is far more sensible than conventional ways of operating.

But remember that my most fundamental principle is that you have to think for yourself.

WHY I WROTE THIS BOOK AND HOW YOU CAN GET THE MOST OUT OF IT

If you are inside Bridgewater, I am passing these principles on in my own words so that you can see the dream and the approach through my eyes. Bridgewater will evolve from where it is now based on what you and others in the next generation of leadership want and how you go about getting it. This book is intended to help you. How you use it is up to you. Whether or not this culture continues is up to you and those who succeed me in the leadership role. It is my responsibility to not be attached to Bridgewater being the way *I* would want it to be. It is most important that you and others who succeed me make your own independent choices. Like a parent with adult children, I want you all to be strong, independent thinkers who will do well without me. I have done my best to bring you to this point; now is the time for you to step up and for me to fade away.

If you are outside Bridgewater and thinking about how these principles might apply to your organization, this book is meant to prompt your thinking, not to give you an exact formula to follow. You don't have to adopt all or any of these principles, though I do recommend that you consider them all. Many people who run other organizations have adopted some of these principles, modified others, and rejected many. Whatever you want to do with them is fine with me. These principles provide a framework you can modify to suit your needs. Maybe you will pursue the same goal and maybe you won't; chances are that, in either case, you will collect some valuable stuff. If you share my goal of having your organization be a real idea meritocracy, I believe this book will be invaluable for you because I'm told that no organization has thought through or pushed the concepts of how to make a real idea meritocracy as far as Bridgewater. If doing that is important to you and you pursue it with unwavering determination you will encounter your own barriers, you will find your own ways around them, and you will get there, even if imperfectly.

While these principles are good general rules, it's important to remember that every rule has exceptions and that no set of rules can ever substitute for common sense. Think of these principles as being like a GPS. A GPS helps you get where you're going, but if you follow it blindly off a bridge—well, that would be your fault, not the GPS's. And just as a GPS that gives bad directions can be fixed by updating its software, it's important to raise and discuss exceptions to the principles as they occur so they can evolve and improve over time.

No matter what path you choose to follow, your organization is a machine made up of culture and people that will interact to produce outcomes, and those outcomes will provide feedback about how well your organization is working. Learning from this feedback should lead you to modify the culture and the people so your organizational machine improves.

This dynamic is so important that I've organized Work Principles around it in three sections: To Get the Culture Right, To Get the People Right, and To Build and Evolve Your Machine. Each chapter within these sections begins with a higher-level principle. Reading these will give you a good sense of the main concepts in each chapter.

Under these higher-level principles there are a number of supporting principles built around the many different types of decisions that need to be made. These principles are meant for reference. Though you might want to skim through them, I recommend using them as one would use an encyclopedia or search engine to answer a specific question. For example, if you have to fire (or transfer) someone, you should use the Table of Principles and go to the section of principles about that. To make this easier, at Bridgewater we created a tool called the "Coach" that allows people to type in their particular issue and find the appropriate principles to help them with it.[37] I will soon be

---

[37] Because *Principles* is an evolving document, with new principles being added and old ones getting refined all the time, they will be changed. You will be able to find them in my forthcoming Principles app, which you can learn about at www.principles.com.

making that available to the public, along with many of the other management tools you'll read about in the final section of the book.

My main objective is not to sell you on these principles but to share the most valuable lessons I've learned over my more than forty-year journey. My goal is to get you to think hard about the tough tradeoffs that you will face in many types of situations. By thinking about the tradeoffs behind the principles, you will be able to decide for yourself which principles are best for you.

This brings me to my most fundamental work principle:

● Make your passion and your work one and the same and do it with people you want to be with.

Work is either 1) a job you do to earn the money to pay for the life you want to have or 2) what you do to achieve your mission, or some mix of the two. I urge you to make it as much 2) as possible, recognizing the value of 1). If you do that, most everything will go better than if you don't.

Work Principles is written for those for whom work is primarily the game that you play to follow your passion and achieve your mission.

TO GET THE CULTURE RIGHT . . .

You have to work in a culture that suits you. That's fundamental to your happiness and your effectiveness. You also must work in a culture that is effective in producing great outcomes, because if you don't, you won't get the psychic and material rewards that keep you motivated. In this section on culture I will share my thoughts on how to match your culture to your needs, and I will explain the type of culture that I wanted and that has worked so well for me: an idea meritocracy.

In Chapter One, I explain what an idea meritocracy looks like, and explore why radical truth and radical transparency are essential for it to work well. Being radically truthful and radically transparent are probably the most difficult principles to internalize, because they are so different from what most people are used to. Because this way of being is frequently misunderstood, I tried especially hard to be crystal clear in conveying why we operate this way and how it works in practice.

In Chapter Two, we will turn our attention to why and how to build a culture that fosters meaningful relationships. Besides being rewarding themselves, meaningful relationships enable the radical truth and transparency that allow us to hold each other accountable for producing excellence.

I believe that great cultures, like great people, recognize that making mistakes is part of the process of learning, and that continuous learning is what allows an organization to evolve successfully over time. In Chapter Three, we will explore the principles for doing that well.

Of course, an idea meritocracy is based on the belief that pulling people's thinking together and stress-testing it produces better outcomes than when people keep their disparate thoughts in their own heads. Chapter Four contains principles for "getting in sync" well. Knowing how to have thoughtful disagreements is key.

Idea meritocracies carefully weigh the merits of its members' opinions. Since many opinions are bad and virtually everyone is confident that theirs are good, the process of being able to sort through them well is important to understand. Chapter Five explains our system for believability-weighted decision making.

Since disagreements sometimes remain even after decisions are made, one also needs principles for resolving them that are clearly communicated, consistently adhered to, and universally recognized as fair. I go over these in Chapter Six.

MAKE YOUR IDEA MERITOCRACY WORK IN A WAY THAT SUITS YOU

While all of what you read here may seem challenging and complicated in practice, if you believe as I do that there is no better way to make decisions than to have believable people open-mindedly and assertively surface, explore, and resolve their differences, then you will figure out what it takes to operate that way. If an idea meritocracy doesn't work well, the fault doesn't lie in the concept; it lies in people not valuing it enough to make sure that it works.

If you take nothing else away from this book, you owe it to yourself to see what it's like to experience an idea meritocracy. If it makes sense to you, I hope you will take the plunge. It won't take long for you to understand what a radical difference it will make to your work and your relationships.

To have an Idea
Meritocracy:

1) Put your honest
thoughts on the table

2) Have thoughtful
disagreement

3) Abide by
agreed-upon ways
of getting past
disagreement

1 Trust in Radical Truth and Radical Transparency

Understanding what is true is essential for success, and being radically transparent about everything, including mistakes and weaknesses, helps create the understanding that leads to improvements. That's not just a theory; we have put this into practice at Bridgewater for over forty years, so we know how it works. But like most things in life, being radically truthful and transparent has cons as well as pros, which I will describe as accurately as possible in this chapter.

Being radically truthful and transparent with your colleagues and expecting your colleagues to be the same with you ensures that important issues are apparent instead of hidden. It also enforces good behavior and good thinking, because when you have to explain yourself, everyone can openly assess the merits of your logic. If you are handling things well, radical transparency will make that clear, and if you are handling things badly, radical transparency will make that clear as well, so it helps to maintain high standards.

Radical truth and radical transparency are fundamental to having a real idea meritocracy. The more people can see what is happening—the good, the bad, and the ugly—the more effective they are at deciding the appropriate ways of handling things. This approach is also invaluable for training: Learning is compounded and accelerated when everyone has the opportunity to hear what everyone else is thinking. As a leader, you will get the feedback essential for your learning and for the continual improvement of the organization's decision-making rules. And seeing firsthand what's happening and why builds trust and allows people to make the independent assessments of the evidence that a functioning idea meritocracy requires.

ADAPTING TO RADICAL TRUTH AND RADICAL TRANSPARENCY

It takes getting used to. Virtually everyone who joins Bridgewater believes intellectually that radical truth and radical transparency are what they want, because, after careful thought, that's what they signed up for. Yet most find it difficult to adjust to it because they struggle with the "two yous" as explained in Understand That People Are Wired Very Differently. While their "upper-level yous" understand the benefits of it, their "lower-level yous" tend to react with a flight-or-fight response. Adapting typically takes about eighteen months, though it varies from individual to individual, and there are those who never successfully adapt to it.

Some people tell me it's inconsistent with human nature to operate this way—that people need to be protected from harsh truths and that such a system could never work in practice. Our experience—and our success—have proven that wrong. While it's true that our way of being is not what most people are used to, that doesn't make it unnatural, any more than the hard physical exercise athletes and soldiers do is unnatural. It is a fundamental law of nature that you get stronger only by doing difficult things. While our idea meritocracy is not for everyone, for those who do adapt to it—which is about two-thirds of those who try it—it is so liberating and effective that it's hard for them to imagine any other way to be. What most people like best is knowing there is no spin.

RADICAL TRUTH AND
TRANSPARENCY IN PRACTICE

To give you an idea of what radical truth and transparency look like, I'll share a difficult situation we faced a few years ago when our Management Committee began thinking about reorganizing our back office. Our back office provides the services we need to support our trading in the markets, including trade confirmations, settlements, record maintenance, and accounting. We had built this team up over many years and it was full of hardworking, close-knit employees who were part of our extended family. But at the time we were seeing a need for new capacities that would stretch us beyond what we could do in-house. This led our COO, Eileen Murray, to devise an innovative strategy for spinning off this team and having them incorporated into a tailor-made group within the Bank of New York/Mellon. It was just an exploratory conversation at first; we had no idea whether we would pursue it, how we would pursue it, or what that would ultimately mean for the members of our back office team.

Put yourself in the shoes of the Management Committee. When would you tell the back office team that you were thinking of spinning off their group into another company? Would you wait until the picture was clear? In most organizations this kind of strategic decision would typically be kept under wraps until it was a done deal, because bosses generally think it's bad to create uncertainty among employees. We believe the opposite: that the only responsible way to operate is truthfully and transparently, so that people know what's really going on and can help us sort through any issues that arise. In this case, Eileen led a town-hall meeting with the back office team right away. In the way typical of leaders at Bridgewater, she explained that there was a lot she didn't know and there were a lot of questions that she wouldn't be able to answer. This was the harsh reality at that moment, and while it did create uncertainty, had she followed the more traditional approach of being less open, the inevitable rumors and speculation would've made things much worse.

Though the group ultimately did get spun off, we continue to have wonderful relationships with the people in it. Not only did they cooperate fully throughout the transition, they still come to our Christmas and Fourth of July parties and remain a part of our extended family. Today, we have an award-winning back office because of the innovative things this change allowed us to do. Most importantly, since we were operating openly even while we hadn't figured things out, the back office team had their confidence in our truthfulness and consideration for them reinforced, and they returned it in kind.

For me, not telling people what's really going on so as to protect them from the worries of life is like letting your kids grow into adulthood believing in the Tooth Fairy or Santa Claus. While concealing the truth might make people happier in the short run, it won't make them smarter or more trusting in the long run. It's a real asset that people know they can trust what we say. For that reason I believe that it's almost always better to shoot straight, even when you don't have all the answers or when there's bad news to convey. As Winston Churchill said, "There is no worse course in leadership than to hold out false hopes soon to be swept away." People need to face harsh and uncertain realities if they are going to learn how to deal with them—and you'll learn a lot about the people around you by seeing how well they do.

1.1 Realize that you have nothing to fear from knowing the truth.

If you're like most people, the idea of facing the unvarnished truth makes you anxious. To get over that, you need to understand intellectually why untruths are scarier than truths and then, through practice, get accustomed to living with them.

If you're sick, it's natural to fear your doctor's diagnosis—what if it's cancer or some other deadly disease? As scary as the truth may turn out to be, you will be better off knowing it in the long run because it will allow you to seek the most appropriate treatment. The same holds for learning painful truths about your own strengths and weaknesses. Knowing and acting on the truth is what we call the "big deal" at Bridgewater. It's important not to get hung up on all those emotion- and ego-laden "little deals" that can distract you from the overall mission.

1.2 Have integrity and demand it from others.

Integrity comes from the Latin word *integritas*, meaning "one" or "whole." People who are one way on the inside and another way on the outside—i.e., not "whole"—lack integrity; they have "duality" instead. While presenting your view as something other than it is can sometimes be easier in the moment (because you can avoid conflict, or embarrassment, or achieve some other short-term goal), the second- and third-order effects of having integrity and avoiding duality are immense. People who are one way on the inside and another on the outside become conflicted and often lose touch with their own values. It's difficult for them to be happy and almost impossible for them to be their best.

Aligning what you say with what you think and what you think with what you feel will make you much happier and much more successful. Thinking solely about what's accurate instead of how it is perceived pushes you to focus on the most important things. It helps you sort through people and places because you'll be drawn to people and places that are open and honest. It's also fairer to those around you: Making judgments about people so that they are tried and sentenced in your head, without asking for their perspective, is both unethical and unproductive. Having nothing to hide relieves stress and builds trust.

a. Never say anything about someone that you wouldn't say to them directly and don't try people without accusing them to their faces. Criticism is welcomed and encouraged at Bridgewater, but there is never a good reason to bad-mouth people behind their backs. It is counterproductive and shows a serious lack of integrity, it doesn't yield any beneficial change, and it subverts both the person being bad-mouthed and the environment as a whole. Next to being dishonest, it is the worst thing you can do in our community.

Managers should not talk about people who work for them if they are not in the room. If someone is not present at a meeting where something relevant to them is discussed, we always make sure to send them a recording of the meeting and other relevant information.

b. Don't let loyalty to people stand in the way of truth and the well-being of the organization. In some companies, employees hide their employer's mistakes, and employers do the same in return. This is unhealthy and stands in the way of improvement because it prevents people from bringing their mistakes and weaknesses to the surface, encourages deception, and eliminates subordinates' right of appeal.

The same thing applies to the idea of personal loyalty. I have regularly seen people kept in jobs that they don't deserve because of their personal relationship to the boss, and this leads to unscrupulous managers trading on personal loyalties to build fiefdoms for themselves. Judging one person by a different set of rules than another is an insidious form of corruption that undermines the meritocracy.

I believe in a healthier form of loyalty founded on openly exploring what is true. Explicit, principled thinking and radical transparency are the best antidotes for self-dealing. When everyone is held to the same principles and decision making is done publicly, it is difficult for people to pursue their own interests at the expense of the organization's. In such an environment, those who face their challenges have the most admirable character; when mistakes and weaknesses are hidden, unhealthy character is rewarded instead.

1.3 Create an environment in which everyone has the right to understand what makes sense and no one has the right to hold a critical opinion without speaking up.

Whether people have the independence and character to fight for the best answers will depend upon their nature, but you can encourage them by creating an atmosphere in which everyone's first thought is to ask: "Is it true?"

a. Speak up, own it, or get out. In an idea meritocracy, openness is a responsibility; you not only have the privilege to speak up and "fight for right" but are obliged to do so. This extends especially to principles. Just like everything else, principles need to be questioned and debated. What you're not allowed to do is complain and criticize privately—either to others or in your own head. If you can't fulfill this obligation, then you must go.

Of course open-mindedly exploring what's true with others is not the same thing as stubbornly insisting that only you are right, even after the decision-making machine has settled an issue and moved on. There will inevitably be cases where you must abide by some policy or decision that you disagree with.

b. Be extremely open. Discuss your issues until you are in sync with each other or until you understand each other's positions and can determine what should be done. As someone I worked with once explained, "It's simple—just don't filter."

c. Don't be naive about dishonesty. People lie more than most people imagine. I learned that by being in the position of being responsible for everyone in the company. While we have an exceptionally ethical group of people, in all organizations there are dishonest people who have to be dealt with in practical ways. For example, don't believe most people who are caught being dishonest when they say that they've seen the light and will never do it again because chances are they will. Dishonest people are dangerous, so keeping them around isn't smart.

At the same time, let's be practical. If I tried to limit my relationships to people who never lied, I'd have nobody to work with. While I have extremely high standards when it comes to integrity, I don't view it in a black-white, one-strike-and-you're-out way. I look at the severity, the circumstances, and the patterns to try to understand whether I am dealing with a person who is a habitual liar and will lie to me again, or with a person who is fundamentally honest yet imperfect. I consider the significance of the dishonesty itself (Was the person stealing a piece of cake or were they committing a felony?) as well as the nature of our existing relationship (Is it my spouse telling the lie, a casual acquaintance, or an employee?). Treating such cases differently is appropriate because a basic law of justice is that the punishment should fit the crime.

1.4 Be radically transparent.

If you agree that a real idea meritocracy is an extremely powerful thing, it should not be a great leap for you to see that giving people the right to see things for themselves is better than forcing them to rely on information processed for them by others. Radical transparency forces issues to the surface—most importantly (and most uncomfortably) the problems that people are dealing with and how they're dealing with them—and it allows the organization to draw on the talents and insights of all its members to solve them. Eventually, for people who get used to it, living in a culture of radical transparency is more comfortable than living in the fog of not knowing what's going on and not knowing what people really think. And it is incredibly effective. But, to be clear, like most great things it also has drawbacks. Its biggest drawback is that it is initially very difficult for most people to deal with uncomfortable realities. If unmanaged, it can lead to people getting involved with more things than they should, and can lead people who aren't able to weigh all the information to draw the wrong conclusions.

For example, bringing all an organization's problems to the surface and regarding every one of them as intolerable may lead some people to wrongly conclude that their organization has more intolerable problems than another organization that keeps its issues under wraps. Yet which organization is more likely to achieve excellence? One that highlights its problems and considers them intolerable or one that doesn't?

Don't get me wrong: Radical transparency isn't the same as total transparency. It just means much more transparency than is typical. We do keep some things confidential, such as private health matters or deeply personal problems, sensitive details about intellectual property or security issues, the timing of a major trade, and at least for the short term, matters that are likely to be distorted, sensationalized, and harmfully misunderstood if leaked to the press. In the following principles, you will get a good explanation of when and why we've found it helpful to be transparent and when and why we've found it inappropriate.

Frankly, when I started off being so radically transparent, I had no idea how it would go; I just knew that it was extremely important and that I had to fight hard and find ways to make it happen. I pushed the limits and was surprised by how well it worked. For example, when I started taping all our meetings our lawyers told us we were crazy because we were creating evidence that could be used against us in court or by regulators such as the SEC. In response, I theorized that radical transparency would reduce the risk of our doing anything wrong—and of not dealing appropriately with our mistakes—and that the tapes would in fact protect us. If we were handling things well, our transparency would make that clear (provided, of course, that all parties are reasonable, which isn't something you can always take for granted), and if we were handling things badly, our transparency would ensure that we would get what we deserve, which, in the long run, would be good for us.

I didn't know for sure at the time, but our experience has proven this theory correct time and again. Bridgewater has had uncommonly few legal or regulatory encounters, largely because of our radical transparency. That's because it's tougher to do bad things and easier to find out what's true and resolve claims through radical transparency. Over the last several decades, we have not had a single material legal or regulatory judgment against us.

Naturally, growing bigger and more successful attracts more media attention, and reporters know that salacious and controversial stories draw more eyeballs than balanced ones. Bridgewater is especially vulnerable to this kind of reporting because, with our culture of bringing problems to the surface and sharing them transparently within the company, we leave ourselves open to leaks. Would it be better not to be transparent and so avoid such problems?

I've learned that the people whose opinions matter most are those who know us best—our clients and our employees—and that our radical transparency serves us well with them. Not only has it led to our producing better results, but it also builds trust with our employees and clients so that mischaracterizations in the press roll off their backs. When we discuss such situations with them, they say that for us to not operate transparently would scare them much more.

Having this sort of understanding and support to do the right things has been immeasurably valuable. But we wouldn't have known about these great payoffs if we hadn't so steadfastly pushed the limits of this truth and transparency.

a. Use transparency to help enforce justice. When everyone can follow the discussion leading up to a decision—either in real time in person or via taped records and email threads—justice is more likely to prevail. Everyone is held accountable for their thinking and anyone can weigh in on who should do what according to shared principles. Absent such a transparent process, decisions would be settled behind closed doors by those who have the power to do whatever they want. With transparency, everyone is held to the same high standards.

b. Share the things that are hardest to share. While it might be tempting to limit transparency to the things that can't hurt you, it is especially important to share the things that are most difficult to share, because if you don't share them you will lose the trust and partnership of the people you are not sharing with. So, when faced with the decision to share the hardest things, the question should not be whether to share but how. The following principles will help you do this well.

c. Keep exceptions to radical transparency very rare. While I would like virtually total transparency and wish that everyone would handle the information they have access to responsibly to work out what's true and what to do about it, I realize that's an ideal to be approached but never fully achieved. There are exceptions to every rule, and in very rare cases, it is better not to be radically transparent. In those unusual cases, you will need to figure out a way that preserves the culture of radical transparency without exposing you and those you care about to undue risks.

When weighing an exception, approach it as an expected value calculation, taking into consideration the second- and third-order consequences. Ask yourself whether the costs of making the case transparent and managing the risks of that transparency outweigh the benefits. In the vast majority of cases, they don't. I've found that the most common reasons to limit broad transparency are:

1. Where the information is of a private, personal, or confidential nature and doesn't meaningfully impact the community at large.
2. Where sharing and managing such information puts the long-term interests of the Bridgewater community, its clients, and our ability to uphold our principles at risk (for instance, our proprietary investment logic or a legal dispute).

3. Where the value of sharing the information broadly with the community is very low and the distraction it would cause would be significant (compensation, for instance).

What I'm saying is that I believe one should push the limits of being transparent while remaining prudent. Because we tape virtually everything—including our mistakes and weaknesses—for everyone to see, we are a target-rich environment for media that thrives on sensationalistic or critical gossip and can find ways of having information leaked to them. In one case when we faced the problem of having information leaked to the press that was intentionally distorted and hurt our recruiting efforts, we were forced to institute some controls on ultrasensitive information, so that only a significant number of ultratrustworthy people received it in real time, and it was distributed to others after a delay. The information was the sort that, in a typical company, would be shared with just a handful but at Bridgewater was shared with nearly a hundred trusted people. In other words, while our radical transparency in that case wasn't total, I pushed its limits in a practical way. It served us well because the people who most needed the transparency got it right away and most everyone understood that the commitment to being transparent remained very much intact, even in challenging circumstances. People know that my intent is to always push the limits of trying to be transparent and that the only things that would prevent me from doing that will be the interests of the company and that I will tell them if I can't be transparent and why. It is in our culture to be that way and that fosters trust, even when the transparency is less than we would like it to be.

d. Make sure those who are given radical transparency recognize their responsibilities to handle it well and to weigh things intelligently. People cannot be given the privilege of receiving information and then use the information to harm the company, so rules and procedures must be in place to ensure that doesn't happen. For example, we provide great transparency inside Bridgewater on the condition that Bridgewater citizens do not leak it outside; if they do, they will be dismissed for cause (for unethical behavior). Additionally, the rules for how issues are explored and decisions are made must be maintained, and because different people have different perspectives, it's important that the paths for resolving them are followed. For example, some people are going to make big deals out of little deals, come up with their own wrong theories, or have problems seeing how things are evolving. Remind them of the risks that the company takes to give them that transparency and their responsibilities to handle the information that they get responsibly. I have found that people appreciating this transparency and knowing that they will lose it if it is not handled well leads them to enforce good behavior with each other.

e. Provide transparency to people who handle it well and either deny it to people who don't handle it well or remove those people from the organization. It is the right and responsibility of management, and not the right of all employees, to determine when exceptions to radical transparency should be made. Management should restrict transparency sparingly and wisely because every time they do, it undermines the idea meritocracy and people's trust.

f. Don't share sensitive information with the organization's enemies. Both inside and outside of any organization, there are some people who will intentionally cause the organization harm. If these enemies are within your organization, you need to call them out to resolve this conflict through the organization's system for achieving such resolutions, because working with enemies within your "extended family" will undermine you and the "family." If the enemies are outside your organization and will use the information to harm you, of course don't share it.

1.5 Meaningful relationships and meaningful work are mutually reinforcing, especially when supported by radical truth and radical transparency.

The most meaningful relationships are achieved when you and others can speak openly to each other about everything that's important, learn together, and understand the need to hold each other accountable to be as excellent as you can be. When you have such relationships with those you work with, you pull each other through challenging times; at the same time, sharing challenging work draws you closer and strengthens your relationships. This self-reinforcing cycle creates the success that allows you to pursue more and more ambitious goals.

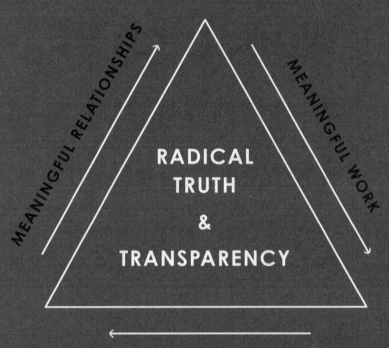

2 Cultivate Meaningful Work and Meaningful Relationships

Meaningful relationships are invaluable for building and sustaining a culture of excellence, because they create the trust and support that people need to push each other to do great things. If the overwhelming majority of people care about having an excellent community, they will take care of it, which will yield both better work and better relationships. Relationships have to be genuine, not forced; at the same time, the culture of the community will have a big influence on how people value relationships and how they behave with each other. To me, a meaningful relationship is one in which people care enough about each other to be there whenever someone needs support and they enjoy each other's company so much that they can have great times together both inside and outside of work. I literally love many of the people I work with, and I respect them deeply.

I have often been asked whether relationships at Bridgewater are more like those of a family or those of a team, the implication being that in a family there is unconditional love and a permanent relationship, while in a team the attachment is only as strong as the person's contribution. Before answering this question, I want to emphasize that either is good by me, because both families and teams provide meaningful relationships and that neither is anything like a typical job at a typical company, where the relationships are primarily utilitarian. But to answer the question directly, I wanted Bridgewater to be like a family business in which family members have to perform excellently or be cut. If I had a family business and a family member wasn't performing well, I would want to let them go because I believe that it isn't good for either the family member (because staying in a job they're not suited to stands in the way of their personal evolution) or the company (because it holds back the whole community). That's tough love.

To give you an idea of how Bridgewater's culture developed and how it's different from what you'd find at most companies, I will tell you about how we handled benefits in our early days. When the company was just me and a small group of people, I didn't provide employees with health insurance; I assumed that they would buy it on their own. But I did want to help the people I shared my life with during their times of need. If someone I worked with got seriously sick and couldn't afford proper care, what was I going to do, stand by and not help them? Of course I'd help them financially, to whatever extent I could. So when I did begin providing health insurance to my employees, I felt that I was insuring myself against the money I knew I'd give them if they were injured or fell ill as much as I was insuring them.

Because I wanted to make certain that they received the best care possible, the policies I provided allowed them to go to any doctor they chose and spend whatever amount was required. On the other hand, I didn't protect them against the little things. For example, I didn't provide dental insurance any more than I provided car insurance, because I felt that it was their own responsibility to protect their teeth, just as it was their own responsibility to take care of their car. If they needed dental insurance, they could pay for it out of their own pocket. My main point is that I didn't approach benefits in the impersonal, transactional way most companies do, but more like something I provided for my family. I was more than generous with some things and expected people to take personal responsibility for others.

When I treated my employees like extended family, I found that they typically behaved the same way with each other and our community as a whole, which was much more special than having a strictly quid pro quo relationship. I can't tell you how many people would do anything in their power to help our community/company and wouldn't want to work anywhere else. This is invaluable.

As Bridgewater grew, my ability to have quality personal contact with everyone faded, but this wasn't a problem because the broader community embraced this way of being with each other. This didn't just happen; we did a lot to help it along. For example, we put into place a policy that we would pay for half of practically any activities that people want to do together up to a set cap (we now support more than a hundred clubs and athletic and common-interest groups); we paid for food and drink for those who hosted potluck dinners at their houses; and we bought a house that employees can use for events and celebrations. We have Christmas, Halloween, Fourth of July, and other parties that often include family members. Eventually, others who valued this kind of relationship took responsibility for it and it spread to become a cultural norm so that I could just sit back and watch beauty happen.

What about the person who doesn't give a damn about all of this meaningful relationship stuff, who just wants to go into work, do a good job, and receive fair compensation? Is that okay? Sure it is, and it's common for a significant percentage of employees. Not everyone feels the same or is expected to feel the same about the community. It's totally okay to opt out. We have all sorts of people and respect whatever they want to do on their own time, as long as they abide by the law and are considerate. But these are not the folks who will provide the community with the skeletal strength of commitment that is essential for it to be extraordinary over very long periods of time.

No matter how much one tries to create a culture of meaningful relationships, the organization is bound to have some bad (intentionally harmful) people in it. Being there isn't good for them or the company so it's best to find out who they are and remove them. We have found that the higher the percentage of people who really care about the organization, the fewer the number of bad people there are, because the people who really care protect the community against them. We have also found that our radical transparency helps make it clearer which are which.

2.1 Be loyal to the common mission and not to anyone who is not operating consistently with it.

Loyalty to specific people who are not in tight sync with the mission and how to achieve it will create factionalism and undermine the well-being of the community. It is often the case, and quite beautiful, that personal loyalties exist. However, it is also often the case, and quite ugly, when personal loyalties come into conflict with the organization's interests.

2.2 Be crystal clear on what the deal is.

To have a good relationship, you must be clear with each other about what the quid pro quo is—what is generous, what is fair, and what is just plain taking advantage—and how you will be with each other.

One important thing that typically divides people is how they approach their work. Are they working just for their paycheck or are they looking for something more? Each of us has our own views about what is most important. I've made a lot of money through my work, but I see my job as much more than as a way to make money—it's how I choose to live out my values around excellence, meaningful work, and meaningful relationships. If the people I worked with were primarily interested in making money, we would have conflicts whenever we had to choose between upholding our values and making an easy buck. Don't get me wrong—of course I understand that people don't work for personal satisfaction alone, and that a job must be economically viable. But we all have definite ideas about what we value and what we want our relationships to be like, and employers and employees have to be in sync on such things.

Naturally there will be disagreement and negotiation, but some things cannot be compromised and you and your employees must know what those things are. This is especially true if you're seeking to create an environment that has shared values, a deep commitment to the mission, and high standards of behavior.

At Bridgewater, we expect people to behave in a manner that is consistent with how people in high-quality, long-term relationships behave—that is, with a high level of mutual consideration for each other's interests and a clear understanding of who is responsible for what. On the surface, that sounds nice and straightforward, but what exactly does that mean? It is important to be clear.

Take for example a case in which an employee's family member is diagnosed with a severe illness, or an employee dies tragically, leaving his or her family in a precarious situation. These things happen far more often than any of us would like them to, and there are of course customs and laws that define the basic accommodations and benefits (such as personal vacation days, short- and long-term disability insurance, and life insurance) that are required. But how do you determine what kinds of assistance should be provided beyond that? What are the principles for deciding how to handle each specific situation fairly—which may not always mean doing the same thing in every case?

None of this is easy, but the following principles provide some guidance.

a. Make sure people give more consideration to others than they demand for themselves. This is a requirement.

Being considerate means allowing other people to mostly do what they want, so long as it is consistent with our principles, policies, and the law. It also means being willing to put others ahead of your own desires. If the people on both sides of an argument approach their disagreements in this way, we will have many fewer disputes about who is offending whom.

Still, judgments will have to be made and lines will have to be drawn and set down in policies.

This is the overarching guideline: It is more inconsiderate to prevent people from exercising their rights because you are offended by them than it is for them to do whatever it is that offends you. That said, it is inconsiderate not to weigh the impact of one's actions on others, so we expect people to use sensible judgment in not doing obviously offensive things. There are some behaviors that are clearly offensive to many people, and it is appropriate to specify and prohibit them in clear policies. The list of those specifics, and the policies pertaining to them, arise from specific cases. Applying this principle to them is done in much the same way that case law is created.

b. Make sure that people understand the difference between fairness and generosity. Sometimes people mistake generosity for not being fair. For example, when Bridgewater arranged for a bus to shuttle people who live in New York City to our Connecticut office, one employee asked, "It seems it would be fair to also compensate those of us who spend hundreds of dollars on gas each month, particularly in light of the New York City bus." This line of thinking mistakes an act of generosity for some for an entitlement for everyone.

Fairness and generosity are different things. If you bought two birthday gifts for two of your closest friends, and one cost more than the other, what would you say if the friend who got the cheaper gift accused you of being unfair? Probably something like, "I didn't have to get you any gift, so stop complaining." At Bridgewater, we are generous with people (and I am personally generous), but we feel no obligation to be measured and equal in our generosity.

Generosity is good and entitlement is bad, and they can easily be confused, so be crystal clear on which is which. Decisions should be based on what you believe is warranted in a particular circumstance and what will be most appreciated. If you want to have a community of people who have both high-quality, long-term relationships and a high sense of personal responsibility, you can't allow a sense of entitlement to creep in.

c. Know where the line is and be on the far side of fair. The line is what's fair, appropriate, or required, as distinct from what's generous, in light of the defined quid pro quo relationship between parties. As mentioned earlier, you should expect people to behave in a manner consistent with how people in high-quality, long-term relationships behave—with a high level of mutual consideration for each other's interests and a clear understanding of who is responsible for what. Each should operate on the far side of fair, by which I mean giving more consideration to others than you demand for yourself. This is different from how people in most commercial relationships generally behave, as they tend to focus more on their own interests than on the interests of others or of the community as a whole. If each party says "You deserve more," "No, you deserve more," rather than "I deserve more," you are more likely to have generous, good relationships.

d. Pay for work. While it isn't all about the quid pro quo between the company and the employee, this balance must be economically viable for the relationships to be sustainable. Set policies that clearly define this quid pro quo, and be measured, but not excessively precise, when shifting it around. While you should by and large stick to the arrangement, you should also recognize that there are rare, special times when employees will need a bit of extra time off and there are times that the company will require employees to give it extra hours. The company should pay for above-normal work one way or another, and employees should be docked for below-normal work. The give-and-take should roughly equal out over time. Within reasonable boundaries, nobody should worry about the exact ebbs and flows. But if the needs of one side change on a sustained basis, the financial arrangement will need to be readjusted to establish a new, appropriate relationship.

2.3 Recognize that the size of the organization can pose a threat to meaningful relationships.

When there were just a few of us, we had meaningful relationships because we knew and liked each other. When we grew to between fifty and a hundred people, we had a community; when we grew beyond that, the sense of community began to slip because we didn't all know each other in the same way. That's when I realized that having groups (departments) of around a hundred (give or take about fifty) that are bound collectively by our common mission was the best way to scale the meaningful relationship. While bigger companies tend to be more impersonal, that is just another challenge that has to be figured out.

2.4 Remember that most people will pretend to operate in your interest while operating in their own.

For example, most people will operate in a way that maximizes the amount of money they will get and that minimizes the amount of work they have to do to get it.

To see this, just leave someone unsupervised and allow them to bill you for what they have done. Be especially wary of this conflict of interest when people are advising you on matters that will affect how much money they earn—such as the lawyer who spends a lot of billable hours giving you advice, or the salesperson who advises you on what to purchase while receiving a commission on the amount that you spend. You can't imagine how many people I meet who are eager to "help" me.

Don't be naive. Strive for the highest possible percentage of your population having meaningful work and meaningful relationships while recognizing that there will always be some percentage of the population who won't care for the community and/or will do it harm.

2.5 Treasure honorable people who are capable and will treat you well even when you're not looking.

They are rare. Such relationships take time to build and can only be built if you treat such people well.

3 Create a Culture in Which It Is Okay to Make Mistakes and Unacceptable Not to Learn from Them

Everyone makes mistakes. The main difference is that successful people learn from them and unsuccessful people don't. By creating an environment in which it is okay to safely make mistakes so that people can learn from them, you'll see rapid progress and fewer significant mistakes. This is especially true in organizations where creativity and independent thinking are important, as success will inevitably require the acceptance of failure as a part of the process. As Thomas Edison once said, "I have not failed. I've just found ten thousand ways that do not work."

Mistakes will cause you pain, but you shouldn't try to shield yourself or others from it. Pain is a message that something is wrong and it's an effective teacher that one shouldn't do that wrong thing again. To deal with your own and others' weaknesses well you must acknowledge them frankly and openly and work to find ways of preventing them from hurting you in the future. It's at this point that many people say, "No thanks, this isn't for me—I'd rather not have to deal with these things." But this is against your and your organization's best interests—and will keep you from achieving your goals. It seems to me that if you look back on yourself a year ago and aren't shocked by how stupid you were, you haven't learned much. Still, few people go out of their way to embrace their mistakes. It doesn't have to be that way.

Remember back in Life Principles, when I told the story about the time that Ross, then our head of trading, forgot to put in a trade for a client? The money just sat there in cash and by the time the mistake was discovered it had cost the client (actually Bridgewater, because we had to make good on it) a *lot* of money. It was terrible and I could easily have fired Ross to make the point that nothing less than perfection will be accepted. But that would have been counterproductive. I would have lost a good man and it would have only encouraged other employees to hide their mistakes, creating a culture that would not only be dishonest but crippled in its ability to learn and grow. If Ross hadn't experienced that pain, he and Bridgewater would have been the worse for it.

The point I made by not firing Ross was much more powerful than firing him would have been—I was demonstrating to him and others that it was okay to make mistakes and unacceptable not to learn from them. After the dust settled, Ross and I worked together to build an error log (we now call it the Issue Log), in which traders recorded all their mistakes and bad outcomes so we could track them and address them systematically. It has become one of the most powerful tools we have at Bridgewater. Our environment is one in which people understand that remarks such as "You handled that badly" are meant to be helpful rather than punitive.

Of course, in managing others who make mistakes, it is important to know the difference between 1) capable people who made mistakes and are self-reflective and open to learning from them, and 2) incapable people, or capable people who aren't able to embrace their mistakes and learn from them. Over time I've found that hiring self-reflective people like Ross is one of the most important things I can do.

Finding this kind of person isn't easy. I've often thought that parents and schools overemphasize the value of having the right answers all the time. It seems to me that the best students in school tend to be the worst at learning from their mistakes, because they have been conditioned to associate mistakes with failure instead of opportunity.

This is a major impediment to their progress. Intelligent people who embrace their mistakes and weaknesses substantially outperform their peers who have the same abilities but bigger ego barriers.

3.1 Recognize that mistakes are a natural part of the evolutionary process.

If you don't mind being wrong on the way to being right you'll learn a lot—and increase your effectiveness. But if you can't tolerate being wrong, you won't grow, you'll make yourself and everyone around you miserable, and your work environment will be marked by petty back-biting and malevolent barbs rather than by a healthy, honest search for truth.

You must not let your need to be right be more important than your need to find out what's true. Jeff Bezos described it well when he said, "You have to have a willingness to repeatedly fail. If you don't have a willingness to fail, you're going to have to be very careful not to invent."

a. Fail well. Everyone fails. Anyone you see succeeding is only succeeding at the things you're paying attention to—I guarantee they are also failing at lots of other things. The people I respect most are those who fail well. I respect them even more than those who succeed. That is because failing is a painful experience while succeeding is a joyous one, so it requires much more character to fail, change, and then succeed than to just succeed. People who are just succeeding must not be pushing their limits. Of course the worst are those who fail and don't recognize it and don't change.

b. Don't feel bad about your mistakes or those of others. Love them! People typically feel bad about their mistakes because they think in a shortsighted way about the bad outcome and not about the evolutionary process of which mistakes are an integral part. I once had a ski instructor who had also given lessons to Michael Jordan, the greatest basketball player of all time. Jordan, he told me, reveled in his mistakes, seeing each of them as an opportunity to improve. He understood that mistakes are like those little puzzles that, when you solve them, give you a gem. Every mistake that you make and learn from will save you from thousands of similar mistakes in the future.

3.2 Don't worry about looking good— worry about achieving your goals.

Put your insecurities away and get on with achieving your goals. Reflect and remind yourself that an accurate criticism is the most valuable feedback you can receive. Imagine how silly and unproductive it would be to respond to your ski instructor as if he were blaming you when he told you that you fell because you didn't shift your weight properly. It's no different if a supervisor points out a flaw in your work process. Fix it and move on.

a. Get over "blame" and "credit" and get on with "accurate" and "inaccurate." Worrying about "blame" and "credit" or "positive" and "negative" feedback impedes the iterative process that is essential to learning. Remember that what has already happened lies in the past and no longer matters except as a lesson for the future. The need for phony praise needs to be unlearned.

3.3 Observe the patterns of mistakes to see if they are products of weaknesses.

Everyone has weaknesses and they are generally revealed in the patterns of mistakes they make. The fastest path to success starts with knowing what your weaknesses are and staring hard at them. Start by writing down your mistakes and connecting the dots between them. Then write down your "one big challenge," the weakness that stands the most in the way of your getting what you want. Everyone has at least one big challenge. You may in fact have several, but don't go beyond your "big three." The first step to tackling these impediments is getting them out into the open.

3.4 Remember to reflect when you experience pain.

Remember this: *The pain is all in your head.* If you want to evolve, you need to go where the problems and the pain are. By confronting the pain, you will see more clearly the paradoxes and problems you face. Reflecting on them and resolving them will give you wisdom. The harder the pain and the challenge, the better.

Because these moments of pain are so important, you shouldn't rush through them. Stay in them and explore them so you can build a foundation for improvement. Embracing your failures—and confronting the pain they cause you and others—is the first step toward genuine improvement; it is why confession precedes forgiveness in many societies. Psychologists call this "hitting bottom." If you keep doing this you will convert the pain of facing your mistakes and weaknesses into pleasure and "get to the other side" as I explained in Embrace Reality and Deal with It.

a. Be self-reflective and make sure your people are self-reflective. When there is pain, the animal instinct is flight-or-fight. Calm yourself down and reflect instead. The pain you are feeling is due to things being in conflict—maybe you've come up against a terrible reality, such as the death of a friend, and are unable to accept it; maybe you've been forced to acknowledge a weakness that challenges the idea you'd had of yourself. If you can think clearly about what's behind it, you will learn more about what reality is like and how to better deal with it. Self-reflectiveness is the quality that most differentiates those who evolve quickly from those who don't. Remember: **Pain + Reflection = Progress.**

b. Know that nobody can see themselves objectively. While we should all strive to see ourselves objectively, we shouldn't expect everyone to be able to do that well. We all have blind spots; people are by definition subjective. For this reason, it is everyone's responsibility to help others learn what is true about themselves by giving them honest feedback, holding them accountable, and working through disagreements in an open-minded way.

c. Teach and reinforce the merits of mistake-based learning. To encourage people to bring their mistakes into the open and analyze them objectively, managers need to foster a culture that makes this normal and that penalizes suppressing or covering up mistakes. We do this by making it clear that one of the worst mistakes anyone can make is not facing up to their mistakes. This is why the use of the Issue Log is mandatory at Bridgewater.

3.5 Know what types of mistakes are acceptable and what types are unacceptable, and don't allow the people who work for you to make the unacceptable ones.

When considering the kinds of mistakes you are willing to allow in order to promote learning through trial and error, weigh the potential damage of a mistake against the benefit of incremental learning. In defining what latitude I'm willing to give people, I say, "I'm willing to let you scratch or dent the car, but I won't put you in a position where there's a significant risk of your totaling it."

PAIN

+

REFLECTION

=

PROGRESS

4 Get and Stay in Sync

Remember that for an organization to be effective, the people who make it up must be aligned on many levels—from what their shared mission is, to how they will treat each other, to a more practical picture of who will do what when to achieve their goals. Yet alignment can never be taken for granted because people are wired so differently. We all see ourselves and the world in our own unique ways, so deciding what's true and what to do about it takes constant work.

Alignment is especially important in an idea meritocracy, so at Bridgewater we try to attain alignment consciously, continually, and systematically. We call this process of finding alignment "getting in sync," and there are two primary ways it can go wrong: cases resulting from simple misunderstandings and those stemming from fundamental disagreements. Getting in sync is the process of open-mindedly and assertively rectifying both types.

Many people mistakenly believe that papering over differences is the easiest way to keep the peace. They couldn't be more wrong. By avoiding conflicts one avoids resolving differences. People who suppress minor conflicts tend to have much bigger conflicts later on, which can lead to separation, while people who address their mini-conflicts head on tend to have the best and the longest-lasting relationships. Thoughtful disagreement—the process of having a quality back-and-forth in an open-minded and assertive way so as to see things through each other's eyes—is powerful, because it helps both parties see things they've been blind to. But it's not easy. While it is straightforward to have a meritocracy in activities in which there is clarity of relative abilities (because the results speak for themselves such as in sports, where the fastest runner wins the race), it is much harder in a creative environment (where different points of view about what's best have to be resolved). If they're not, the process of sorting through disagreements and knowing who has the authority to decide quickly becomes chaotic. Sometimes people get angry or stuck; a conversation can easily wind up with two or more people spinning unproductively and unable to reach agreement on what to do.

For these reasons, specific processes and procedures must be followed. Every party to the discussion must understand who has what rights and which procedures should be followed to move toward resolution. (We've also developed tools for helping do this, which you can review at the end of this book.) And everyone must understand the most fundamental principle for getting in sync, which is that people must be open-minded and assertive at the same time. Thoughtful disagreement is not a battle; its goal is not to convince the other party that he or she is wrong and you are right, but to find out what is true and what to do about it. It must also be nonhierarchical, because in an idea meritocracy communication doesn't just flow unquestioned from the top down. Criticisms must also come from the bottom up.

For example, this email was sent to me by someone who worked for me after a meeting with clients. All the senior people at Bridgewater, including me, are routinely criticized and judged by our subordinates.

From: Jim H
To: Ray; Lionel K; Greg J; Randal S; David A
Subject: Feedback on ABC Meeting . . .

Ray- you deserve a "D-" for your performance today in the ABC meeting and everyone that was in the room that saw you agrees on that harsh assessment (give or take half a grade). This was especially disappointing for two reasons: 1) You have been great in previous meetings where the subject matter to be covered was the same, and 2) We held a specific planning meeting yesterday to ask you to focus tightly on culture and portfolio structuring because we had only 2 hours to have you cover those two topics, me cover the investment process, have Greg do the observatory and have Randal do implementation. Instead, you took a total of 62 minutes (I measured) but worse, you rambled for 50 minutes on what I think was portfolio structuring topics and only then got to culture and you talked about that for 12 minutes. It was obvious to all of us that you did not prepare at all because there is no way you could have been that disorganized at the outset if you had prepared.

Similarly I'd like to share another case in which one of our senior managers observed a conversation between Greg Jensen, who was then CEO, and a junior employee, and felt that Greg was speaking to that employee in a way that discouraged dissent and independent thinking. She raised this in feedback she gave Greg. Greg disagreed, asserting that he was simply reminding the employee of relevant principles and her responsibilities to either adhere to them or openly question them. The two sought to get in sync through a series of emails, and when that didn't work, they raised their disagreement to the Management Committee. A case based on the meeting in question was sent to the entire company so everyone could judge for themselves who was right and who was wrong. It was a good learning exercise that Greg and the senior manager appreciated. We used it to reflect on our written principles for handling situations like this and they both got a lot of useful feedback. If we hadn't laid out our principles and used them to judge cases like this, we would have people with power making decisions however they wanted instead of in mutually agreed-upon ways.

The principles that follow flesh out how we do this. If they are adhered to, you will be well aligned with others and your idea meritocracy will hum with productivity. If they are not, it will grind to a halt.

4.1 Recognize that conflicts are essential for great relationships . . .

. . . because they are how people determine whether their principles are aligned and resolve their differences. Everyone has his or her own principles and values, so all relationships entail a certain amount of negotiation or debate over how people should be with each other. What you learn about each other will either draw you together or drive you apart. If your principles are aligned and you can work out your differences via a process of give-and-take, you will draw closer together. If not, you will move apart. Open discussion of differences ensures that there are no misunderstandings. If that doesn't happen on an ongoing basis, gaps in perspective will widen until inevitably there is a major clash.

a. Spend lavishly on the time and energy you devote to getting in sync, because it's the best investment you can make. In the long run, it saves time by increasing efficiency, but it's important that you do it well. You will need to prioritize what you are going to get in sync about and who you are going to get in sync with because of time constraints. Your highest priority should be the most important issues with the most believable and most relevant parties.

4.2 Know how to get in sync and disagree well.

It is harder to run an idea meritocracy in which disagreements are encouraged than a top-down autocracy in which they are suppressed. But when believable parties to disagreements are willing to learn from each other, their evolution is faster and their decision making is far better.

The key is in knowing how to move from disagreement to decision making. It is important that the paths for doing this are clear so that who is responsible for doing what is known. (This is the reason I created a tool called the Dispute Resolver, which lays out the paths and makes clear to everyone if they are holding on to a different point of view rather than moving it along to resolution. You can read about it in the tools appendix.)

It is essential to know where the ultimate decision-making authority lies—i.e., how far the power of the argument will carry relative to the power of the assigned authority. While arguing and especially after a decision is rendered, everyone in the idea meritocracy must remain calm and respectful of the process. It is never acceptable to get upset if the idea meritocracy doesn't produce the decision that you personally wanted.

a. Surface areas of possible out-of-syncness. If you and others don't raise your perspectives, there's no way you will resolve your disputes. You can surface the areas of disagreement informally or put them on a list to go over. I personally like to do both, though I encourage people to list their disagreements in order of priority so I/we can more easily direct them to the right party at the right time.

The nubbiest questions (the ones that there is the greatest disagreement about) are the most important ones to thrash out, as they often concern differences in people's values or their approaches to important decisions. It's especially important to bring these issues to the surface and examine their premises thoroughly and unemotionally. If you don't, they will fester and cause rot.

b. Distinguish between idle complaints and complaints meant to lead to improvement. Many complaints either fail to take into account the full picture or reflect a closed-minded point of view. They are what I call "chirping," and are generally best ignored. But constructive complaints may lead to important discoveries.

c. Remember that every story has another side. Wisdom is the ability to see both sides and weigh them appropriately.

4.3 Be open-minded and assertive at the same time.

Being effective at thoughtful disagreement requires one to be open-minded (seeing things through the other's eyes) and assertive (communicating clearly how things look through your eyes) and to flexibly process this information to create learning and adaptation.

I have found that most people have problems being assertive and open-minded at the same time. Typically they are more inclined to be assertive than open-minded (because it's easier to convey how they see things than to understand how others do, and also because people tend to have ego attachments to being right) though some people are too willing to accept others' views at the expense of their own. It's important to remind people that they have to do both—and to remember that decision making is a two-step process in which one has to take in information as well as decide. It also helps to remind people that those who change their minds are the biggest winners because they learned something, whereas those who stubbornly refuse to see the truth are losers. With practice, training, and constant reinforcement, anyone can get good at this.

a. Distinguish open-minded people from closed-minded people. Open-minded people seek to learn by asking questions; they realize how little they know in relation to what there is to know and recognize that they might be wrong; they are thrilled to be around people who know more than they do because it represents an opportunity to learn something. Closed-minded people always tell you what they know, even if they know hardly anything. They are typically uncomfortable being around those who know a lot more than they do.

b. **Don't have anything to do with closed-minded people.** Being open-minded is much more important than being bright or smart. No matter how much they know, closed-minded people will waste your time. If you must deal with them, recognize that there can be no helping them until they open their minds.

c. **Watch out for people who think it's embarrassing not to know.** They're likely to be more concerned with appearances than actually achieving the goal; this can lead to ruin over time.

d. **Make sure that those in charge are open-minded about the questions and comments of others.** The person responsible for a decision must be able to explain the thinking behind it openly and transparently so that everyone can understand and assess it. In the event of disagreement, an appeal should be made to either the decision maker's boss or an agreed-upon, knowledgeable group of others, generally people more knowledgeable than and senior to the decision maker.

e. **Recognize that getting in sync is a two-way responsibility.** In any conversation, there is a responsibility to express and a responsibility to listen. Misinterpretations and misunderstandings are always going to happen. Often, difficulty in communication is due to people having different ways of thinking (e.g., left-brained thinkers talking to right-brained thinkers). The parties involved should always consider the possibility that one or both of them misunderstood and do a back-and-forth so that they can get in sync. Very simple tricks—like repeating what you're hearing someone say to make sure you're actually getting it—can be invaluable. Start by assuming you're either not communicating or listening well instead of blaming the other party. Learn from your miscommunications so they don't happen again.

f. Worry more about substance than style. This is not to say that some styles aren't more effective than others with different people and in different circumstances, but I often hear people complaining about the style or tone of a criticism in order to deflect from its substance. If you think someone's style is an issue, box it as a separate issue to get in sync on.

g. Be reasonable and expect others to be reasonable. You have a responsibility to be reasonable and considerate when you are advocating for your point of view and should never let your "lower-level you" gain control, even if the other person loses his or her temper. Their bad behavior doesn't justify yours.

If either party to a disagreement is too emotional to be logical, the conversation should be deferred. Pausing a few hours or even a few days in cases where decisions do not have to be made immediately is sometimes the best approach.

h. Making suggestions and questioning are not the same as criticizing, so don't treat them as if they are. A person making suggestions may not have concluded that a mistake *will* be made—they could just be making doubly sure that the person they're talking to has taken all the risks into consideration. Asking questions to make sure that someone hasn't overlooked something isn't the same thing as saying that he or she *has* overlooked it ("watch out for the ice" vs. "you're being careless and not looking out for the ice"). Yet I often see people react to constructive questions as if they were accusations. That is a mistake.

4.4 If it is your meeting to run, manage the conversation.

There are many reasons why meetings go poorly, but frequently it is because of a lack of clarity about the topic or the level at which things are being discussed (e.g., the principle/machine level, the case-at-hand level, or the specific-fact level).

a. **Make it clear who is directing the meeting and whom it is meant to serve.** Every meeting should be aimed at achieving someone's goals; that person is the one responsible for the meeting and decides what they want to get out of it and how they will do so. Meetings without someone clearly responsible run a high risk of being directionless and unproductive.

b. **Be precise in what you're talking about to avoid confusion.** It is often best to repeat a specific question to be sure both questioner and responder are crystal clear on what is being asked and answered. In an email, this is often as simple as cutting and pasting the questions into the body of the text.

c. **Make clear what type of communication you are going to have in light of the objectives and priorities.** If your goal is to have people with different opinions work through their differences to try to get closer to what is true and what to do about it (open-minded debate), you will run your meeting differently than if its goal is to educate. Debating takes time, and that time increases exponentially depending on the number of people participating in the discussion, so you have to carefully choose the right people in the right numbers to suit the decision that needs to be made. In any discussion try to limit the participation to those whom you value most in light of your objectives. The worst way to pick people is based on whether their conclusions align with yours. Group-think (people not asserting independent views) and solo-think (people being unreceptive to the thoughts of others) are both dangerous.

d. **Lead the discussion by being assertive and open-minded.** Reconciling different points of view can be difficult and time-consuming. It is up to the meeting leader to balance conflicting perspectives, push through impasses, and decide how to spend time wisely.

A common question I get is: What happens when someone inexperienced offers an opinion? If you're running the conversation, you should be weighing the potential cost in the time that it takes to explore their opinion versus the potential gain in being able to assess their thinking and gain a better understanding of what they're like. Exploring the views of people who are still building their track record can give you valuable insights into how they might handle various responsibilities. Time permitting, you should work through their reasoning with them so they can understand how they might be wrong. It's also your obligation to open-mindedly consider whether they're right.

e. Navigate between the different levels of the conversation. When considering an issue or situation, there should be two levels of discussion: the case at hand and the relevant principles that help you decide how the machine should work. You need to clearly navigate between these levels in order to handle the case well, test the effectiveness of your principles, and improve the machine so similar cases will be handled better in the future.

f. Watch out for "topic slip." Topic slip is random drifting from topic to topic without achieving completion on any of them. One way to avoid it is by tracking the conversation on a whiteboard so that everyone can see where you are.

g. Enforce the logic of conversations. People's emotions tend to heat up when there is disagreement. Remain calm and analytical at all times; it is more difficult to shut down a logical exchange than an emotional one. Remember too that emotions can shade how people see reality. For example, people will sometimes say, "I feel like (something is true)" and proceed as though it's a fact, when other people may interpret the same situation differently. Ask them, "Is it true?" to ground the conversation in reality.

h. Be careful not to lose personal responsibility via group decision making. Too often groups will make a decision to do something without assigning personal responsibilities, so it is not clear who is supposed to follow up by doing what. Be clear in assigning personal responsibilities.

i. **Utilize the "two-minute rule" to avoid persistent interruptions.** The two-minute rule specifies that you have to give someone an uninterrupted two minutes to explain their thinking before jumping in with your own. This ensures that everyone has time to fully crystallize and communicate their thoughts without worrying they will be misunderstood or drowned out by a louder voice.

j. **Watch out for assertive "fast talkers."** Fast talkers are people who articulately and assertively say things faster than they can be assessed as a way of pushing their agenda past other people's examination or objections. Fast talking can be especially effective when it's used against people worried about appearing stupid. Don't be one of those people. Recognize that it's your responsibility to make sense of things and don't move on until you do. If you're feeling pressured, say something like "Sorry for being stupid, but I'm going to need to slow you down so I can make sense of what you're saying." Then ask your questions. All of them.

k. **Achieve completion in conversations.** The main purpose of discussion is to achieve completion and get in sync, which leads to decisions and/or actions. Conversations that fail to reach completion are a waste of time. When there is an exchange of ideas, it is important to end it by stating the conclusions. If there is agreement, say it; if not, say that. Where further action has been decided, get those tasks on a to-do list, assign people to do them, and specify due dates. Write down your conclusions, working theories, and to-do's in places that will lead to their being used as foundations for continued progress. To make sure this happens, assign someone to make sure notes are taken and follow-through occurs.

There is no reason to get angry because you still disagree. People can have a wonderful relationship and disagree about some things; you don't have to agree on everything.

l. **Leverage your communication.** While open communication is very important, the challenge is to do it in a time-efficient way—you can't have individual conversations with everyone. It is helpful to identify easy ways of sharing, like open emails posted on an FAQ board or sending around videotapes or audio recordings of key meetings. (I call such approaches "leverage.") The challenges become greater the higher you go in the reporting hierarchy because the number of people affected by your actions and who also have opinions and/or questions grows so large. In such cases, you will need even greater leverage and prioritization (for example by having some of the questions answered by a well-equipped party who works for you or by asking people to prioritize their questions by urgency or importance).

4.5 Great collaboration feels like playing jazz.

In jazz, there's no script: You have to figure things out as you go along. Sometimes you need to sit back and let others drive things; other times, you blare it out yourself. To do the right thing at the right moment you need to really listen to the people you're playing with so that you can understand where they're going.

All great creative collaboration should feel the same way. Combining your different skills like different instruments, improvising creatively, and at the same time subordinating yourself to the goals of the group leads to playing great music together. But it's important to keep in mind what number of collaborators will play well together: A talented duo can improvise beautifully, as can a trio or quartet. But gather ten musicians and no matter how talented they are, it's probably going to be too many unless they're carefully orchestrated.

a. 1+1=3. Two people who collaborate well will be about three times as effective as each of them operating independently, because each will see what the other might miss—plus they can leverage each other's strengths while holding each other accountable to higher standards.

b. 3 to 5 is more than 20. Three to five smart, conceptual people seeking the right answers in an open-minded way will generally lead to the best answers. It may be tempting to convene a larger group, but having too many people collaborate is counterproductive, even if the members of the larger group are smart and talented. The symbiotic advantages of adding people to a group grow incrementally (2+1=4.25) up to a point; beyond that, adding people actually subtracts from effectiveness. That is because 1) the marginal benefits diminish as the group gets larger (two or three people might be able to cover most of the important perspectives, so adding more people doesn't bring much more) and 2) larger group interactions are less efficient than smaller ones. Of course, what's best in practice depends on the quality of the people and the differences of the perspectives that they bring and how well the group is managed.

4.6 When you have alignment, cherish it.

While there is nobody in the world who will share your point of view on everything, there are people who will share your most important values and the ways in which you choose to live them out. Make sure you end up with those people.

4.7 If you find you can't reconcile major differences—especially in values—consider whether the relationship is worth preserving.

There are all kinds of different people in the world, many of whom value different kinds of things. If you find you can't get in sync with someone on shared values, you should consider whether that person is worth keeping in your life. A lack of common values will lead to a lot of pain and other harmful consequences and may ultimately drive you apart. It might be better to head all that off as soon as you see it coming.

5 Believability Weight Your Decision Making

I n typical organizations, most decisions are made either auto-
cratically, by a top-down leader, or democratically, where everyone shares their opinions and those opinions that have the most
support are implemented. Both systems produce inferior decision
making. That's because the best decisions are made by an idea meritocracy with believability-weighted decision making, in which the most
capable people work through their disagreements with other capable
people who have thought independently about what is true and what
to do about it.

It is far better to weight the opinions of more capable decision
makers more heavily than those of less capable decision makers.
This is what we mean by "believability weighting." So how do you
determine who is capable at what? The most believable opinions are
those of people who 1) have repeatedly and successfully accomplished
the thing in question, and 2) have demonstrated that they can logically explain the cause-effect relationships behind their conclusions.
When believability weighting is done correctly and consistently, it is
the fairest and the most effective decision-making system. It not only
produces the best outcomes but also preserves alignment, since even
people who disagree with the decision will be able to get behind it.

But for this to be the case, the criteria for establishing believability must be objective and trusted by everybody. At Bridgewater everyone's believability is tracked and measured systematically, using tools such as Baseball Cards and the Dot Collector that actively record and weigh their experience and track records. In meetings we regularly take votes about various issues via our Dot Collector app, which displays both the equal-weighted average and the believability-weighted results (along with each person's vote).

Typically, if both the equal-weighted average and the believability-weighted votes align, we consider the matter resolved and move on. If the two types of votes are at odds, we try again to resolve them and, if we can't, we go with the believability-weighted vote. Depending on what type of decision it is, in some cases, a single "Responsible Party" (RP) can override a believability-weighted vote; in others, the believability-weighted vote supersedes the RP's decision. But in all cases believability-weighted votes are taken seriously when there is disagreement. Even in cases in which the RPs can overrule the believability-weighted vote, the onus is on the RP to try to resolve the dispute before overruling it. In my forty years at Bridgewater, I never made a decision contrary to the believability-weighted decision because I felt that to do so was arrogant and counter to the spirit of the idea meritocracy, though I argued like hell for what I thought was best.

To give you an example of what this process looks like in action, during the spring of 2012 our research teams used believability-weighted decision making to resolve a disagreement about what would happen next as the European debt crisis was heating up. At that time, the borrowing and debt-service needs of the governments of Italy, Ireland, Greece, Portugal, and especially Spain had reached levels that far exceeded their abilities to pay. We knew that the European Central Bank would either have to make unprecedented purchases of government bonds or allow the debt crisis to worsen to the point where defaults and the breakup of the Eurozone would probably occur. Germany was adamantly opposed to a bailout. It was clear that the fates of these countries' economies, and of the Eurozone itself, depended on how well Mario Draghi, the president of the European Central Bank, orchestrated the ECB's next move. But what would he do?

Like analyzing a chess board to visualize the implications and inclinations of the different moves of the different players, each of us looked at the situation from every angle. After a lot of discussion we remained split: About half of us thought the ECB would print more money to buy the bonds and about half thought they wouldn't, because breaking with the Germans would threaten the Eurozone even more. While such thoughtful and open exchanges are essential, it's also critical to have mutually agreed-upon ways of resolving them to arrive at the best decision. So we used our believability-weighting system to break the stalemate.

We did that using our Dot Collector tool, which helps us surface the sources of our disagreements in people's different thinking characteristics and work our way through them based on their believabilities. People have different believability weightings for different qualities, like expertise in a particular subject, creativity, ability to synthesize, etc. These dots are determined by a mixture of ratings, both from peers and tests of different sorts. By looking at these attributes, and also understanding which thinking qualities are most essential to the situation at hand, we can make the best decisions.

In this case, we took a believability-weighted vote, with the qualities chosen being both subject-matter expertise and ability to synthesize. Using the Dot Collector, it became clear that those with greater believability believed Draghi would defy Germany and print money, so that is what we went with. A few days later, European policymakers announced a sweeping plan to buy unlimited quantities of government bonds, so we got it right. While the believability-weighted answer isn't always the best answer, we have found that it is more likely to be right than either the boss's answer or an equal-weighted referendum.

Regardless of whether or not you use this kind of technology and structured process for believability weighting, the most important thing is that you get the concept. Simply look down on yourself and your team when a decision needs to be made and consider who is most likely to be right. I assure you that, if you do, you will make better decisions than if you don't.

5.1 Recognize that having an effective idea meritocracy requires that you understand the merit of each person's ideas.

Having a hierarchy of merit is not only consistent with an idea meritocracy but essential for it. It's simply not possible for everyone to debate everything all the time and still get their work done. Treating all people equally is more likely to lead away from truth than toward it. But at the same time, all views should be considered in an open-minded way, though placed in the proper context of the experiences and track records of the people expressing them.

Imagine if a group of us were getting a lesson in how to play baseball from Babe Ruth, and someone who'd never played the game kept interrupting him to debate how to swing the bat. Would it be helpful or harmful to the group's progress to ignore their different track records and experience? Of course it would be harmful and plain silly to treat their points of view equally, because they have different levels of believability. The most productive approach would be to allow Ruth to give his instructions uninterrupted and then take some time afterward to answer questions. But because I'm pretty extreme in believing that it is important to obtain understanding rather than accepting doctrine at face value, I would encourage the new batter not to accept what Ruth has to say as right just because he was the greatest slugger of all time. If I were that new batter, I wouldn't stop questioning Ruth until I was confident I had found the truth.

a. If you can't successfully do something, don't think you can tell others how it should be done. I have seen some people who have repeatedly failed at something hold strongly to their opinions of how it should be done, even when their opinions are at odds with those who have repeatedly done it successfully. That is dumb and arrogant. They should instead ask questions and seek believability-weighted votes to help them get out of their intransigence.

b. Remember that everyone has opinions and they are often bad. Opinions are easy to produce; everyone has plenty of them and most people are eager to share them—even to fight for them. Unfortunately many are worthless or even harmful, including a lot of your own.

5.2 Find the most believable people possible who disagree with you and try to understand their reasoning.

Having open-minded conversations with believable people who disagree with you is the quickest way to get an education and to increase your probability of being right.

a. Think about people's believability in order to assess the likelihood that their opinions are good. While it pays to be open-minded, you also have to be discerning. Remember that the quality of the life you get will depend largely on the quality of the decisions that you make as you pursue your goals. The best way to make great decisions is to know how to triangulate with other, more knowledgeable people. So be discerning about whom you triangulate with and skilled in the way you do it.

The dilemma you face is trying to understand as accurately as you can what's true in order to make decisions effectively while realizing many of the opinions you will hear won't be worth much, including your own. Think about people's believability, which is a function of their capabilities and their willingness to say what they think. Keep their track records in mind.

b. **Remember that believable opinions are most likely to come from people 1) who have successfully accomplished the thing in question at least three times, and 2) who have great explanations of the cause-effect relationships that lead them to their conclusions.** Treat those who have neither as not believable, those who have one as somewhat believable, and those who have both as the most believable. Be especially wary of those who comment from the stands without having played on the field themselves and who don't have good logic, as they are dangerous to themselves and others.

c. **If someone hasn't done something but has a theory that seems logical and can be stress-tested, then by all means test it.** Keep in mind that you are playing probabilities.

d. **Don't pay as much attention to people's conclusions as to the reasoning that led them to their conclusions.** It is common for conversations to consist of people sharing their conclusions rather than exploring the reasoning that led to those conclusions. As a result, there is an overabundance of confidently expressed bad opinions.

e. **Inexperienced people can have great ideas too, sometimes far better ones than more experienced people.** That's because experienced thinkers can get stuck in their old ways. If you've got a good ear, you will be able to tell when an inexperienced person is reasoning well. Like knowing whether someone can sing, it doesn't take a lot of time. Sometimes a person only has to sing a few bars for you to hear how well they can sing. Reasoning is the same—it often doesn't take a lot of time to figure out if someone can do it.

f. **Everyone should be up-front in expressing how confident they are in their thoughts.** A suggestion should be called a suggestion; a firmly held conviction should be presented as such—particularly if it's coming from someone with a strong track record in the area in question.

5.3 Think about whether you are playing the role of a teacher, a student, or a peer . . .

. . . and whether you should be teaching, asking questions, or debating. Too often people flail in their disagreements because they either don't know or don't think about how they should engage effectively; they just blurt out whatever they think and argue. While everyone has the right and obligation to make sense of everything, basic rules for engagement should be followed. Those rules and how you should follow them depend on your relative believabilities. For example, it would not be effective for the person who knows less to tell the person who knows more how something should be done. It's important to get the balance between your assertiveness and your open-mindedness right, based on your relative levels of understanding of the subject.

Think about whether the person you're disagreeing with is more or less believable than you. If you are less believable, you are more of a student and should be more open-minded, primarily asking questions in order to understand the logic of the person who probably knows more. If you're more believable, your role is more of a teacher, primarily conveying your understanding and answering questions. And if you are approximate peers, you should have a thoughtful exchange as equals. When there is a disagreement about who is more believable, be reasonable and work it through. In cases when you can't do this alone effectively, seek out the help of an agreed-upon third party.

In all cases, try to see things through the other person's eyes so that you can obtain understanding. All parties should remember that the purpose of debate is to get at truth, not to prove that someone is right or wrong, and that each party should be willing to change their mind based on the logic and evidence.

a. It's more important that the student understand the teacher than that the teacher understand the student, though both are important. I have often seen less believable people (students) insist that the more believable people (teachers) understand their thinking and prove why the teacher is wrong before listening to what the teacher (the more believable party) has to say. That's backward. While untangling the student's thinking can be helpful, it is typically difficult and time-consuming and puts the emphasis on what the student sees instead of on what the teacher wants to convey. For that reason, our protocol is for the student to be open-minded first. Once the student has taken in what the teacher has to offer, both student and teacher will be better prepared to untangle and explore the student's perspective. It is also more time-efficient to get in sync this way, which leads to the next principle.

b. Recognize that while everyone has the right and responsibility to try to make sense of important things, they must do so with humility and radical open-mindedness. When you are less believable, start by taking on the role of a student in a student-teacher relationship—with appropriate humility and open-mindedness. While it is not necessarily you who doesn't understand, you must assume this until you have seen the issue through the other's eyes. If the issue still doesn't make sense to you and you think that your teacher just doesn't get it, appeal to other believable people. If you still can't reach an agreement, assume you are wrong. If, on the other hand, you are able to convince a number of believable people of your point of view, then you should make sure your thinking is heard and considered by the person deciding, probably with the help of the other believable parties. Remember that those who are higher in the reporting hierarchy have more people they are trying to sort through on an expected value basis to get the best thinking and more people who want to tell them what they think, so they are time-constrained and have to play the probabilities. If your thinking has been stress-tested by other believable people who support you, it has a greater probability of being heard. Conversely, those higher in the reporting hierarchy must strive to achieve the goal of getting in sync with those lower in the hierarchy about what makes sense. The more people get in sync about what makes sense, the more capable and committed people will be.

5.4 Understand how people came by their opinions.

Our brains work like computers: They input data and process it in accordance with their wiring and programming. Any opinion you have is made up of these two things: the data and your processing or reasoning. When someone says, "I believe X," ask them: *What data are you looking at? What reasoning are you using to draw your conclusion?*

Dealing with raw opinions will get you and everyone else confused; understanding where they come from will help you get to the truth.

a. If you ask someone a question, they will probably give you an answer, so think through to whom you should address your questions. I regularly see people ask totally uninformed or nonbelievable people questions and get answers that they believe. This is often worse than having no answers at all. Don't make that mistake. You need to think through who the right people are. If you're in doubt about someone's believability, find out.

The same is true for you: If someone asks you a question, think first whether you're the right person to answer it. If you're not believable, you probably shouldn't have an opinion about what they're asking, let alone share it.

Be sure to direct your comments or questions to the believable Responsible Party or Parties for the issues you want to discuss. Feel free to include others if you think that their input is relevant, while recognizing that the decision will ultimately rest with whoever is responsible for it.

b. Having everyone randomly probe everyone else is an unproductive waste of time. For heaven's sake don't bother directing your questions to people who aren't responsible or, worse still, throw your questions out there without directing them at all.

c. **Beware of statements that begin with "I think that . . ."** Just because someone thinks something doesn't mean it's true. Be especially skeptical of statements that begin with "I think that I . . ." since most people can't accurately assess themselves.

d. **Assess believability by systematically capturing people's track records over time.** Every day is not a new day. Over time, a body of evidence builds up, showing which people can be relied on and which cannot. Track records matter, and at Bridgewater tools such as Baseball Cards and the Dot Collector make everyone's track records available for scrutiny.

5.5 Disagreeing must be done efficiently.

Working oneself through disagreements can be time-consuming, so you can imagine how an idea meritocracy—where disagreement is not just tolerated but encouraged—could become dysfunctional if it's not managed well. Imagine how inefficient it would be if a teacher ran a large class by asking each of the students individually what they thought, and then debated with all of them, instead of conveying their own views first and taking questions later.

People who want to disagree must keep this in mind and follow the tools and protocols for disagreeing well.

a. **Know when to stop debating and move on to agreeing about what should be done.** I have seen people who agree on the major issues waste hours arguing over details. It's more important to do big things well than to do the small things perfectly. But when people disagree on the importance of debating something, it probably should be debated. Operating otherwise would essentially give someone (typically the boss) a de facto veto.

b. Use believability weighting as a tool rather than a substitute for decision making by Responsible Parties. Believability-weighted decision making is a way of supplementing and challenging the decisions of Responsible Parties, not overruling them. As Bridgewater's system currently exists, everyone is allowed to give input, but their believability is weighted based on the evidence (their track records, test results, and other data). Responsible Parties can overrule believability-weighted voting but only at their peril. When a decision maker chooses to bet on his own opinion over the consensus of believable others, he is making a bold statement that will be proven right or wrong by the results.

c. Since you don't have the time to thoroughly examine everyone's thinking yourself, choose your believable people wisely. Generally speaking, it's best to choose three believable people who care a lot about achieving the best outcome and who are willing to openly disagree with each other and have their reasoning probed. Of course the number three isn't set in stone; the group could be larger or smaller. Its ideal size depends on the amount of time available, how important the decision is, how objectively you can assess your own and others' decision-making abilities, and how important it is to have a lot of people understand the reasoning behind the decision.

d. When you're responsible for a decision, compare the believability-weighted decision making of the crowd to what you believe. When they're at odds, you should work hard to resolve the disagreement.

If you are about to make a decision that the believability-weighted consensus thinks is wrong, think very carefully before you proceed. It's likely that you're wrong, but even if you're right, there's a good chance that you'll lose respect by overruling the process. You should try hard to get in sync, and if you still can't do that, you should be able to put your finger on exactly what it is you disagree with, understand the risks of being wrong, and clearly explain your reasons and logic to others. If you can't do those things, you probably should suspend your own judgment and go with the believability-weighted vote.

5.6 Recognize that everyone has the right and responsibility to try to make sense of important things.

There will come a point in all processes of thinking things through when you are faced with the choice of requiring the person who sees things differently from you to slowly work things through until you see things the same way, or going along with the other person, even though their thinking still doesn't seem to make sense. I recommend the first path when you are disagreeing about something important and the latter when it's unimportant. I understand that the first path can be awkward because the person you are speaking to can get impatient. To neutralize that I suggest you simply say, "Let's agree that I am a dumb shit but I still need to make sense of this, so let's move slowly to make sure that happens."

One should always feel free to ask questions, while remembering one's obligation to remain open-minded in the discussions that follow. Record your argument so that if you can't get in sync or make sense of things, you can send it out so others can decide. And of course, remember that you are operating in an idea meritocracy—be mindful of your own believability.

a. Communications aimed at getting the best answer should involve the most relevant people. As a guide, the most relevant people to probe are your managers, direct reports, and/or agreed experts. They are the most impacted by and most informed about the issues under discussion, and so they are the most important parties to be in sync with. If you can't get in sync, you should escalate the disagreement by raising it to the appropriate people.[38]

---

[38] The most appropriate people are either the people you both report to (which we call the point of the pyramid in an organizational chart) or someone you mutually agree will be a good arbiter.

b. Communication aimed at educating or boosting cohesion should involve a broader set of people than would be needed if the aim were just getting the best answer. Less experienced, less believable people may not be necessary to decide an issue, but if the issue involves them and you aren't in sync with them, that lack of understanding will in the long run likely undermine morale and the organization's efficiency. This is especially important in cases where you have people who are both not believable and highly opinionated (the worst combination). Unless you get in sync with them, you will drive their uninformed opinions underground. If, on the other hand, you are willing to be challenged, you will create an environment in which all criticisms are aired openly.

c. Recognize that you don't need to make judgments about everything. Think about who is responsible for something (and their believability), how much you know about it, and your own believability. Don't hold opinions about things you don't know anything about.

5.7 Pay more attention to whether the decision-making system is fair than whether you get your way.

An organization is a community with a set of shared values and goals. Its morale and smooth functioning should always take precedence over your need to be right—and besides, you could be wrong. When the decision-making system is consistently well-managed and based on objective criteria, the idea meritocracy is more important than the happiness of any one of its members—even if that member is you.

6 Recognize How to Get Beyond Disagreements

I t is the rare dispute that is resolved to both parties' equal satisfaction. Imagine you are having an argument with your neighbor about a tree of theirs that has fallen onto your property. Who is responsible for its removal? Who owns the firewood? Who pays for the damage? While you might not be able to resolve the disagreement yourselves, the legal system has procedures and guidelines that allow it to determine what's true and what to do about it, and once it renders its judgment it's done, even if one of you didn't get what you wanted. That's just the way life is.

At Bridgewater, our principles and policies work in essentially the same way, providing a path for settling disputes that's not unlike what you'd find in the courts (though it's less formal). Having such a system is essential in an idea meritocracy, because you can't just encourage people to think independently and fight for what they believe is true. You also have to provide them with a way to get past their disagreements and move forward.

Managing this well is especially important at Bridgewater because we have so much more thoughtful disagreement than other places. While in most cases people disagreeing can work things out on their own, it is still often the case that people can't agree on what's true and what to do about it. In those cases, we follow our procedures for believability-weighted voting and go with the verdict; or, in the cases where the RP wants to do it his/her way contrary to the vote and has the power to do so, we accept that and move on.

In the end, people who join our idea meritocracy agree to abide by our policies and procedures and the decisions that come out of them, just as if they had taken a dispute to court and had to abide by its procedures and the resulting verdict. This requires them to separate themselves from their own opinion and avoid getting angry when a decision doesn't go their way. If people don't follow the agreed-upon paths, they don't have the right to complain about either the people they disagree with or the idea-meritocratic system itself.

In those rare cases where our principles, policies, and procedures fail to make clear how a disagreement should be resolved, it is everyone's responsibility to raise that fact so the process can be clarified and improved.

6.1 Remember: Principles can't be ignored by mutual agreement.

Principles are like laws—you can't break one simply because you and someone else agree to break it. Remember that it's everyone's obligation to speak up, own it, or get out. If you don't think the principles provide the right way to resolve a problem or disagreement, you need to fight to change the principles, not just do what you want to do.

a. The same standards of behavior apply to everyone. Whenever there is a dispute, both parties are required to have equal levels of integrity, to be open-minded and assertive, and to be equally considerate. The judges must hold the parties to the same standards and provide feedback consistent with these standards. I have often seen cases in which the feedback wasn't appropriately balanced for various reasons (to hold the stronger performer to a higher standard, to spread the blame). This is a mistake. The person in the wrong needs to receive the strongest message. Not operating this way could lead them to believe that the problem wasn't caused by them, or was caused by both parties equally. Of course, the message should be conveyed calmly and clearly rather than emotionally to maximize its effectiveness.

6.2 Make sure people don't confuse the right to complain, give advice, and openly debate with the right to make decisions.

Everyone does not report to everyone. Responsibilities and authorities are assigned to individuals based on assessments of their ability to handle them. People are given the authority that they need to achieve outcomes and are held accountable for their ability to produce them.

At the same time, they are going to be stress-tested from both directions—i.e., by those they report to and by those who report to them. The challenging and probing that we encourage is not meant to second-guess their every decision but to improve the quality of their work over time. The ultimate goal of independent thinking and open debate is to provide the decision maker with alternative perspectives. It doesn't mean that decision-making authority is transitioned to those who are probing them.

a. When challenging a decision and/or a decision maker, consider the broader context. It's important to view individual decisions in the broadest possible context. For example, if the Responsible Party being challenged has a vision, and the decision being disputed involves a small detail of that overall vision, the decision needs to be debated and evaluated within the context of that larger vision.

6.3 Don't leave important conflicts unresolved.

While it's easier to avoid confrontations in the short run, the consequences of doing so can be massively destructive in the long term. It's critical that conflicts actually get resolved—not through superficial compromise, but through seeking the important, accurate conclusions. In most cases, this process should be made transparent to relevant others (and sometimes the entire organization), both to ensure quality decision making and to perpetuate the culture of openly working through disputes.

a. Don't let the little things divide you when your agreement on the big things should bind you. Almost every group that agrees on the big things ends up fighting about less important things and becoming enemies even though they should be bound by the big things. This phenomenon is called the narcissism of small differences. Take the Protestants and Catholics. Though both are followers of Christ, some of them have been fighting for hundreds of years, even though many of them are unable to articulate the differences that divide them, and most of those who can articulate the differences realize that they are insignificant relative to the big important things that should bind them together. I once saw a close family have an irrevocable blow-out at a Thanksgiving dinner over who would cut the turkey. Don't let this narcissism of small differences happen to you. Understand that nobody and nothing is perfect and that you are lucky to have by-and-large excellent relationships. See the big picture.

b. Don't get stuck in disagreement—escalate or vote! By practicing open-mindedness and assertiveness, you should be able to resolve most disagreements. If not, and if your dispute is one-on-one, you should escalate to a mutually agreed-upon believable other. All things being equal, that should be someone higher in your reporting chain, such as your boss. When a group can't reach an agreement, the person responsible for the meeting should take a believability-weighted vote.

6.4 Once a decision is made, everyone should get behind it even though individuals may still disagree.

A decision-making group in which those who don't get what they want continue to fight rather than work for what the group has decided is destined to fail—you can see this happening all the time in companies, organizations, and even political systems and nations. I'm not saying that people should pretend they like the decision if they don't, or that the matter in question can't be revisited at a future date. What I am saying is that in order to be effective, all groups that work together have to operate with protocols that allow time for disagreements to be explored, but in which dissenting minority parties recognize that group cohesion supersedes their individual desires once they have been overruled.

The group is more important than the individual; don't behave in a way that undermines the chosen path.

a. See things from the higher level. You are expected to go to the higher level and look down on yourself and others as part of a system. In other words, you must get out of your own head, consider your views as just some among many, and look down on the full array of points of view to assess them in an idea-meritocratic way rather than just in your own possessive way. Seeing things from the higher level isn't just seeing other people's point of view; it's also being able to see every situation, yourself, and others in the situation as though you were looking down on them as an objective observer. If you can do this well, you will see the situation as "another one of those," see it through everyone's eyes, and have good mental maps or principles for deciding how to handle it.

Almost all people initially find it difficult to get beyond seeing things through just their own eyes, so I've developed policies and tools such as the Coach (which connects situations to principles) that help people do this. With practice many people can learn to develop this perspective, though others never do. You need to know which type of person you and the people around you are. If you can't do this well on your own, seek the help of others. Recognize that many people cannot see things from the higher level and distinguish those who can from those who can't, and either get rid of those who can't or have good guardrails in place to protect yourself and the organization against this inability.

By the way, it is of course okay to continue to disagree on some things as long as you don't keep fighting, thereby undermining the idea meritocracy. If you continue to fight the idea meritocracy, you must go.

b. Never allow the idea meritocracy to slip into anarchy. In an idea meritocracy, there is bound to be more disagreement than in a typical organization, but when it's taken to an extreme, arguing and nitpicking can undermine the idea meritocracy's effectiveness. At Bridgewater, I have encountered some people, especially junior people, who mistakenly think they are entitled to argue about whatever they want and with whomever they please. I have even seen people band together to threaten the idea meritocracy, claiming that their right to do so comes from the principles. They misunderstand my principles and the boundaries within the organization. They must abide by the rules of the system, which provide paths for resolving disagreements, and they mustn't threaten the system.

c. Don't allow lynch mobs or mob rule. Part of the purpose of having a believability-weighted system is to remove emotion from decision making. Crowds get emotional and seek to grab control. That must be prevented. While all individuals have the right to have their own opinions, they do not have the right to render verdicts.

6.5 Remember that if the idea meritocracy comes into conflict with the well-being of the organization, it will inevitably suffer.

That's just a matter of practicality. As you know I believe that what's good must work well, and that having the organization work well is of paramount importance.

a. Declare "martial law" only in rare or extreme circumstances when the principles need to be suspended. While all these principles exist for the well-being of the community, there may come times when adhering to them could threaten the community's well-being. For example, we encountered a time when there were leaks to the media of some things that we made radically transparent within Bridgewater. People at Bridgewater understood that our transparency about our weaknesses and mistakes was being used to present distorted and harmful pictures of Bridgewater, so we had to lessen our level of transparency until we resolved that problem. Rather than just lessening this degree of transparency, I explained the situation and declared "martial law," meaning that this was a temporary suspension of the full degree of radical transparency. That way, everyone would know both that it was an exceptional case and that we were entering a time when the typical way of operating would be suspended.

b. Be wary of people who argue for the suspension of the idea meritocracy for the "good of the organization." When such arguments win out, the idea meritocracy will be weakened. Don't let that happen. If people respect the rules of the idea meritocracy, there will be no conflict. I know that from my experiences over decades. However, I also know that there will be people who put what they want above the idea meritocracy and threaten it. Consider those people to be enemies of the system and get rid of them.

6.6 Recognize that if the people who have the power don't want to operate by principles, the principled way of operating will fail.

Ultimately, power will rule. This is true of any system. For example, it has repeatedly been shown that systems of government have only worked when those with the power value the principles behind the system more than they value their own personal objectives. When people have both enough power to undermine a system and a desire to get what they want that is greater than their desire to maintain the system, the system will fail. For that reason the power supporting the principles must be given only to people who value the principled way of operating more than their individual interests (or the interests of their faction), and people must be dealt with in a reasonable and considerate way so that the overwhelming majority will want and fight for that principle-based system.

TO GET THE
PEOPLE
RIGHT . . .

While we talked about an organization's culture in the last section, its people are even more important because they can change the culture for better or for worse. A culture and its people are symbiotic—the culture attracts certain kinds of people and the people in turn either reinforce or evolve the culture based on their values and what they're like. If you choose the right people with the right values and remain in sync with them, you will play beautiful jazz together. If you choose the wrong people, you will all go over the waterfall together.

Steve Jobs, who everyone thought was the secret to Apple's success, said, "The secret to my success is that we've gone to exceptional lengths to hire the best people in the world." I explain this concept in the next chapter, Remember That the WHO Is More Important than the WHAT. Anyone who runs a successful organization will tell you the same.

Yet most organizations are bad at recruiting. It starts with interviewers picking people they like and who are like them instead of focusing on what people are really like and how well they will fit in their jobs and careers. As I describe in Chapter Eight, Hire Right, Because the Penalties for Hiring Wrong Are Huge, to hire well, one needs a more scientific process that precisely matches people's values, abilities, and skills with the organization's culture and its career paths. You and your candidate need to get to know each other. You have to let them interview your organization and you have to honestly convey to them what it's like, warts and all, and be crystal clear about what you can expect from each other.

But even then, after you both say yes, you won't know if you have a good fit until you've lived together in your work and your relationships for a while. The "interviewing" process doesn't end when employment begins, but transitions into a rigorous process of training, testing, sorting, and most importantly, getting in sync, which I describe in Chapter Nine, Constantly Train, Test, Evaluate, and Sort People.

I believe that the ability to objectively self-assess, including one's own weaknesses, is the most influential factor in whether a person succeeds, and that a healthy organization is one in which people compete not so much against each other as against the ways in which their lower-level selves get in the way. Your goal should be to hire people who understand this, equip them with the tools and the information they need to flourish in their jobs, and not micromanage them. If they can't do the job after being trained and given time to learn, get rid of them; if they can, promote them.

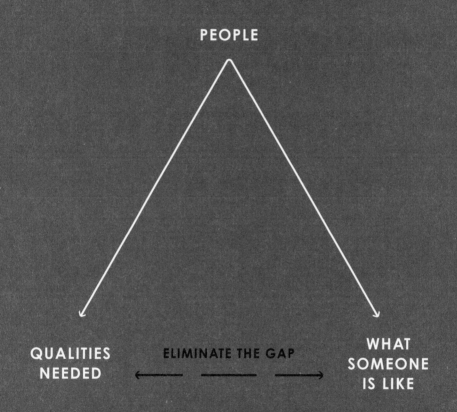

7 Remember That the WHO Is More Important than the WHAT

People often make the mistake of focusing on what should be done while neglecting the more important question of who should be given the responsibility for determining what should be done. That's backward. When you know what you need in a person to do the job well and you know what the person you're putting into it is like, you can pretty well visualize how things will go.

I remember one case where one of our most talented rising executives was putting together a transition plan so that he could move on to another role. He arrived at a meeting with the Management Committee with binders full of process flows and responsibility maps, detailing every aspect of the area he'd been responsible for, and explained how he'd automated and systemized as much of it as possible to make it foolproof. It was an impressive presentation, but it quickly became clear that he didn't have an answer for who was going to take his place and what would happen if they saw things differently and put together a different plan. Who would oversee the machine he'd built, probe it for problems, and constantly improve it or decide to get rid of it? What qualities would such a person need to produce the same excellent results that he had—i.e., what were the important job specifications we should match the person against? Where would we go to recruit such a person?

While these kinds of questions seem obvious in retrospect, time and again I see people overlooking them. Not knowing what is required to do the job well and not knowing what your people are like is like trying to run a machine without knowing how its parts work together.

When I was younger I didn't really understand the saying, "Hire someone better than you." Now, after decades of hiring, managing, and firing people, I understand that to be truly successful I need to be like a conductor of people, many of whom (if not all) can play their instruments better than I can—and that if I was a *really* great conductor, I would also be able to find a better conductor than me and hire him or her. My ultimate goal is to create a machine that works so well that I can just sit back and watch beauty happen.

I cannot emphasize enough how important the selection, training, testing, evaluation, and sorting out of people is.

In the end, what you need to do is simple:

1. Remember the goal.
2. Give the goal to people who can achieve it (which is best) or tell them what to do to achieve it (which is micromanaging and therefore less good).
3. Hold them accountable.
4. If they still can't do the job after you've trained them and given them time to learn, get rid of them.

7.1 Recognize that the most important decision for you to make is who you choose as your Responsible Parties.

If you put your goals in the hands of RPs who can execute those goals well, and if you make it clear to them that they are personally responsible for achieving those goals and doing the tasks, they should produce excellent results.

The same goes for yourself. If your designer/manager-you doesn't have a good reason to be confident that your worker-you is up to a given task, it would be crazy to let yourself do the task without seeking the supervision of believable parties. You know that there are a lot of incompetent people in the world trying to do things they're not good at, so the chances are good that you are one of them. That's just a reality and it's okay for you to accept it and deal with it in a way that produces good outcomes.

a. Understand that the most important RPs are those responsible for the goals, outcomes, and machines at the highest levels. Give me someone who can be responsible for an entire area—someone who can design, hire, and sort to achieve the goal—and I can be comfortable things will go well. These are the most important people to choose and manage well. Senior managers must be capable of higher-level thinking, and understand the difference between goals and tasks—otherwise you will have to do their jobs for them. The ability to see and value goals is largely innate, though it improves with experience. It can be tested for, though no tests are perfect.

7.2 Know that the ultimate Responsible Party will be the person who bears the consequences of what is done.

So long as you bear the consequences of failure, you are the ultimate Responsible Party. For example, while you might choose to delegate the responsibility of figuring out how to handle your illness to a doctor, it is your responsibility to pick the right one, since you will bear the consequences if he does a bad job. Or if you were building a house, would you go to an architect and say "show me the kinds of houses I can build" or would you tell the architect what kind of house you want to live in? This is especially true when it comes to money. If you delegate the oversight responsibility for your finances to others, they typically won't hold themselves as accountable for your money as they would their own and they won't fire themselves if they are doing a bad job. Only the ultimate RP can do that.

When putting someone in a position of responsibility, make sure their incentives are aligned with their responsibilities and they experience the consequences of the outcomes they produce. As an example, structure their deals so that they do well or badly based on how well or badly you do in the areas they are responsible for. This is fundamental for good management.

a. Make sure that everyone has someone they report to. Even a company's owners have bosses, in their case, the investors whose money is being spent to achieve their goals. If the owners are self-funded, they still have to make their clients and employees happy. And they can't escape the responsibility of making sure that their costs are acceptable and their goals are being met. Even if a person's job is unique, someone needs to be holding them accountable at all times.

7.3 Remember the force behind the thing.

Most people see the things around them without considering the forces that created them. In most cases those forces were specific people with specific qualities who worked in specific ways. Change the people and you change how things develop; replace creators with noncreators and you stop having creations.

People tend to personify organizations ("Apple is a creative company") while mistakenly depersonalizing their results, thus losing sight of who did what to produce them. That's misguided because companies don't make decisions—people do.

So who are the people in your organization behind the results and culture that make it special? Think about who they are and how they work together to make it what it is.

8 Hire Right, Because the Penalties for Hiring Wrong Are Huge

R emember back in Understand That People Are Wired Very Differently when I described Bridgewater's hit-or-miss hiring practices in its early days? At the very beginning, we just hired people we liked. But too many of them turned out to be bad fits. Because we liked them, we were reluctant to give up on them, and things often went from bad to worse. So we started hiring like most companies do, by looking at résumés, narrowing the lists, and then interviewing to get a gut feel for who was right. But the questions we asked our candidates, unlike the questions on a scientifically constructed personality test, were unlikely to elicit answers truly indicative of what they were like.

What we were doing, essentially, was looking at prospective employees through our own biased perspectives. Those of us who were linear thinkers tended to want to hire linear thinkers; those of us who were lateral thinkers tended to want to hire lateral thinkers. We all thought the type we chose would perform best in all jobs, and as a result we weren't able to accurately predict who would succeed and who would fail in our very unusual environment. As a result, we continued to make a lot of bad hires.

Eventually we learned from our mistakes and failures that we could improve our hiring results in two ways: 1) by always being crisp and clear on exactly what kind of person we were looking for, and 2) by developing our vocabulary for and means of evaluating people's abilities at a much more granular level. This chapter lays out in detail the principles we've learned for doing this. While we still make too many hiring mistakes, we have significantly reduced the odds of making them by following these processes, which we continually try to improve.

At a high level, we look for people who think independently, argue open-mindedly and assertively, and above all else value the intense pursuit of truth and excellence, and through it, the rapid improvement of themselves and the organization. Because we treat work as more than just what we do to make a living, we look at every potential hire not just as an employee but as someone we'd want share our lives with. We insist that the people we work with are considerate and have a high sense of personal accountability to do the difficult, right things. We look for people with generous natures and high standards of fairness. Most important, they must be able to put their egos aside and assess themselves candidly.

Whether you choose to look for these same traits or others, the most important thing you can do is understand that hiring is a high-risk gamble that needs to be approached deliberately. A lot of time, effort, and resources go into hiring and developing new employees before it's clear whether or not they are good fits. Months or even years and countless dollars can be wasted in training and retraining. Some of those costs are intangible, including loss of morale and a gradual diminishment of standards as people who aren't excellent in their roles bump into each other; other costs from bad outcomes can be measured all too easily in dollars and cents. So whenever you think you are ready to make someone an offer, think one last time about the important things that might go wrong and what else you can do to better assess those risks and raise your probability of being right.

8.1 Match the person to the design.

When building a "machine," design precedes people because the type of people you will need will depend on the design. As you design, create a clear mental image of the attributes required for each person to do their job well. It is futile to give responsibilities to people who do not have the qualities required to succeed. It frustrates, and inevitably angers, all parties, which is damaging to the environment.

In order to match a person to the design, start by creating a spec sheet so that there will be a consistent set of criteria that can be applied from recruiting through performance reviews. Bridgewater's spec sheets use the same bank of qualities as our Baseball Cards.

Don't design jobs to fit people; over time, this almost always turns out to be a mistake. This often happens when someone you are reluctant to let go doesn't work out, and there is an inclination to try to find out what else that person can do. Frequently managers fail to be objective about their own strengths and weaknesses, and put themselves into roles that they're not a click for.

a. Think through which values, abilities, and skills you are looking for (in that order). Values are the deep-seated beliefs that motivate behaviors and determine people's compatibilities with each other. People will fight for their values, and they are likely to fight with people who don't share them. Abilities are ways of thinking and behaving. Some people are great learners and fast processors; others possess the ability to see things at a higher level. Some focus more on the particulars; still others think creatively or logically or with supreme organization. Skills are learned tools, such as being able to speak a foreign language or write computer code. While values and abilities are unlikely to change much, most skills can be acquired in a limited amount of time (e.g., software proficiency can be learned) and often change in worth (today's most in-demand programming language is likely to be obsolete in a few years).

It is important for you to know what mix of qualities is important to fit each role and, more broadly, what values and abilities are required in people with whom you can have successful relationships. In picking people for long-term relationships, values are most important, abilities come next, and skills are the least important. Yet most people make the mistake of choosing skills and abilities first and overlooking values. We value people most who have what I call the three C's: character, common sense, and creativity.

If your people are bound by a sense of community and mission and they are capable, you will have an extraordinary organization. Some people will value the mission and community and others won't. Since at Bridgewater the key shared values that maintain our culture are meaningful work and meaningful relationships, radical truth and radical transparency, an open-minded willingness to explore harsh realities including one's own weaknesses, a sense of ownership, a drive for excellence, and the willingness to do the good but difficult things, we look for highly capable people who deeply want all of those things.

b. Make finding the right people systematic and scientific. The process for choosing people should be systematically built out and evidence-based. You need to have a people-hiring machine in which the goals are clearly stated so that the outcomes can be compared with them and the machine (the design and the people) producing the outcomes can evolve to improve.

Organizations typically hire people by having job candidates' resumes reviewed by semi-random people based on semi-random criteria, which leads them to invite in candidates to have semi-random groups of people ask the candidates semi-random questions and then make their choices of whom to offer jobs based on the consensus of how they liked them. You need to make sure that each one of those steps is done more systematically and purposefully. For example, you should think through what questions are asked and how the different answers candidates give differentiate them in the ways that you are seeking to differentiate them. You should also save all of those answers so you can learn about how indicative they might be of subsequent behaviors and performance. I do not mean that the human dimension or art of the hiring process should be eliminated—the personal values and esprit de corps part of a relationship are critically important and can't be fully measured by data. Sometimes the twinkle in the eye and the facial expressions are telling. However, even for those areas where people's subjective interpretations are important, you can still use data and a scientific approach to be more objective—for example, you can capture data to assess the track records of those making the interpretations.

c. Hear the click: Find the right fit between the role and the person. Remember that your goal is to put the right people in the right design. First understand the responsibilities of the role and the qualities needed to fulfill them, then ascertain whether an individual has them. When you're doing this well, there should almost be an audible "click" as the person you're hiring fits into his or her role.

d. Look for people who sparkle, not just "any ol' one of those." Too many people get hired because they are just "one of those." If you're looking for a plumber you might be inclined to fill the job with the first experienced plumber you interview, without ascertaining whether he has the qualities of an outstanding plumber. Yet the difference between an ordinary plumber versus an outstanding one is huge. When reviewing any candidate's background, you must identify whether they have demonstrated themselves to be extraordinary in some way. The most obvious demonstration is outstanding performance within an outstanding peer group. If you're less than excited to hire someone for a particular job, don't do it. The two of you will probably make each other miserable.

e. Don't use your pull to get someone a job. It is unacceptable to use your personal influence to help someone get a job because doing so undermines the meritocracy. It's not good for the job seeker, because it conveys they did not really earn it; it is not good for the person doing the hiring, because it undermines their authority; and it is not good for you because it demonstrates you will compromise merit for friends. It is an insidious form of corruption and it must not be tolerated. The most you can do at Bridgewater in this respect is to provide a reference for someone you know well enough to endorse. Even though Bridgewater is my company, I have never deviated from this policy.

8.2 Remember that people are built very differently and that different ways of seeing and thinking make people suitable for different jobs.

Some ways of thinking will serve you well for some purposes and serve you poorly for others. It is highly desirable to understand one's own and others' ways of thinking and their best applications. Some qualities are more suitable for some jobs. For example, you might not want to hire a highly introverted person as a salesman. That's not to say an introvert can't do that job; it's just that a gregarious person is likely to be more satisfied in the role and do a better job.

If you're not naturally good at one type of thinking, it doesn't mean you're precluded from paths that require it. It does, however, require that you either work with someone who has that required way of thinking (which works best) or learn to think differently (which is difficult or even impossible).

On the other hand, sometimes I see people dealing with each other, especially in groups, without regard for these differences. They are like the parable of the blind men touching different parts of an elephant and arguing about what it is. Just think about how much better it would be if people were open-minded enough to realize that none of them have the complete picture. Both people expressing their own views and those considering others' views need to take each other's differences into account. These differences are real, so it's dumb to pretend they don't exist.

a. Understand how to use and interpret personality assessments. Personality assessments are valuable tools for getting a quick picture of what people are like in terms of their abilities, preferences, and style. They are often more objective and reliable than interviews.

b. Remember that people tend to pick people like themselves, so choose interviewers who can identify what you are looking for. If you're looking for a visionary, pick a visionary to do the interview in which you probe for vision. If you are looking for a mix of qualities, assemble a group of interviewers who embody those qualities collectively. Don't choose interviewers whose judgment you don't trust (in other words, make sure they are believable).

c. Look for people who are willing to look at themselves objectively. Everybody has strengths and weaknesses. The key to success is understanding one's weaknesses and successfully compensating for them. People who lack that ability fail chronically.

d. Remember that people typically don't change all that much. This is especially true over short periods of time like a year or two, yet most people want to assume that when someone does something wrong the person will learn the lesson and change. That's naive. It is best to assume that they won't change unless there is good evidence to the contrary that they will.

It's better to bet on changes you have seen than those you hope for.

8.3 Think of your teams the way that sports managers do: No one person possesses everything required to produce success, yet everyone must excel.

Teams should operate like those in professional sports, where different skills are required to play different positions. Excellence in each is mandatory, the success of the mission is uncompromisable, and members that don't measure up may need to be cut. When teams operate with such high standards and shared values, extraordinary relationships are likely to develop.

8.4 Pay attention to people's track records.

People's personalities are pretty well formed before they come to you, and they've been leaving their fingerprints all over the place since childhood; anyone is fairly knowable if you do your homework. You have to get at their values, abilities, and skills: Do they have a track record of excellence in what you're expecting them to do? Have they done the thing you want them to do successfully at least three times? If not, you're making a lower-probability bet, so you want to have really good reasons for doing so. That doesn't mean you should never allow yourself or others to do anything new; of course you should. But do it with appropriate caution and with guardrails. That is, have an experienced person oversee the inexperienced person, yourself included (if you fit that description).

a. **Check references.** Don't rely exclusively on the candidate for information about their track record: Talk to believable people who know them, look for documented evidence, and ask for past reviews from their bosses, subordinates, and peers. As much as possible, you want to get a clear and objective picture of the path that they have chosen for themselves and how they have evolved along the way. I've seen plenty of people who claimed to be successful elsewhere operate ineffectively at Bridgewater. A closer look often revealed that they were either not as successful as they portrayed themselves or they got credit for others' accomplishments.

b. Recognize that performance in school doesn't tell you much about whether a person has the values and abilities you are looking for. Largely because they are the easiest to measure, memory and processing speed tend to be the abilities that determine success in school, so school performance is an excellent gauge of these qualities. School performance is also a good gauge of a person's determination to succeed, as well as their willingness and ability to follow directions. But when it comes to assessing a candidate's common sense, vision, creativity, or decision-making abilities, school records are of limited value. Since those traits are the most important, you must look beyond school to ascertain whether an applicant has them.

c. While it's best to have great conceptual thinkers, understand that great experience and a great track record also count for a lot. There are all sorts of jobs and they require all types of people to handle them. I am frequently biased toward finding the entrepreneur type—a clever, open-minded scrapper who will find the best solution—and I have often been disappointed. On the other hand, sometimes I have found a master craftsman who has devoted decades to his specialty who I could completely rely on. What keeps coming to my mind is Malcolm Gladwell's rule that it takes ten thousand hours of doing something to build expertise—and the value of looking at batting averages to judge how well a person can hit. One way you can tell how well a talented rookie will do relative to a proven star is to get them into a debate with each other and see how well they each hold up.

d. Beware of the impractical idealist. Idealistic people who have moralistic notions about how people should behave without understanding how people really do behave do more harm than good.

As a global macroeconomist and businessman and as a philanthropist I have seen this repeatedly in all those domains. I have come to believe that as well-intentioned as they are, impractical idealists are dangerous and destructive, whereas practical idealists make the world a better place. To be practical one needs to be a realist—to know where people's interests lie and how to design machines that produce results, as well as metrics that measure those benefits in relation to the costs. Without such measures, waste will limit or erase the benefits, and with them the benefits will keep flowing.

e. Don't assume that a person who has been successful elsewhere will be successful in the job you're giving them. No matter how good you are at hiring, some of your hires won't work out. Know how the people you're considering operate and visualize how that will produce successful results. Knowing what they did is valuable only insofar as it helps you figure out what they are like.

f. Make sure your people have character and are capable. The person who is capable but doesn't have good character is generally destructive, because he or she has the cleverness to do you harm and will certainly erode the culture. In my opinion, most organizations overvalue the abilities piece and undervalue the character piece because of a shortsighted focus on getting the job done. In doing so, they lose the power of the great relationships that will take them through both good and bad times.

Don't get me wrong, I'm not saying that you should compromise capabilities for character. The person with good character and poor abilities also creates problems. While likable, he or she won't get the job done and is painfully difficult to fire because doing so feels like shooting the loyal dog you can't afford to keep anymore—but he must go. Ultimately, what you need in the people you work with are excellent character *and* excellent capabilities, which is why it's so hard to find great people.

8.5 Don't hire people just to fit the first job they will do; hire people you want to share your life with.

Turnover is costly and inefficient because of the time it takes for people to get to know each other and the organization. Both the people you work with and the company itself will evolve in ways you can't anticipate. So hire the kind of people you want to share a long-term mission with. You will always have uses for great people.

a. Look for people who have lots of great questions. Smart people are the ones who ask the most thoughtful questions, as opposed to thinking they have all the answers. Great questions are a much better indicator of future success than great answers.

b. Show candidates your warts. Show your job prospects the real picture, *especially* the bad stuff. Also show them the principles in action, including the most difficult aspects. That way you will stress-test their willingness to endure the real challenges.

c. Play jazz with people with whom you are compatible but who will also challenge you. You need people who share your tastes and style but who can also push and challenge each other. The best teams, whether in music, in sports, or in business, do all those things at the same time.

8.6 When considering compensation, provide both stability and opportunity.

Pay people enough so that they're not under financial stress, but not so much that they become fat and happy. You want your people to be motivated to perform so they can realize their dreams. You don't want people to accept a job for the security of making a lot more money— you want them to come for the opportunity to *earn* it through hard and creative work.

a. Pay for the person, not the job. Look at what people in comparable jobs with comparable experience and credentials make, add some small premium over that, and build in bonuses or other incentives so they will be motivated to knock the cover off the ball. Never pay based on the job title alone.

b. Have performance metrics tied at least loosely to compensation. While you will never fully capture all the aspects that make for a great work relationship in metrics, you should be able to establish many of them. Tying performance metrics to compensation will help crystallize your understanding of your deal with people, provide good ongoing feedback, and influence how the person behaves on an ongoing basis.

c. Pay north of fair. By being generous or at least a little north of fair with others I have enhanced both our work and our relationships and most people have responded in kind. As a result, we have gained something even more special than money in the form of mutual caring, respect, and commitment.

d. Focus more on making the pie bigger than on exactly how to slice it so that you or anyone else gets the biggest piece. The best negotiations are the ones with someone in which I say, "You should take more," and they argue back, "No you should take more!" People who operate this way with each other make the relationship better and the pie bigger—and both benefit in the long run.

8.7 Remember that in great partnerships, consideration and generosity are more important than money.

Someone who doesn't have much can be more generous giving a little than a rich person giving a lot. Some people respond to the generosity while others respond to the money. You want the first type with you, and you always want to treat them generously.

When I had nothing, I was as generous as I could be with people who appreciated my generosity more than the higher levels of compensation others could afford to give them. For that reason, they stayed with me. I never forgot that, and I made a point of making them rich when I had the opportunity to do so. And they in turn were generous to me in their own way when I needed their generosity most. We both got something much more valuable than money—and we got the money too.

Remember that the only purpose of money is to get you what you want, so think hard about what you value and put it above money. How much would you sell a good relationship for? There's not enough money in the world to get you to part with a valued relationship.

a. **Be generous and expect generosity from others.** If you're not generous with others and others aren't generous with you, you won't have a quality relationship.

8.8 Great people are hard to find so make sure you think about how to keep them.

Make sure you're following the suggestions made earlier, like building meaningful relationships and constantly getting in sync. Most importantly, you have to encourage people to speak up about how things are going for them. Ensuring that their personal development is proceeding appropriately is important too. Close advice from an active mentor should last at least one year.

When you know
what someone is like,
you know what you
can expect from them.

9 Constantly Train, Test, Evaluate, and Sort People

Both your people and your design must evolve for your machine to improve. When you get personal evolution right, the returns are exponential. As people get better and better, they are more able to think independently, probe, and help you refine your machine. The faster they evolve, the faster your outcomes will improve.

Your part in an employee's personal evolution begins with a frank assessment of their strengths and weaknesses, followed by a plan for how their weaknesses can be mitigated either through training or by switching to a different job that taps into their strengths and preferences. At Bridgewater, new employees are often taken aback by how frank and direct such conversations can be, but it's not personal or hierarchical—no one is exempt from this kind of criticism. While this process is generally difficult for both managers and their subordinates, in the long run it has made people happier and Bridgewater more successful. Remember that most people are happiest when they are improving and doing the things that suit them naturally and help them advance. So learning about your people's weaknesses is just as valuable (for them and for you) as is learning their strengths.

Even as you help people develop, you must constantly assess whether they are able to fulfill their responsibilities excellently. This is not easy to do objectively since you will often have meaningful relationships with your reports and may be reluctant to evaluate them accurately if their performance isn't at the bar. By the same token, you may be tempted to give an employee who rubs you the wrong way a worse evaluation than he or she deserves. An idea meritocracy requires objectivity. Many of the management tools we have developed were built to do just that, providing us with an unbiased picture of people and their performance independent of the biases of any one manager. This data is essential in cases where a manager and a report are out of sync on an assessment and others are called in to resolve the dispute.

A few years ago, one of our employees was serving in a trial role as a department head. The prior department head had left the firm, and Greg, who was then CEO, was assessing whether this employee, who had previously been a deputy, had the right abilities to step into the role. The employee thought he did; Greg and others thought he did not. But this decision was not as simple as the CEO "making the call." We want decisions to be more evidence-based. As a result of our Dot Collector system of constant feedback, we had literally hundreds of data points on the specific attributes required for the job, including synthesis, knowing what he didn't know, and managing at the right level. So we put all this data onto the screen and stared hard at it together. We then asked the employee to look at that body of evidence and reflect on what he would do if he were in the position of deciding whether he'd hire himself for the job. Once he was able to step back and look at the objective evidence, he agreed to move on and try another role at Bridgewater more suited to his strengths.

Helping people acquire skills is easy—it's typically a matter of providing them with appropriate training. Improvements in abilities are more difficult but essential to expanding what a person can be responsible for over time. And changing someone's values is something you should never count on. In every relationship, there comes a point when you must decide whether you are meant for each other— that's common in private life and at any organization that holds high standards. At Bridgewater, we know that we cannot compromise on the fundamentals of our culture, so if a person can't get to the bar in an acceptable time frame, he or she must leave.

Every leader must decide between 1) getting rid of liked but incapable people to achieve their goals and 2) keeping the nice but incapable people and not achieving their goals. Whether or not you can make these hard decisions is the strongest determinant of your own success or failure. In a culture like Bridgewater's, you have no choice. You must choose excellence, even though it might be difficult at the moment, because it's best for everyone.

9.1 Understand that you and the people you manage will go through a process of personal evolution.

No one is exempt from this process. Having it go well depends on people's abilities to make frank assessments of strengths and weaknesses (most importantly weaknesses). While it's generally as difficult for managers to give this feedback as it is for their subordinates to hear it, in the long run it makes people happier and the organization more successful.

a. Recognize that personal evolution should be relatively rapid and a natural consequence of discovering one's strengths and weaknesses; as a result, career paths are not planned at the outset. The evolutionary process is about discovering people's likes and dislikes as well as their strengths and weaknesses; it occurs when people are put into jobs they are likely to succeed at, but in which they have to stretch themselves. Each person's career will evolve based on what we all learn about what the person is like.

They should be given enough freedom to learn and think for themselves while being coached so they are prevented from making unacceptable mistakes. The feedback they receive should help them reflect on whether their problems are the kind that can be resolved by additional learning or stem from natural abilities that are unlikely to change. Typically it takes from six to twelve months to get to know a new employee in a by-and-large sort of way, and about eighteen months for them to internalize and adapt to the culture. During this time there should be periodic mini-reviews and several major ones. Following each of these assessments, new assignments should be made that are tailored to their likes and dislikes and strengths and weaknesses. This is an iterative process, in which the accumulated experiences of training, testing, and adjusting direct the person to ever more suitable roles and responsibilities. At Bridgewater, it is typically both a challenging and rewarding process that benefits the individual by providing better self-understanding and greater familiarity with various jobs. When it results in a parting of ways, it's usually because people find they cannot be excellent and happy in any job at the firm.

b. Understand that training guides the process of personal evolution. Trainees must be open-minded; the process requires them to suspend their egos while they discover what they are doing well and what they are doing poorly and decide what to do about it. The trainer must be open-minded as well, and it's best if at least two believable trainers work with each trainee in order to triangulate their views about what the trainee is like. This training is an apprentice relationship; it occurs as the trainer and trainee share experiences, much like when a ski instructor skis alongside his student. The process promotes growth, development, and transparency around where people stand, why they stand where they stand, and what they can do about improving it. It hastens not just their own personal evolution but the evolution of the organization.

c. Teach your people to fish rather than give them fish, even if that means letting them make some mistakes. Sometimes you need to stand by and let someone make a mistake (provided it's not too serious) so they can learn. It's a bad sign if you are constantly telling people what they should do; micromanagement typically reflects inability on the part of the person being managed. It's also not a good thing for you as a manager. Instead of micromanaging, you should be training and testing. Give people your thoughts on how they might approach their decisions, but don't dictate to them. The most useful thing you can do is to get in sync with them, exploring how they are doing things and why.

d. Recognize that experience creates internalized learning that book learning can't replace. There are huge differences between memory-based book learning and hands-on, internalized learning. A medical student who has learned to perform an operation in a medical school class has not learned it in the same way as a doctor who has already conducted several operations. People who excel at book learning tend to call up from memory what they have learned in order to follow stored instructions. People who have internalized their learning use the thoughts flowing from their subconscious without thinking, in the same way they walk down the street. Understanding these differences is essential.

9.2 Provide constant feedback.

Most training comes from doing and getting in sync about performance. Feedback should reflect what is succeeding and what is not in proportion to the actual situation, rather than in an attempt to balance compliments and criticisms. Remember that you are responsible for achieving your goals, and you want your machine to function as intended. For it to do so, the employees you supervise must meet expectations, and only you can help them understand whether they are stacking up. As their strengths and weaknesses become clearer, responsibilities can be more appropriately tailored to make the machine work better and to facilitate personal evolution.

9.3 Evaluate accurately, not kindly.

Nobody ever said radical honesty was easy. Sometimes, especially with new employees who have not yet gotten used to it, an honest assessment feels like an attack. Rise to a higher level and keep your eye on the bigger picture and counsel the person you are evaluating to do the same.

a. In the end, accuracy and kindness are the same thing. What might seem kind but isn't accurate is harmful to the person and often to others in the organization as well.

b. Put your compliments and criticisms in perspective. It helps to clarify whether the weakness or mistake under discussion is indicative of a trainee's total evaluation. One day I told one of our new research people what a good job I thought he was doing and how strong his thinking was. It was a very positive initial evaluation. A few days later I heard him chatting away at length about stuff that wasn't related to work, so I warned him about the cost to his and our development if he regularly wasted time. Afterward I learned that he thought he was on the brink of being fired. My comment about his need for focus had nothing to do with my overall evaluation. Had I explained myself better when we sat down that second time, he could have put my comment into perspective.

c. Think about accuracy, not implications. It's often the case that someone receiving critical feedback gets preoccupied with the implications of that feedback instead of whether it's true. This is a mistake. As I'll explain later, conflating the "what is" with the "what to do about it" typically leads to bad decision making. Help others through this by giving feedback in a way that makes it clear that you're just trying to understand what's true. Figuring out what to do about it is a separate discussion.

d. Make accurate assessments. People are your most important resource and truth is the foundation of excellence, so make your personnel evaluations as precise and accurate as possible. This takes time and considerable back-and-forth. Your assessment of how Responsible Parties are performing should be based not on whether they're doing it your way but on whether they're doing it in a good way. Speak frankly, listen with an open mind, consider the views of other believable and honest people, and try to get in sync about what's going on with the person and why. Remember not to be overconfident in your assessments, as it's possible you are wrong.

e. Learn from success as well as from failure. Radical truth doesn't require you to be negative all the time. Point out examples of jobs done well and the causes of their success. This reinforces the actions that led to the results and creates role models for those who are learning.

f. Know that most everyone thinks that what they did, and what they are doing, is much more important than it really is. If you ask everybody in an organization what percentage of the organization's success they're personally responsible for, you'll wind up with a total of about 300 percent.[39] That's just the reality, and it shows why you must be precise in attributing specific results to specific people's actions. Otherwise, you'll never know who is responsible for what—and even worse, you may make the mistake of believing people who wrongly claim to be behind great accomplishments.

9.4 Recognize that tough love is both the hardest and the most important type of love to give (because it is so rarely welcomed).

The greatest gift you can give someone is the power to be successful. Giving people the opportunity to struggle rather than giving them the things they are struggling for will make them stronger.

---

[39] We did this at Bridgewater and the figure came out to 301 percent.

Compliments are easy to give but they don't help people stretch. Pointing out someone's mistakes and weaknesses (so they learn what they need to deal with) is harder and less appreciated, but much more valuable in the long run. Though new employees will come to appreciate what you are doing, it is typically difficult for them to understand it at first; to be effective, you must clearly and repeatedly explain the logic and the caring behind it.

a. Recognize that while most people prefer compliments, accurate criticism is more valuable. You've heard the expression "no pain no gain." Psychologists have shown that the most powerful personal transformations come from experiencing the pain from mistakes that a person never wants to have again—known as "hitting bottom." So don't be hesitant to give people those experiences or have them yourself.

While it is important to be clear to people about what they are doing well, it is even more important to point out their weaknesses and have them reflect on them.

Problems require more time than things that are going well. They must be identified and understood and addressed, while things that are running smoothly require less attention. Instead of celebrating how great we are, we focus on where we need to improve, which is how we got to be so great.

9.5 Don't hide your observations about people.

Explore them openly with the goal of figuring out how you and your people are built so that the right people can be put in the right jobs.

a. Build your synthesis from the specifics up. By synthesizing, I mean converting a lot of data into an accurate picture. Too many people make assessments of people without connecting them to specific data. When you have all the specifics that we have at Bridgewater—the dots, meeting tapes, etc.—you can and must work from the specifics up and see the patterns in the data. Even without such tools, other data such as metrics, testing, and the input of others can help you form a more complete picture of what the person is like, as well as examine what they did.

b. Squeeze the dots. Every observation of a person potentially tells you something valuable about how they operate. As I explained earlier, I call these observations "dots." A dot is a piece of data that's paired with your inference about what it means—a judgment about what someone might have decided, said, or thought. Most of the time we make these inferences and judgments implicitly and keep them to ourselves, but I believe that if they are collected systematically and put into perspective over time, they can be extremely valuable when it's time to step back and synthesize the picture of a person.

c. Don't oversqueeze a dot. Remember: A dot is just a dot; what matters is how they add up. Think of each individual dot as an at-bat in baseball. Even great hitters are going to strike out many times, and it would be foolish to evaluate them based on one trip to the plate. That's why stats like on-base percentage and batting average exist.

In other words, any one event has many different possible explanations, whereas a pattern of behavior can tell you a lot about root causes. The number of observations needed to detect a pattern largely depends on how well you get in sync after each observation. A quality discussion of how and why a person behaved a certain way should help you understand the larger picture.

d. Use evaluation tools such as performance surveys, metrics, and formal reviews to document all aspects of a person's performance. It's hard to have an objective, open-minded, emotion-free conversation about performance if there is no data to discuss. It's also hard to track progress. This is part of the reason I created the Dot Collector. I also recommend thinking about other ways that people's responsibilities can be put in metrics. One example: You can have people note whether they did or didn't do things on checklists, which you can then use to calculate what percentage of tasks they complete. Metrics tell us whether things are going according to plan—they are an objective means of assessment and they improve people's productivity.

9.6 Make the process of learning what someone is like open, evolutionary, and iterative.

Articulate your assessment of a person's values, abilities, and skills up front and share it; listen to their and others' responses to your description; organize a plan for training and testing; and reassess your conclusions based on the performance you observe. Do this on an ongoing basis. After several months of discussions and real-world tests, you and your report should both have a pretty good idea of what he or she is like. Over time this exercise will crystallize suitable roles and appropriate training or it will reveal that it's time for the person to find a more appropriate job somewhere else.

a. Make your metrics clear and impartial. To help you build your perpetual motion machine, have a clear set of rules and a clear set of metrics to track how people are performing against those rules—and predetermined consequences that are determined formulaically based on the output of those metrics.

The more clear-cut the rules are, the less arguing there will be about whether someone did something wrong. For example, we have rules about how employees can manage their own investments in a way that doesn't conflict with how we manage money for clients. Because these rules are clear-cut, there's no room for argument when a breach occurs.

Having metrics that allow everyone to see everyone else's track record will make evaluation more objective and fair. People will do the things that will get them higher grades and will argue less about them. Of course, since most people have a number of things to do that are of different importance, different metrics have to be used and weighted appropriately. The more data you collect, the more immediate and precise the feedback will be. That is one of the reasons I created the Dot Collector tool to work as it does (providing lots of immediate feedback); people often use the feedback that they get during a meeting to course-correct in the meeting in real time.

Once you have your metrics, you can tie them to an algorithm that spits out consequences. They can be as simple as saying that for every time you do X you will earn Y amount of money (or bonus points), or it can be more complex (for example, tying the weighted mix of metrics grades to various algorithms that provide the estimated compensation or bonus points).

While this process will never be exact, it will still be good in even its crudest form, and over time it will evolve to be terrific. Even when flawed, the formulaic output can be used with discretion to provide a more precise evaluation and compensation; over time it will evolve into a wonderful machine that will do much of your managing better than you could do it on your own.

b. Encourage people to be objectively reflective about their performance. Being able to see yourself from a higher level is essential for personal evolution and achieving your goals. So you and the people who report to you should be looking at the evidence of their performance together; for this to go well, you need lots and lots of evidence and an objective point of view. If required, use agreed-upon others to triangulate the picture the evidence presents.

c. Look at the whole picture. In reviewing someone, the goal is to see the patterns and to understand the whole picture. No one can be successful in every way (if they are extremely meticulous, for example, they might not be able to be fast, and vice versa). Assessments made in reviews must be concrete; they're not about what people *should* be like but what they *are* like.

d. For performance reviews, start from specific cases, look for patterns, and get in sync with the person being reviewed by looking at the evidence together. While feedback should be constant, reviews are typically periodic; their purpose is to bring together the accumulated evidence of what a person is like as it pertains to their job performance. If the constant feedback is done well, it will become like a constant review as the bits and pieces will add up to the whole. A review should contain few surprises, because you should continuously be striving to make sense of how the person is doing their job. If you think their job is being done badly, you should have been probing to identify and address the root causes of their underperformance on a case-by-case basis. It's difficult for people to identify their own weaknesses; they need the appropriate probing (not nit-picking) of specific cases by others to get at the truth of what they are like and how they are fitting into their jobs.

In some cases it won't take long to see what a person is like; in other cases it's a lot harder. But over time and with a large enough sample of cases, their track records (the level and the steepness up or down in the trajectories that they are responsible for, rather than the occasional wiggles) should paint a clear picture of what you can expect from them. If there are performance issues, it is either because of design problems (perhaps the person has too many responsibilities) or fit/abilities problems. If the problems are due to the person's inabilities, these inabilities are either because of the person's innate weaknesses in doing that job (e.g., someone who's five foot two probably shouldn't be a center on the basketball team) or because of inadequate training. A good review, and getting in sync throughout the year, should get at these things. Make sure to make your assessment relative to the absolute bar, not just the progress over time. What matters most is not just outcomes but how responsibilities were handled. The goal of a review is to be clear about what the person can and can't be trusted to do based on what they are like. From there, you can determine what to do about it.

e. Remember that when it comes to assessing people, the two biggest mistakes you can make are being overconfident in your assessment and failing to get in sync on it. If you believe that something is true about someone, it's your responsibility to make sure that it is true and that the person you're assessing agrees. Of course, in some cases it may be impossible to get in sync (if you believe that someone was dishonest and they insist that they weren't, for example), but in a culture of truth and transparency it is an obligation to share your view and let others express theirs.

f. Get in sync on assessments in a nonhierarchical way. In most organizations, evaluations run in only one direction, with the manager assessing the managee. The managee typically disagrees with the assessment, especially if it is worse than his or her self-assessment, because most people believe themselves to be better than they really are. Managees also have opinions about managers that they wouldn't dare bring up in most companies, so misunderstandings and resentments fester. This perverse behavior undermines the effectiveness of the environment and the relationships between people. It can be avoided by getting in sync in a high-quality way.

Your reports have to believe that you're not their enemy—that your sole goal is to move toward the truth; that you are trying to help them and so will not enable their self-deception, perpetuate a lie, or let them off the hook. This has to be done in an honest and transparent way, because if someone believes they are being pigeonholed unfairly the process won't work. As equal partners, it is up to both of you to get to the truth. When each party is an equal participant, no one can feel cornered.

g. Learn about your people and have them learn about you through frank conversations about mistakes and their root causes. You need to be clear in conveying your assessments to your reports and open-minded in listening to their replies so you can work on setting their training and career paths together. Recognizing and communicating people's weaknesses is one of the most difficult things managers have to do. It's important for the party receiving feedback to be sympathetic to the person trying to give it, because it's not easy—it takes character on the part of both participants to get to the truth.

h. Understand that making sure people are doing a good job doesn't require watching everything that everybody is doing at all times. You just have to know what they are like and get a sampling. Regular sampling of a statistically reliable number of cases will show you what a person is like and what you can expect from them. Select which of their actions are critical enough to need preapproval and which can be examined later. But be sure to do the audit, because people will tend to give themselves too much slack or could cheat when they see that they're not being checked.

i. Recognize that change is difficult. Anything that requires change can be difficult. Yet in order to learn and grow and make progress, you must change. When facing a change, ask yourself: Am I being open-minded? Or am I being resistant? Confront your difficulties head-on, force yourself to explore where they come from, and you'll find that you'll learn a lot.

j. Help people through the pain that comes with exploring their weaknesses. Emotions tend to heat up during most disagreements, especially when the subject is someone's weaknesses. Speak in a calm, slow, and analytical manner to facilitate communication. Put things in perspective by reminding them that their pain is the pain that comes with learning and personal evolution—and that knowing the truth will put them on the path to a much better place. Consider asking them to go away and reflect when they are calm, and have a follow-up conversation a few days later.

Ultimately, to help people succeed you have to do two things: First let them see their failures so clearly that they are motivated to change them, and then show them how to either change what they are doing or rely on others who are strong where they are weak. While doing the first without the second can be demoralizing to the people you are trying to help, doing them both should be invigorating, especially when they start experiencing the benefits.

9.7 Knowing how people operate and being able to judge whether that way of operating will lead to good results is more important than knowing what they did.

Knowing what people are like is the best indicator of how well they are likely to handle their responsibilities in the future. At Bridgewater, we call this "paying more attention to the swing than the shot." Since good and bad outcomes can arise from circumstances that might not have had anything to do with how the individual handled the situation, it is preferable to assess people based on both their reasoning and their outcomes. I probe their thinking in a very frank way so as not to let them off the hook. Doing this has taught me a lot about how to assess others' logic, and how to have better logic myself. When both the outcomes and the thinking behind them are bad, and when this happens a number of times, I know I don't want them to do that type of thinking anymore.

For example, if you're a poker player and you play a lot of poker, you will win some hands and lose others and on any given night you might walk away with less money than a lesser player who's gotten lucky. It would be a mistake to judge the quality of a player based on just one outcome. Instead, look at how well someone does what they do and the outcomes they produce over time.

a. If someone is doing their job poorly, consider whether it is due to inadequate learning or inadequate ability. Think of people's performance as being made up of two things: learning and ability, as shown on page 437. A weakness that is due to a lack of experience or training can be fixed, while a weakness that is due to a lack of ability can't be. Failing to distinguish between these causes is a common mistake among managers, because managers are often reluctant to appear unkind or judgmental. Also, they know that people assessed this way tend to push back. This is another one of those situations in which you must force yourself to be practical and realistic.

b. Training and testing a poor performer to see if he or she can acquire the required skills without simultaneously trying to assess their abilities is a common mistake. Skills are readily testable, so they should be easy to determine. Abilities, especially right-brained abilities, are more difficult to assess. When thinking about why someone is a poor performer, openly consider whether it is a problem with their abilities.

9.8 Recognize that when you are really in sync with someone about their weaknesses, the weaknesses are probably true.

When you reach an agreement, it's a good sign you've arrived at truth, which is why getting to that point is such a great achievement. This is one of the main reasons that the person being evaluated must be an equal participant in the process. When you do agree, make a formal record of it. This information will be a critical building block for future success.

a. When judging people, remember that you don't have to get to the point of "beyond a shadow of a doubt." Perfect understanding isn't possible; trying to get to it wastes time and stalls progress. Instead, work toward developing a mutually agreed-upon, by-and-large understanding of what someone is like that has a high level of confidence behind it. When necessary, take the time to enrich this understanding.

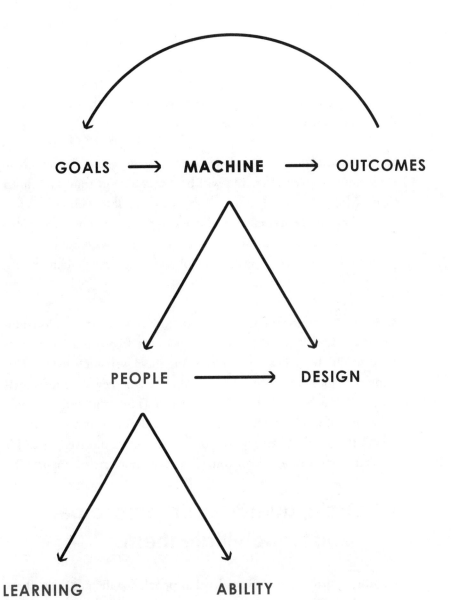

b. It should take you no more than a year to learn what a person is like and whether they are a click for their job. You should be able to roughly assess someone's abilities after six to twelve months of close contact, numerous tests, and getting in sync. A more confident assessment will probably take about eighteen months. This timeline will of course depend on the job, the person, the amount of contact with them, and how well you get in sync.

c. Continue assessing people throughout their tenure. As you get to know your people better, you will be better able to train and direct them. Most importantly, you will be able to assess their core values and abilities more accurately and make sure they complement yours. Don't rest with your initial evaluation, however. Always ask yourself if you would have hired them for that job knowing what you know now. If not, get them out of the job.

d. Evaluate employees with the same rigor as you evaluate job candidates. I find it puzzling that interviewers freely and confidently criticize job candidates without knowing them well but won't criticize employees for similar weaknesses even though they have more evidence. That is because they view criticism as harmful and feel more protective of a fellow employee than they do of an outsider. If you believe that truth is best for everyone, then you should see why this is a mistake, and why frank and ongoing evaluations are so important.

9.9 Train, guardrail, or remove people; don't rehabilitate them.

Training is part of a plan to develop people's skills and help them evolve. Rehabilitation is an attempt to create significant changes in people's values and/or abilities. Since values and abilities are difficult to change, rehabilitation is typically impractical. Since people with inappropriate values and inadequate abilities can have a devastating impact on the organization, they should be fired. If rehabilitation is attempted, it is generally best directed by professionals over extended periods of time.

Remember that if you are expecting people to be much better in the near future than they have been in the past, you are probably making a serious mistake. People who repeatedly operate in a certain way will probably continue to operate that way because that behavior reflects what they're like. Since people generally change slowly, you should expect slow improvement (at best). Instead, you need to change the people or change the design. Since changing the design to accommodate people's weaknesses is generally a bad idea, it is better to sort the people. Sometimes good people "lose their boxes" (they get fired from their role) because they can't evolve into Responsible Parties soon enough. Some of them might be good in another position, in which case they should be reassigned within the company; some of them will not and should leave.

a. **Don't collect people.** It is much worse to keep someone in a job unsuitable for them than it is to fire or reassign them. Consider the enormous costs of not firing someone unsuited for a job: the costs of bad performance; the time and effort wasted trying to train them; and the greater pain of firing someone who's been around awhile (say, five years or more) compared with letting someone go after just a year. Keeping people in jobs they are not suited for is terrible for them because it allows them to live in a false reality while holding back their personal evolution, and it is terrible for the community because it compromises the meritocracy and everyone pays the price. Don't let yourself be held hostage to anyone; there is always someone else. Never compromise your standards or let yourself be squeezed.

b. **Be willing to "shoot the people you love."** It is very difficult to fire people you care about. Cutting someone that you have a meaningful relationship with but who isn't an A player in their job is difficult because ending good relationships is hard, but it is necessary for the long-term excellence of the company. You may have a need for the work they're doing (even if it's not excellent) and find it hard to make a change. But they will pollute the environment and fail you when you really need them.

Doing this is one of those difficult, necessary things. The best way to do it is to "love the people you shoot"—do it with consideration and in a way that helps them.

c. When someone is "without a box," consider whether there is an open box that would be a better fit or whether you need to get them out of the company. Recognize that if they failed in that job, it is because of some qualities they have. You will need to understand what those qualities are and make sure they don't apply to any new role. Also, if you learn that they don't have the potential to move up, don't let them occupy the seat of someone who can.

Remember that you're trying to select people with whom you want to share your life. Everyone evolves over time. Because managers develop a better idea of a new hire's strengths and weaknesses and their fit within the culture than what emerges from the interview process, they are well positioned to assess them for another role if the one they were hired for doesn't work out.

Whenever someone fails at a job, it's critical to understand why they failed and why those reasons won't pose the same problems in a new job.

d. Be cautious about allowing people to step back to another role after failing. Note I said "be cautious." I didn't say never, because it depends on the circumstances. On the one hand, you want people to stretch themselves and experiment with new jobs. You don't want to get rid of a great person just because he or she tried something new and failed. But on the other hand, if you look at most people in this situation, by and large you'll regret allowing them to step back.

There are three reasons for this: 1) You're giving up a seat for someone else who might be able to advance, and people who can advance are better to have than people who can't; 2) The person stepping back could continue to want to do what they aren't capable of doing, so there's a real risk of them job slipping into work they're not a fit for; 3) The person may experience a sense of confinement and resentment being back in a job that they probably can't advance beyond. Keeping them is generally viewed as the preferable short-run decision but in the long run it's probably the wrong thing to do. This is a hard decision. You need to understand deeply what the person in this situation is like and weigh the costs carefully before deciding.

9.10 Remember that the goal of a transfer is the best, highest use of the person in a way that benefits the community as a whole.

Both affected managers should be in sync that the new role is the best, highest use or escalate up the chain to make a determination. The manager wanting to recruit the person is responsible for not causing a disruption. An informal conversation to see if someone is interested is fine, but there should be no active recruiting prior to getting in sync with the existing manager. The timing of the move should be decided by the existing manager in consultation with relevant parties.

a. Have people "complete their swings" before moving on to new roles. There should always be follow-through, not interruption, unless a pressing reason exists (when, say, a person would be a great click for another job that needs to be filled immediately). In a company where things are evolving quickly and people are expected to speak openly, it is natural that there will be a steady stream of opportunities for employees to move into new roles. But if too many people jump from one job to another without fulfilling their responsibilities, the resulting discontinuity, disorder, and instability will be bad for managers, bad for the culture, and bad for the people moving, because they won't be adequately tested in their ability to move things to completion.

As a guideline, a year in a job is sufficient before having conversations about a new role, although this isn't black and white—the range could easily vary depending on the circumstances.

9.11 Don't lower the bar.

You reach a point in all relationships when you must decide whether you are meant for each other—that's common in private life and at any organization that holds very high standards. At Bridgewater, we know that we cannot compromise on the fundamentals of our culture, so if a person cannot operate within our requirements of excellence through radical truth and transparency in an acceptable time frame, he or she must leave.

Tough love is both the hardest and the most important type of love to give.

TO BUILD AND

EVOLVE YOUR

MACHINE . . .

Most people get caught up in the blizzard of things coming at them. In contrast, successful people get above the blizzard so they can see the causes and effects at play. This higher-level perspective allows them to see themselves and others objectively as a machine, to understand who can and cannot do what well, and how everyone can fit together in a way that will produce the best outcomes.

Now that you've learned the best ways to approach your machine's two key components—its culture and its people—I'd like to turn to principles for managing and improving your machine.

In the next chapter, I will go over my high-level principles for applying higher-level thinking to conceptualize your organization as a machine. This isn't just a thought experiment; thinking in a machinelike way also has important practical ramifications for how you manage your team and how you design roles, responsibilities, and workflows.

In Chapter Ten, Manage as Someone Operating a Machine to Achieve a Goal, I apply this approach to organizational design at its highest level.

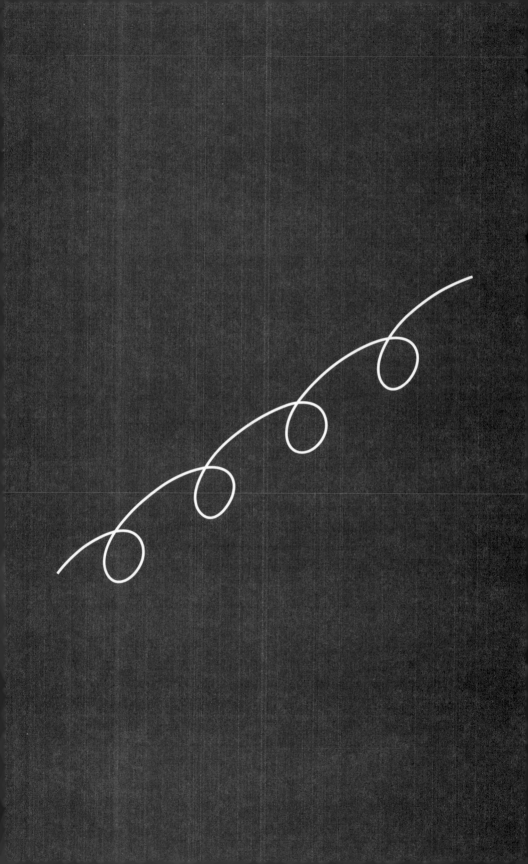

Once you understand how to build and run your machine, your next objective is to figure out how to improve it. We do this through the 5-Step Process I described as 1) identifying our goals, 2) encountering our problems; 3) diagnosing those problems to get at their root causes; 4) designing changes to get around the problems; and 5) doing what is needed. Think of any organization you know and you will see that they go through this evolutionary process with varying degrees of success. The world is littered with once-great organizations that deteriorated because the initial waves of excellence faded and the leadership failed to adequately adapt by changing the people and the designs. There are also a few organizations that keep reinventing themselves to go on to new heights of greatness.

The subsequent chapters of this section explain how the 5-Step Process works within an organization, and what you need to do to make sure you get the most out of it. To be effective, you must look down upon your machines as would an organizational engineer, comparing the outputs with the goals, and constantly modifying the people and the designs to make the outputs better. Most importantly, you must orchestrate your people. How well you do this will determine your success.

Finally, you'll read two chapters on making sure the idea meritocracy runs as designed, both at the day-to-day and the strategic level. Chapter Fifteen, Use Tools and Protocols to Shape How Work Is Done, describes the importance of systemization and tools to ensure the idea meritocracy functions as intended. And in Chapter Sixteen, And for Heaven's Sake, Don't Overlook Governance! I explain that while, at first, I underestimated the importance of governance to ensuring that an organization operates effectively over time, as I've transitioned myself out of running Bridgewater day to day, I've learned a number of important principles for how governance should function in an idea meritocracy.

10 Manage as Someone Operating a Machine to Achieve a Goal

No matter what work you do, at a high level you are simply setting goals and building machines to help you achieve them. I built the machine that is Bridgewater by constantly comparing its actual outcomes to my mental map of the outcomes that it *should* be producing, and finding ways to improve it.

I won't say anything specific about how you should set your own organization's goals other than that the high-level principles about goal setting I covered in Life Principles apply equally to individuals and organizations. I will, however, point out that in running your organization, you and the people you work with must be clear on how your lower-level goals—whether they're to produce things cost-effectively, achieve high customer satisfaction, help a certain number of people in need, whatever—grow out of your higher-level goals and values.

No matter how good you are at design, your machine will have problems. You or some other capable mechanic needs to identify those problems and look under the hood of the machine to diagnose their root causes. You or whoever is diagnosing those problems has to understand what the parts of the machine—the designs and the people— are like and how they work together to produce the outcomes. The people are the most important part, since most everything, including the designs themselves, comes from people. Unless you have a clear understanding of your machine from a higher level—and can visualize all its parts and how they work together—you will inevitably fail at this diagnosis and fall short of your potential.

At Bridgewater, the high-level goal of all of our machines is to create excellent outcomes for our clients—in the returns on their investments, of course, but also in the quality of our relationship and our thought partnership in understanding global economies and markets more broadly. Before we had anything else at Bridgewater, we had this commitment to excellence. Maintaining these extremely high standards has always been a challenge, especially as the pace of our growth and change accelerated. In the next several chapters, I will walk you through a case in which our client service outcomes began to slip and show how we used the 5-Step Process to improve our machine.

But first, I want to share some high-level principles for building and evolving the machine that is any organization.

10.1 Look down on your machine and yourself within it from the higher level.

Higher-level thinking isn't something that's done by higher-level beings. It's simply seeing things from the top down. Think of it as looking at a photo of yourself and the world around you from outer space. From that vantage, you can see the relationships between the continents, countries, and seas. Then you can get more granular, by zooming into a closer-up view of your country, your city, your neighborhood, and finally your immediate environment. Having that macro perspective gives you much more insight than you'd get if you simply looked around your house through your own eyes.

a. Constantly compare your outcomes to your goals. You must always be simultaneously trying to accomplish the goal and evaluating the machine (the people and the design), as all outcomes are reflections of how the machine is running. Whenever you identify a problem with your machine, you need to diagnose whether it is the result of a flaw in its design or in the way your people are handling their responsibilities.

Sample size is important. Any problem can be a one-off imperfection or a symptom of root causes that will show up as problems repeatedly. If you look at enough problems, which one it is will become clear.

b. Understand that a great manager is essentially an organizational engineer. Great managers are not philosophers, entertainers, doers, or artists. They are engineers. They see their organizations as machines and work assiduously to maintain and improve them. They create process-flow diagrams to show how the machine works and to evaluate its design. They build metrics to light up how well each of the individual parts of the machine (most importantly, the people) and the machine as a whole are working. And they tinker constantly with its designs and its people to make both better.

They don't do this randomly. They do it systematically, always keeping the cause-and-effect relationships in mind. And while they care deeply about the people involved, they cannot allow their feelings for them or their desire to spare them discomfort to stand in the way of the machine's constant improvement. To do otherwise wouldn't be good for either the individuals on the team or the team that the individuals are a part of.

Of course, the higher up you are in an organization, the more important vision and creativity become, but you still must have the skills required to manage/orchestrate well. Some young entrepreneurs start with the vision and creativity and then develop their management skills as they scale their companies; others start with management skills and develop vision as they climb the ladder. But like great musicians, all great managers have both creativity and technical skills. And no manager at any level can expect to succeed without the skill set of an organizational engineer.

c. **Build great metrics.** Metrics show how the machine is working by providing numbers and setting off alert lights in a dashboard. Metrics are an objective means of assessment and they tend to have a favorable impact on productivity. If your metrics are good enough, you can gain such a complete and accurate view of what your people are doing and how well they are doing it that you can almost manage via the metrics alone.

In constructing your metrics, imagine the most important questions you need answered in order to know how things are going and imagine what numbers will give you the answers to them. Don't look at the numbers that you have and try to adapt them to your purposes, because you won't get what you need. Instead start with the most important questions and imagine the metrics that will answer them.

Remember that any single metric can mislead; you need enough evidence to establish patterns. And of course the information that goes into the metrics must be assessed for accuracy. A reluctance to be critical can be detected by looking at the average grade each grader gives; those giving higher average grades might be easy graders and vice versa. Similarly helpful are "forced rankings," in which people must rank co-worker performance from best to worst. Forced rankings are essentially the same thing as "grading on a curve." Metrics that allow for independent grading across departments and groups are especially valuable.

d. **Beware of paying too much attention to what is coming at you and not enough attention to your machine.** If you keep your focus on each individual task, you will inevitably get bogged down. If instead you pay attention to building and managing your machines, you will be rewarded many times over.

e. **Don't get distracted by shiny objects.** No matter how complete any project or plan, there will always be things that come out of nowhere and look like the most important or urgent or attractive thing to focus on. These shiny objects may be traps that will distract you from thinking in a machinelike way, so be on your guard for them and don't let yourself be seduced.

10.2 Remember that for every case you deal with, your approach should have two purposes . . .

. . . 1) to move you closer to your goal, and 2) to train and test your machine (i.e., your people and your design). The second purpose is more important than the first because it is how you build a solid organization that works well in all cases. Most people focus more on the first purpose, which is a big mistake.

a. Everything is a case study. Think about what type of case it is and what principles apply to that type of case. By doing this and helping others to do this you'll get better at handling situations as they repeat over and over again through time.

b. When a problem occurs, conduct the discussion at two levels: 1) the machine level (why that outcome was produced) and 2) the case-at-hand level (what to do about it). Don't make the mistake of just having the case-at-hand discussion, because then you are micromanaging (i.e., you are doing your managee's thinking and your managee will mistakenly think that's okay). When having the machine-level discussion, think clearly how things should have gone and explore why they didn't go that way. If you are in a rush to determine what to do and you have to tell the person who works for you what to do, make sure to explain what you are doing and why.

c. When making rules, explain the principles behind them. You don't want the people you work with to merely pay lip service to your community's rules; they should have a high sense of ethics that makes them want to abide by them and hold others accountable for abiding by them, while also working to perfect them. The way to achieve this is via principles that are sound and that have been tested through open discussion.

d. Your policies should be natural extensions of your principles.
Principles are hierarchical—some are overarching and some are less important—but they all should inform the policies that guide your individual decisions. It pays to think those policies through to ensure that they are consistent with each other and the principles they are derived from.

When faced with a case that doesn't have a clear policy to follow (for example, what to do about an employee whose job is to travel but who faces potential health risks because of his travel), one can't just snatch an answer out of the blue without regard for higher-level principles. Policymakers must make policy in the same way that the judicial system creates case law—iteratively and incrementally, by dealing with specific cases and interpreting the law as it applies to them.

That is how I have tried to operate. When a case arises, I lay out the principles behind how I am handling it and get in sync with others to see if we agree on those principles or must modify them to make them better. By and large, that's how all Bridgewater's principles and policies were developed.

e. While good principles and policies almost always provide good guidance, remember that there are exceptions to every rule. While everyone has the right to make sense of things—and is in fact obliged to challenge principles and policies if they conflict with what they believe is the best approach—that's not the same thing as having the right to change them. Changes in policies must be approved by those who made them (or someone else who has been made responsible for evolving them).

When someone wishes to make an exception to an important policy at Bridgewater, they must write up a proposed alternative policy and escalate their request to the Management Committee.

Exceptions should be extremely rare because policies that have frequent exceptions are ineffective. The Management Committee will formally consider it and either reject it, amend it, or adopt it.

10.3 Understand the differences between managing, micromanaging, and not managing.

Great managers orchestrate rather than do. Like the conductor of an orchestra, they do not play an instrument, but direct their people so that they play beautifully together. Micromanaging, in contrast, is telling the people who work for you exactly what tasks to do or doing their tasks for them. Not managing is having them do their jobs without your oversight and involvement. To be successful, you need to understand these differences and manage at the right level.

a. Managers must make sure that what they are responsible for works well. They can do this by 1) managing others well (as explained above), 2) job slipping down to do work they're not responsible for because others can't do their jobs well, or 3) escalating what they can't manage well. The first choice is optimal; the second signals that a change is needed in the people and the design; the third choice is harder still but mandatory.

b. Managing the people who report to you should feel like skiing together. Like a ski instructor, you need to have close contact with your people on the slopes so that you can assess their strengths and weaknesses as they are doing their jobs. There should be a good back-and-forth as they learn by trial and error. With time you will be able to decide what they can and can't handle on their own.

c. An excellent skier is probably going to be a better ski coach than a novice skier. Believability applies to management too. The better your track record, the more value you can add as a coach.

d. You should be able to delegate the details. If you keep getting bogged down in details, you either have a problem with managing or training, or you have the wrong people doing the job. The real sign of a master manager is that he doesn't have to do practically anything. Managers should view the need to get involved in the nitty-gritty as a bad sign.

At the same time, there's danger in thinking you're delegating details when you're actually being too distant from what's important and essentially are not managing. Great managers know the difference. They strive to hire, train, and oversee in a way in which others can superbly handle as much as possible on their own.

10.4 Know what your people are like and what makes them tick, because your people are your most important resource.

Develop a full profile of each person's values, abilities, and skills. These qualities are the real drivers of behavior, so knowing them in detail will tell you which jobs a person can and cannot do well, which ones they should avoid, and how the person should be trained. These profiles should change as the people change.

If you don't know your people well, you don't know what you can expect from them. You're flying blind and you have no one to blame but yourself if you don't get the outcomes you're expecting.

a. Regularly take the temperature of each person who is important to you and to the organization. Probe your key people and urge them to bring up anything that might be bothering them. These problems might be ones you are unaware of, or they may be misunderstood by the person raising them. Whatever the case, it is essential that they be brought out into the open.

b. Learn how much confidence to have in your people—don't assume it. No manager should delegate responsibilities to people they don't know well. It takes time to learn about people and how much confidence you can vest in them. Sometimes new people are offended when their managers don't have confidence in how they are carrying out their responsibilities. They think it's a criticism of their abilities when it's simply a matter of the manager being realistic about the fact that he or she hasn't had enough time or direct experience with them to form a point of view.

c. Vary your involvement based on your confidence. Management largely consists of scanning and probing everything you are responsible for to identify suspicious signs. Based on what you see, you should vary your degree of digging, doing more for people and areas that look suspicious, and less where what you see instills confidence. At Bridgewater a host of tools (Issue Logs, metrics, daily updates, checklists) produce objective performance-related data. Managers should review and spot-check them regularly.

10.5 Clearly assign responsibilities.

Eliminate any confusion about expectations and ensure that people view their failures to complete their tasks and achieve their goals as personal failures. The most important person on a team is the one who is given the overall responsibility for accomplishing the mission. This person must have both the vision to see what should be done and the discipline to make sure it's accomplished.

a. Remember who has what responsibilities. While that might sound obvious, people often fail to stick to their own responsibilities. Even senior people in organizations sometimes act like young kids just learning to play soccer, running after the ball in an effort to help but forgetting what position they are supposed to play. This can undermine rather than improve performance. So make sure that people remember how the team is supposed to work and play their positions well.

b. **Watch out for "job slip."** Job slip is when a job changes without being explicitly thought through and agreed to, generally because of changing circumstances or a temporary necessity. Job slip often leads to the wrong people handling the wrong responsibilities and confusion over who is supposed to do what.

10.6 Probe deep and hard to learn what you can expect from your machine.

Constantly probe the people who report to you while making sure they understand that it's good for them and everyone else to surface their problems and mistakes. Doing so is required to make sure you're getting what you want, even from people who are doing their jobs well (though they can be given a bit more leeway).

Probing shouldn't just come from the top down. The people who work for you should constantly challenge you, so that you can become as good as you can be. In doing so, they will understand that they are just as responsible for finding solutions as you are. It's much easier for people to remain spectators than to become players. Forcing them onto the field strengthens the whole team.

a. **Get a threshold level of understanding.** When managing an area, you need to gain a rich enough understanding of the people, processes, and problems around you to make well-informed decisions. Without that understanding, you will believe the stories and excuses you are told.

b. **Avoid staying too distant.** You need to know your people extremely well, provide and receive regular feedback, and have quality discussions. And while you don't want to get distracted by gossip, you have to be able to get a quick download from the appropriate people. Your job design needs to build in the time to do these things. If it doesn't, you run the risk of not managing. The tools I have developed give me windows into what people are doing and what they are like, and I follow up on problems.

c. Use daily updates as a tool for staying on top of what your people are doing and thinking. I ask each person who reports to me to take about ten to fifteen minutes to write a brief description of what they did that day, the issues pertaining to them, and their reflections. By reading these updates and triangulating them (i.e., seeing other people's takes on what they are doing together), I can gauge how they are working together, what their moods are, and which threads I should pull on.

d. Probe so you know whether problems are likely to occur before they actually do. If problems take you by surprise, it is probably because you are either too far removed from your people and processes or you haven't adequately visualized how the people and processes might lead to various outcomes. When a crisis is brewing, contact should be close enough that there will be no surprises.

e. Probe to the level below the people who report to you. You can't understand how the person who reports to you manages others unless you know their direct reports and can observe how they behave.

f. Have the people who report to the people who report to you feel free to escalate their problems to you. This is a great and useful form of upward accountability.

g. Don't assume that people's answers are correct. People's answers could be erroneous theories or spin, so you need to occasionally double-check them, especially when they sound questionable. Some managers are reluctant to do this, feeling it is the equivalent of saying they don't trust their people. These managers need to understand that this process is how trust is earned or lost. Your people will learn to be much more accurate in what they tell you if they understand this—and you will learn who you can rely on.

h. Train your ear. Over time, you'll hear the same verbal cues indicating that someone is thinking about something badly or failing to apply principles appropriately. For example, listen for the anonymous "we" as a cue that someone is likely depersonalizing a mistake.

i. Make your probing transparent rather than private. This helps assure the quality of the probing (because others can make their own assessments), and it will reinforce the culture of truth and transparency.

j. Welcome probing. It's important to welcome probing of yourself because no one can see themselves objectively. When you are being probed, it's essential to stay calm. Your emotional "lower-level you" will probably react to probing with something like, "You're a jerk because you're against me and making me feel bad," whereas your thoughtful "higher-level you" should be thinking, "It's wonderful that we can be completely honest like this and have such a thoughtful exchange to help assure that I'm doing things well." Listen to your higher-level you and don't lose sight of how difficult it can be for the person doing the probing. Besides helping to make the organization and your relationship with the person who is probing you go well, working yourself through this difficult probing will build your character and your equanimity.

k. Remember that people who see things and think one way often have difficulty communicating with and relating to people who see things and think another way. Imagine you had to describe what a rose smells like to someone who lacks a sense of smell. No matter how accurate your explanation, it will always fall short of the actual experience. The same thing is true of differences in ways of thinking. They are like blind spots, and if you have one (which we all do), it can be challenging to see what's there. Working through these differences requires a lot of patience and open-mindedness, as well as triangulating with other people who can help fill in the picture.

l. **Pull all suspicious threads.** It's worth pulling all suspicious threads because: 1) Small negative situations can be symptomatic of serious underlying problems; 2) Resolving small differences of perception may prevent more serious divergence of views; and 3) In trying to create a culture that values excellence, constantly reinforcing the need to point out and stare at problems—no matter how small—is essential (otherwise you risk setting an example of tolerating mediocrity).

Prioritization can be a trap if it causes you to ignore the problems around you. Allowing small problems to go unnoticed and unaddressed creates the perception that it's acceptable to tolerate such things. Imagine that all your little problems are small pieces of trash you're stepping over to get to the other side of a room. Sure, what's on the other side of the room may be very important, but it won't hurt you to pick up the trash as you come to it, and by reinforcing the culture of excellence it will have positive second- and third-order consequences that will reverberate across your whole organization. While you don't need to pick up every piece, you should never lose sight of the fact that you're stepping over the trash nor that it's probably not as hard as you think to pick up a piece or two as you go on your way.

m. **Recognize that there are many ways to skin a cat.** Your assessment of how Responsible Parties are doing their jobs should not be based on whether they're doing it your way but whether they're doing it in a good way. Be careful about expecting a person who achieves success one way to do it a different way. That's like insisting that Babe Ruth improve his swing.

10.7 Think like an owner, and expect the people you work with to do the same.

It's a basic reality that if you don't experience the consequences of your actions, you'll take less ownership of them. If you are an employee, and you get a paycheck for turning up and pleasing your boss, your mind-set will inevitably be trained to this cause-effect relationship. If you are a manager, make sure you structure incentives and penalties that encourage people to take full ownership of what they do and not just coast by. This includes straightforward things such as spending money like it's their own and making sure their responsibilities aren't neglected when they're out of the office. When people recognize that their own well-being is directly connected to that of their community, the ownership relationship becomes reciprocal.

a. Going on vacation doesn't mean one can neglect one's responsibilities. Thinking like an owner means making sure that your responsibilities are handled well regardless of what comes up. While you are away on vacation, it's your responsibility to make sure nothing drops. You can do that via a combination of good planning and coordination before you go and staying on top of things while you are away. This needn't take much time—it can be as little as an hour of good checking from afar and it doesn't even have to be every day, so you can typically slip it in when it's convenient.

b. Force yourself and the people who work for you to do difficult things. It's a basic law of nature: You must stretch yourself if you want to get strong. You and your people must act with each other like trainers in gyms in order to keep each other fit.

10.8 Recognize and deal with key-man risk.

Every key person should have at least one person who can replace him or her. It's best to have those people designated as likely successors and to have them apprentice and help in doing those jobs.

10.9 Don't treat everyone the same —treat them appropriately.

It's often said that it is neither fair nor appropriate to treat people differently. But in order to treat people appropriately you *must* treat them differently. That is because people and their circumstances are different. If you were a tailor you wouldn't give all of your customers the same size suit.

It is, however, important to treat people according to the same set of rules. That's why I've tried to flesh out Bridgewater's principles in enough depth that differences are accounted for. For example, if someone has worked at Bridgewater for many years, that factors into how they are treated. Likewise, while I find all dishonesty intolerable, I don't treat all acts of dishonesty and all people who are dishonest the same.

a. **Don't let yourself get squeezed.** Plenty of people have threatened me over the years by saying they'd quit, bring a lawsuit, embarrass me in the press—you name it. While some people have advised me that it's easier to just make such things go away, I've found doing that is almost always shortsighted. Giving in not only compromises your values, it telegraphs that the rules of the game have changed and opens you up to more of the same. Fighting for what's right can be hard in the short term, of course. But I'm willing to take the punch. What I worry about is doing the right thing and not about what people think about me.

b. Care about the people who work for you. If you aren't working with people you care about and respect, your job probably isn't the one for you. I will be there for anyone who really needs me; when a whole community operates this way, it is very powerful and rewarding. Personal contact at times of personal difficulty is a must.

10.10 Know that great leadership is generally not what it's made out to be.

I don't use the word "leadership" to describe what I do or what I think is good because I don't believe that what most people think of as "good leadership" is effective. Most people think a good leader is a strong person who engenders confidence in others and motivates them to follow him/her, with the emphasis on "follow." The stereotypical leader often sees questioning and disagreement as threatening and prefers people do what they're told. As an extension of this paradigm, the leader bears the main burden of decision making. But because such leaders are never as all-knowing as they try to appear, disenchantment and even anger tends to set in. That's why people who once loved their charismatic leaders often want to get rid of them.

This traditional relationship between "leaders" and "followers" is the opposite of what I believe is needed to be most effective, and being maximally effective is the most important thing a "leader" must do. It is more practical to be honest about one's uncertainties, mistakes, and weaknesses than to pretend they don't exist. It is also more important to have good challengers than good followers. Thoughtful discussion and disagreement is practical because it stress-tests leaders and brings what they are missing to their attention.

One thing that leaders should not do, in my opinion, is be manipulative. Sometimes leaders will use emotions to motivate people to do things that they would not do after reflecting clearly. When dealing with intelligent people in an idea meritocracy, it is essential that one always appeal to their reason rather than their base emotions.

The most effective leaders work to 1) open-mindedly seek out the best answers and 2) bring others along as part of that discovery process. That is how learning and getting in sync occurs. A truly great leader is appropriately uncertain but well equipped to deal with that uncertainty through open-minded exploration. All else being equal, I think the kind of leader who looks and acts like a skilled ninja will beat the kind of leader who looks and acts like a muscular action hero every time.

a. Be weak and strong at the same time. Sometimes asking questions to gain perspective can be misperceived as being weak and indecisive. Of course it's not. It's necessary in order to become wise and it is a prerequisite for being strong and decisive.

Always seek the advice of wise others and let those who are better than you take the lead. The objective is to have the best understanding to make the best possible leadership decisions. Be open-minded and assertive at the same time and get in tight sync with those who work with you, recognizing that sometimes not all or even the majority of people will agree with you.

b. Don't worry about whether or not your people like you and don't look to them to tell you what you should do. Just worry about making the best decisions possible, recognizing that no matter what you do, most everyone will think you're doing something—or many things—wrong. It is human nature for people to want you to believe their own opinions and to get angry at you if you don't, even when they have no reason to believe that their opinions are good. So, if you're leading well, you shouldn't be surprised if people disagree with you. The important thing is for you to be logical and objective in assessing your probabilities of being right.

It is not illogical or arrogant to believe that you know better than the average person, so long as you are appropriately open-minded. In fact, it is not logical to believe that what the average person thinks is better than what you and the most insightful people around you think, because you have earned your way into your higher-than-average position and you and those insightful people are more informed than the average person. If the opposite were true, then you and the average man shouldn't have your respective jobs. In other words, if you don't have better insights than them, you shouldn't be a leader—and if you do have better insights than them, don't worry if you are doing unpopular things.

So how should you deal with your people? Your choices are either to ignore them (which will lead to resentment and your ignorance of what they are thinking), blindly do what they want (which wouldn't be a good idea), or encourage them to bring their disagreements to the surface and work through them so openly and reasonably that everyone will recognize the relative merits of your thinking. Have the open disagreement and be happy to either win or lose the thought battles, as long as the best ideas win out. I believe that an idea meritocracy will not only produce better results than other systems but will also ensure more alignment behind appropriate yet unpopular decisions.

c. Don't give orders and try to be followed; try to be understood and to understand others by getting in sync. If you want to be followed, either for egotistical reasons or because you believe it more expedient to operate that way, you will pay a heavy price in the long run. When you are the only one thinking, the results will suffer.

Authoritarian managers don't develop their subordinates, which means those who report to them stay dependent. This hurts everyone in the long run. If you give too many orders, people will likely resent them, and when you aren't looking, defy them. The greatest influence you can have over intelligent people—and the greatest influence they will have on you—comes from constantly getting in sync about what is true and what is best so that you all want the same things.

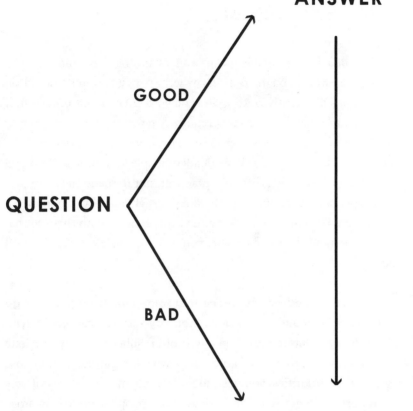

SYNTHESIZED
ANSWER

GOOD

QUESTION

BAD

WHAT WE DID

1) ....
2) ....
3) ....

10.11 Hold yourself and your people accountable and appreciate them for holding you accountable.

Holding people accountable means understanding them and their circumstances well enough to assess whether they can and should do some things differently, getting in sync with them about that, and, if they can't adequately do what is required, removing them from their jobs. It is not micromanaging them, nor is it expecting them to be perfect (holding particularly overloaded people accountable for doing everything excellently is often impractical, not to mention unfair).

But people can resent being held accountable, and you don't want to have to tell them what to do all the time. Reason with them so that they understand the value of what you're doing, but never let them off the hook.

a. If you've agreed with someone that something is supposed to go a certain way, make sure it goes that way—unless you get in sync about doing it differently. People will often subconsciously gravitate toward activities they like rather than what's required. If they lose sight of their priorities, you need to redirect them. This is part of why it's important to get frequent updates from people about their progress.

b. Distinguish between a failure in which someone broke their "contract" and a failure in which there was no contract to begin with. If you didn't make an expectation clear, you can't hold people accountable for it not being fulfilled. Don't assume that something was implicitly understood. Common sense isn't actually all that common—*be explicit*. If responsibilities keep falling between the cracks, consider editing the design of your machine.

c. **Avoid getting sucked down.** This occurs when a manager is pulled down to doing the tasks of a subordinate without acknowledging the problem. The sucked-down phenomenon bears some resemblance to job slip, since it involves the manager's responsibilities slipping into areas that should be left to others. But while job slipping can make sense on a temporary basis to push through to a goal, it's also generally a signal that a part of the machine is broken and needs fixing. The sucked-down phenomenon is what happens when a manager chronically fails to properly redesign an area of responsibility to keep him or herself from having to do the job that others should be capable of doing well. You can tell this problem exists when the manager focuses more on getting tasks done than on operating his or her machine.

d. **Watch out for people who confuse goals and tasks, because if they can't make that distinction, you can't trust them with responsibilities.** People who can see the goals are usually able to synthesize too. One way to test this: If you ask a high-level question like "How is goal XYZ going?" a good answer will provide a synthesis up-front of how XYZ is going overall and, if needed, will support it by accounting for the tasks that were done to achieve it. People who see the tasks and lose sight of the goals will just describe the tasks that were done.

e. **Watch out for the unfocused and unproductive "theoretical should."** A "theoretical should" occurs when people assume that others or themselves should be able to do something when they don't actually know whether they can (as in "Sally should be able to do X, Y, Z"). Remember that to really accomplish things you need believable Responsible Parties who have a track record of success in the relevant area.

A similar problem occurs when people discuss how to solve a problem by saying something vague and depersonalized like "We should do X, Y, Z." It is important to identify who these people are by name rather than with a vague "we," and to recognize that it is their responsibility to determine what should be done.

It is especially pointless for a group of people who are not responsible to say things like "We should . . ." to each other. Instead, those people should be speaking to the Responsible Party about what should be done.

10.12 Communicate the plan clearly and have clear metrics conveying whether you are progressing according to it.

People should know the plans and designs within their departments. If you decide to diverge from an agreed-upon path, be sure to communicate your thoughts to the relevant parties and get their views so that you are all clear about the new direction. This allows people to buy into the plan or express their lack of confidence and suggest changes. It also makes clear what the goals are and who is keeping up his or her end of the bargain and who is falling short. Goals, tasks, and assigned responsibilities should be reviewed at department meetings at least once a quarter, perhaps as often as once a month.

a. Put things in perspective by going back before going forward. Before moving forward with a new plan, take the time to reflect on how the machine has been working up till now.

Sometimes people have problems putting current conditions into perspective or projecting into the future. Sometimes they forget who or what caused things to go well or poorly. By asking them to "tell the story" of how we got here, or by telling the story yourself, you highlight important items that were done well or poorly in relation to their consequences, draw attention to the bigger picture and the overarching goals, specify the people who are responsible for specific goals and tasks, and help achieve agreement. Being able to connect all these items at multiple levels is essential for people to understand the plan, give feedback on it, and eventually believe in it.

10.13 Escalate when you can't adequately handle your responsibilities . . .

. . . and make sure that the people who work for you are proactive about doing the same. Escalating means saying you don't believe you can successfully handle a situation and that you are passing the Responsible Party job to someone else. The person you are escalating to—the person to whom you report—can then decide whether to coach you through it, take control themselves, have someone else handle it, or do something else.

It's critical that escalation not be seen as a failure but as a responsibility. All Responsible Parties will eventually face tests that they don't know whether they can handle; what's important is raising their concerns so their boss knows about the risks and both the boss and the escalating RP can get in sync about what to do about it. There is no greater failure than to fail to escalate a responsibility you cannot handle. Make sure your people are proactive; demand that they speak up when they can't meet agreed-upon deliverables or deadlines. Such communication is essential to get in sync both on the case at hand and on what the person handling it is like.

11 Perceive and Don't Tolerate Problems

On your way to your goals, you will inevitably encounter problems. To be successful you must perceive and not tolerate them. Problems are like coal thrown into a locomotive engine because burning them up—inventing and implementing solutions for them—propels us forward. Every problem you find is an opportunity to improve your machine. Identifying and not tolerating problems is one of the most important and disliked things people can do.

For a lot of people identifying problems is difficult to do. Most people would rather celebrate all the things that are going well while sweeping problems under the rug. Those people have their priorities exactly backward, and there is little that can be more harmful to an organization. Don't undermine your progress in pursuit of a pat on the back; celebrate finding out what is *not* going well so you can make it go better. Thinking about problems that are difficult to solve may make you anxious, but *not* thinking about them (and therefore not dealing with them) should make you even more anxious.

Having this kind of anxiety about what can go wrong is extremely useful. It is what drives one to develop systems and metrics for monitoring the outcomes your machine is producing and motivates those who manage well to constantly taste-test the outputs of the system and to look for problems in its nooks and crannies. Having that constant worry and doing the double-checking is important to maintaining quality control. Making sure that little problems don't exist is important because, if they're allowed to continue, they will grow into big problems. To convey the point, I will tell you about a case in which we initially failed to maintain excellence, then perceived the problem, got at its root causes, designed changes, and pushed those changes through to produce excellent results.

When I started Bridgewater, I was responsible for everything. I made the company's investment decisions and its management decisions and then I built the organization to support me and eventually to carry on excellently without me. As Bridgewater grew, the standard I set was uncompromising and straightforward: The analysis we provide to clients should always be of the same quality it would be if I did it myself. That's because when clients ask what "we" think, they aren't asking what just anyone thinks—they want to know what I and the other CIOs, who are in charge of our investments, are thinking. To achieve that goal, Bridgewater's Client Service Department either handles the questions they get from clients themselves or passes them on to people with various levels of expertise who are assigned to answer questions based on their level of difficulty. The client advisor (who is a knowledgeable professional designed to be the interface between Bridgewater and the client) has to understand the questions well enough to know who they should be routed to, and they need to review the answers before they go back to the client to ensure they are excellent. To be certain that always happens, I created a checks-and-balances system in which some of our best investment thinkers both draft memos to clients themselves and quality-control their colleagues' work, grading it to provide traceable metrics that can be followed to monitor how well things are going and make changes as needed.

In 2011, as a part of my management transition, I handed the oversight of this process to others, and several months later one of the people in the Client Service Department began noticing problems. It started with one memo, which two senior investment advisors noticed had gone out the door to a client even though it contained errors. Though these were minor errors, they were important errors to me. With my prodding, the new management team began investigating other memos and discovered that this poorly prepared memo wasn't just a one-off; it was symptomatic of a more widespread breakdown in the quality control machine. Worse still, the investigation revealed the Responsible Parties were failing to perceive and diagnose these problems. And most worrisome, it wasn't clear that, without my pushing, anyone else would have taken the time to investigate.

This initial failure to perceive and not tolerate problems did not happen for lack of caring; it happened because most of the people in the process paid more attention to getting the tasks done than assessing whether the goals were being achieved. They had become more like rubber stampers than craftsmen, while the top people who were supposed to "taste the soup" to make sure it was excellent were focused on other things.

Discovering this was disappointing to all of us, because it showed that the high standards that for so long had been the reasons for our success were slipping. Facing this reality was painful, but ultimately healthy. The existence of a problem like this one—whether from a flaw in the design of one's machine or from one's own or others' inabilities—is not shameful. Acknowledging a weakness isn't the same thing as accepting it. It's a necessary first step toward overcoming it. The pain one feels, whether from shame and embarrassment, or frustration at one's inability to get the better of it, is like the pain one feels at getting flabby that motivates one to go to the gym. As you'll see in the following chapters, facing this problem led to important innovations and improvements.

The following principles flesh out how to perceive and not tolerate the problems that come your way.

11.1 If you're not worried, you need to worry—and if you're worried, you don't need to worry.

That's because worrying about what can go wrong will protect you and not worrying about what will go wrong will leave you exposed.

11.2 Design and oversee a machine to perceive whether things are good enough or not good enough, or do it yourself.

This is usually done by having the right people—people who will probe, who can't stand inferior work or products, and who can synthesize well—and by having good metrics.

a. Assign people the job of perceiving problems, give them time to investigate, and make sure they have independent reporting lines so that they can convey problems without any fear of recrimination. Without these things in place, you can't rely on people raising all the problems you need to hear about.

b. Watch out for the "Frog in the Boiling Water Syndrome." Apparently, if you throw a frog into a pot of boiling water it will jump out immediately, but if you put it in room-temperature water and gradually bring it to a boil, it will stay in the pot until it dies. Whether or not that's true of frogs, I see something similar happen to managers all the time. People have a strong tendency to slowly get used to unacceptable things that would shock them if they saw them with fresh eyes.

c. Beware of group-think: The fact that no one seems concerned doesn't mean nothing is wrong. If you see something that seems unacceptable to you, don't assume that the fact that others also know about it and aren't screaming means it's not a problem. This is an easy trap to fall into—and a deadly one. Whenever you see badness, point it out to the Responsible Party and hold them accountable for doing something about it. Never stop saying, "This meal stinks!"

d. To perceive problems, compare how the outcomes are lining up with your goals. This means comparing the outcomes that the machine is producing to your visualization of the outcomes you expected so that you can note any deviations. If you expect improvement to be within a specific range . . .

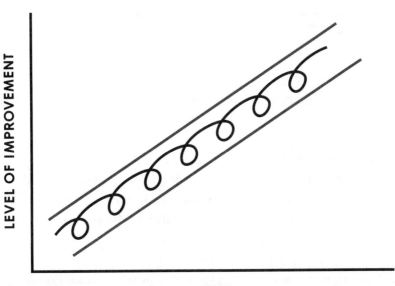

... and it ends up looking like this ...

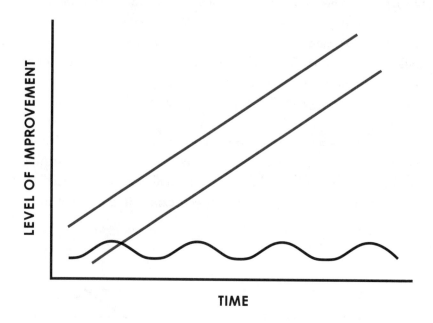

... you will know that you need to get at the root cause to deal with it. If you don't, the trajectory will probably continue.

e. "Taste the soup." Think of yourself as a chef and taste the soup before it goes out to the customers. Is it too salty or too bland? Managers need to do that too, or have someone in their machine do it for them, for every outcome they're responsible for. People who are delegated this task are called "taste testers."

f. Have as many eyes looking for problems as possible. Encourage people to bring problems to you. If everyone in your area feels responsible for the area's well-being and no one is afraid to speak up, you will learn about problems when they are still easy to fix and haven't caused serious damage. Stay in sync with the people who are closest to the most important functions.

g. "Pop the cork." It's your responsibility to make sure communications from your people flow freely, so encourage it by giving them plenty of opportunities to speak up. Don't just expect them to provide you with regular and honest feedback—explicitly ask them for it.

h. Realize that the people closest to certain jobs probably know them best. At the very least, they have perspectives you need to understand, so make sure you see things through their eyes.

11.3 Be very specific about problems; don't start with generalizations.

For example, don't say, "Client advisors aren't communicating well with the analysts." Be specific: Name which client advisors aren't doing this well and in which ways. Start with the specifics and then observe patterns.

a. Avoid the anonymous "we" and "they," because they mask personal responsibility. Things don't just happen by themselves—they happen because specific people did or didn't do specific things. Don't undermine personal accountability with vagueness. Instead of the passive generalization or the royal "we," attribute specific actions to specific people: "Harry didn't handle this well." Also avoid "We should . . ." or "We are . . ." and so on. Since individuals are the most important building blocks of any organization and since individuals are responsible for the ways things are done, mistakes must be connected to those individuals by name. Someone created the procedure that went wrong or made the faulty decision. Glossing over that can only slow progress toward improvement.

11.4 Don't be afraid to fix the difficult things.

In some cases, people accept unacceptable problems because they are perceived as too difficult to fix. Yet fixing unacceptable problems is a lot easier than not fixing them, because not fixing them will lead to more stress, more work, and chronic bad outcomes that could get you fired. So remember one of the first principles of management: You need to look at the feedback you're getting on your machine and either fix your problems or escalate them, if need be, over and over again. There is no easier alternative than bringing problems to the surface and putting them in the hands of good problem solvers.

a. Understand that problems with good, planned solutions in place are completely different from those without such solutions. Unidentified problems are the worst; identified problems without planned solutions are better, but worse for morale; identified problems with a good planned solution are better still; and solved problems are best. It's really important to know which category a problem belongs to. The metrics you use to track the progress of your solution should be so clear and intuitive that they are obvious extensions of the plan.

b. Think of the problems you perceive in a machinelike way. There are three steps to doing this well: First, note the problem; then determine who the RPs to raise it to are; and finally decide when the right time to discuss it is. In other words: what, who, when. Then follow through.

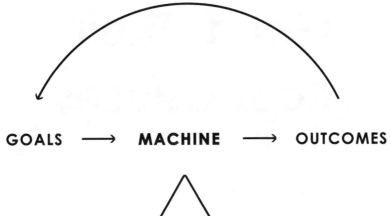

GOALS ⟶ **MACHINE** ⟶ OUTCOMES

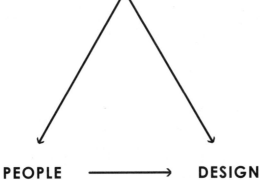

PEOPLE ⟶ **DESIGN**

12 Diagnose Problems to Get at Their Root Causes

When you encounter problems, your objective is to specifically identify the root causes of those problems—the specific people or designs that caused them—and to see if these people or designs have a pattern of causing problems.

What are the most common reasons for failing to diagnose well?

The most common mistake I see people make is dealing with their problems as one-offs rather than using them to diagnose how their machine is working so that they can improve it. They move on to fix problems without getting at their root causes, which is a recipe for continued failure. A thorough and accurate diagnosis, while more time-consuming, will pay huge dividends in the future.

The second most common mistake people make is to depersonalize the diagnosis. Not connecting problems to the people who failed and not examining what it is about them that caused the failure will not lead to improvements of the individuals or the machines.

The third biggest reason for failure is to not connect what one is learning in one diagnosis to what was learned in prior ones. It is important to determine whether the root cause of a particular problem ("Harry was careless") is part of a larger pattern ("Harry is often careless") or not ("It's unlike Harry to be careless").

In the case of our client service analytics team, I knew that unless we got to the root cause of the problems, standards would continue to decline. Bridgewater's other leaders agreed. So I led a series of diagnostic sessions with the team, getting everyone at every level into the room to probe and find out what had gone wrong. I started with my mental map of how things should've gone—based on the machine I'd built—and asked the new managers to describe what had actually happened. Bad outcomes don't just *happen*; they occur because specific people make, or fail to make, specific decisions. A good diagnosis always gets to the level of determining what it is about those people that led to the bad outcomes. This can be uncomfortable but if someone isn't suited for a job, they need to be moved out of it so that the same mistakes won't keep occurring. Of course, nobody is perfect; everyone makes mistakes. So it is important to look at people's track records and their specific strengths and weaknesses in doing a diagnosis.

Coming out of these sessions, a few things were clear: Several of the new line managers who the top managers had brought in to run client service analytics didn't have the right skills, synthesis abilities, or levels of caring to oversee the quality-control process; and the top managers were far too distant from the area and not probing adequately to make sure that everything was going well. This was the "what is"—the reality we faced that produced our problems. It wasn't a pretty picture, but it was exactly what we needed to know in order to move to the next step of designing the changes we had to make.

The following principles flesh out how to diagnose well, beginning with a basic overview.

12.1 To diagnose well, ask the following questions:

1. **Is the outcome good or bad?**
2. **Who is responsible for the outcome?**
3. **If the outcome is bad, is the Responsible Party incapable and/or is the design bad?**

If you keep those big questions in mind and anchor back to them, you should do well. What follows is a guide for getting the answers to these big-picture questions, mostly using a series of simple either/or questions to help you get to the synthesis you are looking for at each step. You should think of these as the answers you need before moving to the next step, leading all the way to the final diagnosis.

You can, but don't need to, follow these questions or this format exactly. Depending on your circumstances, you may be able to move through these questions quickly or you may need to ask some different, more granular questions.

Is the outcome good or bad? And who is responsible for the outcome? If you can't quickly get in sync that the outcome was bad and who specifically was responsible, you're probably already headed for the weeds (in other words, into a discussion of tiny, irrelevant details).

If the outcome is bad, is the RP incapable and/or is the design bad? The goal is to come to this synthesis, though to get there you may need to examine how the machine worked in this instance and build the synthesis from there.

How should the machine have worked? You may have a mental map of who should have done what, or you may need to fill it in using other people's mental maps. In any case, you need to learn who was responsible for doing what and what the principles say about how things should've gone. Keep it simple! At this stage, a common pitfall is to delve into a granular examination of procedural details rather than stay at the level of the machine (the level of who was responsible for doing what). You should be able to crystallize your mental map in just a few statements, each connected to a specific person. If you are delving into details here, you are probably off track. Once you've established the mental map the key question is:

Did the machine work as it should have? Yes or no.

If not, what didn't go as it should have? What broke? This is called the proximate cause and this step should be easy to get to if you laid out the mental map clearly. You can do this via yes/no questions as well because it should just require referring back to the key components of your mental map and pinpointing which the RP or RPs didn't do well.

Say your mental map of how the machine should have worked has two steps: that Harry should have either 1) done his assignment on time or 2) escalated that he couldn't. All you have to do is pinpoint the two steps. 1) Did he do it on time? Yes or no. And if not, 2) did he escalate? Yes or no.

It should be this simple. But this is when the conversation often gets dragged into gobbledygook, where someone goes into a detailed explanation of "what they did." Remember: It's your job to guide the conversation toward an accurate and clear synthesis.

You also have to synthesize whether the problem was meaningful—that is, whether a capable person would have made the same mistake given the circumstances, or whether it's symptomatic of something worth digging into. Don't focus too much on rare events or the trivial problems—nothing and no one is perfect—but be sure you are not overlooking a clue to a systemic machine problem. It's your job to make that determination.

Why didn't things go as they should have? This is where you have synthesized the root cause in order to determine whether the RP is capable or not—or whether the issue is with the design. In order to anchor back to a synthesis rather than get lost in the details you might:

- Try to tie the failure to the 5-Step Process. Which step was not done well? Everything ultimately fits into those five steps. But you may need to get more specific, so:
- Try to crystallize the failure as a specific key attribute or set of attributes. Ask yes/no questions: Did the RP not manage well? Not perceive problems well? Not execute well?
- Importantly, ask yourself this question: If X attribute is done well next time, will the bad outcome still occur? This is a good way of making sure you are logically connecting the outcome back to the case. Think of it this way: If your mechanic replaced that part in your car, would that fix it?
- If the root cause is a faulty design, don't stop there. Ask who was responsible for the faulty design and whether they are capable of designing well.

Is the root cause a pattern? (Yes or no.) Any problem can be a one-off imperfection—or it could be a symptom of a root cause that will show up repeatedly. You need to determine which it is. In other words, if Harry failed to do the assignment due to reliability:

- Does Harry have a reliability problem in general?
- If so, is reliability required for the role?
- Is Harry's failure due to training or abilities?

How should the people/machines evolve as a result? Confirm that the short-term resolution of the issue has been addressed, as needed. Determine the steps to be taken for long-term solutions and who is responsible for those steps. Specifically:

- Are there responsibilities that need to be assigned or clarified?
- Are there machine designs that need to be reworked?

- Are there people whose fit for their roles needs to be reevaluated?

For example, if you've determined that 1) it's a pattern, 2) the RP is missing an attribute that's required for the role, and 3) the attribute is missing due to the RP's ability (not their training)—then you've likely been able to determine the answer to your most important question: the person is not capable and needs to be sorted from the role.

The following principles further flesh out how to diagnose well.

a. Ask yourself: "Who should do what differently?" I often hear people complaining about a particular outcome without attempting to understand the machine that caused it. In many cases, these complaints come from people who are seeing the cons of some decision but not the pros and don't know how the Responsible Party weighed them to come to a decision. Since all outcomes ultimately come from people and designs, asking yourself "Who should do what differently?" will point you in the direction of the kind of understanding that you need to actually change outcomes in the future (versus just chirping about them).

b. Identify at which step in the 5-Step Process the failure occurred. If a person is chronically failing, it is due to a lack of training or a lack of ability. Which is it? At which of the five steps did the person fail? Different steps require different abilities and if you can identify which abilities are lacking, you'll go a long way toward diagnosing the problem.

c. Identify the principles that were violated. Identify which principles apply to the case at hand, review them, and see if they would have helped. Think for yourself which principles are best for handling similar cases. This will help solve not only this problem but other problems like it.

d. Avoid Monday morning quarterbacking. Evaluate the merits of a past decision based not on what you know now but only on what you could have reasonably known at the time the decision was made. Every decision has pros and cons; you can't evaluate choices in retrospect without the appropriate context. Do this by asking yourself, "What should a quality person have known and done in that situation?" Also, have a deep understanding of the person who made the decision (how they think, the type of person they are, whether they learned from the situation, and so on).

e. Don't confuse the quality of someone's circumstances with the quality of their approach to dealing with the circumstances. One can be good and the other can be bad, and it's easy to confuse which is which. Such confusion is especially common in organizations that are doing new things and evolving fast but haven't yet gotten the kinks out.

I have always described Bridgewater as being "terrible and terrific at the same time." For nearly forty years, we have consistently produced extraordinary results while struggling with lots of problems. It is easy to look at messy circumstances, think things must be terrible, and get frustrated. But the real challenge is to look at the long-term successes these messy circumstances have produced and understand how essential they are to the evolutionary process of innovation.

f. Identifying the fact that someone else doesn't know what to do doesn't mean that you know what to do. It's one thing to point out a problem; it's another to have an accurate diagnosis and a quality solution. As described earlier, the litmus test for a good problem solver is 1) they are able to logically describe how to handle the problem and 2) they have successfully solved similar problems in the past.

g. Remember that a root cause is not an action but a reason. Root causes are described in adjectives, not verbs, so keep asking "why" to get at them. Since most things are done or not done because someone decided to do them or not do them in a certain way, most root causes can be traced to specific people who have specific patterns of behavior. Of course, a normally reliable person can make the occasional error and if that's the case, then it can be forgiven, but when a problem is attributable to a person, you have to ask why they made the mistake—and you have to be as accurate in diagnosing a fault in a person as you would be if he or she were a piece of equipment.

A root cause discovery process might proceed like this:

The problem was due to bad programming.

Why was there bad programming?
Because Harry programmed it badly.

Why did Harry program it badly?
Because he wasn't well trained and because he was in a rush.

Why wasn't he well trained?
Did his manager know that he wasn't well trained and let him do the job anyway, or did he not know?

Consider how personal the questioning is. It doesn't stop at "Because Harry programmed it badly." You must go deeper in order to understand what about the people and/or the design led to the failure. This is difficult for both the diagnoser and the RPs, and it often results in people bringing up all kinds of irrelevant details. Be on your guard because people will often look to cover themselves by diving into the weeds.

h. To distinguish between a capacity issue and a capability issue, imagine how the person would perform at that particular function if they had ample capacity. Think back on how the person performed in similar functions when they had ample capacity. If the same kinds of problems came up, then the problem is very likely one of capabilities.

i. Keep in mind that managers usually fail or fall short of their goals for one (or more) of five reasons.

1. They are too distant.
2. They have problems perceiving bad quality.
3. They have lost sight of how bad things have become because they have gotten used to it.
4. They have such high pride in their work (or such large egos) that they can't bear to admit they are unable to solve their own problems.
5. They fear adverse consequences from admitting failure.

12.2 Maintain an emerging synthesis by diagnosing continuously.

If you don't look into significant bad outcomes as they occur, you won't be able to understand what things they are symptomatic of or how they are changing through time—i.e., are they getting better or worse?

12.3 Keep in mind that diagnoses should produce outcomes.

If they don't, there's no purpose to them. At a minimum, a diagnosis should take the form of theories about root causes and clarity about what information needs to be gathered to find out more. At best, it should lead directly to a plan or design to fix the problem or problems.

a. Remember that if you have the same people doing the same things, you should expect the same results. Einstein defined insanity as doing the same thing over and over and expecting different results. Don't fall into this trap because you'll have a hard time getting out of it.

12.4 Use the following "drill-down" technique to gain an 80/20 understanding of a department or sub-department that is having problems.

A drill-down is a process that allows you to gain an understanding of the root causes of the biggest problems in a department or area so you can design a plan to make the area excellent. Drill-downs are not diagnoses, but a form of broad and deep probing. They're not intended to uncover the causes of every problem: only the 20 or so percent of causes that produce 80 percent of the suboptimal effects. A drill-down takes place in two steps and is then followed by design and execution steps. If done well, the two drill-down steps can be done in about four hours. It is very important that the steps be done separately and independently, so as not to go in too many directions at once. Let me take you through the drill-down process, offering guidance and examples for each step.

Step 1: List the Problems. Quickly inventory all the core problems. Be very specific, as this is the only way to effectively find solutions. Don't generalize or use the plural "we" or "they." Name the names of the people experiencing the problems.

- Have all the relevant people from the area under scrutiny participate in the drill-down; you will benefit from their insights and it will drive their ownership of the solution.
- Don't focus on rare events or the trivial problems—nothing is perfect—but be sure they are not symptoms of systematic machine problems.
- Don't try to find solutions yet. Your focus in this step is strictly on listing the problems.

Step 2: Identify the Root Causes. For each problem, identify the deep-seated reason behind the actions that caused each problem. Most problems happen for one of two reasons: 1) It isn't clear who the Responsible Party is, or 2) The Responsible Party isn't handling his/her responsibilities well.

You must distinguish proximate causes from root causes. Proximate causes are the reasons or actions that led to the problem. When you start describing the qualities behind these reasons or actions, you are getting closer to the root cause.

To get at the root cause, keep asking "Why?" For example:

Problem:
The team is continually working late and is on the verge of burning out.

Why?
Because we don't have enough capacity to meet the demand put on the team.

Why?
Because we inherited this new responsibility without additional staff.

Why?
Because the manager did not understand the volume of work before accepting the responsibility.

Why?
Because the manager is bad at anticipating problems and creating plans. [Root Cause]

Do not exclude any relevant people from the drill-down: Besides losing the benefit of their ideas, you'll disenfranchise them from the game plan and reduce their sense of ownership. At the same time, remember that people tend to be more defensive than self-critical. It is your job as a manager to get at truth and excellence, not to make people happy. For example, the correct path might be to fire some people and replace them with better people, or put them in jobs they might not want. Everyone's objective must be to get at the best answers, not the answers that will make the most people happy.

You may find that multiple problems identified in Step 1 share the same root cause. Because you are doing a drill-down in a quick session, your root cause diagnoses may only be provisional—essentially alerts about things to watch out for.

When Step 2 is completed, take a break to reflect; then come up with a plan.

Step 3: Create a Plan. Step away from the group and develop a plan that addresses the root causes. Plans are like movie scripts, where you visualize who will do what through time to achieve the goals. They are developed by iterating through multiple possibilities, weighing the likelihood of goal achievement versus costs and risks. They should have specific tasks, outcomes, Responsible Parties, tracking metrics, and timelines. Allow the key people involved to discuss the plan thoroughly. Not everyone needs to agree on the plan but the Responsible Parties and other key people must be in sync.

Step 4: Execute the Plan. Execute the agreed-upon plan and transparently track its progress. At least monthly, report on the planned and actual progress to date and the expectations for the coming period, and hold people publicly accountable for delivering their outcomes successfully and on time. Make adjustments to the plan as required to reflect reality.

12.5 Understand that diagnosis is foundational to both progress and quality relationships.

If you and others are open-minded and engage in a quality back-and-forth, not only will you find better solutions, you will also get to know each other better. It is an opportunity for you to assess your people and to help them grow—and vice versa.

13 Design Improvements to Your Machine to Get Around Your Problems

Once you've successfully diagnosed the problems standing in the way of your achieving your goals, you need to design paths for solving them. Designs need to be based on deep and accurate understandings (which is why diagnosis is so important); for me, it's an almost visceral process of staring at problems and using the pain they cause me to stimulate my creative thinking.

This is exactly how it was for the team responsible for client service analytics—and especially for Bridgewater's co-CEO David McCormick, who was then head of the Client Service Department. Coming out of the diagnosis, he moved quickly to design and implement changes. He fired the team members who had allowed standards to slip and reflected deeply on what new designs he could implement to get the right people into the right roles. In selecting his new Responsible Parties for client service analytics, he picked one of our top investment thinkers who also had extremely high standards (and was very outspoken about cases where he saw them slipping) and paired him with one of our most experienced managers, who knew how to build the right process flows and make sure everything that needed to happen would go precisely as planned.

But that wasn't all. When coming up with a design, it's important to take time to reflect and make sure you're looking at the problems from the highest level. David knew it would be a mistake to look only at this one part of the department, because the same slip in quality that had happened there was likely to have occurred in other places too. He needed to think creatively to come up with a design that would build a durable culture of pervasive excellence throughout the entire department. This led to his invention of "Quality Day," biannual meetings in which members of the Client Service Department would review each other's mock presentations and memos and give direct feedback on what was good and what wasn't. More importantly, the meetings were a chance to step back and assess whether the ways of ensuring quality were working as expected—by bringing in a bunch of tough, independent thinkers to offer criticism and get the process realigned on what good looks like.

Of course, there were many more details to all of David's plans for transforming the department. But the important thing is how all the details and plans extended from a high-level visualization of what was required. Only when you have such a sketch can you begin to fill it in with specifics. Those specifics will be your tasks; write them down so you don't forget them.

While the best designs are drawn from a rich understanding of actual problems, when you're just starting out on something, you often have to design based on anticipated problems as opposed to actual ones. That's why having systematic ways of tracking issues (the Issue Log) and what people are like (the Dot Collector) is so useful: Instead of just relying on your best guesses of what might go wrong, you can look at data from prior "at bats" for yourself and others and come to the design process with understanding rather than having to start from scratch.

The most talented designers I know are people who can visualize over time, running through different collections of people from the scale of small teams to entire organizations, accurately anticipating the kinds of results they'll produce. They excel at design and systemization. Hence the overriding principle of this chapter: Design and systemize your machine. Creativity is also important to this process, as is character, because the most important problems to design around are often the hardest, and you need to come up with original ways of addressing them and be willing to make hard choices (especially when it comes to people and who should do what).

The following principles delve into designing and how to do it well.

13.1 Build your machine.

Focus on each task or case at hand and you will be stuck dealing with them one by one. Instead, build a machine by observing what you're doing and why, extrapolating the relevant principles from the cases at hand, and systemizing that process. It typically takes about twice as long to build a machine as it does to resolve the task at hand, but it pays off many times over because the learning and efficiency compound into the future.

13.2 Systemize your principles and how they will be implemented.

If you have good principles that guide you from your values to your day-to-day decisions but you don't have a systematic way of making sure they're regularly applied, they're not of much use. It's essential to build your most important principles into habits and help others do so as well. Bridgewater's tools and culture are designed to do just that.

a. Create great decision-making machines by thinking through the criteria you are using to make decisions while you are making them. Whenever I make an investment decision, I observe myself making it and think about the criteria I used. I ask myself how I would handle another one of those situations and write down my principles for doing so. Then I turn them into algorithms. I am now doing the same for management and I have gotten in the habit of doing it for all my decisions.

Algorithms are principles in action on a continuous basis. I believe that systemized, evidence-based decision making will radically improve the quality of management. Human managers process information spontaneously using poorly thought-out criteria and are unproductively affected by their emotional biases. These all lead to suboptimal decisions. Imagine what it would be like to have a machine that processes high-quality data using high-quality decision-making principles/criteria. Like the GPS in your car, it would be invaluable, whether you follow all of its suggestions or not. I believe that such tools will be essential in the future, and as I write these words, I am a short time away from getting a prototype online.

13.3 Remember that a good plan should resemble a movie script.

The more vividly you can visualize how the scenario you create will play out, the more likely it is to happen as you plan. Visualize who will do what when and the result they'll produce. This is your mental map of your machine. Recognize that some people are better or worse at visualization. Accurately assess your own abilities and those of others so you can use the most capable people to create your plans.

a. Put yourself in the position of pain for a while so that you gain a richer understanding of what you're designing for. Either literally or vicariously (through reading reports, job descriptions, etc.), temporarily insert yourself into the workflow of the area you're looking at to gain a better understanding of what it is that you are dealing with. As you design, you'll be able to apply what you've learned, and revise the machine appropriately as a result.

b. Visualize alternative machines and their outcomes, and then choose. A good designer is able to visualize the machine and its outcomes in various iterations. First they imagine how Harry, Larry, and Sally can operate in various ways with various tools and different incentives and penalties; then they replace Harry with George, and so on, thinking through what the products and people and finances would look like month by month (or quarter by quarter) under each scenario. Then they choose.

c. Consider second- and third-order consequences, not just first-order ones. The outcome you get as a first-order consequence might be desirable, while the second- or third-order consequences could be the opposite. So focusing solely on first-order consequences, which people tend to do, can lead to bad decision making. For example, if you asked me if I'd like to not have rainy days, I probably would say yes if I didn't consider the second- and third-order consequences.

d. Use standing meetings to help your organization run like a Swiss clock. Regularly scheduled meetings add to overall efficiency by ensuring that important interactions and to-do's aren't overlooked, eliminating the need for inefficient coordination, and improving operations (because repetition leads to refinement). It pays to have standardized meeting agendas that ask the same feedback questions in each meeting (such as how effective the meeting was) and nonstandard meeting agendas that include things done infrequently (such as quarterly budget reviews).

e. Remember that a good machine takes into account the fact that people are imperfect. Design in such a way that you produce good results even when people make mistakes.

13.4 Recognize that design is an iterative process. Between a bad "now" and a good "then" is a "working through it" period.

That "working through it" period is when you try out different processes and people, seeing what goes well or poorly, learning from the iterations, and moving toward the ideal systematic design. Even with a good future design picture in mind, it will naturally take some mistakes and learning to get to a good "then" state.

People frequently complain about this kind of iterative process because it tends to be true that people are happier with nothing at all than with something imperfect, even though it would be more logical to have the imperfect thing. That kind of thinking doesn't make sense, so don't let it distract you.

a. Understand the power of the "cleansing storm." In nature, cleansing storms are big infrequent events that clear out all the overgrowth that's accumulated during good times. Forests need these storms to be healthy—without them, there would be more weak trees and a buildup of overgrowth that stifles other growth. The same is true for companies. Bad times that force cutbacks so only the strongest and most essential employees (or companies) survive are inevitable and can be great, even though they seem terrible at the time.

13.5 Build the organization around goals rather than tasks.

Giving each department a clear focus and the appropriate resources to achieve its goals makes the diagnosis of resource allocations more straightforward and reduces job slip. As an example of how this works, at Bridgewater we have a Marketing Department (goal: to market) that is separate from our Client Service Department (goal: to service clients), even though they do similar things and there would be advantages to having them work together. But marketing and servicing clients are two distinct goals; if they were merged, the department head, salespeople, client advisors, analysts, and others would be giving and receiving conflicting feedback. If asked why clients were receiving relatively poor attention, the answer might be: "We have incentives to raise sales." If asked why they weren't making sales, the merged department might explain that they need to take care of their clients.

a. **Build your organization from the top down.** An organization is the opposite of a building: Its foundation is at the top, so make sure you hire managers before you hire their reports. Managers can help design the machine and choose the people who complement it. People overseeing departments need to be able to think strategically as well as run the day-to-day. If they don't anticipate what's coming up, they'll run the day-to-day off a cliff.

b. **Remember that everyone must be overseen by a believable person who has high standards.** Without strong oversight, there is potential for inadequate quality control, inadequate training, and inadequate appreciation of excellent work. Never just trust people to do their jobs well.

c. **Make sure the people at the top of each pyramid have the skills and focus to manage their direct reports and a deep understanding of their jobs.** A few years ago, someone at Bridgewater proposed that our facilities group (the people who take care of the building and grounds, food service, office supplies, etc.) should begin to report to our head of technology because of the overlap in the two areas (computers are a facility too, they use electricity, and so on). But having the people who are responsible for janitorial services and meals report to a technology manager would be as inappropriate as having technology people report to the person taking care of facilities. These functions, even if they're considered "facilities" in the broadest sense, are very different, as are the respective skill sets. Similarly, at another time, we talked about putting the folks who work on client agreements under the same manager as those who do counterparty agreements. But that would have been a mistake because the skills required to reach agreements with clients are very different from the skills required to reach agreements with counterparties. It would be wrong to conflate both departments under the general heading of "agreements," because each calls for specific knowledge and skills.

d. In designing your organization, remember that the 5-Step Process is the path to success and that different people are good at different steps. Assign specific people to do each of these steps based on their natural inclinations.

For example, the big-picture visionary should be responsible for goal setting, the taste tester should be assigned the job of identifying and not tolerating problems, the logical detective who doesn't mind probing people should be the diagnoser, the imaginative designer should craft the plan to make the improvements, and the reliable taskmaster should make sure the plan gets executed. Of course, some people can do more than one of these things—generally people do two or three well. Virtually nobody can do them all well. A team should consist of people with all of these abilities and they should know who is responsible for which steps.

e. Don't build the organization to fit the people. Managers will often take the people who work in their organization as a given and try to make the organization work well with them. That's backward. Instead, they should imagine the best organization and then make sure the right people are chosen for it. Jobs should be created based on the work that needs to be done, not what people want to do or which people are available. You can always search outside to find the people who click best for a particular role. First come up with the best work-flow design, then sketch it out on an organizational chart, visualize how the parts interact, and specify what qualities are required for each job. Only after all that is done should you choose the people to fill the slots.

f. Keep scale in mind. Your goals must be the right size to warrant the resources that you allocate to them. An organization might not be big enough to justify having both a sales and an analytics group, for example. Bridgewater successfully evolved from a one-cell organization, in which most people were involved in everything, to a multi-cellular organization because we retained our ability to focus efficiently as we grew.

Temporarily sharing or rotating resources is fine and is not the same as a merging of responsibilities. On the other hand, the efficiency of an organization decreases as the number of people and/or its complexity increases, so keep things as simple as possible. And the larger the organization, the more important are information technology management and cross-departmental communication.

g. Organize departments and sub-departments around the most logical groupings based on "gravitational pull." Some groups naturally gravitate toward one another. That gravitational pull might be based on common goals, shared abilities and skills, workflow, physical location, and so forth. Imposing your own structure without acknowledging these magnetic pulls will likely result in inefficiency.

h. Make departments as self-sufficient as possible so that they have control over the resources they need to achieve their goals. We do this because we don't want to create a bureaucracy that forces departments to requisition resources from a pool that lacks the focus to do the job.

i. Ensure that the ratios of senior managers to junior managers and of junior managers to their reports are limited to preserve quality communication and mutual understanding. Generally, the ratio should not be more than 1:10, and preferably closer to 1:5. Of course, the appropriate ratio will vary depending on how many people your direct reports have reporting to them, the complexity of the jobs they're doing, and a manager's ability to handle several people or projects at once. The number of layers from top to bottom and the ratio of managers to their direct reports will limit the size of an effective organization.

j. Consider succession and training in your design. This is a subject I wish I had thought about much earlier in my career. To ensure that your organization continues to deliver results, you need to build a perpetual motion machine that can work well without you. This involves

505

more than the mechanics of your own "stepping out," but the selection and training and governance of the new leaders who "step up," and most importantly, the preservation of the culture and its values.

The best approach I've seen for doing this is what companies and organizations like GE, 3G, and the Chinese Politburo do, which is to build a pyramid-like "succession pipeline" in which the next generation of leaders is exposed to the thinking and decision making of the current leaders so they can both learn and be tested.

k. Don't just pay attention to your job; pay attention to how your job will be done if you are no longer around. I wrote about key-man risk earlier, which applies the most to those with the largest areas of responsibility, especially the head of an organization. If that's you, then you should designate the people who could replace you and have them do your job for a while so they can be vetted and tested. These results should be documented in a manual that the appropriate people can go to if you should be hit by a bus. If all the key people in the organization do this, you will have a strong "farm team," or at least a clear understanding of vulnerabilities and a plan to deal with them. Remember that a ninja manager is somebody who can sit back and watch beauty happen—i.e., an orchestrator. If you are always trying to hire somebody who is as good as or better than you at your job, that will both free you up to go on to other things and build your succession pipeline.

Beyond that, visualizing your replacement is an enlightening and productive experience. In addition to taking stock of what you are doing and coming up with both bad and good names, you will start to think about how to get your best people into slots that don't yet exist. Knowing that you will have to test them by letting them do your job without interference, you will be motivated to train them properly before the test. And, of course, the stress-testing will help you learn and adapt, which will lead to better results.

l. Use "double-do" rather than "double-check" to make sure mission-critical tasks are done correctly. Double-checking has a much higher rate of errors than double-doing, which is having two different people do the same task so that they produce two independent answers. This not only ensures better answers but will allow you to see the differences in people's performance and abilities. I use double-do's in critical areas such as finance, where large amounts of money are at risk.

And because an audit is only as effective as the auditor is knowledgeable, remember that a good double-check can only be done by someone capable of double-doing. If the person double-checking the work isn't capable of doing the work himself, how could he possibly evaluate it accurately?

m. Use consultants wisely and watch out for consultant addiction. Sometimes hiring an external consultant is the best fit for your design. Doing so can get you precisely the amount of specialized expertise you need to tackle a problem. When you can outsource you don't have to worry about managing, and that's a real advantage. If a position is part-time and requires highly specialized knowledge, I would prefer to have it done by consultants or outsiders.

At the same time, you need to beware of the chronic use of consultants to do work that should be done by employees. This will cost you in the long run and erode your culture. Also make sure you are careful not to ask consultants to do things that they don't normally do. They will almost certainly revert to doing things in their usual way; their own employers will demand that.

When evaluating whether to use a consultant, consider the following factors:

1. **Quality Control.** When someone doing work for you is an employee, you are responsible for the quality of their work. But when the person working for you works for another company, you're operating by their standards, so it's important to know whether their standards are as high or higher than yours.

2. **Economics.** If a full-time person is required, it is almost certainly more cost-effective to create a position. Consultants'

daily rates add up to considerably more than the annualized cost of a full-time person.

3. **Institutionalization of Knowledge.** Someone who is around your environment on an ongoing basis will gain knowledge and an appreciation of your culture that no outsider can.

4. **Security.** Having outsiders do the job substantially increases your security risks, especially if you can't see them at work (and monitor whether they follow proper precautions, like not leaving sensitive documents on their desks).

You have to consider whether you should be outsourcing or developing capabilities in-house. Though temps and consultants are good for a quick fix, they won't augment your capacities in the long term.

13.6 Create an organizational chart to look like a pyramid, with straight lines down that don't cross.

The whole organization should look like a series of descending pyramids, but the number of layers should be limited to minimize hierarchy.

a. Involve the person who is the point of the pyramid when encountering cross-departmental or cross-sub-departmental issues. Imagine an organizational chart as a pyramid that consists of numerous pyramids.

When issues involve parties not in the same part of the pyramid, it is generally desirable to involve the person who is at the point of the pyramid, and thus has the perspective and knowledge to weigh the trade-offs and make informed decisions.

b. Don't do work for people in another department or grab people from another department to do work for you unless you speak to the person responsible for overseeing the other department. If there is a dispute about this, it needs to be resolved at the point of the pyramid.

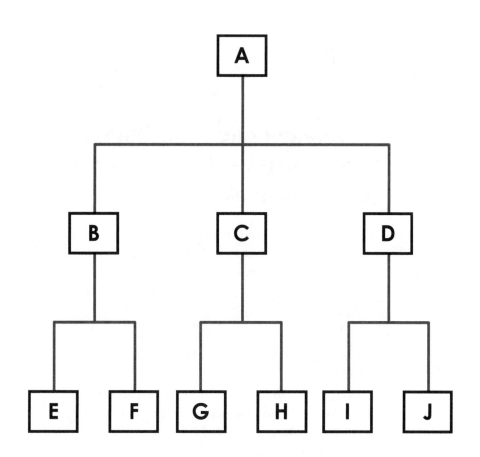

c. Watch out for "department slip." This happens when a support department mistakes its responsibility to provide support with a mandate to determine how the thing they are supporting should be done. An example of this sort of mistake would be if the facilities group thought it should determine what facilities we should have. While support departments should know the goals of the people they're supporting and provide feedback regarding possible choices, they are not the ones to determine the vision.

13.7 Create guardrails when needed— and remember it's better not to guardrail at all.

Even when you find people who are great clicks for your design, there will be times when you'll want to build guardrails around them. No one is perfect, everyone has strengths and weaknesses, and as hard as you look, you won't always be able to find everything you want in one person. So look down on your machine and the people you choose for your roles, and think about where you might need to supplement your design by adding people or processes to ensure that each job is done excellently.

Remember, guardrailing is meant to help people who can by and large do their jobs well—it's intended to help good people perform better, not to help failing people reach the bar. If you're trying to guardrail someone who is missing the core abilities required for their job, you should probably just fire them and look for someone else who will be a better click.

A good guardrail typically takes the form of a team member whose strengths compensate for the weaknesses of the team member who needs to be guardrailed. A good guardrailing relationship should be firm without being overly rigid. Ideally, it should work like two people dancing—they're literally pushing against each other, but with a lot of mutual give-and-take. Of course, having someone in a job who needs to be guardrailed is not as good as having someone in a job who will naturally do the right things. Strive for that.

a. Don't expect people to recognize and compensate for their own blind spots. I constantly see people form wrong opinions and make bad decisions, even though they've made the same kinds of mistakes before—and even though they know that doing so is illogical and harmful. I used to think that they would avoid these pitfalls when they became aware of their blind spots, but typically that's not the case. Only very rarely do I hear someone recuse himself from offering an opinion because they aren't capable of forming a good one in a particular area. Don't bet on people to save themselves; proactively guardrail them or, better yet, put them in roles in which it's impossible for them to make the types of decisions they shouldn't make.

b. Consider the clover-leaf design. In situations where you're unable to identify one excellent Responsible Party for a role (which is always best), find two or three believable people who care deeply about producing excellent results and are willing to argue with each other and escalate their disagreements if necessary. Then set up a design in which they check and balance each other. Though it's not optimal, such a system will have a high probability of effectively sorting the issues you need to examine and resolve.

13.8 Keep your strategic vision the same while making appropriate tactical changes as circumstances dictate.

Bridgewater's values and strategic goals have been the same since the beginning (to produce excellent results, meaningful work, and meaningful relationships through radical truth and transparency) but its people, systems, and tools have changed over forty-plus years as we have grown from a one-person company to a 1,500-person organization—and they can continue to change while maintaining values and strategic goals as newer generations replace older ones. That can happen for organizations in much the same way as it happens for families and communities. To help nurture that, it is desirable to reinforce the traditions and reasons for them, as well as to make sure the values and strategic goals are imbued in the successive leaders and the population as a whole.

a. Don't put the expedient ahead of the strategic. People often tell me they can't deal with the longer-term strategic issues because they have too many pressing issues they need to solve right away. But rushing into ad hoc solutions while kicking the proverbial can down the road is a "path to slaughter." Effective managers pay attention both to imminent problems and to problems that haven't hit them yet. They constantly feel the tug of the strategic path because they worry about not getting to their ultimate goal and they are determined to continue their process of discovery until they do. While they might not have the answer right away, and they might not be able to come up with it by themselves, through a combination of creativity and character they eventually make all the necessary upward loops.

b. Think about both the big picture and the granular details, and understand the connections between them. Avoid fixating on irrelevant details. You have to determine what's important and what's unimportant at each level. For example, imagine you are designing a house. First you need to start with the big picture: Your house will sit on a plot of land, and you have to think through where the water comes from, how the house gets hooked up to the power grid, and so on. Then you need to decide how many rooms it will have, where the doors will go, where you need windows, and so on. When designing the plan, you need to think about all of these things and connect them, but that doesn't mean that you actually need to go out and pick the hinges for the door yourself. You just need to know that you'll need a door with hinges and how it fits into the bigger picture of the house.

13.9 Have good controls so that you are not exposed to the dishonesty of others.

Don't assume that people are operating in your interest rather than their own. A higher percentage of the population than you might imagine will cheat if given the opportunity. When offered the choice of being fair with you or taking more for themselves, most people will take more for themselves. Even a tiny amount of cheating is intolerable, so your happiness and success will depend on your controls. I have repeatedly learned this lesson the hard way.

a. Investigate and let people know you are going to investigate. Investigate and explain to people that you are going to investigate so there are no surprises. Security controls should not be taken personally by the people being checked, just like a teller shouldn't view the bank counting the money in the drawer (rather than just accepting the teller's count) as an indication that the bank thinks the teller is dishonest. Explain that concept to employees so that they understand it.

But even the best controls will never be foolproof. For that reason (among many others), trustworthiness is a quality that should be appreciated.

b. Remember that there is no sense in having laws unless you have policemen (auditors). The people doing the auditing should report to people outside the department being audited, and auditing procedures should not be made known to those being audited. (This is one of our few exceptions to radical transparency.)

c. Beware of rubber-stamping. When a person's role involves reviewing or auditing a high volume of transactions or things that other people are doing, there's a real risk of rubber-stamping. One particularly risky example is expense approvals. Make sure you have ways to audit the auditors.

d. Recognize that people who make purchases on your behalf probably will not spend your money wisely. This is because 1) it is not their money and 2) it is difficult to know what the right price should be. For example, if somebody proposes a price of $125,000 for a consulting project, it is unpleasant, difficult, and confusing to figure out what the market rate is and then negotiate a better price. But the same person who's reluctant to negotiate with the consultant will bargain furiously when he is hiring someone to paint his own house. You need to have proper controls, or better yet, a part of the organization that specializes in this kind of thing. There's retail and there's wholesale. You want to pay wholesale whenever possible.

e. Use "public hangings" to deter bad behavior. No matter how carefully you design your controls and how rigorously you enforce them, malicious and grossly negligent people will sometimes find a way around them. So when you catch someone violating your rules and controls, make sure that everybody sees the consequences.

13.10 Have the clearest possible reporting lines and delineations of responsibilities.

This applies both within and between departments. Dual reporting causes confusion, complicates prioritization, diminishes focus on clear goals, and muddies the lines of supervision and accountability—especially when the supervisors are in two different departments. When situations require dual reporting, managers need to be informed. Asking someone from another department to do a task without consulting with his or her manager is strictly prohibited (unless the request will take less than an hour or so). However, appointing co-heads of a department or a sub-department can work well if the managers are in sync and combine complementary and essential strengths; dual reporting in that case can work well if properly coordinated.

a. Assign responsibilities based on workflow design and people's abilities, not job titles. Just because someone is responsible for "Human Resources," "Recruiting," "Legal," "Programming," and so forth, doesn't necessarily mean they are the appropriate person to do everything associated with those functions. For example, though HR people help with hiring, firing, and providing benefits, it would be a mistake to give them the responsibility of determining who gets hired and fired and what benefits are provided to employees.

b. Constantly think about how to produce leverage. Leverage in an organization is not unlike leverage in the markets; you're looking for ways to achieve more with less. At Bridgewater, I typically work at about 50:1 leverage, meaning that for every hour I spend with each person who works for me, they spend about fifty hours working to move the project along. At our sessions, we go over the vision and the deliverables, then they work on them, and then we review the work, and they move forward based on my feedback—and we do that over and over again. The people who work for me typically have similar relationships with those who work for them, though their ratios are typically between 10:1 and 20:1. I am always eager to find people who can do things nearly as well as (and ideally better than) I can so that I can maximize my output per hour.

Technology is another great tool for providing leverage. To make training as easy to leverage as possible, document the most common questions and answers through audio, video, or written guidelines, and then assign someone to organize them and incorporate them into a manual, which is updated on a regular basis.

Principles themselves are a form of leverage—they're a way to compound your understanding of situations so that you don't need to exert the same effort each time you encounter a problem.

c. Recognize that it is far better to find a few smart people and give them the best technology than to have a greater number of ordinary people who are less well equipped. Great people and great technology both enhance productivity. Put them together in a well-designed machine and they improve it exponentially.

d. Use leveragers. Leveragers are people who can go from conceptual to practical effectively and do the most to get your concepts implemented. Conceptualizing and managing takes only about 10 percent of the time needed for implementing, so if you have good leveragers, you can devote a lot more of your time to what's most important to you.

13.11 Remember that almost everything will take more time and cost more money than you expect.

Virtually nothing goes according to plan because one doesn't plan for the things that go wrong. I personally assume things will take about one and a half times as long and cost about one and a half times as much because that's what I've typically experienced. How well you and the people working with you manage will determine your expectations.

14 Do What You Set Out to Do

The organization, like the individual, has to push through to results in order to succeed—this is step five in the 5-Step Process.

While recently cleaning up a huge pile of work products from the 1980s and 1990s, I came across boxes and boxes full of research. There were thousands of pages, most covered with my scribbles, and I realized that they represented just a fraction of the effort I'd put in. At our fortieth-year celebration I was given copies of the almost ten thousand Bridgewater *Daily Observations* that we'd published. Every one of them expressed our deepest thinking and research about markets and economies. I also stumbled across the manuscript of an eight-hundred-page book that I wrote but then got too busy to publish, and countless other memos and letters to clients, research reports, and versions of the book you're reading now. Why did I do all these things? Why do others work so hard to achieve their goals?

From what I can see, we do it for different reasons. For me, the main reason is that I can visualize the results of pushing through so intensely that I experience the thrill of success even while I'm still struggling to achieve it. Similarly, I can visualize the tragic results of not pushing through. I am also motivated by a sense of responsibility; I have a hard time letting people I care about down. But that's just what's true for me. Others describe their motivation as attachment to the community and its mission. Some do it for approval and some do it for financial rewards. All these are perfectly acceptable motivations and should be used and harmonized in a way consistent with the culture.

The way one brings people together to do this is key. This is what most people call "leadership." What are the most important things that a leader needs to do in order to get their organizations to push through to results? Most importantly, they must recruit individuals who are willing to do the work that success requires. While there might be more glamour in coming up with the brilliant new ideas, most of success comes from doing the mundane and often distasteful stuff, like identifying and dealing with problems and pushing hard over a long time. This was certainly the case with the Client Service Department. Through a lot of relentless hard work in the years since the original problem turned up, the department has become an example to other teams at Bridgewater—and our client satisfaction levels remain consistently high. The great irony of all this is that none of our clients ever even noticed the problems we saw with the memos. Sending out work not up to our standards was bad—and I'm glad it was corrected. But it could've been much worse, tarnishing our reputation for delivering pervasive excellence. Once that happens, it becomes much harder to restore trust.

14.1 Work for goals that you and your organization are excited about . . .

. . . and think about how your tasks connect to those goals. If you're focused on the goal, excited about achieving it, and recognize that doing some undesirable tasks to achieve the goal is required, you will have the right perspective and will be appropriately motivated. If you're not excited about the goal that you're working for, stop working for it. Personally, I like visualizing exciting new and beautiful things that I want to make into realities. The excitement of visualizing these ideas and my desire to build them out is what pulls me through the thorny realities of life to make my dreams happen.

a. Be coordinated and consistent in motivating others. Managing groups to push through to results can be done emotionally or intellectually, and by carrots or by sticks. While we each have our own reasons for working, there are unique challenges and advantages to motivating a community. The main challenge is the need to coordinate, i.e., to get in sync on the reasons for pursuing a goal and the best way to do it. For example, you wouldn't want one group to be motivated and compensated so differently from another (one gets big bonuses for example, and another doesn't under the same set of circumstances) that the differences cause problems. The main advantage of working in groups is that it's easier to design a group to include all the qualities needed to be successful than to find all those qualities in one person. As with the steps in the 5-Step Process, some people are great at one step and some are terrible at that step. But it doesn't matter which is the case when everyone is clear on each other's strengths and weaknesses and the group is designed to deal with those realities.

b. Don't act before thinking. Take the time to come up with a game plan. The time you spend on thinking through your plan will be virtually nothing in relation to the amount of time that will be spent doing, and it will make the doing radically more effective.

c. Look for creative, cut-through solutions. When people are facing thorny problems or have too much to do, they often think that they need to work harder. But if something seems hard, time-consuming, and frustrating, take some time to step back and triangulate with others on whether there might be a better way to handle it. Of course, many things that need getting done are just a slog, but it's often the case that there are better solutions out there that you're not seeing.

521

14.2 Recognize that everyone has too much to do.

How to do more than we think we can is a puzzle we all struggle with. Other than working harder for longer hours, there are three ways to fix the problem: 1) having fewer things to do by prioritizing and saying no, 2) finding the right people to delegate to, and 3) improving your productivity.

Some people spend a lot of time and effort accomplishing very little while others do a lot in the same amount of time. What differentiates people who can do a lot from those who can't is creativity, character, and wisdom. Those with more creativity invent ways to do things more effectively (for instance by finding good people, good technologies, and/or good designs). Those with more character are better able to wrestle with their challenges and demands. And those with more wisdom can maintain their equanimity by going to the higher level and looking down on themselves and their challenges to properly prioritize, realistically design, and make sensible choices.

a. Don't get frustrated. If nothing bad is happening to you now, wait a bit and it will. That is just reality. My approach to life is that it is what it is and the important thing is for me to figure out what to do about it and not spend time moaning about how I wish it were different. Winston Churchill hit the nail on the head when he said, "Success consists of going from failure to failure without loss of enthusiasm." You will come to enjoy this process of careening between success and failure because it will determine your trajectory.

It makes no sense to get frustrated when there's so much that you can do, and when life offers so many things to savor. Your path through any problem is outlined in these principles—and in others you'll discover yourself. There's nothing you can't accomplish if you think creatively and have the character to do the difficult things.

14.3 Use checklists.

When people are assigned tasks, it is generally desirable to have them captured on checklists. Crossing items off a checklist will serve as both a task reminder and a confirmation of what has been done.

a. **Don't confuse checklists with personal responsibility.** People should be expected to do their whole job well, not just the tasks on their checklists.

14.4 Allow time for rest and renovation.

If you just keep *doing*, you will burn out and grind to a halt. Build downtime into your schedule just as you would make time for all the other stuff that needs to get done.

14.5 Ring the bell.

When you and your team have successfully pushed through to achieve your goals, celebrate!

15 Use Tools and Protocols to Shape How Work Is Done

Words alone aren't enough.

That's something I learned from watching people struggle to get themselves to do things that are in their best interests. After I shared these principles with the people at Bridgewater and refined them, nearly everyone saw the connection between the principles and our excellent results and wanted to operate in accordance with them. But there's a big difference between *wanting* to do something and actually being able to do it. Assuming people will do what they intellectually want to do is like assuming that people will lose weight simply because they understand why it's beneficial for them to do it. It won't happen until the proper habits are developed. In organizations, that happens with the help of tools and protocols.

Take a minute to think about how this applies to your reading of this book, or reading books in general. How often have you read a book describing some behavioral change you've wanted to make but then failed to? How much behavioral change do you think will result from this book if you don't have tools and protocols to help you? My guess is hardly any. Just as you can't learn many things by reading a book (how to ride a bike, speak a language, etc.), it's nearly impossible to change a behavior without practicing it. That is why I plan to make the tools that I describe in the Appendix publicly available.

15.1 Having systemized principles embedded in tools is especially valuable for an idea meritocracy.

That is because an idea meritocracy needs to operate in accordance with agreed-upon principles and to be evidence-based and fair instead of following the more autocratic and arbitrary decisions of the CEO and his or her lieutenants. Rather than be above the principles, the people responsible for running the organization must be evaluated, chosen, and—if needed—replaced in an evidence-based way according to rules, just like everyone else in the organization. Their strengths and weaknesses, like everyone's, must be taken into consideration. Collecting objective data about all people is essential for this. And you need good tools to convert data into decisions in agreed-upon ways. Moreover, the tools allow the people and the system to work together in a symbiotic way to improve each other.

a. To produce real behavioral change, understand that there must be internalized or habituated learning. Thankfully, technology has made internalized learning much easier today than it was when books were the primary way of conveying knowledge. Don't get me wrong, the book was a powerful invention. Johannes Gutenberg's printing press allowed easy dissemination of knowledge that helped people build on each other's learnings. But experiential learning is so much more powerful. Now that technology makes it so easy to create experiential/virtual learning, I believe that we are on the brink of another step-change improvement in the quality of learning that will be as great as or even greater than Gutenberg's.

We have been trying to create internalized learning at Bridgewater for a long time, so how we do it has evolved a lot. Since we tape virtually all our meetings, we have been able to create virtual learning case studies that allow everyone to participate without actually being in the room. People see the meeting transpire as though they were in it, and then the case study pauses and asks them for their own thinking on the matter at hand. In some cases, they input their reactions in real time as they watch. Their thinking is recorded and compared with others' using expert systems that help us all understand more about how we think. With this information, we can better tailor their learning and their job assignments to their thinking styles.

That is just one example of a number of tools and protocols we have developed to help our people learn and operate by our principles.

b. Use tools to collect data and process it into conclusions and actions. Imagine that virtually everything important going on in your company can be captured as data, and that you can build algorithms to instruct the computer, as you would instruct a person, to analyze that data and use it in the way you agreed it should be used. In that way, you and the computer on your behalf could look at each person and all the people together and provide tailored guidance, just like your GPS provides you guidance by knowing all the traffic patterns and routes. You don't have to make it mandatory to follow that guidance, though you can. Generally speaking, the system operates like a coach. And the coach can learn about its team: Data is collected about what people do so that if they make more insightful moves or less insightful moves, learning will occur and be used to create improvements. Because the thinking behind the algorithms is available to everyone, anyone can assess the quality of the logic and its fairness, and have a hand in shaping it.

c. Foster an environment of confidence and fairness by having clearly-stated principles that are implemented in tools and protocols so that the conclusions reached can be assessed by tracking the logic and data behind them. In all organizations, it's always the case that some of the people judged to be ineffective will argue that those judgments are wrong. When that happens, a data- and rules-based system with clearly laid-out criteria allows less room for such arguments and greater belief that the system is fair. Though the system won't be perfect, it is much less arbitrary—and can much more easily be examined for bias—than the much less specified and much less open decision making of individuals with authority. My ideal is to have a process in which everyone contributes criteria for good decision making and those criteria are assessed and selected by appropriately assigned (believable) people. If people maintain the right balance of open-mindedness and assertiveness so they understand where they are and aren't believable to make decisions, having these open discussions on the criteria for assessing and managing people can be very powerful in building and reinforcing the idea meritocracy.

We have early-stage tools that achieve these things and we are striving to refine them so that our people management system operates as effectively as our investment management system.

Even with its imperfections, our evidence-based approach to learning about people, guiding them, and sorting them is much fairer and more effective than the arbitrary and subjective management systems that most organizations still rely on. I believe that the forces of evolution will push most organizations toward systems that combine human and computer intelligence to program principles into algorithms that substantially improve decision making.

In the Appendix, I've provided detailed descriptions of a number of the tools and protocols that support this idea-meritocratic approach and reinforce the behaviors that people need to operate consistently with it. They are designed to help us achieve our goals of 1) learning what people are like, 2) sharing what people are like, 3) providing personalized training and development, 4) offering guidance and oversight in specific situations, and 5) helping managers sort people into the right roles or out of the company based on what they are like and what is required.

You don't need to use these same tools and protocols for your own idea meritocracy, but you should have ways of producing the internalized learning that it will require. While ours have evolved a lot, yours don't have to be as fancy or automated. For example, providing a form or a template to help guide people through the steps required for them to manage their work or carry out a process will yield better results than expecting them to just remember—or figure it out—on their own.

How you decide to use tools and protocols is up to you. The main point I want to make here is that they're important.

16 And for Heaven's Sake, Don't Overlook Governance!

All that I've said thus far will be useless if you don't have good governance. Governance is the oversight system that removes the people and the processes if they aren't working well. It is the process that checks and balances power to assure that the principles and interests of the community as a whole are always placed above the interests and power of any individual or faction. Because power will rule, power must be put in the hands of capable people in key roles who have the right values, do their jobs well, and will check and balance the power of others.

I didn't realize the importance of this sort of governance until after I transitioned out of the CEO role, because I was an entrepreneur and company builder (as well as an investment manager) who largely did what I thought was best. While I needed and developed double-checks on myself—I created a Management Committee that I put above me so that I had to report to it—I always had the power of my equity to change things, though I never used it. Some might say that I was a benevolent despot because while I had all the power (the complete voting rights), I exercised my power in an idea-meritocratic way, recognizing that the good of the whole was best for us all, and that

I needed to be double-checked. I certainly did not create the sort of governance system appropriate for Bridgewater, given its scale.

For example, Bridgewater didn't have a board of directors overseeing the CEOs, there were no internal regulations, no judicial system for people to appeal to, and no enforcement system, because we didn't need them. I, with the help of others, simply created the rules and enforced them, though everyone had the right to appeal and overturn my and others' judgments. Our principles were the equivalent of what the Articles of Confederation had been to the United States in its first years, and our policies were like our laws, but I never created a formal way of operating such as a "Constitution" or a justice system to enforce them and resolve disputes. As a result, when I stepped out and passed the power to others, confusions about decision rights arose. After conferring with some of the world's greatest experts on governance, we put a new system in place based on these principles. Still, I want to make clear that I don't consider myself an expert on governance and can't vouch for the following principles as much as I can vouch for the previous ones, because they are still new as of this writing.

16.1 To be successful, all organizations must have checks and balances.

By checks, I mean people who check on other people to make sure they're performing well, and by balances, I mean balances of power. Even the most benevolent leaders are prone to becoming more autocratic, if for no other reason than because managing a lot of people and having limited time to do it requires them to make numerous difficult choices quickly, and they sometimes lose patience with arguments and issue commands instead. And most leaders are not so benevolent that they can be trusted to put the organization's interests ahead of their own.

a. Even in an idea meritocracy, merit cannot be the only determining factor in assigning responsibility and authority. Appropriate vested interests also need to be taken into consideration. For example, the owners of a company might have vested interests that they are perfectly entitled to that might be at odds with the vested interests of the people in the company who, based on the idea meritocracy, are most believable. That should not lead the owners to simply turn over the keys to those leaders. That conflict has to be worked out. Since the purpose of the idea meritocracy is to produce the best results, and the owners have the rights and powers to assess that, of course they will make the determination— though I recommend they choose wisely.

b. Make sure that no one is more powerful than the system or so important that they are irreplaceable. For an idea meritocracy, it is especially important that its governance system is more powerful than any individual—and that it directs and constrains its leaders rather than the other way around. The Chinese leader Wang Qishan drew my attention to what happened in ancient Rome when Julius Caesar revolted against the government, defeated his fellow general Pompey, seized control of the Republic from the Senate, and named himself emperor for life. Even after he was assassinated and governance by the Senate was restored, Rome would never again be what it was; the era of civil strife that followed was more damaging than any foreign war.

c. Beware of fiefdoms. While it's great for teams and departments to feel a strong bond of shared purpose, loyalty to a boss or department head cannot be allowed to conflict with loyalty to the organization as a whole. Fiefdoms are counterproductive and contrary to the values of an idea meritocracy.

d. Make clear that the organization's structure and rules are designed to ensure that its checks-and-balances system functions well. Every organization has its own way of doing this. The diagram on the next page is a sketch of my conceptualization of how this should work for Bridgewater, which is currently an organization of about 1,500 people. The principles it follows, however, are universal; I believe that all organizations need some version of this basic structure.

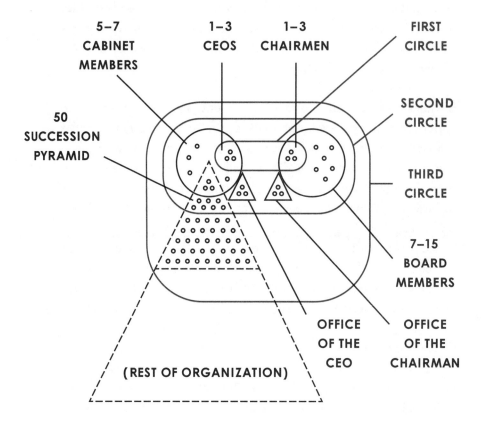

5-7
CABINET
MEMBERS

1-3
CEOS

1-3
CHAIRMEN

FIRST
CIRCLE

SECOND
CIRCLE

THIRD
CIRCLE

7-15
BOARD
MEMBERS

50
SUCCESSION
PYRAMID

OFFICE
OF THE
CEO

OFFICE
OF THE
CHAIRMAN

(REST OF ORGANIZATION)

There are one to three chairmen working with seven to fifteen board members supported by staff, whose purpose is primarily to assess whether: 1) The people running the company are capable; 2) The company is operating in accordance with its agreed-upon principles and rules. The board has the power to select and replace the CEOs, but doesn't engage in the micromanagement of the firm nor the people running it, though in the event of an emergency, they can drop into a more active role. (They can also help the CEOs to the extent they want it.) While Bridgewater's idea meritocracy is ideally all-inclusive, there need to be various circles of authority, trust and access to information, and decision-making authority, which are shown in the chart's three circles.

e. Make sure reporting lines are clear. While this is important throughout the organization, it is especially important that the reporting lines of the board (those doing the oversight) are independent of the reporting lines of the CEOs (those doing the management), though there should be cooperation between them.

f. Make sure decision rights are clear. Make sure it's clear how much weight each person's vote has so that if a decision must be made when there is still disagreement, there is no doubt how to resolve it.

g. Make sure that the people doing the assessing 1) have the time to be fully informed about how the person they are checking on is doing, 2) have the ability to make the assessments, and 3) are not in a conflict of interest that stands in the way of carrying out oversight effectively. In order to assess well, one has to gain a threshold level of understanding and that takes time. Some people have the ability and the courage to hold people accountable, while most don't; having such ability and courage is essential. And the person doing the assessing must not have conflicts of interest—such as being in a subordinate position to the person they are intended to check on—that stand in the way of holding them accountable, including recommending that they be fired.

h. **Recognize that decision makers must have access to the information necessary to make decisions and must be trustworthy enough to handle that information safely.** That doesn't mean that all people must have access and be trustworthy. It is possible to have subcommittees who have access to sensitive information and make recommendations to the board that are substantiated with enough information to make good judgments, but without disclosing the highly sensitive particulars.

16.2 Remember that in an idea meritocracy a single CEO is not as good as a great group of leaders.

Dependence on one person produces too much key-man risk, limits the range of expertise (because nobody is good at everything), and fails to establish adequate checks and balances. It also creates a burden because there's generally too much to do. That's why we have a co-CEO model at Bridgewater that is essentially a partnership of two or three people who lead the firm.

At Bridgewater the CEOs are overseen by a board largely via the executive chairman or chairmen. In our idea meritocracy, the CEOs are also held accountable by the employees of the company, even though these employees are subordinate to the CEOs. The challenge of having two or three people is for them to dance well together. If they can't do that, and coordinate well with the chairmen, they have to notify the executive chairman or chairmen so changes can be made.

For the same reason we have more than one CEO overseeing management of the company, we have more than one chief investment officer (there are currently three).

16.3 No governance system of principles, rules, and checks and balances can substitute for a great partnership.

All these principles, rules, and checks and balances won't be worth much if you don't have capable people in positions of power who instinctually want to operate for the good of the community based on the agreed-upon principles. A company's leaders must have wisdom, competence, and the ability to have close, cooperative, and effective working relationships characterized by both thoughtful disagreement and commitment to following through with whatever the idea-meritocratic process decides.

We work with others
to get three things:

1) Leverage to accomplish
our chosen missions in
bigger and better ways than
we could alone.

2) Quality relationships
that together make for a
great community.

3) Money that allows us to
buy what we need and want
for ourselves and others.

WORK PRINCIPLES: PUTTING IT ALL TOGETHER

Since the relative importance of these three things varies by person, it is up to you to determine the quantities and mix you want. The important thing to realize is that they are mutually supportive. If you want to accomplish your mission, you will be better off having quality relationships with people committed to that mission and financial resources to put behind it. Similarly, if you want to have a great work community, you will need a shared mission and financial resources to support you, and if you want to make the most money possible, you will need clear goals and tight relationships to achieve them. In my life, I have been lucky to have much more of all three of these than I could have ever imagined. I have tried to convey the approach that worked for me—an idea meritocracy in which meaningful work and meaningful relationships are the goals and radical truth and radical transparency are the ways of achieving them—so that you can decide what, if any of it, is of use to you.

Recognizing that I gave you a pile of principles that could be confusing, I want to make sure that the headline I'm trying to get across comes through. It is that of all approaches to decision making, **an idea meritocracy is the best.**[40] It's almost too obvious to warrant saying, but I will anyway: Knowing what you can and cannot expect from each person and knowing what to do to make sure the best ideas win out are the best way to make decisions. Idea-meritocratic decision making is better than traditional autocratic or democratic decision making in almost all cases.

That's not just theory. While there is no such thing as utopia just like there is no such thing as perfect, there is great—and there isn't much doubt that the results of this idea-meritocratic approach have been pretty great for Bridgewater for more than forty years. Because this approach can work equally well in most organizations, I wanted to lay it out clearly and in detail. While you needn't follow this idea-meritocratic approach exactly as I've done it, the big question is: Do you want to work in an idea meritocracy? If so, what is the best way for you to do that?

An idea meritocracy requires people to do three things: 1) Put their honest thoughts on the table for everyone to see, 2) Have thoughtful disagreements where there are quality back-and-forths in which people evolve their thinking to come up with the best collective answers possible, and 3) Abide by idea-meritocratic ways of getting past the remaining disagreements (such as believability-weighted decision making). While an idea meritocracy doesn't have to operate exactly in any particular way, it does have to by and large follow those three steps. Don't worry about remembering all the particular principles that I gave you in this book. Just go after having an idea meritocracy and figure out what works for you by encountering your trade-offs and coming up with your principles for handling them.

In my case, I wanted meaningful work and meaningful relationships, and I believed that being radically truthful and radically transparent were required to get those. Then I went after them and encountered problems that forced me to make choices. By writing down how I made these choices, I was able to flesh out my principles, which led

---

[40] I'm not saying that it is always the best, as there are some cases where it's not. I'm saying that I believe that it is almost always the best if it can be implemented well.

me to shape Bridgewater's idea meritocracy with the people I worked with so that it would work well for us. As you set out on your own and encounter your own impediments, you might want to refer back to these principles because chances are that I've encountered many of the same impediments, did my wrestling with how to handle them, and laid out my thinking in principles. And then write down your own.

Of course, people's abilities to influence how their group works vary, and I don't know your circumstances. But I do know that if you want to work in an idea-meritocratic way, you can find your own way of doing that. Maybe it will be by helping shape your organization from the top, maybe it will be by choosing the right organization for you, and maybe it will be by simply dealing with the people you work with in an idea-meritocratic way. No matter your position, you can always practice being open-minded and assertive at the same time, and thinking about your and others' believabilities when deciding what to do.

Above all else, my wishes for you are that: 1) You can make your work and your passion one and the same; 2) You can struggle well with others on your common mission to produce the previously mentioned rewards; 3) You can savor both your struggles and your rewards; and 4) You will evolve quickly and contribute to evolution in significant ways.

It's up to you to decide what you want to get out of life and what you want to give.

CONCLUSION

As I said at the outset, my goal is to pass along the principles that worked well for me; what you do with them is up to you.

I of course hope that they will help you visualize your own audacious goals, navigate through your painful mistakes, have quality reflections, and come up with good principles of your own that you will systematically follow to produce outcomes that vastly exceed your expectations. I hope that they will help you do these things both individually and when working with others. And, since your journey and evolution will certainly be a struggle, I hope that these principles will help you struggle and evolve well. Perhaps they will even inspire you and others to put your principles in writing and collectively figure out what's best in an idea-meritocratic way. If I could tilt the world even one degree more in that direction, that would thrill me.

Along these lines, there is more to come. Because I know that having tools and protocols is necessary to helping people convert what they want to do into actually doing it, I will soon be making the ones we've created available to you.

I feel I have now done the best I can to pass along my Life and Work Principles. Of course, we aren't done with our struggles until we die. Since my latest struggle has been to pass along whatever I have that has been of value, I feel a certain sense of relief to have gotten these principles out to you, and a sense of contentment as I end this book and turn my attention to passing along my economic and investment principles.

TOOLS AND PROTOCOLS FOR BRIDGEWATER'S IDEA MERITOCRACY

What follows is a quick overview of many of the tools and processes currently in use at Bridgewater. It's my intention to soon share many of these with the wider world in a Principles app so you can try them out for yourself.

COACH

Because there are too many principles for anyone to keep top of mind enough to apply appropriately to whatever situation they face, and because it's easier to ask for advice than to seek it out in a book, I created Coach. Coach's platform is populated with a library of common situations, or "ones of those" (e.g., disagreeing with an assessment someone made, someone lied or did something unethical, etc.), which are linked to the relevant principles to help people handle them. As people use Coach, they give feedback on the quality of advice it provides, essentially coaching the Coach so that it can deliver better and better advice. Over time, Coach has become increasingly effective in much the same way Siri has.

DOT COLLECTOR

The **Dot Collector** is an app used in meetings that allows people to express their thoughts and see others' thoughts in real time, and then helps them collectively reach an idea-meritocratic decision. It surfaces people's thinking, analyzes it, and uses the information to help people make real-time decisions better in a few ways. Specifically:

- Participants continuously record their assessments of each other by giving them "dots," positive or negative, on any number of several dozen attributes. These dots are laid out in a grid that updates dynamically, so that everyone in the conversation can see one another's thinking as the meeting progresses. Doing this helps people shift their perspectives from being stuck in their own heads with their own opinions to looking down on everyone's views. Seeing things through everyone's eyes naturally causes most people to adopt the higher-level view in which they recognize that their own perspective is just one of many, so they ask themselves which criteria are best for deciding how to resolve the issue at hand. In this way it promotes open-minded, idea-meritocratic, collective decision making.
- It helps people make better decisions by providing advice in the same way a GPS does. By taking data on what everyone in the room is like, the app is able to give people individualized coaching, which is especially important when their own opinions are unlikely to be right. We have found that helping people through such times can be invaluable.
- The Dot Collector highlights what we call "nubby questions"—cases where the pattern of answers and attributes of people on different sides of an issue suggest that there's an important disagreement to be resolved. For example, it will alert you automatically if you disagree with the believability-weighted majority on a given issue and give you guidance on the appropriate steps to take to resolve that disagreement in an evidence-based way.

- It enables believability-weighted voting. The Dot Collector provides both a polling interface where people can vote yes or no (or provide a numerical rating) and a back-end system of believability weighting, which allows us to look at vote results on both equal-weighted and believability-weighted bases, not as just simple majorities but also based on which way the people whose views have the most merit voted. While this may sound complicated, it's simply a way of helping people keep track of believability without having to remember who is more believable at what.

BASEBALL CARDS

In addition to collecting "dots" about people in meetings, we collect data on our people in numerous other ways (reviews, tests, the choices people make, etc.). All these dots are analyzed via computerized algorithms based on stress-tested logic in order to create pointillist pictures of what people are like. That logic is typically shared with and vetted by the people in the company to help its objectivity and believability. We then capture these pictures in **Baseball Cards**, which are a simple way of presenting a person's strengths and weaknesses and the evidence behind them (in much the same way as a baseball card does for a professional baseball player).

I found that we needed to have these and refer to them regularly because without them, people tended to interact with each other without any regard to who was good or bad at what. For example, Baseball Cards are useful in meetings, where they allow people to assess the qualities of whoever is expressing a point of view to determine the merit of that opinion. As a supplement to Baseball Cards, we developed another tool called the People Profile, which takes all the data from Baseball Cards (which have grown complex over time) to provide a simple, text-based summary of what each person is like. Over time, this is meant to provide employees with a systemized synthesis that captures Bridgewater's best thinking about what someone is like. We work with the people being assessed to compare these pictures with the assessed person's own perceptions. In this way of seeking alignment between the process and the person's self-perception, both the processes and the confidences in the perceptions are improved.

In order to match people to jobs, I developed the **Combinator**, which takes the data from the Baseball Cards and allows one to look at people based on their key attributes and compare them to one another. If you're looking for a certain type of person to fill a role, you can enter a few names of people who fit the image, and the Combinator will call up the precise data on what those people are like, synthesize the key qualities that make them that way, and then search the database to help you find other similar people. The Combinator can also be used to generate job specifications (based on the type of person you are looking for) that you can apply both inside and outside the company.

ISSUE LOG

The **Issue Log** is our primary tool for recording our mistakes and learning from them. We use it to bring all problems to the surface, so we can put them in the hands of problem solvers to make systematic improvements. It acts like a water filter that catches garbage. Anything that goes wrong must be "issue logged" with the severity of the issue and who is responsible for it specified, so that it's easy to sort through most problems. Issue logs also provide paths for diagnosing problems and the information pertaining to them. In that way, they also provide effective metrics of performance, as they allow you to measure the numbers and types of problems coming up (and identify the people who are contributing to them and fixing them).

The Issue Log is a good example of a tool that changed habits and perceptions. A common challenge people had at first was openly pointing out mistakes, because some people instinctively viewed pointing out mistakes as hurtful to the people who made them. Once they got used to doing this, they realized the benefit of it and they got in the good habit of doing it. Now most people can't do without it.

PAIN BUTTON

I believe *Pain+Reflection=Progress*. In other words, pain is an important signal that there is something to be learned, and if you reflect on your pain well, you will almost always learn something important. That prompted me to create the **Pain Button**.

The moment someone experiences pain is the best time for them to record what the pain is like, but it's a bad time to reflect because it's hard to keep a clear head. So the app is designed to let people record the emotions they are feeling (anger, disappointment, frustration, etc.) as they feel them and then come back at a later time to reflect on them using guided reflection questions. The tool prompts the people who experienced the pain to specify what they will do to deal with that situation, so that the pain is mitigated in the future (for example, have a quality conversation with the person who is causing the pain, etc.). There is a part of the app that shows the frequency of the pain and the causes of the pain and whether the actions were followed through and productive. In that way, one receives a sort of biofeedback connection among the pain that occurred, the diagnosis of it, the plan for improvement so that the problems are reduced or eliminated, the following through on these plans, and the results produced. The tool creates a template for looping toward improvement that everyone can see. It allows you to share your entries with others or keep them to yourself. Some people have described the Pain Button as like having a psychologist in your pocket, although better as it's always available and a hell of a lot cheaper.

DISPUTE RESOLVER

Disputes need clear paths toward resolution. That is especially so in an idea meritocracy where people are expected to disagree and create paths for resolving disagreements. The **Dispute Resolver** provides paths for resolving disagreements in an idea-meritocratic way. It asks a series of questions used to guide the people through the resolution process. One of its features is that it locates believable people who can help determine whether a disagreement is worth taking up at a higher management level. The app also makes clear to everyone that if they have a different point of view from others, it's up to them to express it and work to get in sync—instead of privately holding on to the view and not putting it on the table. Whether you have a tool like the Dispute Resolver or not, you must have a clear and fair system to resolve disputes in order to ensure there is a real idea meritocracy. Otherwise the person with greater power could pull rank on the person with lesser power.

We also have a number of tools that help us complete and oversee our day-to-day work and stay in sync regarding how things are going.

DAILY UPDATE TOOL

For years, I have asked each person who reports to me to take about ten to fifteen minutes to write a brief email of what they did that day, the issues pertaining to them, and their reflections. By reading these updates and triangulating them (in other words, seeing different people's takes on what they are doing), I can gauge how they are working together, what their moods are, and which threads I should pull. Over the last few years, I've developed this into a software application that pulls these updates into a dashboard, which makes them much easier to track, record metrics, and respond to than dealing with dozens of separate email threads. It also allows people to easily provide helpful data—like their morale, how heavy their workload is, issues they want to escalate—on a daily basis. I and those I work with find this simple tool invaluable in helping us stay in sync. Also, at the company level, it provides valuable information for taking the daily pulse of what's going on (morale, workloads, specific issues, who is doing what, etc.).

CONTRACT TOOL

How often have you ended a meeting with everybody saying we should do this or that, but then everybody walks off and nothing actually happens because people lose track of what was agreed upon? Implicit contracts are pretty much worthless; the commitments people make to each other need to be explicit to be actionable—and firm enough to hold each other accountable. The **Contract Tool** is a simple app that lets people make and monitor their commitments to each other. It helps both the people who requested things, and those who are required to provide those things, to easily stay on top of them.

PROCESS FLOW DIAGRAM

Just as an engineer uses flow charts to understand the workflow of what they're designing, a manager needs a **Process Flow Diagram** to help visualize the organization as a machine. It might have references to an organizational chart that shows who reports to whom, or the org chart might supplement the Process Flow Diagram. Ideally the Process Flow Diagram is made in a way that allows you to both see things simply at a high level and drop down to lower levels of detail as needed (e.g., when looking at a person in the diagram, one can click into their Baseball Card and view other info about them).

At Bridgewater, we've created process maps for every department in the company that show us clearly all the roles and the responsibilities for each role and how the work flows among them to reach intended outcomes.

POLICY AND PROCEDURES MANUALS

This is the compendium of policies and procedures that people can consult as one would an operating manual. It's a living document in which the organization's learning is codified.

METRICS

As the saying goes, "You can't manage what you can't measure." By measuring how your machine is working, you can manage it more easily, especially if you can enlist the help of algorithms to do a lot of your thinking and work for you.

Good metrics come about by first thinking of what information you need to answer your pressing questions and then figuring out how to get it. They do not come about by gathering information and putting it together to see what it tells you. At Bridgewater, we talk about four helpful steps to creating good metrics: 1) know what goal your business is achieving, 2) understand the process for getting to the goal (your "machine" with its *people* and *design*), 3) identify the key parts in the process that are the best places to measure, so you know how your *machine* is working to achieve that goal, and 4) explore how to create levers, tied to those key metrics, that allow you to adjust your process and change your outcomes. To that end, we encourage employees to construct our metrics in conjunction with process flow diagrams and procedures manuals.

The test of the effectiveness of metrics lies in whether they can tell you what and who is doing well and poorly, all the way down to specific people. We aim to have metrics that cascade from the most important matters the CEOs are responsible for at the company level, down through the departments, to the teams within them and the people responsible in each role.

BIBLIOGRAPHY

Aamodt, Sandra, and Sam Wang. *Welcome to Your Brain: Why You Lose Your Car Keys but Never Forget How to Drive and Other Puzzles of Everyday Life*. New York: Bloomsbury Publishing, 2009.

Beauregard, Mario, and Denyse O'Leary. *The Spiritual Brain: A Neuroscientist's Case for the Existence of the Soul*. San Francisco: HarperOne, 2007.

Campbell, Joseph. *The Hero with a Thousand Faces*. Princeton: Princeton University Press, 1949.

Dalai Lama XIV. *Beyond Religion: Ethics for a Whole World*. Boston: Houghton Mifflin Harcourt, 2011.

Dawkins, Richard. *River Out of Eden: A Darwinian View of Life*. New York: Basic Books, 1995.

Duhigg, Charles. *The Power of Habit: Why We Do What We Do in Life and Business*. New York: Random House, 2012.

Durant, Will, and Ariel Durant. *The Lessons of History*. New York: Simon & Schuster, 1968.

Eagleman, David. *Incognito: The Secret Lives of the Brain*. New York: Pantheon Books, 2011.

Gardner, Howard. *Changing Minds: The Art and Science of Changing Our Own and Other People's Minds*. Cambridge: Harvard Business Review Press, 2006.

Gazzaniga, Michael S. *Who's in Charge?: Free Will and the Science of the Brain*. New York: Ecco Books, 2011.

Grant, Adam. *Originals: How Non-Conformists Move the World*. New York: Viking, 2016.

Haier, Richard J. *The Intelligent Brain*. Chantilly, VA: The Great Courses Teaching Company, 2013.

Hess, Edward D. *Learn or Die: Using Science to Build a Leading-Edge Learning Organization*. New York: Columbia Business School Publishing, 2014.

Kahneman, Daniel. *Thinking, Fast and Slow.* New York: Farrar, Straus & Giroux, 2011.

Kegan, Robert. *The Evolving Self: Problem and Process in Human Development.* Cambridge: Harvard University Press, 1982.

Kegan, Robert. *In Over Our Heads: The Mental Demands of Modern Life.* Cambridge: Harvard University Press, 1998.

Kegan, Robert, and Lisa Laskow Lahey. *An Everyone Culture: Becoming a Deliberately Developmental Organization.* Cambridge: Harvard Business Review Press, 2016.

Lombardo, Michael M., Robert W. Eichinger, and Roger P. Pearman. *You: Being More Effective in Your MBTI Type.* Minneapolis: Lominger Limited, 2005.

Mlodinow, Leonard. *Subliminal: How Your Unconscious Mind Rules Your Behavior.* New York: Pantheon Books, 2012.

Newberg, Andrew, MD, and Mark Robert Waldman. *The Spiritual Brain: Science and Religious Experience.* Chantilly, VA: The Great Courses Teaching Company, 2012.

Norden, Jeanette. *Understanding the Brain.* Chantilly, VA: The Great Courses Teaching Company, 2007.

Pink, Daniel H. *A Whole New Mind: Why Right-Brainers Will Rule the Future.* New York: Riverhead Books, 2005.

Plekhanov, G. V. *On the Role of the Individual in History.* Honolulu: University Press of the Pacific, 2003. (Original work published 1898)

Reiss, Steven. *Who Am I? The 16 Basic Desires That Motivate Our Actions and Define Our Personalities.* New York: Berkley, 2002.

Riso, Don Richard, and Russ Hudson. *Discovering Your Personality Type: The Essential Introduction to the Enneagram, Revised and Expanded.* New York: Mariner Books, 2003.

Rosenthal, Norman E, MD. *The Gift of Adversity: The Unexpected Benefits of Life's Difficulties, Setbacks, and Imperfections.* New York: TarcherPerigee, 2013.

Taylor, Jill Bolte. *My Stroke of Insight: A Brain Scientist's Personal Journey.* New York: Penguin Books, 2009.

Thomson, J. Anderson, with Clare Aukofer. *Why We Believe in God(s): A Concise Guide to the Science of Faith.* Charlottesville: Pitchstone Publishing, 2011.

Tokoro, M., and K. Mogi, eds. *Creativity and the Brain.* Singapore: World Scientific Publishing, 2007.

Wilson, Edward O. *The Meaning of Human Existence.* New York: Liveright Publishing Corporation, 2014.

INDEX

abilities, 407–8, 435–36

above-the-line conversations, 247

accountability, 402, 468–70

accuracy, in evaluations, 426–27

advancers, 228

advice, 387

AI (artificial intelligence), 262–65

algorithms, 257–62

alignment, 369

   see also sync, getting in

answers, 189, 459–60

approximations, 244–46

arguing vs. seeking to understand, 190

assertiveness, 362–64, 365–66

assessments of others, 176, 225–31, 430–35, 438, 535

attributes, positive and negative aspects of, 210–14

auditors, 513

bad behavior, 514

badmouthing, 327–28

barriers, 183–87

   blind spot, 185–87, 199, 511

behavior:

   change in, 526–27

   standards of, 386–87

believability, 190

   choosing believable people, 381

   comparing your own with others', 199

   in decision making, 256–57, 307–14, 370–83

   oversight and, 503

   Responsible Parties and, 381

   track records in, 380

   triangulating and, 193–95

   and understanding others' reasoning, 375–76

below-the-line conversations, 247

bets, 253

big picture, 512–13

blame and credit, 352

blind spots, 185–87, 199, 511

brain, 218–25

"by-and-large" statements, 244–46

capability, 299, 414–15, 490
career paths, 423–24
celebration, 523
change, 136, 244, 411, 434, 526–27
character, 299, 414–15
checklists, 523
checks and balances, 532–36
circumstances, 489
cleansing storms, 502
closed-minded people, 196–98,
    362–63
clover-leaf design, 511
collaboration, 368–69, 415
common sense, 251
communication(s):
    aimed at educating or boosting
      cohesion, 383
    aimed at getting best answer, 382
    clarity in, 470
    and different ways of thinking,
      460–61
    leveraging, 367–68
    opportunities for, 479
    precision in, 365
    types of, 365
    see also conversations
compensation, 416–17
complaints, 362, 387
completion, pushing through to,
    177–78
compliments, 426, 428
compromise, 305–7
computer algorithms, 257–62
confidence, 457, 527–29
conflicts:
    important, 388–89
    relationships and, 360
    see also disagreements
conscious vs. unconscious mind,
    218–19

consequences:
    Responsible Parties and, 402
    second- and third-order, 155–56,
      501
consideration, 343–44, 417
consultants, 507–8
controls, 513–14
conversations:
    above-the-line and below-the-line,
      247
    completion in, 367
    logic of, 366
    managing, in meetings, 364–68
    about mistakes, 433–34
    navigating between levels of, 366
    see also communication
creators, 228
credit and blame, 352
criticisms, 329–30, 364, 426, 428
culture and people, 299–305

daily updates, 459
data, 527–29
debating, 380, 387
    see also disagreements
decisions, decision making:
    algorithms and, 257–62
    believability weighting, 256–57,
      307–14, 370–83
    challenging, considering broader
      context for, 387
    choosing Responsible Parties, 401
    complaining, advice-giving, and
      debating vs., 387
    criteria for, 499–500
    decision rights in, 535
    delaying, evaluating benefits vs.
      costs of, 254–55
    and disagreement with consensus,
      381

effective, 234–65
emotions and, 236–37
evidence in, 200–201
as expected value calculations,
251–53
fairness vs. getting your way in, 383
faith in, 201–2
group, 366
information access and, 536
levels and, 247–50
past, evaluating, 488–89
pros and cons in, 253
by Responsible Parties, 381
supporting, in spite of
disagreement, 389–91
as two-step process, 188, 236–37
and who to ask questions of, 238
delegation, 456
departments, 505, 508, 510
desires, 172–73
determination, 134–35, 161–62
difficult things, doing, 462
disagreements, 384–97
efficiency in, 380–81
and getting in sync, 361–62
getting stuck in, 388–89
important, 388–89
on little things, 388
supporting decisions in spite of,
389–91
surfacing, 299–305, 361
thoughtful, 190–92
triangulating and, 193–95
dishonesty, 329–30, 513–14
distractions, 452
doing what you set out to do, 518–23
dots, 237–46, 429
double-doing, 506–7
dreams, 134–35
drill-down technique, 492–94

ego barrier, 183–84
80/20 rule, 246, 492–94
emotions, 219–20, 227, 236–37
empathizing, 189
enemies, 335
escalation, 471
evaluations, 426–27, 429–30, 438
everything and nothing, being, 149
evidence, 161, 200–201
evolution, 142–45, 423–25
as accomplishment and reward,
147–50
death and, 145–47
maximizing, 150–52
mistakes as part of, 351–52
executors, 228
expectations, 173, 176
experience, 376, 413
extroversion, 226

failure, 351, 440–41, 468
fairness, 344–45, 383, 416, 527–29
fast talkers, 367
fears, of what others think, 137
feedback, 425
feelings, 219–20, 227, 236–37
fiefdoms, 533
firing people, 439–40
5-Step Process, 168–81, 488, 504
flexibility, 173
flexors, 228
Frog in the Boiling Water Syndrome,
476
frustration, 522

generosity, 344–45, 417
genetic programming, 215–17
goal(s):
achieving, vs. looking good,
188–89, 352, 363

goal(s) (*cont.*)
building organization around, 502–8
clarity of, 172–74
desires and, 172–73
focusing on, 229, 453
group, and individual incentives, 148
and managing as someone operating a machine, 448–71
motivation for, 520–21
outcomes and, 157–59, 450–51, 477
paths to achieving, 177
right people in the right roles in support of, 231–33
tasks vs., 229, 469, 502–8
unattainable, 173
visualization and, 176
"good," 141–42
governance, 530–37
gravitational pull, 505
great vs. new, 238
group size, 368–69
group-think, 477
guardrails, 510–11

habits, 178, 220–22, 223
higher level, 157–62, 389–90, 450–52
hiring, 404–19
and candidate's success elsewhere, 414
capability and character in, 414–15
interviewers and, 411
for long-term mission, 415
and matching people to the design, 407–10
and objectivity in candidates, 411
of outstanding people, 409
personal influence in, 409–10
and showing candidates the real picture, 415
and suitability for different jobs, 409, 410–11
systematic and scientific approach to, 408–9
track records and, 412–15
honorable people, 347
humility, 180–81, 378
hyperrealist, being, 134–35

idealists, 414
idea meritocracy, 307–14, 320
anarchy in, 390
assigning responsibility and authority in, 532–33
governance and, 533
leaders in, 536
and principles embedded in tools, 526–29
understanding each person's ideas in, 374–75
and well-being of organization, 391–92
ideas, 376
see also opinions
incentives, individual, 148
information, 188, 536
integrity, 327–28
interruptions, 367
introversion, 226
intuiting vs. sensing, 226–27
investigations, 513
"I think that . . ." statements, 380

job slip, 458
job titles, 515
judgments, 189, 383, 436
justice, 332–33

key-man risk, 463, 506
kindness, 426–27
knowing and not knowing, 188, 363

leaders, group of, 536
leadership, 464–66
learning, 136–37, 189
  inadequate, 435–36
  internalized, 425, 526–27
  mistake-based, 354
levels, 246–51
leverage, 515
leveragers, 516
life principles, 131–277
limits, pushing, 152
logic, 251, 366, 376, 527–29
lowering the bar, 442
loyalty, 328, 342
lynch mobs, 390–91

machine, 157
  building, 499
  and comparing outcomes with
    goals, 157–59
  designer of, vs. worker within, 159
  designing improvements to, 496–516
  focusing on goal vs., 453
  higher level and, 157–62
  imperfection and, 501
  looking down on, from higher
    level, 450–52
  management of, 448–71
  paying attention to, 452
  probing and, 458–61
  problems and, 176–77, 476–79,
    480
  visualizing, 500–501
  "working through it" period and,
    501–2
  see also organization

management, 448–71
  authoritarian, 466
  delegation in, 456
  distance and, 458–59
  leadership, 464–66
  and managers as engineers, 451
  managing, micromanaging, and not
    managing in, 455–56
  reasons for failure in, 491
  senior and junior, 505
  sucked-down phenomenon and,
    469
  understanding in, 458
martial law, 391
meaningful work and meaningful
  relationships:
  cultivating, 338–47
  genetic programming for, 215–17
  as mutually reinforcing, 336
  and people operating in their own
    interests, 346–47
  and size of organization, 346
  truth and transparency and,
    137–38
meditation, 199–200
meetings, 364–68, 501
mental maps, 180–81
metrics, 178, 416, 429–30, 452, 470
mind, conscious vs. unconscious,
  218–19
mistakes, 348–55
  acceptable vs. unacceptable, 354
  conversations about, 433–34
  in evolutionary process, 351–52
  feeling bad about, 351–52
  learning and, 354
  letting people make, 424–25
  patterns of, 179, 352–53
mob rule, 390–91
money, 514, 516

motivation, 520–21
must-dos and like-to-dos, 254

nature, 138–47, 150–52
new vs. great, 238
no pain, no gain, 152

objective viewpoint, 159–61, 354,
    431
1+1=3, 368
open-mindedness, 161–62, 198–202,
    363
  assertiveness and, 362–64, 365–66
  radical, 136–38, 182–202, 378
  signs of, 196–98, 362–63
openness, 329
operating methods, 435–36
opinions, 238, 375
  believability of, see believability
  critical, 329–30
  past accomplishments and, 374–75,
    376
  reasoning behind, 379–80
optimizing for the whole, 148
organization(s):
  building to fit people, 504
  checks and balances in, 532–36
  culture and people in, 299–305
  departments in, 505, 508, 510
  goals vs. tasks in, 502–8
  leverage in, 515
  people at tops of pyramids in, 503,
    508
  size of, 346, 504–5
  succession and training in, 463,
    505–6
  top-down organization in, 503
  well-being of, 391–92
  see also machine
organizational chart, 508–10

outcomes, 156–57, 176–77, 435
  and asking who should do what
    differently, 488
  diagnoses and, 491
  goals and, 157–59, 450–51, 477
oversight, 503
owner, thinking like, 462

pain, 152, 153–54, 174, 434–35, 500
  reflection on, 152–55, 198,
    353–54
partnership, 537
pay, 345, 416
peer role, 377–78
people:
  allowing to step back after failure,
    440–41
  assessments of, 225–31, 430–35,
    438, 535
  building organization to fit, 504
  caring about, 464
  confidence in, 457
  finding better fit for, vs. letting go,
    440
  firing, 439–40
  as forces, 403
  hiring, see hiring
  how they operate vs. what they did,
    435–36
  keeping, 418
  keeping in unsuitable job, 439
  knowledge about, 456–57
  observations about, 428–30
  outstanding vs. ordinary, 409, 516
  performance surveys, metrics, and
    reviews for, 416, 429–32
  personal evolution in, 423–25
  and remembering that WHO is
    more important than WHAT,
    398–403

Responsible Parties, 381, 401, 402, 461, 471
right, in the right roles, 231–33
track records of, 412–15
training, testing, evaluating, and sorting, 420–27
transfers of, 441–42
treating appropriately, 463–64
wiring of, 204–33
perceiving vs. planning, 227–28
perfectionism, 246
performance measurements, 416, 429–32
personality assessments, 229–30, 411
perspective, 149–50, 238
plan, 176–78
clarity in communicating, 470
reflection and, 470
as resembling a movie script, 177, 500–501
time needed for, 177, 521
planning vs. perceiving, 227–28
policies, 454
possibilities vs. probabilities, 254
power, 392, 533
precise communications, 365
pressing vs. strategic issues, 512
principles, 255–56, 527–29
agreeing to ignore, 386–87
algorithms and, 257–62
policies and, 454
power and, 392
rules and, 453
suspension of, 391
systemizing, 499–500
tools and, 526–29
violation of, 488
prioritizing, 172
probabilities, 253, 254
probing, 379, 458–61

problem(s), 472–81
big vs. small, 175
and capacity vs. capability, 490
vs. cause for problem, 175
designing improvements to machine to get around, 496–516
diagnosing root causes of, 175–76, 492–95
diagnostic questions for, 485–91
difficult, fixing, 480
drill-down technique and, 492–94
Frog in the Boiling Water Syndrome and, 476
group-think and, 477
identifying, 174–75, 476–80, 478
identifying before solving, 175–76
machine and, 176–77, 476–79, 480
probing and, 459
proximate vs. root causes of, 176
as set of outcomes, 176–77
with solutions vs. without, 480
specificity in identifying, 174, 479
tolerating, 175
two levels of discussion for, 453
progress, 152–55, 495
protocols, 524–29
"public hangings," 514
purchasing, 514
putting out without taking in, 189

questions, 238, 364, 379, 415

reality(ies), 134–35
embracing and dealing with, 132–67
harsh, avoiding, 174
synthesizing, *see* synthesis
see also truth
reason, 251
reasonableness, 364

references, checking, 412–13
refiners, 228
reflection, 176, 470
  on pain, 152–55, 198, 353–54
rehabilitation, 438–41
relationships:
  conflicts and, 360
  diagnosis and, 495
  see also meaningful work and
    meaningful relationships
responsibility(ies), 427, 455
  anonymous "we" and "they" and,
    479
  assigning, 457–48, 515, 532–33
  checklists vs., 523
  and confidence in people, 457
  escalation and, 471
  to make sense of important things,
    382–83
  personal, 366
  reporting lines and delineations of,
    514–16, 535
Responsible Parties (RPs), 381, 401,
    402, 461, 471
rest and renovation, 523
results, of doing the same things, 491
rubber-stamping, 513–14
rules, making, 453

sampling people's work, 434
scale, 504–5
school performance, 413
self-accountability, 173
self-assessment, 225–31
self-management, 232–33
self-reflectiveness, 353–54
sensing vs. intuiting, 226–27
setbacks, 173–74
shapers, 230–31
shoulds, 140–41, 469–70

simplification, 255
skiing, 455
skills, 407–8, 436
solutions, 178–79, 480, 521
speaking up, 329
stories, both sides of, 362
strategic vs. pressing issues, 512
strength(s):
  of others, 161
  in personal evolution, 423–24
  weakness and, 465
stress-testing, 376
student, 377–78
style vs. substance, 364
success:
  5-Step Process and, 179, 504
  learning from, 427
  in life, 134–35
  and right people in the right roles,
    231–33
  trappings of, 173
succession, 463, 505–6
suggestions, 364, 376
suspicious threads, 461
sync, getting in, 356–69, 468
  on assessments, 433
  bringing issues to the surface, 361
  disagreement and, 361–62
  as investment, 360
  major differences and, 369
  as two-way responsibility, 363
synthesis, 237–38, 491
  building from specifics up, 428–29
  logic, reason, and common sense
    in, 251
  time in, 239–46

tasks:
  double-doing, 506–7
  goals vs., 229, 469, 502–8

tasting the soup, 478
teacher, 377–78
teams, 412
testing skills, 436
thinking, 223–24
  feeling vs., 219–20, 227
threats, 463
time, 254, 516, 522
  synthesis and, 239–46
tools, 524–29
topic slip, 366
tough love, 154–55, 305–7, 427–28
track records, 412–15
training, 424, 436, 438–41
transfers, 441–42
transparency, 332–33
  radical, 136–38, 308–14, 322–26,
    330–35
trial and error, 148–49
triangulating, 193–95
truth, 135–36, 326–27
  radical, 137–38, 308–14, 322–30,
    336
  see also reality
two-minute rule, 367

unconscious vs. conscious mind,
  218–19
understanding vs. arguing, 190
updates, 459

vacation, 462
values, 369, 407–8
verbal cues, 460
vision, 511–13
visualization, 176, 230–31, 500–501

"we," anonymous, 460, 479
weaknesses, 159, 436–38
  and finding solutions, 178–79
  others' strengths and, 161
  pain of exploring, 434–35
  patterns of mistakes and, 352–53
  in personal evolution, 423–24
  strength and, 465
wiring, 204–33
work:
  amount of, 522
  habits in, 178
  meaningful, see meaningful work
    and meaningful relationships
  passion and, 317
  pay for, 345, 416
  principles, 270–541
  tools and protocols for, 524–29
Workplace Personality Inventory,
  229–30
worry, 476
worst-case scenario, 194–95

"yous," two, 184–85

ACKNOWLEDGMENTS

My Life and Work Principles are a result of my encounters with reality over many years. Because these encounters were most importantly shaped with Bob Prince, Greg Jensen, Giselle Wagner, Dan Bernstein, David McCormick, Eileen Murray, Joe Dobrich, Paul Colman, Rob Fried, Ross Waller, Claude Amadeo, Randal Sandler, Peter LaTronica, Brian Gold, Osman Nalbantoglu, Brian Kreiter, Tom Sinchak, Tom Waller, Janine Racanelli, Fran Schanne, and Lisa Safian, they are the people to whom I am most grateful.

Bob, Greg, and I have spent the greater parts of our adult lives trying to discover the timeless and universal laws of economies and markets. In the process, we had daily interactions that were typically thoughtful, infrequently bloody, and occasionally euphoric. While our meetings were primarily about economies and markets and led to the discovery of invaluable economic and investment principles, they also taught us a great amount about ourselves and about how people should be with each other. We captured these lessons as life and work principles that were even more valuable. More recently, we did that with Eileen Murray and Dave McCormick, who together replaced me as co-CEOs. Thank you, Dave and Eileen, for contributing to, receiving, and taking care of the boon.

When I first imagined transitioning Bridgewater from a first-generation organization to a second-generation one, I decided to pull together my scattered collection of principles into this recipe book to help others at Bridgewater. Collecting and transforming what started as a messy pile of principles into this beautiful book was an epic effort that Mark Kirby, more than anyone, was responsible for helping me with. I also appreciate Arthur Goldwag's and Mike Kubin's contributions in tightening up and refining the entire manuscript. (Mike did that as a friend.) I further appreciate Arianna Huffington, Tony Robbins, Norm Rosenthal, and Kristina Nikolova for taking the time to read the book and provide valuable suggestions.

Those who enabled me most on a daily basis were "Ray's Angels" (Marilyn Caufield, Petra Koegel, Kristy Merola, and Christina Drossakis), "Ray's Leveragers" (Zack Wieder, Dave Alpert, Jen Gonyo, and Andrew Sternlight—and past leveragers Elise Waxenberg, David Manners-Weber, and John Woody), and "Ray's Researchers" (Steven Kryger, Gardner Davis, and Brandon Rowley—and past researcher Mark Dinner). I am also thankful to Jason Rotenberg, Noah Yechiely, Karen Karniol-Tambour, Bruce Steinberg, Larry Cofsky, Bob Elliott, Ramsen Betfarhad, Kevin Brennan, Kerry Reilly, and Jacob Kline, who are among the next generation who help spark and shape our investment principles; to Jeff Gardner, Jim Haskel, Paul Podolsky, Rob Zink, Mike Colby, Lionel Kaliff, Joel Whidden, Brian Lawlor, Tom Bachner, Jim White, Kyle Delaney, Ian Wang, Parag Shah, and Bill Mahoney, who have personified our principles to our clients; to Dave Ferrucci, who, more than anyone else, has helped me convert the Work Principles into algorithms; and to Jeff Taylor, Steve Elfanbaum, Stuart Friedman, and Jen Healy, who are helping me convert them into common sense for a lot of people. Though my interests and directions have always been diverse, these teams made my missions their missions, and kept me moving forward. Without their help, I wouldn't have accomplished anything close to what I have. Thank you for enduring me and for selflessly supporting me.

Whatever beauty you see in the book's design was the result of Phil Caravaggio's generosity and talent. After I put the original version of Principles online as a PDF, he came to me as a stranger bearing the gift of a gorgeously designed print edition, created with the help of the artistic book designer Rodrigo Corral. Phil, who is a brilliant entrepreneur in his own right, just wanted to thank me because the principles had helped him. The book's beauty astounded me, and Phil's account of what these principles meant to him was another gift that nudged me closer to making the book a reality. Once I decided to make it, Phil went on to work tirelessly with Rodrigo to shape the aesthetic of what you are now holding in your hands—doing so again solely as a gift. Thank you, Phil!

Six years ago, Jofie Ferrari-Adler, Executive Editor at Simon & Schuster, read the principles online, found them valuable, and explained to me why sharing this book was an important thing for me to do to help others. He has been a valued partner in making that happen. In exploring my publishing options, I triangulated with others to find the best agent available. This search led me to Jim Levine. I learned why he is so admired by his clients as he provides his great time, skill, and empathy. Jim guided me through the publishing process, which led me to Jon Karp, Simon & Schuster's President. From the start, Jon wanted my book to be more what I wanted it to be than what he wanted it to be, and he helped me make it happen.

Finally, I'd like to thank my wife, Barbara, and my sons Devon, Paul, Matt, and Mark for putting up with me and my principles—and for giving me the time and space to create both these principles and this book.

ABOUT THE AUTHOR

Ray Dalio, who grew up a very ordinary middle-class kid from Long Island, started the investment company Bridgewater Associates out of his two-bedroom apartment when he was 26 years old, and built it over the next 42 years into what *Fortune* magazine assessed to be the fifth most important private company in the U.S. He did that by creating a unique culture—an idea meritocracy based on radical truth, radical transparency, and believability-weighted decision making—that he believes most people and organizations can use to better achieve their own goals.

Along the way, Dalio became one of the 100 most influential (according to *Time*) and 100 wealthiest (according to *Forbes*) people in the world, and because his unique investment principles changed the industry, *CIO* magazine called him "the Steve Jobs of investing." (Those principles will be conveyed in his next book, *Economic and Investment Principles*.) He believes that his success isn't due to anything special about him—it is the result of principles he learned, largely by making mistakes, from which he also believes most people can benefit.

At 68 years old, Dalio's primary objective is to pass along these principles in case others find them of value.